Will Shortz Presents

GOOD *TIMES* CROSSWORDS

The New York Times

Crossword Puzzles

The #1 Name in Crosswords

Available at your local bookstore or online at nytimes.com/nytstore

St. Martin's Griffin

Will Shortz Presents

GOOD *TIMES* CROSSWORDS
200 Easy *New York Times* Crossword Puzzles

Edited by Will Shortz

ST. MARTIN'S GRIFFIN ❧ NEW YORK

ACROSS

1 What some people do in an online "room"
5 Shoe bottom
9 Swift
14 Circle of light around the sun or moon
15 Bard of ___ (Shakespeare)
16 Microscopic creature
17 "So be it"
18 Nourish
19 Beckett's "Waiting for ___"
20 MAYS
23 Zinc or zirconium
24 Home of Barack Obama's father
25 Radical 1960s org
28 1st to 220th, in Manhattan: Abbr.
29 Israeli-made gun
31 Like hereditary factors
33 English dramatist George
35 Actress Turner
36 MAIZE
42 ___ Mountains (Asia/Europe separator)
43 What the dish ran away with, in "Hey Diddle Diddle"
44 Soda can feature
48 "___ the ramparts we watched . . ."
49 Butter serving
52 One step ___ time
53 Zones
55 Rock with a crystal inside
57 MAZE
60 Tangle
62 "Honest to God!"
63 Place of research: Abbr.
64 With 34-Down, golf's U.S. Open champion of 1994 and 1997
65 Peru's capital
66 "Beetle Bailey" dog
67 West Pointer, e.g.
68 Toward the rising sun
69 First-year college student, usually

DOWN

1 Gorges
2 Small village
3 Native Alaskans
4 South Pacific kingdom
5 Official's call with outspread arms
6 Excess
7 Frederick ___, "My Fair Lady" composer
8 Part of a whodunit that reveals who done it
9 Overcoat sleeve
10 Mine: Fr.
11 Statue's support
12 Nigerian native
13 "Gimme ___!" (rude order)
21 Viscous
22 Soapmaker's supply
26 Flintstones' pet
27 Surgery souvenir
30 Zuider ___ (former inlet in the Netherlands)
32 North Carolina university
33 ___-mell
34 See 64-Across
36 Larva successor
37 In ___ (stuck in the same old same old)
38 Dreamy place
39 Arboreal animals with pouches
40 Anguish
41 Welsh dog
45 One of two for the Ten Commandments
46 Departure's opposite: Abbr.
47 Any of the Fab Four
49 Ballerina's position
50 "___ Fideles"
51 German
54 Courtyards
56 Writer T. S.
58 Singer India.___
59 Vegetarian's no-no
60 Dry, as wine
61 Gun lobbyists' org.

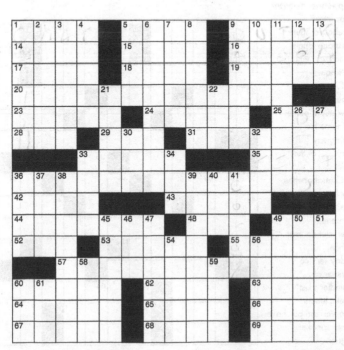

by Janet R. Bender

ACROSS

1 Performed on Broadway, say
6 Cry like a baby
10 Invitation request, for short
14 Actress Christine of "Chicago Hope"
15 Madame Bovary
16 Its license plates say "Birthplace of Aviation"
17 Envision in one's sleep
19 Yawl or yacht
20 Bad thing to have on one's face
21 List ender: Abbr.
22 Transition
24 NPR newsman Adams
26 Where to run some tests
28 Like some bad film scenes
31 Sleepwear component
34 Vegas intro?
35 Scoreboard figure
36 Tombstone letters
37 ___ salts
40 Hog's home
41 Dishful near a restaurant door
43 "How stupid of me!"
44 Nickname for Hemingway
46 Krazy ___ of the comics
47 The Chattahoochee River forms part of it
51 Classic family name in Florence
52 Street caution near a school
53 Sunday service
56 Schindler of "Schindler's List"
58 Genetic letters
60 2006 Verizon purchase
61 Former speaker Gingrich
63 Arrive on the Enterprise via transporter

66 Done
67 Molten flow
68 "Live Free ___" (New Hampshire motto)
69 Take from the top
70 Noted garden site
71 President born on August 4, whose name can be found backward in 17-, 31-, 47- and 63-Across

DOWN

1 John on the Mayflower
2 Freight
3 Clothing retailer starting in 1969
4 Pilot's announcement, for short
5 It's smaller than a penny
6 Online video equipment

7 Start of a Latin conjugation
8 Big name in morning radio
9 Sometime in the future
10 Hearty
11 Squeeze (into)
12 By way of
13 One calling the kettle black, in a phrase
18 Collection of plates
23 Sees red
25 Circle of angels?
27 What some drinkers run up
29 Skip
30 Recipe amts.
32 Fill to capacity and then some
33 Pick up, in a way
37 Dutch cheese
38 Gondolier's need
39 Tailed

40 Rejuvenation location
42 Part of an agenda
45 Friendly
46 Money from Sweden
48 European-style cafe
49 Subject of a Hemingway title
50 Holiday Inn alternative
54 Fabric for theater curtains
55 Part of a record getting the most airplay
57 Peruse
59 Bug chaser?
61 Hide-hair connector
62 Threshold
64 Cry in old Rome
65 Sphere

by Alan Arbesfeld

ACROSS

1 Did a dog trick
6 ___-Ball (game on an incline)
10 "Mamma Mia" quartet
14 Renault 5, in North America
15 Rain cats and dogs
16 Film critic Pauline
17 First few bars
18 Mrs. Dithers in the comics
19 "This ___ joke!"
20 America's so-called Third Coast
22 Clementine's shoe size
23 Playboy or Playgirl-caliber model
24 Item with a magnetic strip, nowadays
26 Tyler of "The Incredible Hulk"
27 What Hail Mary passes rarely result in, briefly
28 One who must be above suspicion, in a saying
32 Ex-governor Palin
33 Hero maker's aid
34 Crèche trio
37 Whole bunch
39 Prefix with normal
40 Hunky sort
43 One who tries
46 Many an autobiographer's need
48 Early Beatle Sutcliffe
51 Original Luddite ___ Ludd
52 Oklahoma's ___ Tree National golf course
53 Like Bill O'Reilly's "zone" on Fox News
55 Clearance rack words
57 Character known for exclaiming the first words of 20-, 28- and 46-Across

60 Like certain sums
61 Ballet bend
62 Perfect Sleeper maker
63 Smooth
64 "___ Enchanted" (Anne Hathaway movie)
65 Range extending to the Arctic Ocean
66 Huge quantities
67 Gray no more, say
68 Longtime CBS boss William

DOWN

1 Cold-shoulder
2 Booth Tarkington title tween
3 Largish combos
4 Unit of purity
5 Racy reading
6 Pet welfare org.
7 Wack job
8 "That's it!"
9 Blackboard accessories
10 Closely related
11 St. Peter's, e.g.
12 Affleck/Lopez as a tabloid twosome
13 Important plant in alternative medicine
21 Father of Goneril
25 Fashion inits.
29 Mother's cry at a dinner table
30 Japanese sliding screen
31 Disposable cleaning aid
32 Lust and envy, for two
34 Ones in high places
35 Post-it component
36 Brainstorming result, perhaps
38 Wack job

41 "Who am ___ say?"
42 Out of order, in a way
44 Refuse to grant
45 Matures
47 Singer with the 1994 #1 hit "Bump N' Grind"
48 Form of a well-thrown pigskin
49 Y.A. known for well-thrown pigskins
50 On edge
54 Mattel's Princess of Power
56 Roget offerings: Abbr.
58 Anger
59 Interpret

by Donna S. Levin

4

ACROSS

1 Intense enthusiasm
5 Townshend of the Who
9 Stock exchanges: Abbr.
13 Diva's solo
14 Praise highly
16 All over again
17 Examiner of heart and life lines
19 "Look twice before crossing," e.g.
20 Soothing ointment
21 Partitioned-off work space
23 N.B.A. official
26 Fishnet stocking material
28 Halloween purchases
29 Left the building
31 Attractiveness
33 Sheets, pillowcases, etc.
34 Look of disdain
35 Beings from out of this world, in brief
38 Pond organism
39 Student at the Citadel
40 Border on
41 "___-haw!" (western rider's cry)
42 Tableware inspired by Scandinavian design
43 Sporty Mazda
44 Call on the carpet
46 Pirate support, stereotypically
47 Iridescent gems
48 Feds who catch counterfeiters
50 Golfer Trevino
51 Enduring literary work
53 The Runnin' Rebels of the N.C.A.A.
55 Came to earth
56 Small bottle in a purse
61 ___ qua non
62 Persona non ___

63 Tennis champ Arthur
64 Four: Prefix
65 First Best Actor winner Jannings
66 Billet-___ (love letter)

DOWN

1 Hit with high voltage
2 Chapter in history
3 Feel sick
4 Gentle creature
5 Skinned, as potatoes
6 Midterms and finals
7 Tiny bit
8 Basic util.
9 Actress Tomei
10 Slow pitch with a little spin
11 Spills the beans
12 ___' Pea (Popeye's boy)
15 Louis Armstrong's instrument

18 Japanese noodle dish
22 1930s boxing champ Max
23 Race with batons
24 Napoleon, on Elba
25 Messy art medium for kids
27 Phone part . . . or a title for this puzzle?
30 What the Hatter and the March Hare drank
32 Sneak preview
34 Sent to the bottom
36 Private pupil
37 Where a 51-Down performs
39 Producing as a result
40 Insurance giant in 2009 news
42 Two-base hits: Abbr.
43 ___ Park (Edison's lab site)
45 Egg-dyeing time

46 Someone from whom you might collect exotic stamps
47 One-toothed dragon of old children's TV
49 Prefix with vitamin
51 See 37-Down
52 Give a darn
54 Prince called "the Impaler," who was the inspiration for Dracula
57 "___ the Walrus"
58 Equal: Prefix
59 Moo ___ pork
60 Evil spell

by Paula Gamache

ACROSS

1 Baking soda meas.
4 Brother of Nintendo's Mario
9 Good thing
14 Oklahoma Indian
15 Beaming
16 Prefix with -path
17 Islamabad's land: Abbr.
18 Nursery purchase
19 In unison
20 Pre-costume ball activity
23 Salt Lake City team
24 Ellipsoidal
25 Uses rubber on
27 "___ life!"
28 Like Buddy Holly's glasses
32 Like Stephen King novels
34 Burning passions
35 Bottom-of-letter abbr.
38 Patient care grp.
39 Angry cry to a vampire
41 Zippo
42 Strong suit
44 Supermodel Evangelista
46 Prepares part of breakfast, say
49 Tee off
53 Long-eared hound
54 Rising star
55 Figure in red
57 Cole Porter musical that's a play within a play
60 Break-in deterrent
62 Pick up bit by bit
63 Tonic go-with
64 $2 on the gray mare, e.g.
65 Bandleader's command
66 Upper-left key
67 Winter accident cause

68 Starts a turn on "Wheel of Fortune"
69 Library admonition

DOWN

1 Head honcho
2 ". . . ___ a fever"
3 Jab with a finger
4 Memory glitch
5 Wrinkly citrus
6 "Axis of evil" land
7 Pungent, like some Asian cuisine
8 One after another
9 Simile words
10 "Well, sorr-r-r-y!"
11 Tartan wearer
12 "___ kleine Nachtmusik"
13 Tot's "piggies"
21 Metro map points: Abbr.
22 Scorecard figure

26 Evaluated, with "up"
28 Western omelet need
29 Conquistador's prize
30 "Y"-sporting collegian
31 Upgrade from a dial-up connection
33 Knight's realm?
35 Letter before gee
36 Hide-hair link
37 Game to 31
39 Like, slangily
40 Gerund end
43 Source of an oil used in aromatherapy
44 Blurt out, say
45 Bad way to run
47 Set a price at
48 Paddock sounds
50 Camera card contents
51 Fixation

52 Word that can precede the starts of 20-, 28-, 46- and 57-Across
54 Number after a period
55 Crow cousins
56 Flier to Ben-Gurion
58 Alien-seeking program: Abbr.
59 Common street name
61 Villain player in "Rocky III"

by Oliver Hill

6

ACROSS

1 Cause for an eyelift
4 Playground shout
9 With 59-Across, novel of 1851
13 Benzoyl peroxide target
14 Bitter
15 Shield border
16 Complain
17 Frigid temps
18 Head of the Egyptian god Thoth
19 Take the lead
21 Sig Ep and others
22 Fish tail?
23 At sea
24 Stable display
25 Stylize anew, as a car seat
27 Rushed (by)
29 Warhol associate ___ Sedgwick
30 Israel's Barak and Olmert
31 Character in 9- & 59-Across
36 Chills, so to speak
37 Sorvino of "Mighty Aphrodite"
40 Cordial offering?
44 "___ is gained as much by good works as by evil": Machiavelli
46 St. Stephen, notably
47 Pronoun in the starts of many letters
49 Netflix offering
50 Simon Says players, say
51 Displays
53 Designate "commercial" or "single-family," e.g.
54 Incline (and a hint to the location in this completed puzzle of the first line of 9- & 59-Across)
55 Recipe direction
56 Hollywood's Kazan
57 Lumberjack competition
58 Change of address, for short
59 See 9-Across
60 Does what a good dog does
61 Halftime features

DOWN

1 Searched high and low
2 ___ Geometry (college course)
3 Four-star leader: Abbr.
4 Grasp
5 They're served with spoon-straws
6 9- & 59-Across
7 Rear
8 QBs' coups
9 Shimmery fabrics
10 Jerry of "Law & Order"
11 Carefree
12 Assented
13 Eponymous French physicist
20 1960 Olympics boxing gold medalist
21 High-school class, informally
24 Musical conclusion
26 "Fool (If You Think It's Over)" singer Chris
28 Onetime Asiatic nomads
30 New York's ___ River
32 Hunts, with "on"
33 Numerical prefix with oxide
34 Qty.
35 What a swallow may swallow
38 Displays
39 Supplements
40 Blown away
41 "In ___, where love is king" (start of "That's Amore")
42 Peaceful
43 Word with hot or blue
44 Reading for home mechanics
45 Rambler maker, once: Abbr.
48 Baklava ingredient
51 One whose shirttail is always untucked, maybe
52 Start of an incantation
54 Sign of success

by Peter A. Collins & Joe Krozel

ACROSS

1 Container for serving wine
7 Kindergarten learning
11 Sounds during backrubs
14 Witty
15 Lunch or dinner
16 Gift at Honolulu airport
17 1966
19 Norse war god
20 Former Treasury secretary Geithner
21 ___ guy (one who gets things done)
22 Flank
23 Drinking cup
26 With 51-Across, roles for 17-, 38- and 62-Across
28 Big part of an elephant
29 Jacob's first wife
32 Pictures at a hospital
33 City on the Black Sea
36 Actress Zellweger
38 1989
42 Theater walkway
43 Came out with
45 Solar phenomenon
48 Laudatory poems
50 A pair
51 See 26-Across
53 Chinese blossom
56 Big name in elevators
57 Fashionable
60 Official with a whistle
61 ___ Tin Tin
62 2008
66 "i" topper
67 French eleven
68 Mark slightly longer than a hyphen
69 ___-cone
70 Be overrun (with)
71 Declares emphatically

DOWN

1 Roman 300
2 Ginger ___
3 Place to pull over
4 Be of help to
5 Physicist Enrico
6 Flub
7 Bullets and BBs
8 Borscht vegetable
9 Chocolate substitute
10 ___-mo
11 Nissan sedan
12 Period of one's prime
13 Fire truck sounds
18 Double curve
22 Emphasize
23 Pooh-bah hired by a board of directors
24 Muslim's pilgrimage
25 Family groups
27 Leaps in ice-skating
30 Like parabolas
31 When doubled, a villain's chuckle
34 Close calls, perhaps
35 One taking to the slopes
37 Static, e.g.
39 Nobel Prize-winning U.N. workers' grp.
40 On empty
41 6:30 p.m. broadcast
44 Female deer
45 Norwegian coastal features
46 Skin soother
47 Like
49 Draw like Albrecht Dürer
52 Where the action is
54 Where the action is
55 Helen who sang "I Am Woman"
58 Jimi Hendrix's "Purple ___"
59 See 62-Down
62 With 59-Down, something flying off the shelves
63 ___ États-Unis
64 Double curve
65 Letter between pi and sigma

by Mike Buckley

8

ACROSS
1 Short
7 Hideout
11 General on a Chinese menu
14 Plugs
15 Right-hand person
16 Help in a heist, say
17 Fountain treat
19 Bearded beast
20 Bearded bloom
21 "Just watch me!"
23 Type size used in typewriters
27 Tangy pie filler
30 Goes postal
32 Penlight batteries
33 Patty Hearst kidnap grp.
34 He flew too close to the sun, in myth
35 "___ du lieber!"
36 Abbr. on an envelope
37 Relative of a certain cobbler
41 Idiosyncrasies
43 Batman and Robin, e.g.
44 Game keeper?
47 Setting for TV's "Newhart"
48 Sharif of "Doctor Zhivago"
50 A little scared
51 Candy bar with maraschinos
54 Big stingers
55 Show deep respect (to)
56 Make
58 Vermeer's "Woman With a ___"
59 Popular Fanta-like soda
66 Those, in Toledo
67 "___ Cop"
68 Robert Ludlum hero searching for his identity

69 Hideout
70 Carriers of Lyme ticks
71 Balloons

DOWN
1 Alert, for short
2 Thing with cups and hooks
3 Harry Potter's best friend
4 Actress Thurman
5 Pays what's due
6 Peter I, II or III
7 Run out, as a subscription
8 Feel ill
9 Uganda's ___ Amin
10 Eye part
11 Rib-eye alternatives
12 Natural seasoning
13 Club chair companion piece
16 Biology lab supply
18 Buildup at a river's mouth

22 IV amounts
23 Yale student
24 Tone ___ (early rapper)
25 Scientist who experienced a great fall?
26 Maryland squad
28 Lens type
29 Diamond Head locale
31 Archipelago unit: Abbr.
35 Lexus competitor
36 Big name in metal foil
38 Dutch dairy product
39 Aid in locating a pirate's treasure
40 Root beer float with chocolate ice cream
41 Amused
42 Not farmed out
45 Passbook abbr.
46 Masthead contents, briefly

48 ___ y Plata (Montana's motto)
49 "Dear me!"
50 Thick carpet
52 66 and others: Abbr.
53 Guadalajara guy
57 Confederate soldiers, for short
60 ___ v. Wade
61 Actor Vigoda
62 Lament
63 http://www.yahoo.com, e.g.
64 Skit-filled NBC show, for short
65 "For ___ a jolly . . ."

by Tony Orbach

ACROSS

1 ___ unto itself
5 Brown fur
10 Is shy, in a way
14 Game Gear company
15 Philanderer, in slang
17 Our genus
18 Madre's hermanos
19 To this point, in verse
20 Intravenous hookup
21 Hamid Karzai, starting in 2004
24 Uppity type
25 Org. concerned with firing practices?
26 One of four generations in a photo
34 Iranian cash
35 Occasion for a proctor
36 Overly
37 "Must've been something ___"
38 Like "King Lear"
41 Keep an appointment
42 When juillet and août occur
43 Get rid of
44 Vacant, in a way
45 Driver's electric convenience
50 Old Ford model
51 Like 26-Down
52 Frances Hodgson Burnett kid-lit novel . . . and a hint to 21-, 26- and 45-Across
59 Piltdown man, notably
60 Longtime label for 38-Down
61 Like a hottie
62 Rocker Quatro
63 Father ___, leper priest of Molokai
64 "Ain't it the truth!"
65 Siesta time, maybe

66 Has-___ (ones who are washed up)
67 Like some sums

DOWN

1 Wirehair of film
2 Son of Eric the Red
3 All worked up
4 Stock transaction made to claim a tax deduction
5 Court worker, for short
6 Sluggishness
7 Mobster's code
8 Dots over eyes?
9 New Mexico skiing locale
10 "Mercy!"
11 Dog-eared
12 Discharge
13 Conciliatory bribe
16 Promo container that's a twofer

22 See 39-Down
23 Apothecary weight
26 "Peer Gynt" composer
27 Gaucho's gear
28 What "-vore" means
29 Like some ions: Abbr.
30 Early sixth-century date
31 Patriot Allen
32 Nary a soul
33 Air controller's place
38 Jerry Garcia's band, for short
39 With 22-Down, stinging insects
40 Hubbub
41 Shows disdain for
43 Snorkel and colleagues: Abbr.
44 Res ___ loquitur
46 "Dynasty" vixen
47 Infant's bodysuit
48 Raising a stink?
49 Hammond products
52 Historic site option

53 Give a paddling, maybe
54 Kvetcher
55 White coat
56 Moore of film
57 Deleted, with "out"
58 Part of Rockefeller Ctr.'s address
59 V-J Day pres.

by Peter A. Collins

10

ACROSS

1 Kitchen V.I.P.'s
6 Towel (off)
10 Rock star, say
14 W.W. II German sub
15 Peak
16 Moore of "G.I. Jane"
17 Tilter at windmills
19 City NNW of Oklahoma City
20 Raised, as livestock
21 "Dee-fense! Dee-fense!" and others
23 Little article accompanying a bigger article
27 For free
28 One of golf's four majors
29 Biblical objects of multiplication
30 Sprinted
31 ___ Carlo (part of Monaco)
32 "Hike!" callers in football, for short
35 Entryway
36 Fabricate, as a signature
37 Multinational currency
38 Umberto ___, author of "The Name of the Rose"
39 Santa's little helpers
40 Cranium contents
41 Hire, as a lawyer
43 Industry in Las Vegas and Atlantic City
44 Plaza
45 Plaza displays
46 Psychology 101, e.g.
47 Number of calories in water
48 Nobelist Wiesel
49 Place to order a Blizzard
55 Softly hit ball in tennis
56 "Render ___ Caesar . . ."
57 Eggs on
58 Writer ___ St. Vincent Millay
59 Aspirin target
60 ___ Gay (W.W. II plane)

DOWN

1 What a cow chews
2 "Entourage" network
3 Ages and ages
4 Online help page
5 Struck accidentally, as the toe
6 Floor finisher
7 Item with earbuds
8 Favorite
9 Detest
10 Think creatively
11 Star of "The Rookie," 2002
12 Fails to mention
13 Jar tops
18 Ahmadinejad's country
22 One who's well off
23 Increase in troop levels
24 Newton with a law named after him
25 Medicine woman of 1990s TV
26 Fencing sword
27 Pagoda instruments
29 Italian 31-Down star Sophia
31 See 29-Down
33 Salt water
34 Hymns, e.g.
36 Came back strong, as allergies
37 Bombeck who wrote "The Grass Is Always Greener Over the Septic Tank"
39 Greek H's
40 Like the works of Handel and Bach
42 "I've got it!"
43 Indiana birthplace of the Jackson 5
44 Sphere or cube
45 Argentine dictator who was ousted in 1955
46 Relinquish
47 Casserole pasta
50 "Gimme ___!" (Alabama cheerleader's cry)
51 Container at many receptions
52 Maniacal leader?
53 Ingredient in some sushi rolls
54 Intelligence-gathering org.

by Anthony J. Salvia

ACROSS

1 Early calculators
6 What it takes not to say "I see you've put on a little weight"
10 Arabian Peninsula land
14 Georgia Music Hall of Fame city
15 Workplace watchdog org.
16 Fashion line named for a sport
17 Conceals, as a card
18 Golda of Israel
19 Just slightly
20 Residential area of California [think Chevy]
23 In the style of
24 Clumsy sort
25 Fresh talk
26 Start of a stampede, maybe [think Ford]
32 "The Simpsons" storekeeper
33 Commuter's option
34 Realm of Tolkien's Middle-earth
37 Subtle flavor
39 Sonora snacks
42 Elbow
43 Locale of many outsourced jobs
45 Altar exchange
47 Be sociable
48 Part of a peace treaty [think Honda]
52 Blue shade
54 Tot's "piggy"
55 Letter-shaped cross
56 Cars suggested by 20-, 26- and 48-Across?
62 Surface figure
63 Trevi Fountain throw-in, once
64 Colonel North, informally
66 Put on the line

67 Dr. ___ (Mike Myers character)
68 The Beav's big brother
69 Rose who surpassed Cobb
70 Religious offshoot
71 Soda shop order

DOWN

1 Roadie's load
2 Meadow calls
3 Rights org.
4 Front-line action
5 Isolated, as a people
6 Mummy's locale
7 On a cruise
8 Casual slacks
9 Takeoff or touchdown site
10 Gem mined in Australia
11 It might have a "wide load" sign
12 It's good when airtight
13 Still in bed
21 Charged
22 At a distance
26 Hawaiian fish, on menus
27 ___ arms (indignant)
28 Going-to-church clothes
29 Actress ___ Scala
30 Conqueror of Valencia, 1094
31 Much Top 40 music
35 Closely related
36 Barbershop call
38 Quirky habit
40 "___ to Billie Joe" (1967 #1 hit)
41 Sir Georg of the Chicago Symphony
44 Play opener
46 Dugongs or manatees
49 Lots and lots

50 Bring back, as a fashion
51 Islamic leader
52 Quick-witted
53 "___ eleison" ("Lord, have mercy")
57 Do some yard work
58 Idle of "Life of Brian"
59 Sentry's order
60 Jazz's Fitzgerald
61 Symbol of smoothness
65 Check out

by Bob Johnson

12

ACROSS

1 Hurts
7 3, 4 or 5, typically, in golf
10 Best-selling computer game from the early 2000s, with "The"
14 When Hamlet says "To be or not to be"
15 Payment promise
16 "I'm ___!" ("Will do!")
17 "___, please" (diner's request)
19 Endangered state bird
20 PC capacity, for short
21 "Full" sign
22 Shot using one's noggin
24 Beethoven dedicatee
27 "___, please" (announcer's request)
29 What to do at a crossroads
31 Postpone yet again
32 Vehement speech
35 Roman household god
36 "___, please" (awards show presenter's request)
40 G.I.'s mail drop
42 "Twelfth Night" duke
43 Malodorous critter
47 Mexican revolutionary played by Brando
51 "___, please" (operator's request)
54 18 oz., maybe, on a cereal box
55 Hardware store boxful
56 Springsteen's birthplace of song
58 Gerber eater
59 Old salt's direction
60 "___, please!" (Henny Youngman's request)
64 Past the golf pin, say
65 Direction from L.A. to K.C.

66 Band with the 1975 #1 hit "One of These Nights"
67 Ferrara family name
68 Blazed a trail
69 Dada, to many

DOWN

1 With 45-Down, something not to criticize
2 Ernest Borgnine title role
3 ___ FireBall (hot candy)
4 Job for a tailor
5 Rejoinder to "'tain't!"
6 Collects splinters, so to speak
7 Embroidery loop
8 Just fine
9 Fraternity hopeful

10 Beethoven keyboard work
11 Like poisonous mushrooms
12 Seat of Nassau County, N.Y.
13 Less lenient
18 401(k) alternative
23 Fangorn in "The Lord of the Rings," e.g.
25 Jedi enemy
26 Falco who played Carmela on "The Sopranos"
28 Familial diagrams
30 Bard's before
33 "I can't sing ___"
34 TiVo, for one
36 Broad-minded
37 Taylor who said "I do" eight times
38 ___ equal footing

39 Wearer of a triple tiara
40 Last Supper guest
41 Some rainwear
44 Come into prominence
45 See 1-Down
46 Dutch brew
48 The Scourge of God
49 Get-one-free deal
50 Swear (to)
52 Microwaved, slangily
53 "The Waste Land" monogram
57 Grace ender
61 "I'd like to buy ___, Pat"
62 Hoopster ___ Ming
63 Chicago Cubs' station

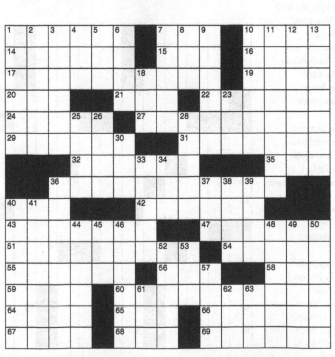

by Gary Cee

ACROSS

1 Fastener that may have a Phillips head
6 "One more thing . . ."
10 Eject, as 16-Across
14 Tara's Scarlett
15 Factory whistle time
16 Material from a volcano
17 Roger Bannister was the first
20 "You've got mail" co.
21 Trudge (along)
22 Sheeplike
23 In the proper manner
24 Agents' customers
26 Women's quarters, in sultans' homes
29 Fan sound
30 Emergency removal of people, for short
31 "Rise and ___!"
32 "Paper or plastic?" item
35 How something may be done, nostalgically
39 Old competitor of Pan Am
40 Heeded the alarm
41 ___ and proper
42 Mensa-eligible
43 Area west of the Mississippi
45 Regardless of
48 500 sheets
49 Visitor in "District 9"
50 Little vegetables that roll
51 Pitchfork-shaped Greek letter
54 Features of yawls or ketches
58 Essayist's newspaper piece
59 Suffix with billion
60 Fabric introduced by DuPont
61 Poetic nights
62 Use a spyglass
63 Sport with shotguns

DOWN

1 Couch
2 Part of a sneeze after "ah-ah-ah . . ."
3 Fidel Castro's brother
4 "To ___ is human . . ."
5 Indian beads used as money
6 Really bother
7 Ear-busting
8 Drunkard
9 Marine ___ (presidential helicopter)
10 Tiny slice of pie
11 Politico Sarah
12 Long jump or 100-meter dash
13 Peddlers peddle them
18 Woes
19 Fabrics with wavy patterns
23 Art ___ (1920s–'30s style)
24 Doorbell
25 Queue
26 Test the weight of
27 Swear to
28 ___ avis
29 Predecessor of bridge
31 Part of a mall
32 Italian port on the Adriatic
33 Closely related
34 Rubies, emeralds, etc.
36 Thin layer
37 "Dang!"
38 E-mail often caught in filters
42 Risks being caught in a radar trap
43 Bog fuel
44 Rodeo ropes
45 Willem of Spider-Man movies
46 Run off to the justice of the peace
47 Patrol car wailer
48 Direct, as for information
50 Whittle down
51 Heap
52 ___ gin fizz
53 "Money ___ everything!"
55 40 winks
56 Expire
57 Noah's vessel

by Fred Piscop

14

ACROSS

1 Moody's rates them
6 Oceanic in scope
10 Early software version
14 Musical work that's often not in English
15 Gross, in kidspeak
16 Cart-pulling beasts
17 Pretentious and showy
18 See 37-Across
20 Uncooked
21 Old woman's home, in a nursery rhyme
23 "___ Was a Lady" (Ethel Merman tune)
24 See 37-Across
28 "___ to please!"
29 "Careful, now!"
30 Woody Allen's trademark emotion
32 It may be worse than a bite
34 Winter hrs. in New Orleans
37 How 18-, 24-, 47- and 56-Across may be defined
41 Director's "Stop!"
42 Tops of many Halloween getups
43 "You ___ be there"
44 Bell-ringing cosmetics company
46 Theater area
47 See 37-Across
52 A pet collar repels them
54 Flip, as a coin
55 Tuna at a sushi bar
56 See 37-Across
59 Rambo type
61 Start the pot
62 Equips for war
63 In-your-face
64 "Guarding ___" (1994 MacLaine movie)
65 First, second, third or home
66 Noodges

DOWN

1 Sows' mates
2 TV host with a book club
3 Food package datum
4 "M*A*S*H" staffers: Abbr.
5 Greets informally
6 Baseball cap part
7 Needed a massage, maybe
8 Precursor of reggae
9 49-Down war god
10 Plant expert's field
11 Give off, as charm
12 Garr or Polo
13 Rice who wrote of vampires
19 Accompaniers of carrots in a Birds Eye package
22 Haw's partner
25 El ___, Tex.
26 Belgrade natives
27 Forming clumps, like drying mud
30 Epitome of simplicity
31 Big Apple sch.
32 Spring sound
33 Land SW of Uru.
34 Utah, Omaha and others, on D-Day
35 Pink elephant sighter
36 Fight ender, for short
38 Tae ___ do
39 Hot car's destination
40 Giant in pasta sauce
44 Responds to a morning alarm
45 Workbench gripper
46 Some football linemen: Abbr.
47 Sunni and Shia, for two
48 "10 ___ or less" (checkout sign)
49 Like Odin or 9-Down
50 Business presentation aid
51 Aids for the stumped
52 Rush week venue, for short
53 Sprinter's assignment
57 Running account at a bar
58 Geologic time
60 Day before a big event

by Steven Ginzburg

15

ACROSS

1 Source of the music for a 2001 theatrical hit
5 Partner of grease
9 Business card number
12 Legendary opera star
15 Shortly
17 Rabid fan
18 "The one beer to have when you're having more than one" sloganeer
19 Fixed, as a tapestry
20 ___ in cat
21 Hubs: Abbr.
22 Come back following renovations, say
24 Admonition to a cell phone user in a theater
25 Comet, for one
28 Seen
31 Bank job
32 Wing, perhaps
34 Laugh syllable
35 E.R.A. part: Abbr.
36 Ad follower
38 Giant slugger
39 Something to stroke
40 O.T. book
41 Fear
43 Part of dressy attire for a woman
45 Foursome
47 Some revenue
49 Contents of a hoedown seat
50 Echo
51 Identity theft targets: Abbr.
53 Theater sign
54 Available, as a London limo
58 Stir-fried entree
60 How a particularly close nephew may be treated
61 Upstage
62 Mythical sea creature
63 Starting point for a long drive?
64 Not much
65 Banks on TV

DOWN

1 Rent-___
2 Wished
3 Arch above the eye
4 Night lights
5 Tell apart
6 Like the sun god Inti
7 Sounds from a 50-Down
8 Old carrier inits.
9 Superfluous person
10 Yank or Ray
11 Gen ___
13 Like some Adventists
14 Round snack items
16 Anne of HBO's "Hung"
23 Cry in "Hair"
24 Intuition
25 Sound from a monastery
26 Army Corps of Engineers construction
27 Quaver
28 Dog doc
29 Colonel's insignia
30 Refuse
33 Bumps
37 California's Fort ___
42 Ticked off
44 Lady Lindy
46 Certain filers
48 Bar closing time, often
50 Sports venue
51 Highlander, e.g.
52 Actress Elisabeth
53 Dressy attire for a man
55 "The Lord ___ shepherd . . ."
56 Enthusiastic audience response
57 Sicilian resort city
59 ___ Na Na

by Jim Hyres

ACROSS

1 Card game in which a player might ask "Got any 8's?"
7 Sluggers' stats
11 B'way's "Les ___"
14 Southwest Indian home
15 Alan of "M*A*S*H"
16 Useful item accompanying a face card in blackjack
17 San ___ (Hearst castle)
18 Coconut source
20 Fall for it
22 "The Simpsons" clerk
25 "The Simpsons" neighbor
26 Raggedy ___
27 Give away temporarily
29 Jilts
33 Brother of Cain and Abel
36 Walk the runway at a fashion show
38 Complains
40 Actress Scala
41 Start something that one shouldn't start
44 Certain camera, for short
45 Sacred song
46 Liberates
47 Head: Fr.
49 Bowler's button
51 Steeple contents
52 Hem's partner
54 Astronaut Grissom
56 Bill the Science Guy
57 Be a sucker
62 Insert in a tape recorder
63 Boxing combo
67 What the rings signify on a tree
68 Verb go-with
69 Hell-___ (rowdy sort)
70 Call to a shepherd
71 State when one's nose is out of joint
72 Hook, line and ___

DOWN

1 Navigational gizmo
2 Yes, in Québec
3 Masc. alternative
4 "Yeah, sure"
5 M.I.T.'s ___ School of Management
6 Gave a toot
7 Transfixed
8 Unexciting
9 Twiddling one's thumbs
10 Latin ballroom dance
11 Algae color
12 Rapper turned actor
13 New York's Tappan ___ Bridge
19 Bronzes at the beach
21 Instill with the three R's
22 "Close but no cigar"
23 Us Weekly rival
24 Disney lyric repeated before "Darling it's better / Down where it's wetter"
28 Lion's lair
30 Lions' hair
31 Tutee
32 Letters on a Coppertone bottle
34 Opportune
35 Big inconvenience
37 Escapee's run
39 Abbr. in personals
42 Where streets meet: Abbr.
43 Globe
48 Grabs dinner
50 English monarchs from Henry VII through Elizabeth I
53 Birds in many birdhouses
55 Egyptian desert
57 Daffy
58 School for princes William and Harry
59 Decorative needle case
60 Period of fasting
61 No, in Nuremberg
62 Taxi
64 "Tut-tut"
65 Itsy-bitsy
66 Hockey's Bobby

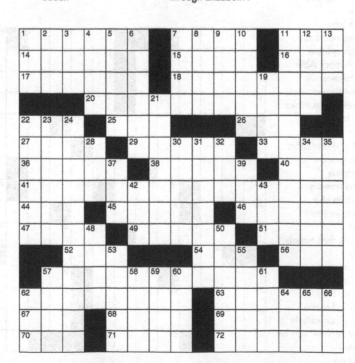

by Andrea Carla Michaels and Ashish Vengsarkar

ACROSS

1 Tight spots
6 "Pronto!"
10 Part of a Latin 101 conjugation
14 Family tree member
15 "Yikes!"
16 Ankle-length, maybe
17 Borrower's limit
19 Up-front
20 Hard to rattle
21 Joe Six-Pack's protrusion
23 Lake former, perhaps
25 Kemo ___ (the Lone Ranger)
26 Little devil's opposite
30 "___ a Rock"
33 Chips go-with
36 Harmless-to-humans slitherer
39 It may be floppy or pointy
40 Hit a serve past
41 ___-Grain (breakfast bar brand)
42 You can't escape it
43 "That's all ___ wrote"
44 Typical visitor to Cooperstown
46 ___ Vecchio (Florence landmark)
48 Night sch. class
49 Gut course
50 Neeson of "Kinsey"
52 Self-importance
54 One cause of deforestation
58 Star, in Paris
63 Visitors to the manger
64 Conflict settled by the Treaty of Paris in 1856
66 Queens tennis stadium
67 1965 Beatles song or movie
68 Use more 3-in-One on
69 "West Side Story" gang
70 Works of 9-Down
71 Word that can follow the ends of 17-, 21-, 36-, 44-, 54- and 64-Across

DOWN

1 Popular ballpoints
2 Concerning, on a memo
3 Pirate or Padre, for short
4 Miami-___ County
5 Bernie Madoff job
6 Co. offering a Buddy List
7 Send via DHL, say
8 Cornerstone word
9 Keats and Horace, for two
10 Pseudopod-forming organism
11 Canadiens' rivals
12 Jump on the ice
13 Facetious nickname for a giant
18 Samovar beverage
22 Military site
24 Apply incorrectly
26 Visibly shocked
27 Cheesy snack
28 Go-ahead
29 J.F.K. posting: Abbr.
31 Starts the kitty
32 Venus de Milo material
34 Skewered Asian fare
35 Concert venue
37 Genetic letters
38 Sedona and Sorento automaker
42 Atlantic state in two time zones: Abbr.
44 Put up with
45 Trapeze artist's attire
47 Straightens (up)
51 Like many a Clint Eastwood character
53 "I didn't know that!"
54 Key with three sharps: Abbr.
55 Item on a docket
56 Ticked off
57 Aswan's river
59 Fit to serve
60 Lottery player's cry of elation
61 Of the flock
62 Writer ___ Stanley Gardner
65 "M*A*S*H" cops, for short

by Alan Arbesfeld

ACROSS

1 Third-party account
7 Key of Beethoven's Seventh: Abbr.
11 Smoked fare, for short
14 J. Lo title role
15 Common command in Basic programming
16 Évian water
17 Arborists
19 ___ Tomé and Príncipe (equatorial land)
20 "Buenos ___!"
21 U.S.N. junior officer: Abbr.
22 Summer hours in Va.
24 Capitalism
30 Cause for an R rating
31 Margaret Mitchell family
32 Jack Horner line ender
35 Allen and Coen
39 Some touch screens, for short
40 Disagree
43 Roman Cath. title
44 Get cozy
45 O.R. figures
46 "It has come to my attention . . ."
48 My ___, Vietnam
50 Tuneful Ford
56 Key that might close a dialog box
57 Letters in a U.R.L.
58 Buffer areas, briefly
60 Former cabinet department
62 Art show that might feature "Fish Magic"
66 Nabokov novel
67 Recovered from
68 University of Oregon city
69 Costa del ___
70 Beats by a hair
71 Colossus locale

DOWN

1 Town line sign abbr.
2 Times Roman typeface feature
3 Find innocent
4 Big Cup maker
5 See 32-Down
6 Become full, as the moon
7 99 of "Get Smart," e.g.
8 "What hath God wrought" sender
9 Court V.I.P.: Abbr.
10 Nativity figure
11 Roused to action
12 Cote call
13 Quid pro ___
18 Compose, in a way
23 Unmerciful Athenian lawgiver
25 Some shoes . . . and a feature of this puzzle's theme

26 Renews, say
27 ___ Park, N.J.
28 Libertine of myth
29 Some hook shapes
32 With 5-Down, ticket words
33 Israel's Dayan
34 For the most part
36 Giggle bit
37 1950s campaign inits.
38 Adolph Ochs's newspaper: Abbr.
41 ___ fats
42 Go like heck
47 Think, colloquially
49 Roy G. Biv part
51 Take three of three, say
52 Still-life pieces
53 12-Down producer
54 Fix firmly: Var.
55 Slate or Salon

59 Jeanne d'Arc et al.: Abbr.
60 "Time ___ . . ."
61 Hubbub
63 Mid first-century year
64 Ballot marker
65 "What the . . . ?"

by Richard Chisholm

ACROSS

1 Home
6 If A > B and B > C, then A > C, e.g.
11 '60s hallucinogen
14 Subtraction from a bank account
15 Cage or Penn
16 Teardrop's starting point
17 Film director's sound?
19 Massachusetts' Cape ___
20 Nun from Ávila
21 "Goodness gracious!"
23 Genetic letters
24 Bard of ___
26 Birth control advocate's fury?
33 Architect Saarinen
34 Old photo tint
35 How some mail-order packages arrive, for short
37 Puts on
38 Barcelona's home
39 Amount between all and none
40 U.S.N. officer
41 Coin toss call
42 1998 Disney film set in China
43 Jazz pianist's court appearance?
46 X-ray vision blocker
47 Letter after wye
48 Bamboo-eating animal
51 Words of longing
56 55-Down's cold war foe
57 Comedian's parents?
60 Ullmann from Norway
61 Submit one's tax return via computer
62 Horses with speckled coats
63 Wages
64 7/4/1776 and 12/7/1941, e.g.
65 This, that and the ___

DOWN

1 Foofaraws
2 Alternative to suspenders
3 News item listing surviving kin
4 Branches off
5 Everlasting
6 Lad's mate
7 Eight: Prefix
8 Classic muscle car
9 Charged particle
10 Onetime center of Italian violin manufacture
11 Edward who wrote humorous verse
12 Working well together, after "in"
13 Say no to
18 Derrière
22 Where London is: Abbr.
24 Venomous, as a snake
25 Conceited
26 Ancient Persian
27 "Get ___ Little Dogies"
28 Get the soap out
29 Caught sight of
30 Dabbling ducks
31 Bacteria in a breakout
32 Not italic
36 China's ___ Xiaoping
38 Chronicle
39 It's guaranteed to hit the mark
41 Dealt with, as an injury
42 Eminent conductor
44 Antiquated
45 Basso Pinza
48 Solid parts of orange juice
49 It's east of Europe
50 Armada
51 Capri, for one
52 Sras. : Mexico :: ___ : France
53 Opposite of nah
54 French department
55 56-Across's cold war foe
58 Three ___ kind
59 Sch. near Harvard

by Bernice Gordon

ACROSS

1 *One attracted to a flame
5 Maker of the Outback
11 ___ pro nobis
14 A single time
15 Smoothing tools
16 Scott Joplin composition
17 *Bygone $20 gold coin
19 "___ Could Turn Back Time" (1989 Cher hit)
20 ___ bit (slightly)
21 Skillful
23 Cause for a blessing
27 Joanne of "Red River"
29 Wrist-elbow connector
30 Baby-sat, say
31 Guitarist Segovia
33 Eye
34 Nanosecond
36 Just enough to wet one's whistle
38 What the answers to all the asterisked clues are
42 U.F.O. fliers
43 "Can't you take ___?"
44 Actress Rowlands
45 Leaning type
47 "To your health!"
49 Was friends with
50 One of Captain Ahab's legs
52 Lifelines?
53 Poet Nash and others
55 "I'm ___!"
57 Hydroelectric facility
58 *President's ride
64 Pub order
65 Brainstorm
66 Rocker Stefani
67 Guy doll
68 Dreaded
69 *Pest you might slap

DOWN

1 Stylish, '60s-style
2 Singer who funded New York's Strawberry Fields memorial
3 Fort Worth sch.
4 Book after Philemon: Abbr.
5 Shot out, as lava
6 Peter Fonda title role
7 Bleated
8 Lee who directed "Taking Woodstock"
9 Second start
10 Secondhand
11 Spherical home in a tree
12 *Mark on a Brit. military pilot's uniform
13 Antsy feeling
18 Lie in a hammock all afternoon, e.g.
22 Karel Capek play
23 Whacked, old-style
24 *Nocturnal songster
25 Grunts
26 First place?
28 Singer Bonnie
32 Morning moisture
34 More than 14-Across
35 ___ Tin Tin
37 High-school jrs. take them
39 Guy's date
40 Pier, during loading or unloading
41 Dr. Frankenstein's assistant
46 Shock's partner
47 Like DNA strands
48 Campus mil. group
49 Old "You press the button, we do the rest" sloganeer
51 Succeed
54 Innocent
56 Do, re or mi
59 Stephen of "The Crying Game"
60 Yolk holder
61 Not rent
62 Teachers' org.
63 M.D. specialty

by Fran and Lou Sabin

ACROSS

1 Dismounted
5 Designer Oscar ___ Renta
9 Last word in the Bible
13 Zippo
14 Athenian marketplace
16 Big, big, big: Prefix
17 Playground situation #1
20 Place for three men of verse
21 Where Springsteen was born
22 "Orinoco Flow" singer, 1989
24 "Right you ___!"
25 Give ___ go
28 Land of Esau's descendants
30 As per schedule
35 ___ me tangere (touch-me-not)
37 "Was it ___ I saw?" (cat's palindrome)
39 Drink you stir
40 Playground situation #2
43 Fab Four member
44 Long, long time
45 "Waiting for the Robert ___"
46 First-string athletic groups
48 "Portnoy's Complaint" author
50 High-fashion inits.
51 Internet access co.
53 Goad
55 Ol' Blue Eyes' family
60 Rash, perhaps
64 1962 Robert Mitchum/Shirley MacLaine film . . . or the outcome of 17- and 40-Across?
66 Vegetable on a vine
67 You can get a rise out of it
68 French 101 verb
69 There's nothing like it
70 December ad word
71 Wild hog

DOWN

1 Voting no
2 Croquet locale
3 Mental flash
4 Oncle's spouse
5 How diaries are written
6 Self-image
7 Anderson of "WKRP in Cincinnati"
8 Boxing venue
9 Femme friend
10 Restaurant reading
11 Coop finds
12 Rocketeer's org.
15 The Jetsons' dog
18 Whistler's whistle
19 From what place
23 Circulation line
25 Part of IUD
26 Namely
27 Coeur d'___, Idaho
29 Bill who said of his TV monologues "It's all been satirized for your protection"
31 Hit, of a sort
32 How you might respond to an offensive remark
33 Styles
34 Aid in show-and-tell
36 Swenson of "Benson"
38 Scout unit
41 Marinara sauce ingredient
42 Gives over for safekeeping
47 "Apologies!"
49 Sharpen
52 Glove material
54 Hardly Mr. Cool
55 Battle town of 1944
56 "Heads ___, tails . . ."
57 Gold rush locale of 1898–99
58 Some distance away
59 Fake
61 Words in a ratio
62 Poet Teasdale
63 Washstand vessel
65 That, to Juanita

by Maura B. Jacobson

22

ACROSS

1 Even a tiny bit
6 Family group
10 Employs
14 Tia ___ (coffee liqueur)
15 Opposite of taped
16 Having everything arranged just so
17 Official with a stopwatch
19 Goat cheese
20 Bragging sort
22 Uncle's partner
25 Going ___ (bickering)
26 Alternatives to woods
27 Sags
29 Pinup's leg
30 Broadcast
31 Resuming the previous speed, in music
35 See 5-Down
39 What 17-, 20-, 56- and 60-Across are?
42 Writer/illustrator Silverstein
43 Stroke gently
44 Owns
45 Firms: Abbr.
47 Subject of a will
49 Stable bedding
52 "The Thin Man" pooch
55 Wild goat
56 One good at forming connections with others
59 "And so . . ."
60 Miser, e.g.
64 Sir Christopher the architect
65 ___ Minor (constellation)
66 Bedtime story?
67 Fill
68 "Leave in," to a proofer
69 Crystal ball users

DOWN

1 Quantity: Abbr.
2 ___ chi ch'uan
3 Where the humerus and ulna are
4 Doesn't level with
5 With 35-Across, view from Cleveland
6 Split
7 Florentine painter Fra Filippo ___
8 Prevent, as disaster
9 Detective ___ Wolfe
10 Not yet in a recognizable shape
11 Take care of
12 All gone, as dinner
13 Constellation elements
18 Stretchables
21 Actress Farrow
22 John or John Quincy
23 Dickens's Heep
24 Oslo's country, to natives
28 La ___, Bolivia
29 Takes it slow
32 Disney deer
33 Mal de ___
34 Lead-in to nuptial
36 Program for kicking a habit
37 Angry, and then some
38 County on the Thames
40 Gangster a k a Scarface
41 Nincompoop
46 "Whoo . . . whoo . . ." caller
48 Cassiterite
49 Gushes
50 ___ firma
51 Thesaurus compiler
52 Toward the left side of a ship
53 Taste or touch
54 Halloween goody
57 Down Under birds
58 Former G.M. make
61 Sign flashed by Churchill
62 Something that may be pricked
63 Apt. divisions

by Mark Feldman

23

ACROSS

1 Playbill listing
5 Bygone J.F.K. landers
9 Fit-for-a-king spread
14 Hodgepodge
15 "We're in trouble!"
16 Tilter's weapon
17 ___-do-well
18 Job-related move, for short
19 Follow, as advice
20 "Tough!"
23 Riverbank cavorter
24 Calendar pgs.
25 Wall and Bourbon, e.g.: Abbr.
27 Grp. that awards merit badges
28 Keenness of mind
32 Problem with an old 45
33 Hindu master
34 More standoffish
35 "Tough!"
38 Completely off drugs
40 Reproduce like salmon
41 Disorderly stack
42 Quantity consumed
44 Took a load off
47 Duke's sports org.
48 Before, to Byron
49 Gladiator's milieu
51 "Tough!"
56 Source of annoyance
57 Wear out the carpet, maybe
58 Up to the job
59 1987 world figure skating champion Brian
60 Botanical balm
61 Womanizer's look
62 Dictionary word in bold type
63 Pound cry
64 Citi Field team

DOWN

1 Swindler's work
2 Native Alaskans
3 Sonora snooze
4 Dessert from Linz
5 "You bet!"
6 Former home of the 64-Across
7 Payment at many a New York bridge
8 "You'll have to demonstrate"
9 Alternative to heels
10 Pricing word
11 Like many automobile braking systems
12 Terrier type, informally
13 Half a score
21 Make use of, as experience
22 Accelerator bit
26 It begins in Mar.
29 Hired ride
30 Thurman of "Kill Bill"
31 Central spot
32 Read the U.P.C. of
33 Laundromat buy
34 "No fooling!"
35 Bit of 1773 Boston Harbor jetsam
36 Hot springs site
37 Cask material
38 When doubled, a dance
39 Speaker's stand
42 Org. that proceeds according to schedule?
43 Take-home amount
44 Navy builder
45 Short sock
46 Cops' stunners
48 Manicurist's tool
50 King's domain
52 "Did you ___?"
53 In the pink
54 Green sci.
55 Sound heard during gridlock
56 Who wrote "All that we see or seem / Is but a dream within a dream"

by Gail Grabowski

ACROSS

1 With 69-Across, ship of 55-Across
5 ___ d'esprit (witty remark)
8 See 67-Across
13 Less receptive
15 Part of some garden statuary
16 Sum of any two opposite faces on a standard die
17 Gossipy type
18 Aptly named ship on a later voyage of 55-Across
20 Body of water sailed in by 55-Across
22 Genetic letters
23 "Quíen Te Dijo ___?" (2003 Latin hit)
24 Cornstarch brand
26 Like most of the voyages of 55-Across
32 ___ scale
34 Salon supply
35 Citizen alternative
36 Vernal mo.
37 Top players
40 Apology starter
41 Copenhagen's ___ Bohr Institute
44 Palm Pilot, e.g.
45 Bigfoot photo, e.g.
46 See 55-Across
50 Pins and needles holder
51 ___ Carlos, Brazil
52 War stat
55 Explorer who sailed into 46-Across in 1609
61 55-Across's destination when returning to Europe
63 Top players
64 More precious
65 Series ender: Abbr.
66 Reach in total
67 With 8-Across, business of 55-Across's backers
68 Stephen of "V for Vendetta"
69 See 1-Across

DOWN

1 Informal greeting
2 Expert server
3 Nickname for someone who shares a name with the 16th president
4 Chains
5 Sport with throws
6 Attorney General Holder
7 Defeat, as an incumbent
8 1992 presidential aspirant Paul
9 Excite, with "up"
10 Declare
11 Laura of "Jurassic Park"
12 "A Day Without Rain" singer
14 Mrs. Gorbachev
19 Psychologist Jung
21 It might produce a line at a party
25 Cosine of zero degrees
26 Hosted
27 Having everything needed
28 Hebrew leader?
29 Island east of Java
30 Swedish retail giant
31 Say "Pretty please?," say
32 Educator Horace
33 Mayberry boy
38 Nabokov title heroine
39 Fen
42 Caustic substance
43 "Told ya!"
45 Tough
47 Regretful type
48 German children
49 "24" agent Jack
52 Bubs
53 "You don't need to wake me"
54 Italian wine region
56 Miles per gallon, e.g.
57 "A place you can go," in a 1979 #2 hit
58 ___-Tibetan languages
59 Hall-of-Fame QB Graham
60 ___ lamp
62 Gumshoe

by Jonathan Gersch

ACROSS

1 Sleep stage, for short
4 Nog ingredient
10 Opposite of subtracts
14 The "E" in 68-Across
15 Relative of a rhododendron
16 Losing roll in a casino
17 Abrupt way to quit
19 Former Big Apple mayor Giuliani
20 More greasy
21 State of weightlessness, as in space
23 Consumer
24 Suffix with cigar
27 Monk's superior
30 Actress Rosie of "Do the Right Thing"
32 Boat rower
33 Purplish
34 Betray by blabbing
36 Brings home for a score
37 B-ball official
40 Chocolaty morsel munched at movies
42 N.F.L. six-pointers
43 Talks off the cuff
45 Bluefin and albacore
47 Join forces
48 V.P. Biden
49 ___ congestion
53 Bolivian capital
54 Chooses, with "for"
56 Southwest Indian
57 Gets around like Superman
59 Flared skirts
61 Saharan country south of Algeria
63 Round, red firecracker
66 Political coalition

67 Quit one's job
68 Classic car inits.
69 High points of a European trip?
70 Annual tennis championship in Queens, N.Y.
71 Advice columnist Landers

DOWN

1 Get back, as lost money
2 Fictional girl at the Plaza Hotel
3 Arthur who wrote "Death of a Salesman"
4 Label G or PG, e.g.
5 Color of a picture-postcard sky
6 ___ of 1812
7 Antlered animal

8 Old, crotchety guy
9 Marvin of Motown
10 Circus performer
11 Narcs' raid
12 Mom's mate
13 Nathan Hale, notably
18 More grim
22 Month-long Islamic observance
25 Hammer or saw
26 Close-fitting sleeveless shirt
28 Roman love poet
29 Fives and ___
31 Africa's fourth-longest river and site of Victoria Falls
35 "___ better to have loved and lost . . ."
36 Hot dog holder
37 Fidel Castro's brother
38 "Giant" writer Ferber

39 Beach footwear
41 Performing pair
44 Type for book titles
46 Form of address in British India
48 Teases playfully
50 Mexican state on the Gulf of California
51 Tarzan and kin
52 Portugal's capital
55 Beetle Bailey's boss
58 Light brown
60 One of the Redgrave sisters
61 Degree for a C.E.O.
62 Entirely
64 That, south of the border
65 ___ Van Winkle

by Lynn Lempel

26

ACROSS

1 Moth-repellent closet material
6 Osprey's claw
11 E.R. hookups
14 Get around
15 First month in México
16 "Just kidding!"
17 *Dangerously unpredictable sort
19 Old "Up, up and away" carrier
20 Even-tempered
21 Last choice on a questionnaire
23 Nasty habit
26 Silverstein of children's literature
27 Christmas carols
28 Take a breath
30 Commercial prefix meaning "low price"
32 Add fuel to, as a fire
33 Harvest
35 "___ first you don't succeed . . ."
38 Sleuth, slangily
39 *Junk
42 Monk's title
43 ___-Seltzer
45 Irish Rose's beau
46 Coming-clean declaration
48 Clued in
50 ___ Boys' Choir
51 Cousin of a foil
53 Bottom of a 40-Down
56 Three-stripers: Abbr.
57 Entrance to a bay
58 They're on your side
60 Bygone muscle car
61 *Inviolable, as rules
66 Abbr. on an input jack
67 Harold who directed "Groundhog Day"
68 May and June, but not July
69 "___ and ye shall receive"
70 "But of course!"
71 Clueless . . . or where the answers to this puzzle's starred clues were all first used

DOWN

1 Animation frame
2 "Evil Woman" band, for short
3 Roy Rogers and Dale Evans, e.g.
4 Marketers' "language"
5 Fishing line holder
6 Show the ropes
7 Photographer Leibovitz
8 War aid program passed by Congress in 1941
9 Conquistador's quest
10 "That is completely the wrong way!"
11 *Likely to happen
12 One of five different ones in "sequoia"
13 Roster at the Oscars
18 Private eye's project
22 Collette of "The Sixth Sense"
23 Scene from a summit
24 Big chipmaker
25 *Jammed
29 Set the pace
31 Cost-of-living stat.
33 Insurgent group
34 Prefix with center or cycle
36 Ain't right?
37 Triumphant cries
40 It may be cocked or cupped
41 Noon, on a sundial
44 Bide-___
47 Healthful claim on labels
49 Joint: Prefix
50 Blood line
51 Summation symbol
52 Nay sayers
54 Any Beatles tune, now
55 Bill of fashion
59 ___ Krabappel of "The Simpsons"
62 "That feels so-o-o good!"
63 Morning hrs.
64 Visit with
65 Luggage inspection org.

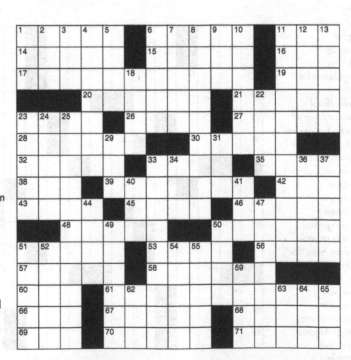

by Paula Gamache

Note: When the puzzle is done, the circled letters will spell, from top to bottom, the name of the town where all the people in this puzzle's theme once lived.

ACROSS

1 & 6 With 22-Across, noted 19th-century writer
11 British rule in India
14 With aloofness
15 It beats nothing
16 Arthur Godfrey's instrument, informally
17 The Ivies, e.g.
18 Where Emirates Airline is based
19 Málaga Mrs.
20 Refrain syllable
22 See 1-Across
24 With 53-Across, noted 19th-century writer
29 Some saloon signs
30 Took in
31 In ___ (as found)
32 The Bakkers' old ministry, for short
33 Meditate (on)
35 Subject of a Debussy piece
36 Places to hibernate
39 Noted 19th-century writer
43 Mushy snowball sound
44 Tre + tre
45 Have influence on
46 1945 Pacific battle site, briefly
47 Solar wind particles
49 "A" in German 101?
50 Little hooter
53 See 24-Across
55 See 70-Across
57 ___ sister
58 Went underground
59 Bull on glue bottles
62 2008 Pixar robot
66 H.S. subj.
67 Pope's triple crown
68 iPhone function
69 Alternative to white
70 & 71 With 55-Across, noted 19th-century writer

DOWN

1 Copacabana locale
2 Georgia Tech's sports org.
3 On
4 Sylvia who wrote "The Bell Jar"
5 Many-headed serpents
6 Glob of gum
7 TV's Kwik-E-Mart clerk
8 Place for a designer's name
9 Circular meas.
10 Monopoly avenue in the light-blue group
11 Rene of "Lethal Weapon" movies
12 Goodyear's Ohio headquarters
13 Casual wear
21 Lively, on a score
23 Tomb artifacts, e.g.
24 Table salt, chemically
25 Friend of Aramis
26 Prepare to drive
27 Bullet point
28 Superstate in Orwell's "1984"
32 Lamentations
34 More artful
37 Galley toiler
38 Coffee spot
40 Cutting-edge features
41 "That hurts!"
42 Daly of "Judging Amy"
48 Didn't skip something
50 Alternative to this and that, with "the"
51 Prone to complaining
52 Rustic retreat
53 Any of us
54 "The Audacity of Hope" author
56 Get caught in ___
60 Muff one
61 Bit of sunshine
63 Head of London?
64 52, in old Rome
65 Days of yore, in days of yore

by Kevin G. Der

28

ACROSS

1 Brown eyes or curly hair
6 Surrender
10 House in Spain
14 Cry of exasperation
15 Salve ingredient
16 Boxer Muhammad and family
17 $500
20 Stoops
21 Not knowledgeable in the ways of the world
22 Prefix with plunk or plop
23 Collection of information in tabular form
25 $5,000
30 Gladden
31 Sort of: Suffix
32 "___ du lieber!"
35 Exactly . . . or where to find 17-, 25-, 43- and 57-Across?
40 China's Chiang ___-shek
41 Tricked
42 Questioned
43 $10,000
47 Not to be missed, as a TV show
50 ". . . boy ___ girl?"
51 Pester
52 Divided in appropriate amounts
57 $1,000
60 Swampy ground
61 Snakes that constrict
62 U.S./Mex./Can. commerce pact
63 Years and years
64 Rodgers and Hart's "___ It Romantic?"
65 Nervous

DOWN

1 Fancy marbles
2 Banister
3 Singer Guthrie
4 Ice house: Var.
5 Stocky
6 Kodak product
7 Majestic shade trees
8 Only one of the Seven Dwarfs to wear glasses
9 Hair-raising cry
10 Ancient Palestine
11 "___ well" ("Don't worry")
12 Kitchen utensil with a mesh
13 So far
18 Sound before "Your, um, fly is open"
19 Take ___ account
23 Waiter's serving
24 Tennis's Arthur
25 Bozo
26 Inter ___ (among other things)
27 Bearers of gold, frankincense and myrrh
28 Biblical suffix
29 "Same for me"
32 Paul who sang "Diana"
33 Middling grades
34 Jekyll's counterpart
36 Undress with the eyes
37 Alaskan city near the Arctic Circle
38 Dance craze of the '90s
39 ___Kosh B'Gosh
43 Hotpoint products
44 "___ sow, so shall . . ."
45 What the weary get, it's said
46 Can. division
47 Molten volcanic material
48 Strip, as a ship
49 Cause unrest?
52 Bit of strategizing
53 Shepard who walked on the moon
54 President just before Wilson
55 Med. specialists who might treat tonsillitis
56 June 6, 1944
58 Hitter's stat
59 "I Spy" co-star Bill, familiarly

by Mark Feldman

ACROSS

1 Christine's lover in "The Phantom of the Opera"
5 Onetime science magazine
9 Philosopher with a "razor"
14 "___ Lama Ding Dong," 1961 hit for the Edsels
15 Paper purchase
16 Best-selling author Bret Easton ___
17 "The Lord ___ shepherd . . ."
18 Only common word in the English language with the consecutive letters MPG
20 Wild animal track
22 Command to a person holding a deck of cards
23 ___ lily
24 What colors may do in hot water
26 Moves back, as a hairline
28 . . . ADQ . . .
31 Carney of "The Honeymooners"
32 Catch some Z's
33 "This tastes horrible!"
37 Really ticked
39 Circus stick
42 "Comin' ___ the Rye"
43 Actress Winona
45 Captain for 40 days and nights
47 "___ approved" (motel sign)
48 . . . KSG . . .
52 "I don't want to hear about it!"
55 Perform really badly
56 Golfer Isao
57 Escape clauses, e.g.
60 Pair of lenses
62 . . . ZKR . . .
65 Cheese sold in red paraffin

66 Cowboy star Lash, who taught Harrison Ford how to use a bullwhip
67 Boat in "Jaws"
68 Trick
69 Rub out
70 Butterfly catchers' needs
71 German admiral Maximilian von ___

DOWN

1 Goddess of discord
2 . . . SPB . . .
3 Burned ceremonially
4 Walloped but good
5 "The Lord of the Rings" baddie
6 Lake ___, created by Hoover Dam
7 ID
8 Bestow
9 Not 'neath
10 Narrowly spaced, as the eyes
11 Aware, with "in"
12 All-Star Danny who played for the 1980s Celtics
13 PC platform released in 1982
19 Mirth
21 Necessary: Abbr.
25 Pairs
27 What Evita asked Argentina not to do for her
28 Fur
29 First anti-AIDS drug
30 Freshen, as a stamp pad
34 Fettered
35 . . . NKC . . .
36 Romance/suspense novelist Tami
38 Rubble, e.g.
40 The "L" in L.A.
41 Marks with graffiti
44 Baseball summary inits.
46 The middle part of 44-Down
49 Crazedly
50 One of about 100 billion in the human brain
51 Snakes
52 Expensive fur
53 Arctic or antarctic
54 "Seven Samurai" director Kurosawa
58 Tucker out
59 Zen Buddhism, e.g.
61 Right-hand man for a man with no right hand
63 Capital of Zambia?
64 Tankful

by Matt Ginsberg

ACROSS
1 Sailor
5 Austen and Flaubert heroines
10 Blitzing linebacker's feat
14 Own
15 Raid target
16 Ask
17 Served as well as possible
18 "El ___" (1983 film)
19 "Gimme a C! . . . ," e.g.
20 See 57-Across
23 Gene of westerns
24 One likely to lend a needed hand
25 "I'm stumped"
28 Meter reading, e.g.
32 Letter in Socrates' name
33 Releases
39 Dominican-born player in the 600 club
40 Writers Fleming and McEwan
42 Center of a 57-Across
43 Box gently
44 Bird's home
45 When repeated, statement after an explosion
47 Wildcatter's find
48 Annual feast
50 Prefix with red
52 ___ choy (Chinese green)
54 Finnish architect Alvar ___
57 Setting for a 20-Across . . . as represented by this puzzle's circled letters
64 Botanical angle
65 Friend in the hood: Var.
66 Flu feature
67 Nincompoop
68 Farm soils
69 Temple cases
70 De novo
71 Dawn
72 Overly docile

DOWN
1 Henry Higgins's creator
2 Home of the Dr Pepper Museum
3 Say with conviction
4 Pandemonium
5 ___ & Young (accounting firm)
6 Hungry cow, maybe
7 Wed
8 Dramatic start
9 Pen filler
10 Hand-held telescope
11 Geographical info
12 Storm's predecessor
13 Richard Petty's racing son
21 Contest at 20 paces
22 Blue
25 Down-home breakfast serving
26 Bear's landing place?
27 Added muscle, with "up"
29 On ___ things
30 Old carrier name
31 ___ Maples Trump
34 One with defib training
35 Chipped part of a statue, maybe
36 Bottom line
37 Economic fig.
38 Shelley's "___ to Naples"
41 Referral for further information
46 "Lovely" Beatles girl
49 Laura's 1960s sitcom hubby
51 Polite denial
53 Artist Frida ___
54 Actress Kruger and others
55 Stop on ___
56 "Thou ___, most ignorant monster": Shak.
57 Cake with a kick
58 Dendrite's counterpart
59 9 ½ narrow, e.g.
60 "Laughing" bird
61 Monster
62 Certain W.M.D.
63 PC site

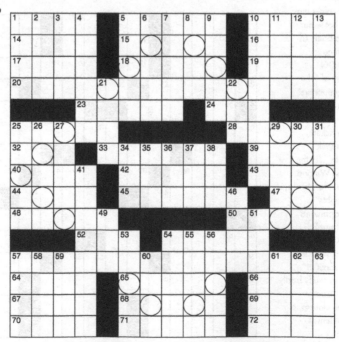

by Tim Wescott

ACROSS

1 Bit of sunlight
4 Effrontery
8 Make equal, as the score
14 Ram's mate
15 Sting, in baby talk
16 Piece of luggage
17 ___-o'-shanter
18 Likely result of pollution along a beach
20 "You ___ wrong!"
22 Peach ___ (dessert)
23 Title bear of 1960s TV
26 Says "Come on, try harder!," say
30 Classic theater name
31 "Le Coq ___"
33 Height: Abbr.
34 "___ Marlene" (W.W. II song)
37 Half of dos
39 Charles Nelson ___, longtime "Match Game" panelist
41 Receptacle for some donations
44 1910s–'20s flivver
45 Make equal, as the score
46 Simplicity
47 Postpone, with "off"
48 Center of a simile
50 Peeved state
52 Crush, with "on"
54 "It's so good," in Paris
59 Bewildered
61 Milan's home
62 Lenten treat
67 Edge
68 Mount where Noah landed
69 President before Wilson
70 Adam's madam
71 Sags
72 "Scat!"
73 Filming locale

DOWN

1 Change the price on at the store
2 In the know
3 The "heel" of the Arabian Peninsula
4 Leave the band and strike out on one's own
5 Exclamation before "How cute!"
6 52, in old Rome
7 "___ at 'em!"
8 Good's opposite
9 Abigail of "Dear Abby"
10 Sir Edward who composed "Pomp and Circumstance"
11 Point on a 13-Down
12 "Made in the ___"
13 Writing implement
19 Darn, as socks
21 Walk purposefully
24 Rejoices
25 ___ means (not at all)
27 Emperor after Nero
28 ___ Island (onetime immigrants' arrival point)
29 Broadway songwriter Jule
32 China and environs, once, with "the"
34 Swellings
35 Has left the office
36 Caused
38 Mel who was #4 at the Polo Grounds
40 "Aha!"
42 Nonsense
43 Sound of crowd disapproval
49 King beaters
51 Really digs
53 Prefix with economics
55 Certain bridge positions
56 Reveals
57 Martini go-with
58 Citi Field player, for short
60 Bar habitués
62 Owned
63 Bobby who was #4 at Boston Garden
64 Chinese "way"
65 "Humbug!"
66 Sci-fi saucer

by Richard Chisholm

ACROSS

1 Pop music's Cass Elliot and Michelle Phillips
6 Wander aimlessly (about)
9 ___ America
13 Frigidaire competitor
14 Debuts on the N.Y.S.E.
16 Court records
17 Member of Sherwood Forest's "merry band"
19 Existing
20 First pro team to play on artificial turf
21 Calif. barrio area
23 Pale as a ghost
25 Company stationery
27 ___ Na Na
28 Old console using Game Paks, briefly
29 Scrap for Spot
30 Turkish title
31 Antique shop item
33 Humiliate
35 Prince Charles, beginning in 1952
41 Blackmailer's evidence
42 Heavenly hunter
43 One signatory to Nafta
46 Belmont Park action
47 Moon jumper of rhyme
49 Claiborne of fashion
50 Cramped spot, slangily
53 Soil: Prefix
54 Fire up
55 Five Nations tribe
57 Blacktop, e.g.
58 Poker player's dream . . . and a hint to the ends of 17-, 25-, 35- and 50-Across
62 ___-European languages
63 "Judge Judy" figure
64 Elzie ___, Popeye's creator

65 Woad and anil, for two
66 Take a shot
67 Snacks often eaten inside out

DOWN

1 Prefix with ware or content
2 Bordeaux buddy
3 Seductive W.W. I spy
4 Unable to sit still
5 Margarita go-with
6 Action figures for boys
7 Words after "deaf as" or "dumb as"
8 Cry accompanying a head slap
9 Cattail's locale
10 Summer refresher

11 "Hogan's Heroes" setting
12 Brand used in 10-Down, maybe
15 Show contempt for
18 Writer ___ Stanley Gardner
22 Gallery event
23 "The Apostle" author Sholem
24 Elisabeth of "Leaving Las Vegas"
26 "Hamlet" soliloquy starter
28 Opposite of everything
32 N.Y.C.'s original subway line
33 Sounds of relief
34 Go astray
36 Just for ___
37 Place for a béret
38 Auto dashboard indicator

39 Pinot ___
40 Automaker Ferrari
43 Log-on name
44 Dresden's state
45 Skee-Ball site
47 One who sings to the cops
48 Like Nash's lama
51 Pranks
52 More coquettish
53 Irene of a Sherlock Holmes story
56 "In that case . . ."
59 "Git!"
60 ___ Paulo, Brazil
61 Four-baggers: Abbr.

by Sharon Delorme

ACROSS

1 Gallows-shaped letter
6 1975 musical with the song "Believe in Yourself," with "The"
9 Perle who inspired "Call Me Madam"
14 Not native
15 Stand buy
16 Sing the praises of
17 Attacked
18 The Caribbean, for one
19 Alternative to Rover or Rex
20 –
23 Wriggly fish
24 Wise old Greek
25 –
30 Subject of some tables
31 Cook's wear
32 "Now I get it!"
33 Essence of a person, one might say
36 What this puzzle's four missing clues spell, in order
41 Slalom section
42 "Frasier" role
43 Inflicted upon
44 Analgesic's target
46 –
48 Teeming
51 Atom ___, 1960s cartoon superhero
52 –
59 Hazardous
60 Tease mercilessly, with "on"
61 Sign up
62 "___ inside" (slogan)
63 Sculpting medium
64 Desolate
65 Plow man
66 In accordance with
67 Fillers of library shelves

DOWN

1 Duds
2 Banned apple spray
3 Dress not for the self-conscious
4 Butcher's stock
5 Non-pro?
6 Bathes
7 Standard of perfection
8 Passion
9 Became engaged
10 Blow the whistle on
11 Thickset
12 Trunk
13 Shorten the sleeves on, e.g.
21 Get an eyeful
22 Univac's predecessor
25 Massachusetts getaway, with "the"
26 Piece of music
27 Scepter toppers
28 "My mama done ___ me"
29 Italian diminutive ending
30 Tue. plus two
32 Wood-smoothing tool
33 Founder and first queen of Carthage
34 Reply to the Little Red Hen
35 In a bit
37 Arrestable offense
38 Endless years
39 What summers do
40 Nervous mannerism
44 Sarah Jessica of "Sex and the City"
45 Tartan pattern
46 Wild ass
47 Paper size: Abbr.
48 Biting
49 Perform very well
50 Coffee grounds and orange peels, typically
51 On the double
53 Tap trouble
54 Dry run
55 Sondheim's "___ the Woods"
56 Fill by force
57 Washington chopping down the cherry tree, e.g.
58 Part of B.P.O.E.

by Richard Silvestri

ACROSS

1 V.I.P.'s vehicle
5 Cry one's eyes out
9 Sudden impulse
13 Tracking dog's clue
14 Double-reed instrument
15 Glistened
16 *Backwoods locale
18 Parts of parkas
19 Averages
20 Colorful shawls south of the border
22 ___ Rica
24 Nintendo competitor
25 Spike who directed "Crooklyn"
26 Fireplace residue
27 *Particle with no electric charge
30 Commercials
31 Obstruction, as in a pipe
33 1950s prez
35 Boozers
36 Outbuildings
38 Sleeping, most likely
42 Golf peg
44 Place to buy a dog or dog food
46 Badminton court divider
49 *Stew made with paprika
51 L.A. campus
52 Ending on a campus e-mail address
53 Anglo-Saxon writing symbol
54 Monteverdi opera hero who descends into Hades
56 Marches in protest outside a workplace
58 Tiny flourish on a letter
60 Liability's opposite
61 Gush (over) . . . or sounds shared by the answer to each starred clue

65 "Crazy" birds
66 Hawaiian garlands
67 To the ___ of the earth
68 B&B's
69 "Fiddlesticks!"
70 Immediately, to a surgeon

DOWN

1 High tennis hit
2 Altar vow
3 *Apollo 11, 12 or 13, e.g.
4 "Ready ___, here . . ."
5 Ka-blam!
6 "Sesame Street" lessons
7 Stir-fry cooker
8 ___ of two evils
9 Cowboy's "Stop!"
10 *Commotion
11 Truly
12 Bungles, with "up"

15 Got smaller
17 Guzzled
21 Selfish sorts
22 Taxis
23 Nobel Peace Prize city
24 Church bell holder
28 Tactfully remove from a job
29 "Yuck!"
32 Winter hours in Minn.
34 Sup
37 U.S. anti-trafficking grp.
39 *Teased hairdo
40 Gaelic
41 Art ___ (1920s–'30s style)
43 Long-feathered wading birds
45 Lacking its wool coat, as a sheep
46 Katmandu native

47 The "Ed" of Con Ed
48 *Home of the University of Arizona
50 Still on the market
55 Roller coaster and bumper cars
57 Male companions for Barbies
58 Branch of Islam predominant in Iran
59 Sunrise direction
62 Above, poetically
63 Tooth decay-fighting org.
64 F.D.R.'s successor

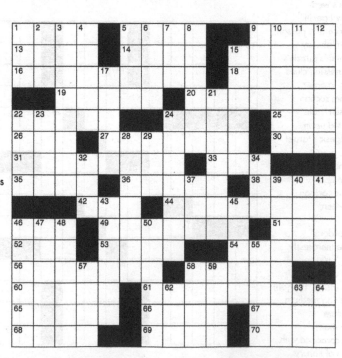

by Lynn Lempel

ACROSS

1 Composer Kurt
6 Basketball backboard attachment
10 It's the truth
14 "Are not!" retort
15 Dame who's a hoot
16 Jacob's twin
17 View from the Oval Office
19 Madams' partners
20 Grab ___ (eat on the run)
21 Wrecks beyond repair
23 Stay-at-home ___
25 Premium Scotch whiskey
28 Sportscaster Hershiser
30 Sip from a flask
31 Greeted the morning
32 First-rate
35 Tandoori-baked bread
37 Event featuring sports stars of yesteryear
42 Not a copy: Abbr.
43 New York's ___ Square
45 "Your 15 minutes of fame ___!"
49 Litter box visitor
51 Sushi bar soup
52 Pastry sold at pizzerias
56 Safety device eschewed by the Flying Wallendas
57 Levels of society
58 Like an unborn baby's position
60 10 C-notes
61 Make an abrupt change . . . and a hint to this puzzle's theme
66 Passbook amts.
67 Smooth, as the way
68 Kovacs of early TV
69 Word after Bay or gray
70 Eyelid woe
71 Aid in pulling an all-nighter

DOWN

1 It was hell, to Sherman
2 Punk rock subgenre
3 "You're on!"
4 Leopold's 1920s codefendant
5 Mr. Spock's forte
6 Found on this page
7 Like a "Ripley's Believe It or Not!" item
8 Cyclops eye count
9 Trousers
10 Addams Family uncle
11 Panini cheese
12 France's Bruni-Sarkozy and others
13 Bit of a fight
18 Greece's capital, in its airport code
22 Tropicana fruit
23 ___ Holliday
24 Folkie Guthrie
26 Partner of oil
27 On ___ with (equal to)
29 Drug sold on blotting paper
33 Visit while on the road, as a motel
34 Broadcast
36 ___ Wednesday
38 Prey for owls
39 Biceps' place
40 The rest of the U.S., to Hawaiians
41 "You're something ___!"
44 Preceder of com or org
45 #2 in a prosecutor's office: Abbr.
46 Newsman Dan
47 Chunnel's home
48 Patriotic chant
50 Chewy coating for an apple
53 Says while choking
54 Tennis do-over
55 Three-star U.S. Army officer
59 Commercial prefix with "flot"
62 Busby or derby
63 Wall creeper
64 Ipanema's locale
65 "___ who?"

by Gary Cee

ACROSS

1 "Whew!"
4 "___ ears!"
9 Weasel-like animal
14 Santa ___, Calif.
15 Big name in skin care
16 Saintly glows
17 Oversimplifies, as educational standards
19 Council of ___, 1545–63
20 Flying A competitor
21 A.E.F.'s conflict
22 Dragon-slaying saint
23 Club official
26 Archangel in Daniel
29 Judge in an impeachment trial
33 Not quite up yet
34 Bud holder, of sorts
35 Ab ___ (from the start)
36 Ballet rail
37 Frank McCourt memoir
38 Barrio quaffs
40 Noted 1945 photo site, briefly
41 It might get a 4.0 A.P.R.
42 Ad music
43 French newspaper since 1944
46 Mississippi's capital
47 Proof of purchase
49 "Hägar the Horrible" creator Dik
52 Part of a geisha's attire
53 Cries of surprise
57 North African capital
58 Job for a dummy?
60 Quick-footed
61 Pilgrimage destination
62 Draft pick?
63 Heroic acts
64 Bob Marley's "___ the Sheriff"
65 Genre for 1- & 22-Across, 22- & 26-Across, 26- & 46-Across and 46- & 49-Across

DOWN

1 Expressed, as a farewell
2 Cross to bear
3 Thanksgiving dish
4 Those with clout
5 Hump day, to an office worker
6 Affirmation
7 Explorer with Sacagawea
8 PC-linking system
9 Lustrous cloth
10 Dawn goddess
11 Uncle Remus title
12 January 1 song word
13 90° from sur
18 "Oh, ___!" (Pooh expression)
22 Dharma's sitcom spouse
24 5K, for one
25 A Swiss Army knife has lots of them
26 1999 Exxon merger partner
27 Blown away
28 PC backup medium
30 Picker-uppers
31 Convex molding
32 Baseball's Al a k a the Hebrew Hammer
34 Sportage automaker
37 Cheshire cat's place
38 End of a Caesarean boast
39 Place to dip a quill
41 Out of work
42 Guadalajara's state
44 Ruby's live-TV victim
45 City on the Loire with a quarter million people
46 "Goldberg Variations" composer, in brief
48 Results of abrasion
49 Thin nail
50 Latest thing
51 Best New American Play award
54 Jalopy
55 Where the traitorous Vidkun Quisling lived
56 1/12 of a recovery program
58 Early 10th-century year
59 It may be felt on your head

by Peter A. Collins

ACROSS

1 John of colonial Jamestown
6 The first "A" in N.A.A.C.P.: Abbr.
10 Bag
14 "Tosca," for one
15 "Get out of here, fly!"
16 Surrounding glow
17 Completely uses up, as a credit card, with "out"
18 Dana Scully's sci-fi partner
20 Prowling feline
22 Nissan sedan
23 Letter-shaped, threaded fastener
24 Washed-up person
25 Course in which to conjugate "amo, amas, amat . . ."
27 "We ___ please"
28 Dull pain
29 Autumn
31 When repeated, bygone newsboy's cry
35 Con's opposite
36 Mystery quality . . . or what 18- and 55-Across and 3- and 32-Down have?
38 Snakelike fish
39 H. Ross ___, candidate of 1992 and 1996
41 Party giver
42 U.S. military vet
43 Ancient Greek city with a mythical lion
45 Learn secondhand
47 Having insurance
50 Large, at Starbucks
51 Twigs for baskets
52 "If I may . . ."
55 Owner of the farm where Woodstock took place
57 Contest submission
58 Writer James
59 Vases
60 Have the wheel of a car
61 Transmit
62 Jab between the ribs, say
63 Mob

DOWN

1 Capital of Italia
2 Milky white gem
3 "Superman" villain
4 Something for nothing
5 Start of a billboard catchphrase meaning "close to the highway"
6 Equally plump
7 Photographed
8 "Red" or "White" baseball team
9 Courteous rejection to a woman
10 House style with a long pitched roof in back
11 Actor Murphy of old westerns
12 Middle of an Oreo
13 Designer Donna
19 Coat named for an Irish province
21 Steep drop-off
24 Sword handles
25 Northern Scandinavian
26 Field unit
27 It acquired Reynolds Metals in 2000
30 Sighed with satisfaction
32 Cowboy who sang the title song from "High Noon"
33 ___ Park (Queens neighborhood)
34 A, in Arabic
36 Nissan S.U.V.
37 None of the above, on a survey
40 Like two jacks in a deck of cards
42 Take away from, as profits
44 Goof
46 Tangle up (in)
47 Unconscious states
48 Missouri river or Indian
49 Reindeer teamed with Prancer
50 Esther 8:9 is the longest one in the Bible
52 Play a practical joke on, slangily
53 Talking horse of '60s TV
54 Brontë's Jane
56 Miracle-___ (plant food)

by Mike Nothnagel

ACROSS

1 Mountains
6 "Shall I compare thee to a summer's day?" has five of these
11 "Spare" thing at a barbecue
14 Eskimo
15 Instrument played with a bow
16 Gate guess: Abbr.
17 Solid with four triangular faces
19 Scoundrel
20 Lone Star Stater's northern neighbor
21 Unnamed person
23 Part of a word: Abbr.
25 Former Chief of staff in the Obama White House
28 Alternative to an iron, in golf
30 Sword fight, e.g.
31 Midway between sober and drunk
32 "Dies ___" (hymn)
33 Seat where people may sing 32-Across
34 Knee's place
35 Start of the Bible
37 Post-W.W. II demographic, informally
41 Bit of wordplay
42 Boar's mate
43 x, y and z, in math
44 Commercial writers
47 1958 sci-fi classic, with "The"
48 Population fig., e.g.
49 High muck-a-muck
52 Lifesaving team, for short
53 Most difficult
54 Loretta who sang "Don't Come Home A-Drinkin' (With Lovin' on Your Mind)"
56 Cobbler's tool

57 Shouter of this puzzle's circled sounds
62 "Didn't I tell you?"
63 John Lennon's "Instant ___!"
64 Explosive
65 Word repeated after "If at first you don't succeed"
66 Bird of prey's dip
67 Previously, in poetry

DOWN

1 Quarry
2 Suffix with propyl
3 Help in buying a car
4 Captain for Spock and McCoy
5 Series of steps between floors
6 "___ been there"

7 Reinforcements
8 Tiny bit to eat
9 Flower
10 Redwood City's county
11 Win back, as losses
12 Online music mart
13 By a hair
18 First thing usually hit by a bowling ball
22 Riddles
23 Big swallow
24 Days of ___
26 Colors
27 Kitten's plaint
29 Part of a pool for diving
34 Like an offer that's under actual value
36 Places for tanning
37 Idiot
38 Reach as far as

39 500 sheets
40 Old transatlantic speedsters
42 Driver's caution to reduce speed
44 Shocked
45 Bureau part
46 Jacob whose ghost appears to Scrooge
47 Fernando ___, painter of plump figures
50 "Nonsense!"
51 Carrion consumer
55 Innocent
58 & 59 Popular music style
60 Go wrong
61 ___ v. Wade

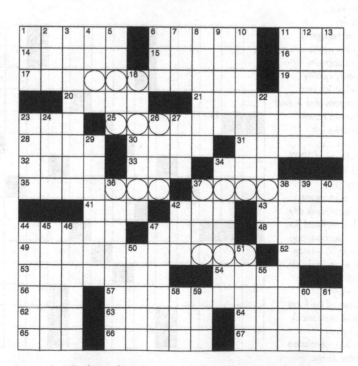

by Chuck Deodene

2

ACROSS

1 Slightly sharp or flat, as a voice
7 Insects in swarms
14 Encroachment
15 Retired Big Apple basketball player?
16 What tests test
17 Expounds upon
18 English racing site
19 "Das Rheingold" goddess
20 Brit's oath
21 Was well-versed in a will?
25 Sawbones
26 Hot time in la cité
27 Make in a cauldron
31 R-rated, maybe
34 Lock
38 Guinevere, to Lancelot?
41 Like some suspects
42 Lunch site
43 Kids' stuff
44 What you might get in a booth
46 Roxy Music co-founder
48 Macramé company's goal?
55 Cyclades island
56 Sorrows
57 Bloopers, e.g.
60 Miss the start, maybe
63 Theme song from "American Gigolo"
64 Select a sweater?
65 Even
66 Trigonometric ratios
67 Run in

DOWN

1 Torre Pendente city
2 Prepares, as the presses
3 What a king may win
4 List preceder
5 Stopped
6 Upholsterer's meas.
7 Oafs
8 Think up
9 Bank drafts: Abbr.
10 "Gimme ___!" (repeated cry of a University of Mississippi cheerleader)
11 Griminess
12 Follow, as advice
13 Woman's golf wear
15 Meanie
19 Blah, blah, blah
22 Woman-chaser
23 Ltr. routing aid
24 Earn
27 ___-ray Disc
28 Dorm heads, for short
29 E-mail address ending
30 Jane of "Father Knows Best"
32 "Huh?"
33 Puts off
35 Kind of boost
36 Short
37 Many figs. on stained-glass windows
39 Norwegian king
40 Numbers game
45 "Uh, hold on! That's wrong!"
47 Like things said after cutting to a commercial
48 Fun
49 "___ Is to Blame" (1986 hit)
50 Of element #76
51 University mil. programs
52 Look through half-closed blinds, e.g.
53 Less healthy
54 Type squiggle
58 Aussie runners
59 Number of dwarfs with Blanche Neige
61 Theta preceder
62 Hosp. staffer
63 Windy City transportation org.

by Mike Torch

ACROSS

1 U.S. disaster relief org.
5 Crackle and Pop's companion
9 "___ la vista, baby!"
14 Lumberjacking tools
15 Gondolier's need
16 Thespian
17 Jeopardy
18 Step after "write"
19 Baseball catcher's position
20 Spring egg distributor
23 Cartoonist Browne
24 Verdi aria "___ tu"
25 Gasoline additive
28 Wad of gum
30 Jetsam's partner
34 One who leaves money under a pillow
37 Fork part
38 Cove
39 "Yoo-___!"
40 Beauty parlor
41 Greenish-blue
42 Head of a major toy outfit
44 Largest city in Pakistan
46 "Big Love" airer
47 Depot: Abbr.
48 Greek letter X
49 Kind of date for an expectant mother
51 Ripley catchphrase that's apropos to 20-, 34- and 42-Across
59 "Keep your ___ the prize"
60 E-mail woe
61 Band's schedule
63 Disagree (with)
64 Heavy book
65 Poet Pound
66 Sloppy
67 Adam and Eve's first residence
68 Landlord's check

DOWN

1 Distant
2 Lighted sign above a door
3 Net
4 Posed, as questions
5 Mention
6 Agrees nonverbally
7 Disembarked
8 ___ Best of the pre-Ringo Beatles
9 Owner of Scrabble
10 Result of a "not guilty" verdict
11 Gobsmack
12 Means ___ end
13 Pretentious
21 Start of prime time, generally
22 Depend (on)
25 Adhere
26 Skater Harding
27 From the extreme north and south of the earth
29 Persian-founded faith
30 Possible sign of rabies
31 George Eliot's "___ Marner"
32 Provide ___ (allow to escape)
33 Group for geniuses
35 Stubborn
36 Charged particle
40 Search high and low
42 Prison weapon
43 What situps tighten up
45 Biden's predecessor as vice president
50 Write in
51 Smile from ear to ear
52 Rochester's beloved governess
53 Pants parts
54 Villa d'___
55 Apple MP3 player
56 Domesticated
57 Seep
58 Chance to play in a game
62 Mafioso informer

by Andrea Carla Michaels and Kent Clayton

ACROSS

1 With 73-Across, former New York governor
6 Enter unannounced, with "in"
11 Military mess workers, for short
14 Improve
15 Lucy's friend on "I Love Lucy"
16 W.W. II female
17 Gila woodpeckers nest in them
18 Layers of paint
19 ___ crossroads
20 Start of a quote by 1-/73-Across
23 Rank below cpl.
25 Not talking
26 What Fred Ott did in the first movie to be copyrighted
27 Crème ___ crème
29 Astronaut's work environment, for short
31 Actress Turner
32 Put down, as an uprising
34 Not ___ eye in the house
36 Brits call it "the pond": Abbr.
37 Middle of the quote
41 "Gimme ___ ding!"
44 ___ gin fizz
45 Fires
49 Memo starter
51 Win the World Series in four games, say
54 Perlman of "Cheers"
55 Sign painter's help
57 Crosses (out)
59 ___ McMuffin
60 End of the quote
63 Prefix with cycle or sex
64 Ancient Aegean region
65 Surgeon's assistant

68 ___ City (Las Vegas nickname)
69 Standing at attention
70 Trojan War epic
71 "___ Te Ching"
72 Drawer holders
73 See 1-Across

DOWN

1 Start of many a Scottish family name
2 Flu fighters: Abbr.
3 One of the three green R's
4 Call ___ question
5 Hatred
6 Turned out
7 Basic building block
8 Gershwin composed one "in blue"

9 Blow one's top
10 Elmer the Bull's mate
11 December celebration
12 "Beware the fury of a ___ man": John Dryden
13 Iran-Contra, e.g.
21 Slangy response to "Why?"
22 Hair goop
23 Instantly, for short
24 Fire: Fr.
28 Matterhorn, e.g.
30 ___ show (carnival attraction)
33 Part of U.C.L.A.
35 Casual greetings
38 "Hamlet" setting
39 Water-skiers' holds
40 Former Mideast inits.
41 Emotion conveyed by wrinkling one's nose

42 Willa Cather's "My ___"
43 Golfer Lee
46 "Toodle-oo!"
47 Unit of gunpowder
48 Slump
50 Cincinnati-to-Pittsburgh dir.
52 Ones living abroad
53 Each
56 "I can't remember if I ___" ("American Pie" lyric)
58 ___ the Hedgehog (video game)
61 Paper cut, e.g.
62 Navigator on the Enterprise
66 Uncle ___
67 Old Tokyo

by Barry Boone

42

ACROSS

1 Valentine's Day figure
5 Computer that once came in "flavors"
9 Channel with hearings
14 Porterhouse order
15 Crowe's role in "A Beautiful Mind"
16 Swordsman who leaves his mark
17 Stop talking, with "up"
18 Three-ingredient breakfast serving?
20 Word before mail or crime
21 TV brand
22 Canadian Thanksgiving mo.
23 Visually assessed
24 Afraid of wine?
29 Straight edges of pizza slices, essentially
31 "Rush!"
32 TV character who jumped the shark, with "the"
33 Former Portuguese colony in China
35 Powder holder
37 ___ pro nobis
38 Ill humor
40 Weapon for 16-Across
42 W.C.
43 Tristan's title
45 "Lay Lady Lay" singer
46 Largest dwarf planet in the solar system
48 Fan's reading
50 Frequent Woody Allen feeling
53 Foreboding cartoons?
56 Mideast ruler: Var.
57 Suffix with velvet
58 It's not gross
59 Wrestling extravaganza enclosure
60 The way of the government?
64 Volcano that devastated Catania
65 Totally wow
66 Very, very
67 Sailed through
68 Old TV parts
69 Not mint
70 Spike Lee's "___ Gotta Have It"

DOWN

1 1-Across, for one
2 1941–42 Allies vs. Japanese battle locale
3 Film that's been speechified?
4 Like some summer school classes
5 Words from an emcee
6 Mime who created Bip
7 Afghans, e.g.
8 Comedian Margaret
9 Brno native
10 More or less
11 Lead-in to law or med
12 Constellation south of Scorpius
13 Dictator Lon ___
19 Having a reddish-brown tinge
25 Tree on a Connecticut state quarter
26 Shout of disapproval exactly like another?
27 As to, on memos
28 White House appointment
30 Decorates, as a cake
34 Pearl Harbor ship
36 Many a party at Kennedy Center
38 '63 role for Liz
39 "No ___, no foul"
41 Cure-alls
44 Canyon area
45 Pass on
47 Blessing elicitor, sometimes
49 Portions of about 11%
51 Dotted-line user
52 Radial patterns
54 Dwarf planet in the asteroid belt
55 Got off the bottom?
60 "___ chance!"
61 Cousin of a cassowary
62 Smidge
63 Baseball's Piniella

by Ricky Ini Liu

ACROSS

1 Actor's representative
6 Group of actors
10 Eye desirously
14 Copy machine powder
15 German king who became an early Holy Roman Emperor
16 Whoppers
17 Rushed, as a decision
18 Throat soother
20 Gin-touting Whitney
21 I.M. provider
22 Slanted
23 Time just after sunset
27 Almost any element whose name ends in -ium
29 12th graders
30 Class for U.S. citizens-to-be
32 "___ you kidding?!"
33 Three: Prefix
34 Letter after sigma
35 Alan who directed and starred in "Betsy's Wedding"
36 Where dishes may pile up
39 Give off
41 Motorists' org.
42 Lowest-ranking G.I.
43 Paper Mate product
44 "Larry King Live" channel
45 Sneaky types
49 Latino's Yankee buddy
51 Go in without a suit
53 Rulers until 1917
55 "What's more . . ."
56 All ___ day's work
57 Problem-solving research institute
59 Shade of yellow
61 Slime
62 Boundary
63 "Winnie-the-Pooh" writer
64 Cheers for the matador
65 Warty hopper
66 Newspapers collectively

DOWN

1 Parthenon's site
2 Only soccer player who can throw the ball
3 Junior naval officer
4 Kind of profit or loss
5 Take a stab at
6 Hot winter drinks
7 Ring-shaped island
8 Disco guy on "The Simpsons"
9 "Animal House" garb
10 Radio blast from the past
11 Chitchat at a sweet sixteen sleepover
12 Ballerina's tight-fitting attire
13 Meeting of the minds, for short?
19 WWW letters
21 From Niger or Nigeria
24 Bandleader's "Let's go!"
25 Wrongful act
26 Low in fat
28 "Back to the Future" actress Thompson
31 Discontinue for now
34 Black or green drink
35 Restless
36 Really big, as a mattress
37 Brinker with storied skates
38 Nobelist Pavlov
39 Clean Air Act org.
40 18-Across ingredient
44 It's popped on New Year's Eve
45 Sent an eye signal
46 Fit for consumption
47 White sale items
48 Bowling scores inferior to strikes
50 Places to make 48-Down
52 Roo's mom in "Winnie-the-Pooh"
54 "Do not change," to an editor
57 Likewise
58 Hustle and bustle
59 Measure of electric current
60 Onetime space station

by Lynn Lempel

44

ACROSS

1. "Attack, Fido!"
6. Lose firmness
9. Greeted at the door
14. Ahead of time
16. Excruciating pain
17. Happen
18. Hefty volumes
19. Western writer Wister
20. Make a pick
21. Guaranteed to happen
22. Aussie outlaw ___ Kelly
23. First cable series to win an Emmy for Outstanding Drama
27. Drag show accessory
28. "Your Moment of ___" ("The Daily Show" feature)
29. Globe: Abbr.
30. Visitor from beyond the solar system
33. Titan, to 9-Down
35. Director Kazan
36. Process involving illegal drug profits, say
39. Prima donnas have big ones
40. Falco of 23-Across
41. Feelings, informally
42. What a high jumper jumps
43. Original N.Y.C. subway line
44. Coop denizen
45. Flip side of the Beatles' "If I Fell"
49. 500 mg., say
52. ___ May Clampett of "The Beverly Hillbillies"
53. ___ in queen
54. One seeking damages
55. Like some tabloid headlines
57. Retreat in fear

59. In pursuit of
60. Carpool, say
61. With 63-Across, name associated with the starts of 17-, 23-, 36-, 45- and 57-Across
62. Bug planter
63. See 61-Across

DOWN

1. Squelch
2. Extremely impressed
3. Like dry mud on cleats
4. Paradise
5. Three-time title for Yogi Berra, in brief
6. Potions professor at Hogwarts
7. Ad agcy. clients
8. "I didn't know that!"
9. Second-largest planet in the solar system
10. Ancient market
11. 1960s movement rejecting traditional gender roles
12. Suffix with labyrinth
13. Albany is its cap.
15. Hilo hello
21. Shell out
23. Lead role on 23-Across
24. Form of oxygen with a sharp odor
25. Speak one's piece
26. Catches, as fly balls
27. Domesticated insects
30. Unicellular organism
31. Boston airport
32. "___ form a more perfect Union . . ."
33. Long-running "S.N.L." rival
34. Arles assent
35. "___ Brockovich"
37. Jim Croce's "bad, bad" Brown
38. At any time
43. "Let me help with the dishes"
44. "Steppenwolf" author
46. Perjurer's admission
47. Provide with gear
48. Good at home repairs
49. Like Mayberry
50. Big name in balers and harvesters
51. Elizabeth of cosmetics
54. Funny Mort
55. It's practiced on "The Practice"
56. Transport for a 30-Across
57. $200 Monopoly properties: Abbr.
58. Rebs' grp.

by Alan Arbesfeld

ACROSS

1 New wing
6 Home of the Bonneville Salt Flats
10 Where "La Dolce Vita" was filmed
14 A-number-one
15 McGwire's friendly home-run rival
16 "Paradise Lost" character
17 User of barley malt
19 Stick in the mud
20 Sharing properties
21 Envelope marking
23 Straight from hell
25 Neighbor of a Thai
26 Rush week participant
30 Emphatic boast of responsibility
35 Fireside chat medium
37 Turf group
38 Slo-___ fuse
39 Start of a count . . . or the letter frequencies in 17-, 30-, 46- and 64-Across
43 Nascar sponsor
44 Satyr's feeling
45 "Amazing" debunker of the paranormal
46 One way to be armed
50 Clairol products
51 Marvel Comics villain with an eyeball-like helmet
52 Largest bird in the Americas
54 Count, as points
58 Go nuts
63 ___ Jannings, Best Actor of 1928
64 "And away go troubles . . ." company
66 "___ speak"
67 Thick serving
68 They're par for the course
69 Apply spin to
70 A-number-one
71 Miller's need

DOWN

1 Police dept. notices
2 Crowd in Cologne?
3 Carpe ___
4 Katz of "Dallas"
5 Title holder
6 Net handle
7 Glider's need
8 Between ports
9 Unbending
10 Musketeer's need
11 Cartoon canine
12 Phoenix landing site, 2008
13 Iowa home of the Cyclones
18 Raga player Shankar
22 What a skull and crossbones signifies
24 Zippo, e.g.
26 "Punkin" cover
27 Wound up costing
28 Masterful
29 Small songbird
31 Patriotic org. since 1890
32 Key shade
33 Throw off
34 Biographer ___ Kearns Goodwin
36 Hogwarts roost
40 Cause for a reprimand from a teacher
41 China's Lao-___
42 Streaking, once
47 Like a jack-o'-lantern
48 Hurts like heck
49 Pick up, in a way
53 "You're ___ friends"
54 Hardy heroine
55 Wildly
56 "Less filling" brand
57 Pullover shirt
59 Robin Hood's beneficiaries, with "the"
60 Abruzzi bell town
61 Treasure chest treasure
62 At one time, at one time
65 Draw upon

by Kelsey Blakley

ACROSS

1 ___ wool (soft material)
6 Heart or kidney
11 Inc., in England
14 Delta alternative, once
15 Rent
16 Lyricist Gershwin
17 Like a story that can't be believed
19 Mink or ermine
20 It's just below the thigh
21 Fall birthstone
22 Streamlined
24 Spouse's servile words
26 Fancy items worn around the neck
27 Military strategy during the 2003 invasion of Iraq
32 ___ the Hutt ("Star Wars" villain)
36 Ad-___
37 Currier's partner in lithography
38 Jazzy Fitzgerald
39 Veep's superior
41 Profound
42 Greek H's
43 Battery for a camera or phone
44 Late
45 Subject of a 1950s "revolution"
49 Classic cigarette brand
50 Novels, e.g.
55 1945 conference site
57 Skye, e.g.
59 Hairstyle that may have a comb stuck in it
60 Sports Illustrated's Sportsman of the Century
61 Prepare to use a rifle
64 "___ Miz"
65 Spacecraft's path
66 Golden Globe winner Nick
67 Abbr. after a phone no.
68 One-footer, say, in golf
69 Much of Chile

DOWN

1 Like a rabbit's foot or four-leaf clover
2 Together
3 Spiked clubs
4 Rode a Schwinn, e.g.
5 Mrs., in Madrid
6 Veteran
7 Singer McEntire
8 France before it was France
9 "Talking" done with the hands: Abbr.
10 Mandela of South Africa
11 Candy with a hole in the middle
12 T on a test
13 Gloomy
18 Ark builder
23 "Well, look at you!"
25 Spanish "that"
26 Newborn
28 Cloudless
29 Spherical cereal
30 Marijuana, slangily
31 Glimpse
32 Give a Bronx cheer
33 Midrange voice type
34 Secretly ban from employment
35 Score after dribbling, say
39 Huff and puff
40 "Gnarly!"
44 Special attention for a patient, in brief
46 Like a clock with hands
47 Recently
48 Property claim
51 Eagle's grasper
52 "Too rich for my blood"
53 Give a grand speech
54 Junctures
55 Where the Clintons got law degrees
56 Trebek who says "And the answer is . . ."
57 Long-range weapon, for short
58 0% fat, say
62 ". . . ___ quit!"
63 Code of life

by James Mulhern and Ashton Anderson

ACROSS

1 Gulf of ___, off the coast of Yemen
5 Animal acquired from an animal shelter, say
8 Coins a nickname for
12 Eyelike windows
13 QB Manning
14 China's Zhou ___
16 With 2-Down, group with the only James Bond theme to hit #1
17 Okra feature
18 With 10-Down, flashy jewelry
19 Ones who stand above the crowd?
21 International alliance
23 Eastern royal
24 Cuban base in the news, in brief
26 Petri dish gel
27 IHOP drinks
29 Silent hellos and goodbyes
31 Daniel of the old frontier
34 A.P. transmission
38 ___ for Africa
39 With 25-Down, start of a nighttime nursery rhyme
41 Not used
42 Dress shirt accessories
44 Wear away
46 Bright double star in Orion
47 Japanese prime minister Taro ___
48 "Put a tiger in your tank" brand
51 On the ball
53 Arctic seabird
57 Italian ice cream treat
59 Emphatic refusal
61 With 50-Down, #1 hit of 1969
62 Prodigal ___
64 With 54-Down, intro to a joke

65 Flew into ___ (got furious)
66 License plate
67 Cover ltr. accompaniers
68 Smartphone introduced in 2002
69 Sellout sign
70 Fake at the rink

DOWN

1 High-end Honda division
2 See 16-Across
3 Great joy
4 Bilbao boy
5 Coke competitor
6 "Do Ya" rock grp.
7 High and low water lines
8 Credit card balance, e.g.
9 Let loose
10 See 18-Across
11 Nick who comes at night
12 Scent
15 Media exec Robert
20 They line up between centers and tackles: Abbr.
22 Orwell's "1984" or Clarke's "2010"
25 See 39-Across
28 Martial artist who starred in "Romeo Must Die"
30 Fencing weapons
31 Tampa Bay footballer, briefly
32 The Buckeyes, for short
33 Klutz
34 Menus with reds, whites and rosés
35 Lennon's "Two Virgins" partner
36 Newsman Koppel
37 Run a tab
40 City near Manchester
43 French cheese
45 Cash who sang "Black Cadillac"
47 20s dispenser
48 She, in Sicily
49 Sudden burst
50 See 61-Across
52 Rock star whose name is spelled out by the middle letters of 16-, 18-, 39-, 61- and 64-Across
54 See 64-Across
55 Donald Duck, to Huey, Dewey and Louie
56 "All systems go" signals
58 Nabisco cookie
60 Squeezed (by)
63 Sculling propeller

by John Farmer

ACROSS

1 Like some cheddar
6 Spicy Asian cuisine
11 Musician's deg.
14 Personnel director, at times
15 "___ Mio"
16 Small island in a river
17 Olympic track-and-field event
19 Toiler on a hill
20 Knock to the ground
21 Latin list ender
23 Simple hanger
24 Beast in an Ogden Nash poem
27 Roasted, in Rouen
28 Childish plea
30 Play and film about a noted 1977 series of interviews
33 Humble abode
35 Make ready for winter flight
36 Loosely woven cotton fabric
40 Vintage synthetic fabric
41 Parts of a tour
44 Indoor dipole antenna, colloquially
49 Subtle glow
50 Melville work set in Tahiti
51 "The Lord is my light and my salvation . . . ," for one
53 Census datum
54 World of espionage
57 Causes of some untimely ends
59 Lunar New Year in Vietnam
60 Five-card draw variation . . . or a hint to 17-, 30-, 36- and 44-Across

64 Leandro's love
65 Bone: Prefix
66 Dementieva of tennis
67 Palacio resident
68 "Beat it!"
69 "Mary Had a Little Lamb," e.g.

DOWN

1 "Zip your lip!"
2 Historic racetrack site
3 Eau de vie from Gascony
4 "Ratatouille" rat chef
5 Green shampoo brand
6 Korean conflict, for one
7 Escort to a seat, slangily
8 Fish-fowl connector
9 Soothing succulent
10 Small salamander

11 "___ moment" (ad catchphrase)
12 Over and done
13 Reach
18 Massage deeply
22 Short opera piece
23 Desk toppers
25 1903–04 cars sold only in red
26 "Just ___!"
29 Washington Irving's Crane
31 No later than, briefly
32 Cpls. and sgts.
34 Actress Russell of "Waitress"
37 "The Lord of the Rings" creature
38 Ooze
39 Collar wearer, often
42 Roll call response
43 Clarence Clemons's instrument

44 Team listing
45 Current measure
46 Young stud
47 Money of exchange
48 ___ machine
52 Made low noises?
55 Spanish eyes
56 Opposite of fem.
58 Star turns in music
61 Basketball position: Abbr.
62 Mauna ___
63 Roll call response

by Paula Gamache

ACROSS

1 Former British rule in India
4 "Bon appetit!"
9 With 46-Down, 1969 album by the 38-Across
14 Yoko ___
15 Spitting nails, so to speak
16 "We're more popular than Jesus now," famously
17 Luau dish
18 Athlete trying to pass the bar?
20 Novelist Ferber
22 It may be worn around the neck at a convention
23 Enters again, as text
25 Egyptian god of death
29 In custody
30 "Nowhere ___" (1966 hit)
32 Where eggs hatch
33 This and this
35 Of the congregation
36 Concert receipts
37 Pallid
38 Group with the four circled members
41 ___ Jones industrials
42 Israeli carrier
44 Big fibs
45 The Supremes and others
47 Sitarist Shankar
48 "Gonna ___ with a little help from my friends"
49 "Open 24 hours" sign, maybe
50 Hitchcock film with a shower scene
52 Injured
55 Silencer?
58 Sketched
59 Toxic herbicide
63 Metal on its way to a refinery
64 Not so good
65 Had
66 Business for Shell or ExxonMobil
67 Like a fuzzy computer image, informally
68 Sound akin to "Harrumph!"
69 Funnyman Brooks

DOWN

1 Cowboy with a lariat
2 Battery terminal
3 Head out to sea, say
4 Quick swim
5 Pressed, as clothes
6 Festive events
7 Short news piece
8 Campbell of "Party of Five"
9 Light blue shades
10 Like eyes seemingly about to pop out
11 Droid
12 Summer in Paris
13 "___ Blues" (song on the White Album)
19 Immediately
21 Yes votes
24 Commoner, for short
26 Library area
27 "How much ___ much?"
28 Mulligan and others
30 One to whom "Ahoy!" is directed
31 Isn't well
33 Dweeb
34 Longtime N.F.L. coach nicknamed Papa Bear
35 Lion's den
39 Corrida charger
40 Long part of a rose
43 Driver's ID
46 See 9-Across
49 Noodge
51 Despises
52 "Beats me!"
53 Like a coincidence that raises the hair on the back of your neck
54 Live (in)
56 Mavens
57 ___ tennis
59 Piercing tool
60 Slime
61 Mess up
62 Summer hours in N.Y.C.

by Ben Pall

ACROSS

1 Eucalyptus
8 Not easily tricked
11 Typewriter type
15 Cast a spell over
16 "Time out" hand signal shape
17 Simon Cowell's former show, for short
18 Introduced to the mix
19 With 64-Across, everything considered
21 Use deep massage on
22 Donated
24 Toothpaste that Bucky Beaver once pitched
25 PC introducer of 1981
27 Where the North Slope slopes
30 Oscar-winning "American Beauty" writer
34 With 43- and 48-Across, everything considered
38 Habit-kicking program
39 "I have no preference"
41 Adriatic, e.g.
42 Stuntman Knievel
43 See 34-Across
44 Having similar properties
45 Actress Long of "Are We There Yet?"
46 Howard who announced "Down goes Frazier!"
47 Pullover style
48 See 34-Across
50 Avoid, with "from"
52 Oust from office
54 Internet access option, for short
55 Melvin of the Nixon cabinet
58 Droner, usually
60 Luke Skywalker's mentor
64 See 19-Across
67 The "O" of Jackie O.

69 Word after gray or Bay
70 Return addressee?: Abbr.
71 Phrases with "as a" in the middle
72 Quad building
73 Pedal next to the brake
74 Gets the better of, slangily

DOWN

1 First or neutral
2 "Go back" computer command
3 The year 1450
4 After "in," and with 44-Down, everything considered
5 "Way cool!"
6 Riddle
7 Sicilian hot spot
8 "Delphine" author Madame de ___

9 Call in tennis
10 Up to now
11 Tin that inspired the Frisbee
12 Inkling
13 Stamford's state: Abbr.
14 Capt. Pierce player
20 Backpacking sort
23 Traveling bag
26 Consumer protection org.
28 For a short time
29 Molt
30 Gladiators' venue
31 Ira who wrote "Rosemary's Baby"
32 Leading
33 Rent payer
35 Out of whack
36 German binoculars maker
37 Long and lean
40 Converse with
43 They carry a charge
44 See 4-Down

46 Publisher ___ Nast
47 #2's, for short
49 City near Raleigh
51 Like paradise
53 Bottomless pit
55 Washerful
56 Early do for Michael Jackson
57 Way of old Rome
59 Parks who wouldn't sit still for injustice
61 Capital on a fjord
62 Prie-___ (prayer bench)
63 Deputy: Abbr.
65 Use a spade
66 Coach Parseghian
68 Soul: Fr.

by Victor Fleming and Bonnie L. Gentry

ACROSS

1 Catalog clothing retailer since 1983
6 Suffragist Carrie Chapman ___
10 Signal receiver
14 Like a clear sky
15 Eastern domestic
16 Golden rule preposition
17 Goodyear offering
19 One cast out of paradise
20 ___ Lanka
21 Weather map symbol
22 Red telephone's connection
24 Israeli or Palestinian
26 Good to go
27 Boy soprano in a Menotti opera
30 Pro- or con-
32 Crooner canned on live TV in 1953
34 Political symbol
38 Act like a rat
39 Salad green
41 Skin cream additive
42 Litigation-prompting insulation
44 Justice replaced by Sotomayor
46 Many Marley fans
48 Song of David
49 "The Creation" composer
52 Bit of Java programming
54 Mountain previously named Peak XV
56 Chaney of the silents
57 Item with underwires
60 "Peter Pan" dog
61 Blackbeard flew one
64 One of American banking's Big Four, for short
65 Talks lovingly
66 River of Lyon
67 Panache
68 Hippie's cross
69 Plays resulting in yardage losses

DOWN

1 Shakes up
2 White House policy appointee
3 Gernreich of fashion
4 "___ tu" (Verdi aria)
5 Sneaky sorts
6 Inside of a toy mouse, perhaps
7 Buddy, in Burgundy
8 North Carolina gridders
9 Lt. Kojak
10 Feature of many muscle cars
11 Destination of Vasco da Gama
12 Put up with
13 Warm and comfy
18 Abner's radio partner
23 Make a misstep
24 Where lost hair may accumulate
25 Syrup source
27 Pond organism
28 ___ best friend
29 One with an "al-" in his name, often
31 Come clean, with "up"
33 Bible book after John
35 Utah ski area
36 Seasonal air
37 Kind of life insurance
40 Pitchers are often put in this
43 Compos mentis
45 Church keys
47 Play in the pool, say
49 Ergo
50 Be of use to
51 Spreader of dirt
53 Place to play stickball
55 Shelter org.
57 Political grouping
58 Needing a bath badly
59 Seemingly forever
62 "M*A*S*H" extra
63 Shelter financing org.

by Allan E. Parrish

ACROSS

1 Sunset direction
5 ___ sign (=)
10 Tempe sch.
13 State as fact
14 Breast-fed
16 Vigor
17 Latvia's capital
18 186,000 miles per second
20 Child's friend
22 Breastbones
23 Central points
24 Nonsense singing
25 Not making any sounds
32 Left-handed Beatle
33 Fetes
34 Prefix with skeleton
35 Not too soft, as pasta
38 Clearasil target
41 Sing like Bing Crosby
42 Taboo
43 Seabird native to the Galápagos Islands
49 "My bad!"
50 Worms, for a fisherman
51 Reveal
54 Only American League player to win a batting crown without hitting a home run
58 French novelist who had an affair with Frédéric Chopin
60 ___ noire
61 60-min. periods
62 Chic
63 "I can't believe ___ the whole thing!"
64 Fast jet, for short
65 ___ Rizzo, Dustin Hoffman role
66 Word that can follow the ends of 18-, 25-, 43- and 58-Across

DOWN

1 Twist out of shape
2 Blackhearted
3 Dreamcast game company
4 Amount of food at a cafeteria checkout
5 Intertwine
6 "Cut that out!"
7 Feel the ___
8 Cigarette's end
9 "___ Go Crazy" (#1 Prince hit)
10 Hasty glance
11 Perceived to be
12 Supply with more recent info
15 Summer clocks are set to it: Abbr.
19 Mexican moolah
21 "Après ___ le déluge"
25 Mimic
26 "Wailing" instrument
27 Status ___
28 15-percenter
29 ___ Fernando Valley
30 PC key
31 Fannie ___ (home financing group)
35 Terrier's bark
36 London lavatory
37 Scooby-___
38 Where to see elephants and elands
39 Schubert's Symphony No. 8 ___ Minor
40 Many an item in Santa's bag
41 ___ Romero, onetime player of the Joker
42 Zilch
43 Tree branches
44 Recluses
45 Like Brahmins in the caste system
46 Old U.S. govt. investments
47 Cool cat
48 Inexpensive pen
52 ___ Pepper
53 Deborah of "The King and I"
54 Diatribe
55 Derrière
56 Jazzy James
57 Bawl
59 Adriatic or Aegean

by Oliver Hill

ACROSS

1 City near the Great Sphinx
6 Mine treasure
9 Macaroni shape
14 Steve who was called Steverino
15 Turkish headgear
16 Golden egg layer of story
17 Rod in a henhouse
18 Magical powder
20 French lady friend
21 Peeved
22 1980s soap opera set at a winery
26 Fury
29 Blue literature
30 Blue hue
31 Cuts with light
34 Homecoming returnees, for short
35 1950s–'60s sitcom that ran on all three networks
40 Tale of Troy
41 Alfred P. ___ Foundation
42 Papyrus plant, e.g.
43 Plucks, as eyebrow hairs
48 Prefix with biology
49 Occasion for pumpkin picking
53 Almost
55 Killer whale
56 Part of a morning routine . . . or a literal hint to 18-, 22-, 35- and 49-Across
59 Knock the socks off
60 Not deigning to consider
61 ___ goo gai pan
62 Turn away
63 Ate in high style
64 Drink with a head
65 Fits one inside the next

DOWN

1 Wine container
2 Six-time baseball All-Star Sandy
3 Repetitively named Philippine province
4 Take out surgically
5 Ottawa's prov.
6 Take out
7 Show again
8 Net mag
9 1-Across is its capital
10 Mine treasure
11 Chic shop
12 C.I.A. forerunner
13 Not yet firm, as cement
19 Univ. dorm supervisors
23 Like some smoothly running machines
24 Tenn. neighbor
25 Wine containers
27 Jamaica exports
28 Atlantic Seaboard states, with "the"
30 Priest's robe
32 Blowup: Abbr.
33 Truth, old-style
34 Ed who played Lou Grant
35 Order after "Aim!"
36 The "A" in A-Rod
37 Get stewed
38 Duped
39 Guitar pedal effect
44 Change over time
45 Homes (in on)
46 Front car in a motorcade
47 Turns on, as a car
49 Not real
50 It might mean "I want a treat!"
51 Andean animal
52 "Disinfect to Protect" brand
54 Christmas light site
56 George Thorogood stutter "B-B-B-B- ___ . . ."
57 A sac fly earns one
58 Nail spot
59 Wave a palm frond at, say

by Jonah Kagan and Victor Fleming

54

ACROSS
1 Whole bunch
4 In an ark, say
8 Monopoly maker
14 Actress Lupino
15 Debtor's worry
16 Irish-themed Vegas casino
17 Bill Gates snapshot?
20 Baseball's Bud
21 "That's a joke, ___!"
22 Raw material, of sorts
23 Turkish V.I.P.
26 Full of energy
28 Banshees' boast?
35 In ___ land
36 Pikake garland
37 Actress Carter who was once Miss World USA
38 Blotter abbr.
39 Comedic soldier during training?
42 Lead role on "Providence"
43 Ten Commandments locale
45 Carrier with a hub at LAX
46 FIFA Player of the Century
47 Words to estate attorneys?
51 "Man ___ Mancha"
52 Reclined
53 Approach shot
56 Spinners at affairs
58 Mushroom producer, for short
62 Advice to the rash, and a hint to this puzzle's theme
66 Francis of "What's My Line?"
67 Prefix with skid
68 Big ___
69 Attached, in a way
70 New driver, typically
71 "Madame Butterfly" wear

DOWN
1 Bread in a jar, perhaps
2 Drooling canine in the funnies
3 Salt, symbolically
4 Nancy's friend in the funnies
5 Get out into the open
6 Sometimes-split charge
7 Son of Seth
8 Start of an elocution class phrase
9 Mother of Peer Gynt
10 Hard to make out
11 Composer Bartók
12 Heavy metal band with the triple-platinum album "Out of the Cellar"
13 Workplace watchdog org.
18 Item often worn with a sash
19 Fuddy-dud
24 Storytelling dance
25 Sidewalk stand buys
27 Hanukkah goodies
28 More than just reduce
29 Jack of "The Great Dictator"
30 Primary strategy
31 Kojak's rank: Abbr.
32 Adams who co-founded Group f/64
33 Pastoral piece
34 Does dock work
39 "Back to the Future" bully
40 "Wiseguy" actor Ken
41 Sections of digestive tracts
44 Like Steve Jobs and Moses
46 Niña companion
48 Codgers
49 Big Indian
50 Like a good deal for both sides
53 Facebook feature
54 Mata ___
55 Trinidad or Tobago
57 Game with 32 cards
59 Old Sinclair rival
60 Bit of theater litter
61 Actress Hatcher
63 Brian who produced U2
64 Phoenix-to-Philly dir.
65 Fr. holy woman

by Jack McInturff

ACROSS

1 ___ Club (discount chain)
5 Pain
9 Country adjacent to the Dominican Republic
14 "Quickly!," on an order
15 Runaway victory
16 More peculiar
17 Blended fruit-flavored drinks
20 Available from a keg
21 Opposite of naughty
22 Hawaii's Mauna ___
23 Christmastime
25 Old-time singer Julius
29 "Jumpin' Jehosaphat!"
31 News anchor Williams
34 Highlands hillside
35 ___ tai (cocktail)
36 Oodles
37 Nothing fancy
39 "Woof!," e.g.
40 Tummy muscles
41 Peacock's distinctive feature
42 Past, present or future
43 TV character who says "It's 1 a.m. Better go home and spend some quality time with the kids"
47 Shorthand pros
48 Before long
49 1970s Dodgers All-Star Ron
52 Harbor vessels
54 Thrust out
56 Words after the starting syllables of 17-, 29- and 43-Across
60 Oven setting
61 Wide-mouthed pitcher
62 What high rollers roll
63 Golf score of two under par
64 Pea holders
65 ". . . ___ and not heard"

DOWN

1 Give permission
2 Unanimously
3 A Gabor sister
4 Cowboy boot feature
5 Wily
6 High-priced
7 What you can do if you don't know the words
8 British prep school
9 Flapjack
10 Stick (to)
11 Uganda's ___ Amin
12 Summer shirt, for short
13 Org. with a 4/15 deadline
18 Silky synthetic fabric
19 Squirter at an auto garage
24 Mummifies
26 Financial adviser Suze
27 Roebuck's partner in retailing
28 Look-___ (twin)
29 Owns
30 Bush spokesman Fleischer
31 Sense of tedium, with "the"
32 C-3PO or R2-D2
33 Informal reply to "Who's there?"
37 Collect $200 in Monopoly
38 52, in old Rome
39 London's Big ___
41 Reason for a 911 call
42 Lone Ranger's companion
44 Call for
45 Combined, as assets
46 Recovers from a bender, with "up"
49 Physics Nobelist Marie
50 Draw out
51 Modern locale of ancient Sheba
53 Rung
55 Country mail rtes.
56 Lincoln, informally
57 Gun rights org.
58 Woofer?
59 Duet number

by Ed Sessa

56

ACROSS
1 Guitarist Paul
4 Sportscaster Albert
8 Singer Baker
13 Humorist Buchwald
14 Comedian Anderson
15 Philosopher Diderot
16 First lady McKinley
17 Director Welles
18 Comedian Sykes
19 Mezzo-soprano Resnik
21 Poet Teasdale
23 Author Fleming
24 Actress Carter
26 Statesman Sharon
28 Director Kubrick
31 Author Waugh
32 Actor Feldman
33 Baseball player Yastrzemski
35 Humorist Bombeck
39 General Bradley
40 Designer Ellis
41 Newsman Huntley
42 Tennis player Sampras
43 Country singer Bryan
44 Dancer Castle
45 Economist Smith
47 Actress Bening
49 Political adviser Hughes
51 Civil rights figure Parks
52 Novelist Radcliffe
53 Keyboardist Saunders
56 Skier McKinney
60 Actress Zellweger
62 Composer Copland
64 TV writer/host Serling
65 Nurse Barton
66 Soap actress Kristen
67 Actress MacGraw
68 Poet Ginsberg
69 Basketball player Archibald
70 Newspaper editor Bradlee

DOWN
1 Place to hibernate
2 Earth, in Essen
3 Unaccompanied
4 A pep talk may boost it
5 Neighbor of Ger.
6 Carriers of water to los océanos
7 ___ cava
8 Pop-up-producing program
9 Cultural grant org.
10 Certain navel
11 Kind of basin
12 Dumb ___ ox
14 In need of company
20 The body's balance regulator
22 Good news on Wall Street
25 Lecture hall
27 Good Humor product
28 Old English bard
29 No light reading
30 "I smell ___"
31 Overdue debt
34 Genesis craft
36 Orator's skill: Abbr.
37 Puzzle completion?
38 Perfectly, after "to"
40 Creator of shavings
44 Bonkers
46 Humiliate
48 Zero
49 Mournful ring
50 Yearly record
52 Old Spanish treasure chest
54 Parade stopper
55 Follower of "ooh" or "tra"
57 Spirited horse
58 Credits listing
59 Tennis edge
61 Bard's "before"
63 Abbr. after many a general's name

by Joe Krozel

57

ACROSS

1 Pilots
6 Biographical info
9 Lab wear
14 "Farewell, François!"
15 Marked, on a ballot
16 Oscar-winning Marisa
17 Gladiolus
19 Ain't how it should be?
20 Spic and Span competitor
21 Asia's ___ Sea
22 Rome-to-Belgrade dir.
23 They're usually aimed at heads
28 Areas between hills
31 Like Death Valley
32 Ancient Greek portico
33 Captured
35 Furthermore
37 Beer may be on it
38 Shake-up in the global balance of power . . . and a hint to the circled letters
42 New Jersey's Fort ___
43 Author Silverstein
44 Originally
45 Digging
47 Jai ___
49 Health menace, briefly
53 Need a nap
56 Actress Peeples
57 Copier unit
58 Doing better at the casino, say
61 Kind of patch
63 It's done outside a lab
65 Idolize
66 School department
67 Renaissance faire sight
68 "The Bells of St. ___"
69 "You got it!"
70 Gripped on a bench

DOWN

1 Latched, in a way
2 Currie who wrote "A Parliamentary Affair"
3 Train company founded in 1900
4 Piddling
5 Some cold ones
6 Armpit
7 Solidify
8 Joseph ___, who lent his name to some ice cream
9 M.V.P. of the first two Super Bowls
10 Some eels
11 Dish that may be prepared in a special pan
12 1900–99, e.g.: Abbr.
13 Do-it-yourselfer's purchase
18 It's a long shot, usually
21 Builds an extension
24 Unwritten rules
25 Wacky
26 Jet engine's output
27 Spring run
29 "How disgusting!"
30 Scatters seeds
34 Something a doctor should do
36 Tram loads
38 Roger Maris, for the Yankees
39 Like some paint
40 Move, to a real-estate broker
41 The Pistons, on a scoreboard
42 "What's the ___?"
46 Famed Chicago livestock owner
48 Keys
50 Negatively charged particles
51 Buchanan's predecessor
52 Listened, poetically
54 Challenges
55 Actor Brynner
59 Year the Vandals sacked Rome
60 River in a 1957 film
61 Impact sound
62 Vitamin no.
63 Former baseball commissioner Vincent
64 Tick off

by Peter A. Collins

58

ACROSS

1 Prefix with dextrous
5 Musketeer with Porthos and Aramis
10 Bart Simpson's brainy sister
14 Detach from a source of dependence
15 Musical beat
16 Desertlike
17 Acupuncture, e.g.
20 Goes "A-a-a-choo!"
21 Tickles the fancy
22 Go up
23 The "A" in P.T.A.: Abbr.
24 Furnace, e.g.
29 "___ side are you on anyway?"
31 Good name for a Dalmatian
32 "___ about had it up to here!"
33 Male deer
34 Surface again, as a driveway
36 Extended family
37 1980s sitcom with an extraterrestrial
38 One-person performance
39 "___ you glad?"
40 Rough-terrain cyclist
44 Helper
45 Oklahoma city
46 Bolts (down)
49 Two-page ads
53 Samoan or Fijian
56 Quod ___ demonstrandum
57 Andrea ___, ill-fated ship
58 Writer Émile
59 TV's warrior princess
60 What to call Spain's Juan Carlos
61 15-percenters: Abbr.

DOWN

1 Fills with wonder
2 Like taking candy from a baby?
3 First, second or third, on a diamond
4 Bank accrual
5 Motionless
6 More uptight
7 "Well, let me think . . ."
8 Unlock, to a bard
9 Popular teen hangout 50+ years ago
10 Gap in a manuscript
11 Pupil surrounder
12 Trig function
13 Fruit beverages
18 Web mag
19 "No more for me"
23 Mighty Dog competitor
24 Greek port where Prince Philip was born
25 ___ Martin (James Bond car)
26 Bathroom floor installer
27 Former Indiana senator Bayh
28 Payment in Monopoly
29 "Kapow!"
30 Circle of angels?
34 Where a hot dog stand may stand
35 "Night" author Wiesel
36 Sideboard
38 Not flexible, as muscles
39 Director Kurosawa
41 Airport near Tokyo
42 Nickname for Elizabeth
43 Live, as a football
46 X-ray ___ (novelty item)
47 Have concern
48 Open up ___ of worms
50 Work like ___
51 Shoulder muscle, briefly
52 Mmes., in Madrid
54 Rank above maj.
55 Abbr. on a clothing sale item

by Tim Darling

ACROSS
1 Lamebrain
5 Kind of TV now converted from digital
11 Wood-shaping tool
14 Gas brand in Canada
15 Where to dock a Sea Ray
16 Monk's title
17 Zealous sort whose schedule may include 27-, 50- and 64-Across
19 Cyclotron bit
20 Weapon using high-arcing ammo
21 Morale booster
22 Early second-century year
23 Desktop picture
25 Japanese dramatic form
26 Suffix with chlor- or sulf-
27 See 17-Across
31 Head honcho
32 Spitfire-flying grp.
33 Rapper Kanye
34 Tax investigator, for short
36 Port of old Rome
38 A/C fig.
40 Spin doctor's concern
43 Golf innovator Callaway and bridge maven Culbertson
45 She-bears, south of the border
47 Barker
48 Like bad losers
50 See 17-Across
53 Printers' measures
54 London facility
55 Greek counterpart of Mars
56 Blond shade
57 River of Florence
59 Material thing
63 "Mamma ___!"
64 See 17-Across

66 Off-road transport, for short
67 One unlikely to compromise
68 Fuel from bogs
69 Word in alumnae bios
70 Big name in small swimsuits
71 Many-axled vehicle

DOWN
1 Appear to be
2 Golf's ___ Aoki
3 Roman Cath. title
4 Word with justice or license
5 Cynical Bierce
6 Scot's denial
7 ___ Sea (Amu Darya's outlet)
8 Kind of will
9 What a flamingo might stand on

10 Country's Brooks
11 Devotee
12 Sci-fi automatons
13 Class clowns, e.g.
18 Monticello or Saratoga
24 Crash-probing agcy.
27 Old hand
28 Refrain syllables
29 Item in a man's medicine chest
30 10th-century Holy Roman emperor
31 Emeril catchword
35 Loaded onto the wrong truck, say
37 Spot in the Seine
39 McCain's alma mater: Abbr.
41 55-Across, e.g.
42 I, to Claudius
44 Save for a rainy day

46 Go along with
48 One on deck
49 Like some job training
51 Novelist ___ de Balzac
52 Movie camera lens settings
54 Northern Scandinavians
58 Mayberry boy
60 "Gotcha"
61 Orioles or Cardinals
62 Bigfoot's Asian cousin
65 Tripper's turn-on

by Steve Dobis

ACROSS

1 Fish tank buildup
6 Go off
9 It flows through Turin
14 Othello, for one
16 Leggy wader
17 Help for a pioneer
18 French first lady __ Bruni-Sarkozy
19 H.S. course
20 More unearthly
22 Real looker
23 Alan Paton's "__, the Beloved Country"
24 Thin nail
26 Milne hopper
27 Symbols of goodness
30 Experiment subject
32 Fall site
33 Flier to Stockholm
34 "Dumb and Dumber" actress
35 Offering from the front desk
37 Classic Steinbeck story, with "The"
40 First-time driver, often
41 United
42 Geraint's love, in Arthurian legend
43 Unable to hear
46 Answers in court
47 Frog predator
48 Influence
49 __ Palmas, capital of the Canary Islands
50 Boundless
52 Paris's __ Garnier
54 Four-time platinum album of 2001
57 Foundation abbr.
59 T-shaped pullover
61 Do a lube job on
62 Animated TV character with buck teeth
63 How an April fool may be done
64 Guinness suffix
65 Important signs

DOWN

1 Proficient
2 __ shark
3 What a tattoo may identify
4 Dull finish?
5 Lawn cutters
6 Subject of the documentary "Smart Television"
7 Volume of reprints
8 Half brother of Ivan V
9 Active ingredient in marijuana: Abbr.
10 Apt attachment to the starts of 14-, 17-, 35- and 43-Across
11 Likely to slip
12 Hoi __
13 How a bump may appear
15 Dull, as London skies
21 Varied
23 Swindlers
25 No more
27 The Beatles' "And I Love __"
28 Stir
29 "The Cossacks" novelist
30 Like apparel donned in a Christmas carol
31 Partner of jeweler Van Cleef
33 Parody
36 Not give up
37 Foul caller
38 Actress Vardalos
39 Gridiron stat: Abbr.
41 Heavy blows
43 Cuts off
44 Prickly plant
45 Slide away
46 Round a corner in Monopoly
49 Brave one
51 Apt attachment to the ends of 30-, 37-, 59- and 62-Across
53 Oceans
54 Be in accord
55 __ Hubbard
56 Gambling venues, briefly
58 Crusading journalist Nellie
60 Do some tailoring

by David J. Kahn

61

ACROSS

1 Willy Wonka creator Dahl
6 Vessels at marinas
11 Boeing 737, e.g.
14 Golfer Palmer, informally
15 Parts to play
16 Firefighter's tool
17 Humor publication since 1952
19 Many a first grader's age
20 What generals command
21 Parks of civil rights fame
22 Educ. institution
25 Docs-to-be
28 Selected
30 Dorm overseers, for short
31 Seniors' org.
32 All-encompassing
38 Tricky operation for extending a plane's flight
41 Causing the most wolf whistles, perhaps
42 To be, to Henri
43 Tit for ___
44 Brides' walkways
46 Lionel products
52 N.Y.C. summer hrs.
53 Ammonia has a strong one
54 Mame on Broadway
56 Fix, as a fight
57 Dirty campaign tactic
62 Take to court
63 Win by ___
64 Actress Shire of "Rocky"
65 Ambulance letters
66 "That's enough out of you!"
67 Nonstop

DOWN

1 Computer capacity, for short
2 ". . . man ___ mouse?"
3 +
4 Peru's largest city
5 "Goodness gracious!"
6 Cornrow, e.g.
7 Falls through the cracks?
8 "He's making ___ and checking . . ."
9 The number at left + 1
10 NNW's opposite
11 Leader of the Argonauts, in myth
12 Be
13 State on the Rio Grande
18 F.B.I. operatives
21 Fixes, as a shoe
22 Rascal
23 Committee leader
24 Mob
26 Language derived from Hindustani
27 7/20/69, for one
29 Splash, as grease
32 Charlemagne's domain: Abbr.
33 Some tech grads
34 Sternward
35 Bibliographical datum
36 When right turns are often allowed
37 Spew out
39 Venetian's lang.
40 Film director Martin
44 Dead set against
45 Really digs
46 Samuel with a code
47 Hatred
48 Venetian rulers of old
49 Dangerous gas
50 "Moi, ___" ("Me, too": Fr.)
51 Cove
55 Former New York cardinal Edward
57 Big ___ (Golden Arches offering)
58 39-Down article
59 ___-de-France
60 Anaïs ___, "Delta of Venus" author
61 Travel aimlessly, with "about"

by Sarah Keller

ACROSS

1 Material for informal jackets or skirts
6 Building block brand
10 City on the Arno
14 "Gentlemen Prefer Blondes" writer Loos
15 Like slander, as opposed to libel
16 Bartlett's abbr.
17 Attendant at a '50s dance?
19 Occupy the throne
20 Animals farmed for their fur
21 Goodyear's Ohio headquarters
22 Personnel concern for Santa?
26 Tuckered out
27 Mule of song
28 Tofu source
29 List-ending abbr.
31 Item made from 20-Across
33 Goofs
36 Hosiery hue
37 One given away by her father, often
39 Secluded valley
41 Washed-up star
43 Grammarian's concern
44 Mandlikova of tennis
45 Krazy ___ of the comics
47 Miami-to-Boston dir.
48 Street urchins
51 Acupuncturist?
54 Pakistan's chief river
55 All lathered up
56 Injure, as the knee
57 Addicted to shopping?
62 Walk wearily
63 The brother in "Am I my brother's keeper?"

64 Item in "Poor Richard's Almanack"
65 Places for props
66 Many adoptees
67 Curtain fabric

DOWN

1 Morse T
2 Brian of ambient music
3 Sip from a flask
4 Response to "Who's there?"
5 Henri who painted "The Dance"
6 Subdued in manner
7 Shake an Etch A Sketch
8 Needle-nosed fish
9 Jolly ___ Saint Nick
10 Ads aimed at hikers and picnickers?
11 Toughen, as to hardship
12 Athenian lawgiver
13 With regard to
18 Inner: Prefix
21 "Chop-chop!," on a memo
22 To be, to Brutus
23 Gate fastener
24 Botanist's study
25 Pinochle lay-down
30 Gift in a long, thin box
32 Money for liquor?
33 Break a commandment
34 Botanist's study
35 Musical repetition mark
37 Gridder Roethlisberger
38 Collect, as rewards
40 Not e'en once

42 Jazz combo member
43 Ideal, but impractical
45 Rounded hills
46 63-Across's father
48 Cirrus cloud formations
49 A spat covers it
50 Dostoyevsky novel, with "The"
52 It might have a single coconut tree
53 Singer Lauper
57 Explorer's aid
58 Actor Vigoda
59 Aykroyd of "Ghostbusters"
60 Swelled head
61 La-Z-Boy spot

by Robert A. Doll

ACROSS

1 "I dare you"
10 The Hawks of the Atlantic 10 conference, informally
15 This very moment
16 Conscious
17 1970 Santana hit
19 Orch. section
20 It might pass une loi
21 Reuters competitor
22 Tiny recipe amount
26 Idol worshiper?
28 Kind of pit, briefly
31 Burgundy or Chablis
32 Evidence in the Watergate scandal
39 "Without ___, the crudeness of reality would make the world unbearable": Shaw
40 Instantly fry
41 In vitro cells
42 Macho types
49 Lone Star State cowboy
50 Trekkies' genre
51 Impulsively
55 Medical insurance portion of Medicare
58 Extinct cousin of the kiwi
59 Break point score, perhaps
62 Artist Lichtenstein
64 Varying wildly
69 Misanthrope
70 Part of a postal address for Disneyland
71 + end
72 Answer to an old riddle alluded to by the starts of 17-, 32-, 42- and 64-Across

DOWN

1 Pointed criticisms
2 Org. that used to bring people to court?
3 Stretch of grass
4 Sam Spade type
5 "Uh-uh, bad!"
6 Tach reading
7 Votes for
8 Gandalf, for one
9 Barely making (out)
10 Took care of business
11 See 32-Down
12 Become blocked
13 Animal with striped legs
14 Start of a counting rhyme
18 Have turkey-serving duty, say
23 U.S. dance grp.
24 It facilitates replying to a MS.
25 Buckingham Palace letters
27 Article in El Mundo
29 Schmo
30 Campus areas
32 Card game for 11-Down
33 Onetime realm of central Eur.
34 "___ be an honor"
35 A writer may work on it
36 Washington pro
37 Christmas ___
38 Carrier to Copenhagen
43 "Oh yeah . . . ," in a text message
44 France's second-busiest port
45 Nitrous ___
46 Brief swim
47 Design deg.
48 Lungful
51 1935 Triple Crown horse
52 Christopher who directed "The Dark Knight"
53 Finnish architect Alvar ___
54 Erin of "Happy Days"
56 Charlie Chaplin persona
57 Ball-rolling game
60 ___ Reader
61 Midwinter phenomenon, sometimes
63 Strangely, it's shorter than a day on Venus
65 Orthographer's ref.
66 Frequent Canadian interjections
67 Vim
68 ___ Fáil, Irish coronation stone

by Jonathan Porat

64

ACROSS

1. Actor Washington who once played Malcolm X
7. Org. for women on the links
11. Karl Marx's "___ Kapital"
14. Mountain climber's tool
15. Got ___ deal (was rooked)
16. Mind reader's "gift"
17. One word that precedes "pit," one that follows it
19. Had a bite
20. Antlered animal
21. Grieves
22. Cereal advertised with a "silly rabbit"
23. "Slipped" backbone part
25. "Don't tell ___ can't . . . !"
26. Sounds during medical checkups
27. One word that precedes "key," one that follows it
33. By eyesight
36. Long-nosed fish
37. Scottish refusal
38. Infant bodysuit
39. Countryish
41. "Let's call ___ day"
42. W.W. II female
44. Pregame morale builder
45. One word that precedes "play," one that follows it
48. Suffix with pont-
49. Cartoonist Chast
50. With 13-Down, "super power" glasses
54. Ostrich or owl
56. Buckaroo ___ (movie character)
59. Plains tribe
60. Insect with a queen
61. One word that precedes "hard," one that follows it
63. "___ bin ein Berliner"
64. Prepare cookies or chicken, e.g.
65. Egyptian temple site
66. "Love ___ neighbor . . ."
67. ___-bitsy
68. Evaluate

DOWN

1. Chopped into small cubes
2. Food-poisoning bacteria
3. Prominent giraffe parts
4. Ringo's drummer son
5. Test
6. Former NBC host Jay
7. Famed tar pits whose name is Spanish for "the tar"
8. Clipping, as shrubs
9. Guys' mates
10. Hole-making tool
11. Start of a Christmas letter
12. ___ Spumante (wine)
13. See 50-Across
18. Ventriloquist's prop
22. However, informally
24. Singer Kristofferson
26. Sudden
28. ___ Kenobi of "Star Wars"
29. Fat substitute brand
30. Risk taker
31. Train track part
32. What a swabbie swabs
33. Invalidate, as a check
34. Fascinated by
35. Fit for sailing
40. Hellish river
43. Music store fixtures
44. Order from Domino's
46. Silent assent
47. Braying animal
51. TV sports broadcasting pioneer Arledge
52. Book of maps
53. "Sunny" egg parts
54. Worms in a can, e.g.
55. 1/36 of a yard
56. Gravy vessel
57. Paul who wrote "My Way"
58. Actress Lupino and others
61. Slugger's stat
62. B&O and Reading: Abbr.

by Patrick Merrell

ACROSS

1 Hipster's jargon
5 Shrewd
10 Yank's foe
13 Black, to bards
14 Outranking
15 "A ___ bagatelle!"
16 *Did a dog trick
18 Toiling away
19 The Wildcats of the Big 12 Conf.
20 Took charge
21 Rebounds, shooting percentage, etc.
22 *One who's often doing favors
27 Tylenol alternative
29 Martínez with three Cy Youngs
30 ___-Rooter
31 Shrimp-on-the-barbie eater
33 Fancy dresser
36 *Affordable, as an apartment
38 *Tugboat rope
40 "Bed-in" participant Yoko ___
41 Most dangerous, as winter roads
43 Pullers in pairs
44 "You can't teach ___ dog . . ."
45 Sprinkle holy water on
46 *Aldous Huxley novel
51 Hawkeye State native
52 "___ on parle français"
53 Mangy mutt
56 Door-busting equipment
57 *Bar patron's request for a refill
61 "Dang it!"
62 Al ___ (pasta order)
63 Italian wine region
64 ID with two hyphens

65 Mythical lecher
66 School attended by 007

DOWN

1 So-and-so
2 Nigerian natives
3 "B," maybe, in an encyclopedia
4 Photo lab abbr.
5 Officer-to-be
6 "Humble" dwelling
7 White House Web address ending
8 Eden exile
9 "___ out!" (ump's call)
10 Mark down for a sale, say
11 Verdi aria
12 ___ Wetsy (old doll)
15 San ___ (Bay Area county)
17 Additional
21 Hinge holder
23 Songwriter Novello
24 Rotational speed meas.
25 Homes for 46-Down
26 ___-proof (easy to operate)
27 Guthrie who sang about Alice's Restaurant
28 Nut case
31 Cornice support
32 Of service
33 Salaries, e.g., to a business owner
34 Leftmost compartment in a till
35 Parker products
37 German indefinite article
39 Lounge around

42 Part of P.E.I.: Abbr.
44 Salt's "Halt!"
45 Creamy cheese
46 Things hidden in the answers to this puzzle's six starred clues
47 Zoo noises
48 "Gimme a break!"
49 Quick with the zingers
50 Autumn shade
54 "Render ___ Caesar . . ."
55 Horse halter
57 PC pop-ups
58 Teachers' org.
59 Neighbor of Que.
60 Singer Corinne Bailey ___

by Peter A. Collins

ACROSS

1 Iditarod vehicle
5 Tay and Lomond
10 Film format sometimes in 3-D
14 Internet cafe offering
15 With 68-Across, "Carry on"
16 ___-Coburg-Gotha (old British royal house)
17 Letter preceding bravo
18 Wallace ___ of "Manhattan"
19 January 1 title word
20 Company with the stock ticker symbol BKS
23 Strawberry Fields pilgrimage figure
24 Page, for example
25 Company with the stock ticker symbol DNA
30 Tree sacred to the Druids
34 Panama, for one
35 Green of "Radio Days"
36 1973 Paul McCartney & Wings hit
37 Russian city on the Oka
39 Company with the stock ticker symbol ZZ
41 Feudin' with
42 Unyielding
44 Syrup brand
46 Stash of cash
47 Herb with antiseptic properties
48 Company with the stock ticker symbol PZZA
50 Order whose members have included five U.S. presidents
52 Rubina ___ of "Slumdog Millionaire"
53 Company with the stock ticker symbol HOG
60 Many diva performances
61 Amtrak debut of 11/17/2000
62 Ophthalmologist's concern
63 Cartel led by a secretary general
64 Former Fox series set in Newport Beach
65 Art Deco architect William Van ___
66 Part of a Zippo
67 Competitor of 39-Across
68 See 15-Across

DOWN

1 DNA collector, perhaps
2 Oscar winner Kedrova
3 Chutzpah
4 Wiest of "Radio Days"
5 Bonny gal
6 Dept. of Labor division
7 Printer's color
8 Elephant rider's seat
9 Many a Muslim
10 Queen in events of 1492
11 Rough up
12 Highway toll unit
13 Struck (out)
21 Seemingly forever
22 Jazz singer who took her surname from pig Latin
25 Pac-Man enemy
26 Image on eco-friendly products
27 Try to prove
28 Time off from l'école
29 Grammy winner ___ Khan
31 Item used with high frequency?
32 Competitor of Aquafina
33 Rips to pieces
36 Vidal's "___ Breckinridge"
38 Often-bawdy verse
40 Michael Phelps workout unit
43 Word on a business card
45 Ventura County's ___ Valley
48 Freudian topic
49 "He who hesitates is lost," e.g.
51 Colleague of Byron and Shelley
53 Pueblo language
54 Actor Guinness
55 Hinds, e.g.
56 Zillions
57 Explorer Cabeza de ___
58 ___ and terminer
59 Endangered state bird
60 Barnyard mother

by Adam Cohen

ACROSS

1 Flexible, electrically
5 Desert plants
10 For fear that
14 Prisoner's knife
15 Be ___ in the neck
16 "Even ___ speak . . ."
17 Cab
18 Window features
19 One at the computer
20 Agent Gold of HBO's "Entourage"
21 Japanese sleuth Mr. ___
22 Primp
23 2000 De Niro/Stiller comedy
27 "Mighty" man who struck out
28 Not written, as a test
29 Makes mistakes
31 Pleased
32 "___ Pinafore"
35 Basic, as issues
40 Toddler
41 Land west of Vietnam
42 Chooses
43 West Germany's capital
44 Alternative to singles, in figure skating
47 What judges do in court
52 First name in W.W. II infamy
53 Commedia dell'___
54 Gold, in Guadalajara
56 Color lightly
57 So yesterday
59 Editing mark
60 Suffix with kitchen
61 Parisian love
62 No. on a bank statement
63 Like show horses' feet
64 Bedsheets, e.g.
65 "___ be in England"

DOWN

1 "The Thin Man" dog
2 The third time's said to be one
3 Strom Thurmond follower of 1948
4 106, to Trajan
5 Truman who wrote "Breakfast at Tiffany's"
6 Lack of interest
7 Something to paddle
8 Even score
9 Ones who are elected
10 Winner's wreath
11 German steel city
12 Bonbon, e.g.
13 Shorebirds
21 The Appalachians, e.g.: Abbr.
22 "The Devil Wears ___"
24 Sunrise direction
25 Explorer Marco
26 "I smell ___"
29 Ambulance worker, for short
30 ___ Speed Wagon (old vehicle)
31 Auto gizmo that talks, in brief
32 Sidewalk game with chalk
33 Big Apple museum, with "the"
34 Sizzling sound
36 Standoffish
37 Half of Mork's goodbye
38 Advice regarding touching a hot stove
39 Actress Spelling
43 Sang loudly, with "out"
44 Chase
45 To the rear, on a ship
46 Suffix with Israel or Manhattan
47 Spouses
48 Singer Piaf
49 The Lone Ranger's faithful friend
50 Bourne of "The Bourne Identity"
51 Build
55 Sgt. Snorkel's four-legged friend
57 Friend
58 French friend
59 ___ Paulo, Brazil

by Andrea Carla Michaels

ACROSS

1 Fiber-___ cable
6 Milan's La ___
11 Sun or moon, to bards
14 "Be-Bop-___" (Gene Vincent hit)
15 Is visibly frightened
16 Zilch
17 They're hard to believe
19 Eerie sighting, for short
20 PT boat crewman: Abbr.
21 Adoptees from shelters
22 Initial stage
24 Beach atmosphere
26 Have the nerve
28 1939 Bette Davis drama
33 Former U.N. chief Kofi ___
36 Take five
37 Free of clutter
39 Clayey soil
40 Paycheck extra
41 Word before Charles or George
42 ___ John's (Domino's competitor)
43 Years, in the Yucatán
44 Not loyal
45 Big pile of cash
48 Top-___ (best)
49 Series beginners
53 Garlic-crushing tool
56 Tumbled
58 Bearded pres.
59 CNN's Dobbs
60 Figure described by the first words of 17-, 28- and 45-Across
64 Galley need
65 Bird-related
66 Potbelly ___
67 Old hand
68 Gossipy sort
69 Vocal qualities

DOWN

1 Hall's partner in pop
2 Make smooth
3 Arkansas River city
4 "___ bite"
5 Sea fed by the Volga
6 Dick and Jane's dog
7 Dodgem units
8 Boxer Laila
9 Ann of the Shakers
10 Place into cubbyholes
11 Burden of proof
12 In widespread use
13 Bad mark on one's reputation
18 The U.S. Virgin Is., e.g.
23 Source of orange-red light
25 Unbreakable stones of legend
26 Cause of atrophy
27 Takes steps
29 Swedish currency
30 Black mamba's secretion
31 Flesh-and-blood
32 Chews the fat
33 Bernese peak
34 Wordsmith Webster
35 California wine valley
38 ___ time (course slot)
40 Barracks locale
44 Most jam-packed
46 Consternation
47 Bargain hunter's event
50 Sported
51 Partner of beyond
52 Monica with nine Grand Slam tournament wins
53 Alka-Seltzer-into-water sound
54 Have a hearty laugh
55 Its symbol looks like an equal sign through a C
56 Autostrada auto
57 Sicilian city
61 N.Y.C.'s Park or Madison
62 Pewter component
63 "Who am ___ say?"

by John Greenman

ACROSS

1 Garden bloom, informally
5 Removes, in a way
10 "Down with," at the Bastille
14 White coat
15 Husband of Bathsheba
16 Pioneer Boone, familiarly
17 Genesis victim
18 Host city of golf's Memorial Tournament
20 Stumped solver's desire
22 Headline in a circular
23 Apt. ad abbr.
24 Write, as a P.S.
25 Component of bronze
28 Scand. land
29 Sound from a masseur's client
30 Hometown to college football's Vandals
33 Project conclusion?
34 O'Connor's successor on the Supreme Court
35 Geraint's lady
36 Where rock's R.E.M. was formed
41 Think ahead
42 Clearance rack abbr.
43 ___-rock (music genre)
44 Paul Revere founded a brass and copper works here
50 Raise a stink?
51 St. Louis-to-Indianapolis dir.
52 Language suffix
53 Rough position?
54 It has two values in blackjack
55 Blow off some hot air
57 Do a soccer mom's chore
59 Birthplace of Vice President Hannibal Hamlin
63 Place to use Easy-Off
64 Summers on the Seine
65 Back 40 units
66 Boggy stuff
67 Turner and Williams
68 Food and water, for two
69 Host who said "I kid you not!"

DOWN

1 Made of whole-wheat flour
2 Sexual instinct
3 Compensation for loss
4 Shoulder muscle, briefly
5 Turkey
6 Tulsa sch.
7 Bits of baloney
8 Lola of "Golden Boy"
9 1862 battle site
10 Hoo-ha
11 Native of one of the Gulf States
12 Lion's kingdom
13 Pie-eyed
19 "Quo Vadis" role
21 Fancy wrap
26 "Heads ___, tails . . ."
27 Things to pick
31 "High Hopes" lyricist
32 Herd orphan
35 Like a flan
36 Set aside
37 In shreds
38 Fish-eating raptor
39 Assayers' samples
40 Exchange new vows
41 Protective wall
44 Tach figure, informally
45 Words before band or army
46 Growl at, say
47 "Twelfth Night" countess
48 Muralist Diego
49 More astute
56 Pit stop change
58 49–0 game, e.g.
60 Magazine output: Abbr.
61 Homer's neighbor
62 Start of summer?

by William Frank Macreery

ACROSS

1 Book balancer, briefly
4 Be in the game or in the band
8 Photography icon Adams
13 Lubricates
15 Taj Mahal feature
16 Any old jerk
17 Injure severely
18 Cloth square for a bedcover
20 Following behind, as a broken-down car
22 Cunning
23 Whole bunch
24 Figure fashioned from dough
28 Service charge
29 Frozen waffle brand
30 All-out
32 Yankee nickname starting in 2004
35 Query
37 Quick barber jobs
40 Clothing with tabs
44 Dwelling with a smoke hole
45 Atlas page
46 Risqué
47 Early Mexican
50 Held on to
52 Some degs. after bachelor's
54 Retailer's enticement
59 Met singer Pinza
61 "Uh-uh"
62 Pop heroes
63 "Stop!" . . . or what you do to 18-, 24-, 40- and 54-Across
67 ___ 500
68 Home of the Minotaur's labyrinth
69 Brink
70 Chief Norse god
71 "The Lion and the Mouse" storyteller
72 Roald who created Willy Wonka
73 Jiffy

DOWN

1 Chris Rock or Ellen DeGeneres
2 Steinway, e.g.
3 Justice Samuel
4 Pronto
5 Singer Rawls or Reed
6 Travelers in horse buggies
7 Scold
8 Deadly cobra
9 Spinoff of CBS's "JAG"
10 Determinant of a "best if used by" date
11 Toastmaster
12 Lerner's "Camelot" partner
14 Russian fish delicacy
19 Printing goof
21 Top part of a disguise
25 "Holy cow!"
26 Mediocre
27 "___, Brute?"
31 Place to make a scene?
32 Likely
33 "The Facts of Life" actress Charlotte
34 Night and day, say
36 Airline whose name is consecutive letters of the alphabet
38 Mingle
39 Hog's place
41 Radiation units
42 ___ Michigan
43 Grp. with clout at the gas pump
48 Sicily's erupter
49 Having an outer layer, as M&M's
51 Taro dish
52 Muhammad's birthplace
53 Sky-blue
55 "The Mary Tyler Moore Show" spinoff
56 Locales for ducks
57 Hit from Grandpa's day
58 Boy band that sang "Girlfriend"
60 Filmmaker Preminger
64 Cool, in the '40s
65 "Yuck!"
66 ___ Aviv

by Lynn Lempel

ACROSS

1 Hockey fake-out
5 Oodles
9 Tortilla chip dip
14 Apple variety
15 Anchor
16 Deuce follower in tennis
17 Marge's sister, to Bart Simpson
19 French river valley with many châteaux
20 Shout at a soccer game
21 Oinker
23 The first "T" in 36-Down
24 Reggae relative
26 Not a good way to buy a car
30 Rowboat implement
31 What a barber has to trim around
32 Suspicious
33 Equestrian's "Stop!"
35 Transport in Duke Ellington's theme song
38 Risk-taker's credo
43 Popular record label
44 Crucifix
46 Reward for a job well done
48 Secret govt. group
51 Stallone's nickname
52 Seasonal Arctic phenomenon
55 Squeeze (out)
56 1972 treaty subj.
57 Darn
58 _____ Report (luxury lifestyle magazine)
60 Jockey's handful
63 What 17-, 26-, 38-, and 52-Across contain
67 Neighbor of Israel
68 "Need You Tonight" band, 1987
69 _____ Minor
70 Shoes that add inches to one's height
71 Deli queue call
72 Flapjack eatery, for short

DOWN

1 24 horas
2 Outback runner
3 Outback hopper
4 Outer: Prefix
5 Aviator Earhart
6 Online guffaw
7 Get-up-and-go
8 Brown eyes or baldness, e.g.
9 "My gal" of song
10 Fuss
11 Hang around
12 Two-seated carriage
13 Had dinner at home
18 Postpaid encl.
22 Soviet labor camp
24 Boar's mate
25 Madeline of "Young Frankenstein"
27 Common knee stain for kids
28 Moonwalking Armstrong
29 Mexican mister
34 Once more
36 Big boom maker
37 Dappled horses
39 Bears: Lat.
40 Supermodel Cheryl
41 Thorny shrub
42 Center of an egg
45 Secret of many a redhead
46 Steakhouse offering
47 Regard highly
49 Most confident
50 "With a wink and _____ . . ."
52 Reedy place
53 Encircle
54 Rough cord
59 _____ B'rith
61 Zippo
62 Carrier to Oslo
64 Hard-core film "rating"
65 Spanish uncle
66 Easy mark

by Daniel Kantor and Jay Kaskel

ACROSS

1. "That's ___ . . ."
4. Moo ___ pork
7. You don't want it beaten out of you
10. A minimus is the smallest one
13. Ritz-___ hotels
15. Expert at interpreting a text
17. It's "ascending" in a Vaughan Williams piece
18. Contents of a lode
19. E'er
21. Justin Timberlake's former group
22. Badlands sight
23. "___ te llamas?" (Spanish 101 question)
26. Hammarskjöld of the U.N.
28. Inspiration for Hunter S. Thompson
31. Egg: Prefix
32. Heir
36. Dudes
37. Blow away
38. La mer, e.g.
39. Uncle of fiction
40. Eyre
43. "Winnie the Pooh and Tigger ___"
44. "Beetle Bailey" dog
45. Not budging
46. Talks one's head off
47. Instrument you blow into
50. Low-lying wetland
53. Air
58. Zagat's readers, informally
59. Ape
60. Cheese for French onion soup
61. It may be hidden under a shirt
62. "___ Mine" (1957 hit by the Platters)
63. Sault ___ Marie
64. Cincinnati-to-New York dir.
65. Pip at the start of "Great Expectations," e.g.

DOWN

1. Prefix with -gon
2. Actress Arlene
3. Chose, as lots
4. Holds back
5. Equine
6. Bad behavior
7. Sub at the office
8. "Lost time is never found again," e.g.
9. Actress Zellweger
10. Flowerpot material
11. Buckwheat's affirmative
12. Electric ___
14. Grassy plain
16. Subtly suggests
20. Elite Eight org.
23. Money-saving restaurant offer
24. Flagrant
25. Like a stereotypically bad professor
27. Man-eating shark
29. Bygone Apple laptop
30. Autos for test-driving
32. Hair lacking care
33. Be in the red
34. Fire
35. Orange or plum
41. Nonentity
42. Boxer Willard defeated by Jack Dempsey for the world heavyweight title
46. Isaac Bashevis Singer story "___ the Yeshiva Boy"
48. Off-Broadway awards
49. Critic Roger
51. Capital of Jordan
52. Singer Frankie
53. Peeved
54. "Gotcha"
55. Ace
56. Highest European volcano
57. One of two in a 47-Across
58. Alphabet trio

by Oliver Hill

ACROSS

1 Prolonged attack
6 Pilot
11 Used a stool
14 Counting everything
15 Pigeon's perch
16 In favor of
17 "Splendor in the Grass" actress
19 Always, in verse
20 Like raw film
21 Fresh from the shower
23 One of 100 in D.C.
24 "Hold on a ___!"
25 Bleated
27 Telecommuter's need
31 Remove a fastener from
34 Emulates Eminem
35 Tampa Bay baseballer
36 Six years, for a 23-Across
37 "Lord, ___ this food" (grace words)
39 Kind of car seen at Indy
40 "___ we there yet?"
41 Blockhead
42 Second-year students, for short
43 Drink with a marshmallow
47 Train's place
48 Pilot's announcement, for short
49 Some AOL communications
52 1993 Aerosmith hit with the lyric "Love is sweet misery"
54 Most kilt wearers
56 Atlanta, for Delta
57 Common remote control holder
60 "What was ___ think?"
61 Happen as a consequence
62 Critic Ebert
63 Freud subj.
64 Looks like
65 Stockholm native

DOWN

1 It may be blocked when you have a cold
2 Nonsensical
3 Consumed
4 Happy
5 Ralph who wrote "Invisible Man"
6 Sheep's coat
7 Smutty
8 Altar vow
9 Freud subject
10 Station porters
11 Ticket locale
12 Geographical statistic
13 Of two minds
18 News bit
22 Romanian money
25 Feathery scarves
26 Concert equipment
27 That guy
28 Words to live by
29 Apiece
30 Loaves with seeds
31 Where the 2002 Winter Olympics were held
32 Adopted son of Claudius
33 Candidate for male modeling
37 Voting group
38 Combination ___
39 "The Fall of the House of Usher" writer
41 Odds
42 Fixed parts of motors
44 Dernier ___ (latest fashion)
45 Dirty old men
46 Perched on
49 Spitting ___
50 Parceled (out)
51 Sound asleep?
52 Word that can follow the ends of 17-, 27-, 43- and 57-Across
53 What wagon wheels may make
54 Pond gunk
55 Pack away
58 Long-distance number starter
59 Exhaust, with "up"

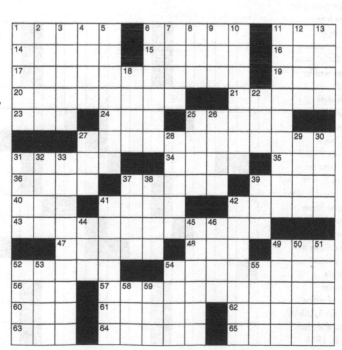

by Tracey Snyder

ACROSS

1 Pickle flavoring
5 Sheetful of cookies
10 Eight: Prefix
14 "The ___ Love"
(hit by 42-Across)
15 Nasty virus
16 Setting for an
Inaugural Address
17 Representation
of a state on
the U.S. flag
18 Silents actress
Normand
19 Jane Austen novel
20 Book by 52-Across,
with "The"
23 Test for coll. seniors
24 Opposite SSW
25 Former body
for 52-Across
27 Dresses like
a justice
29 Synagogue-goer
30 It's not free
of charge
31 Hobbit's enemy
32 "The Bells" poet
33 Frozen waffle
brand
34 Crash site?
36 See 29-Down
38 Winter forecast
39 ___ Office
40 Hobbit's friend
41 52-Across once
passed it, with "the"
42 Rock band fronted by
Michael Stipe
43 Cartoon collectible
44 Senses
48 You can dig it
50 "___ what?"
51 Vintner's
container
52 Oath of office
taker on 1/20/09
56 Not of the cloth
57 May 8, 1945
58 "Oh, woe!"
59 QB Michael

60 Upper echelon
61 ___ Stanley Gardner
62 Actress Lupino
and others
63 Winter forecast
64 Bakery loaves

DOWN

1 Medicinal amount
2 Through regular order
of succession
3 52-Across, starting
1/20/09
4 Old Italian money
5 Valentine candy
message
6 Lets up
7 Sir ___ Belch of
"Twelfth Night"
8 Nile queen, informally
9 Not fully noticed
10 Ancient Greek
theater

11 52-Across had one
with John McCain
12 Cry just before
leaving
13 Solid ___ rock
21 "Mad Money"
network
22 Chop
26 Sufficient, once
28 Transmitted by speech
29 With 36-Across,
52-Across's
number two
32 Suffix for many a
computer
attachment
33 Biblical birthright
seller
34 Variety
35 Spent too much (for)
36 1960s hairdos
37 Home state of
52-Across: Abbr.

41 Kind of bomber
43 What secondary
recipients of
e-mails get
44 Natural
45 "Maybe later"
46 "Hot" food
47 Equilibria
49 Parts of bottles
53 Big name in
computers
54 Actress Sedgwick
55 1930s boxing champ
Max
56 This clue's number
in Roman numerals

by Tim Wescott

ACROSS

1 Electrical bridges
5 Disney output, once
9 Winter warmer
14 Polo on TV
15 Place to pay a toll, perhaps
16 Jude Law title role
17 "___ unrelated note . . ."
18 Buggy place?
19 4×100 meters need
20 Genghis Khan's non-pedigree domain?
23 George ___, longest-reigning English king
24 Round fig.
25 Narrowest winning margin in baseball
28 Rush hour pace
30 Word after pen or gal
32 Newcastle's river
33 Be indisposed
35 In the thick of
37 So last year
38 Non-pedigree essential courses?
42 Monopolist's portion
43 Margin marking
44 Author of "The Island of the Day Before"
45 "___ Houston" of 1980s TV
47 Far from welcoming
48 You can open with them
52 Repugnant
54 Letters on tires
56 Talladega unit
57 Casey's non-pedigree team?
61 Put on the books
63 Trial balloon, e.g.
64 Dr. Pavlov
65 Bat maker's tool
66 Pundit Colmes
67 Be disposed (to)
68 Burgers on the hoof
69 For fear that
70 Bullpen stats

DOWN

1 Like superprecise clocks
2 "The Bathers" painter
3 Head cases?
4 Be a fink
5 Hands over
6 Jump for joy
7 Singles bar delivery
8 Pipe part
9 Salk contemporary
10 Bordeaux wine
11 Words from Alphonse or Gaston
12 Ipanema locale
13 Place for reeds
21 Items in some illicit trade
22 Miranda rights readers
26 "One" on a coin
27 Court divider
29 Cabinet department until 1947
30 Kegger, e.g.
31 "___ losing it?"
34 Elizabethan ballad player, maybe
36 Ernie the Muppet's rubber toy
38 Decked out
39 Frisbee game involving body contact
40 Nonacademic school activities, informally
41 Chaney of "The Wolf Man"
42 Latin 101 word
46 "You got me!"
49 Twist of fiction
50 Potassium source
51 Goes on a spree
53 Out-and-out
54 Results of some bargains
55 Apply spin to
58 Baby bottle?
59 On one's duff
60 Time on a marquee
61 Ways around Chi-town
62 N.L.'er since 2005

by Fred Piscop

76

ACROSS

1 Bother persistently
6 Airing
10 Zilch
14 Lots of screaming and shouting
15 Gleeful giggle
16 Plow team
17 Distrustful
18 Loretta of "M*A*S*H"
19 Alda of "M*A*S*H"
20 "Bad idea!"
23 Archibald or Thurmond of the N.B.A.
24 His and ___
25 6-1, 3-6 and 7-5, in tennis
27 Race, as an engine
30 Sunken ship's locale
34 "Oh!" in Österreich
35 Steps between floors
37 "My sweetie" in a 1957 hit for the Bobbettes
38 "Bad idea!"
41 "___ River" (song from "Show Boat")
42 Passover meal
43 Hush-hush org.
44 Offer advice from around a card table
46 Barfly
47 Ice cream brand
48 Babe in the woods
50 Cornerstone abbr.
52 "Bad idea!"
58 Couturier Christian
59 Elaborate April fool
60 Hall's singing partner
62 Are, in Argentina
63 "You're something ___!"
64 Center Shaquille
65 Kind of carpet
66 Woodwind item
67 Bothersome

DOWN

1 Org. for Patriots and Packers
2 Jean who wrote "The Clan of the Cave Bear"
3 Gardener's gift
4 Arterial trunks
5 Romantic rendezvous
6 Very
7 Small salamander
8 Chicken piece
9 Presidential noes
10 Two-by-two vessel
11 Car bar
12 Letter starter
13 One of the Brontë sisters
21 "Phooey!"
22 Cause of a low Richter reading
25 Give the go-ahead
26 Undercooked meat danger
28 Has dinner
29 Aura, informally
31 Social arrangements that don't always work out
32 ___-weensy
33 Edgar who painted ballerinas
35 Beachgoer's acquisition
36 Work over
39 Central street
40 Shortstop Derek
45 Instrument with 30+ strings
47 Flammable gas
49 Cello feature
51 Bend to go through a doorway, say . . . or what may be in front of the door
52 Fateful day in March
53 Satellite signal receiver
54 Letter after theta
55 Lighten, as a burden
56 Pink-slipped
57 Wood for shipbuilding
61 Wily

by Timothy Powell and Nancy Salomon

ACROSS

1 Li'l Abner creator Al
5 China shop purchase
11 Seminoles' sch.
14 Baseball's Moises or Felipe
15 Play starter
16 "___ only money!"
17 Game with "Out of Gas" cards
19 Certain whiskey
20 Spots for spats
21 High-voltage weapon
23 Had a yen
25 Word with double or free
26 Furrier John Jacob ___
28 Classic Isaac Asimov short-story collection
31 Popular fabric softener
34 Big name in retail jewelry
36 Gives the thumbs-up
37 Composer Satie
38 Some mailings to record execs
39 Go sprawling
40 AOL alternative
41 Nation once known as Dahomey
42 Horses' locks
43 Like newly laid lawns
45 Alternative to a station wagon or convertible
47 Contradict
49 Convertibles, informally
53 Cop's cruiser
56 Check out of a library, e.g.
57 Place for a plug
58 Robert Ludlum protagonist
60 Ugly as ___

61 Former British P.M. Clement ___
62 Larry who won the 1987 Masters
63 Poem of Sappho
64 Start over with, as a lawn
65 Salon sound

DOWN

1 Bar soap brand
2 Flared dress
3 Oompah band tune
4 Exert one's superiority
5 Typewriter formatting feature
6 Prefix with system or sphere
7 Gillette razor
8 Braga of film
9 Vigorous feelings
10 Lab personnel
11 Heir to a throne, typically
12 Eyelid woe
13 Tech's customer
18 ___-weensy
22 "I'll take that as ___"
24 Dunkin' Donuts order
27 Harold of "Ghostbusters"
29 Depression-era migrant
30 Recipe amts.
31 G.O.P. rivals
32 Guesstimate phrase
33 Like the dust in a dust storm
35 Asocial sort
38 Devote wholly
39 Rugrats' outbursts
41 Sylvia Plath novel, with "The"

42 Myopic Mr.
44 Mountain ___ (soda)
46 Applied gently
48 Some bridge seats
50 Sen. Hatch of Utah
51 ___ scheme (investment scam)
52 Remove dust bunnies
53 Colombian cash
54 Drug bust, e.g.
55 58-Across, for Matt Damon
59 Bridal bio word

by Jim Hyres

ACROSS

1 Level
5 Record store section
9 "Natch!"
13 Puzzlemaker Rubik
14 Big name in briefs
16 Played for a cat's-paw
17 Robin Hood's love
19 Like some telegrams
20 Identified
21 Frolicking
23 Blanc who voiced Porky Pig
24 One at the front desk, perhaps
25 Cheer up
28 Business letter abbr.
29 Relief map figs.
30 Some fund-raising orgs.
33 Parade honoree, familiarly
37 Ring around the collar?
38 Nail-biter, perhaps
40 Billy Joel's "___ to Extremes"
41 Come to mind
43 It's handed down
44 Pueblo dweller
45 Catch in the act
47 Storefront shaders
49 Leader deposed in 1955
54 Rescuer of Odysseus
55 1960s role for Diana Rigg
56 ___ Palace (French president's home)
59 Writer O'Flaherty
60 Bearers of a phrase suggested by saying the starts of 17-, 24-, 38- and 49-Across
62 Kick back
63 Safe place
64 Specks in the Seine
65 Gave the nod
66 Test version
67 Thomas who wrote "Utopia"

DOWN

1 Fill-in
2 "Dies ___"
3 Tough to figure out
4 "Blue Moon" composer
5 Roe source
6 Galley need
7 Men in blue
8 Rimes of country music
9 Any character in Clue
10 Take forcibly
11 Zellweger of "Nurse Betty"
12 Neatening tool
15 Plumber's tool
18 Cheesy entree
22 Pick up on
24 Major chipmaker
25 Symbol of goodness
26 It may be D.C.
27 Prefix with center
31 Way back when
32 Wrap in a roll
34 "Layla" has one
35 Totally wowed
36 Deep-six
38 "The Sound of Music" family name
39 Copy cats?
42 Like a ghostwriter
44 Dickens lad
46 Nut producer
48 Rock's Lofgren
49 Molded fare
50 Eskimo boat
51 Totally wow
52 Dry out, in a way
53 Place for pimiento
56 Novelist Ferber
57 One who's "just looking"
58 Latin 101 verb
61 Rent out

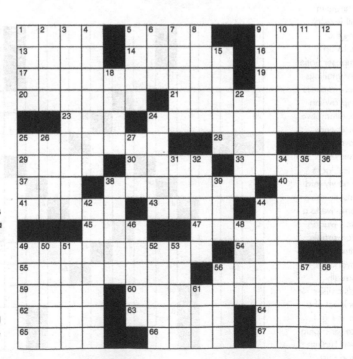

by Michael Langwald

ACROSS

1. Like Louisiana cuisine
6. ___-bodied seaman
10. Grocery carrier
14. Astound
15. Worker in an apron
16. "Get ___ it!"
17. Pinocchio, notably
19. Sport on horseback
20. Game console introduced in 2006
22. Maryland seafood specialty
26. CBS hit with two spinoffs
27. Removes from office
28. Betty Crocker offering
30. Decree
33. Dropped fly ball, e.g.
34. Reason to replace a windshield
35. Superlative suffix
38. Parisian's "But of course!"
40. Query from one who's ready to go
42. What boring things never seem to do
43. Impertinent
45. Arrived after a trip
46. Transport on a camp lake
47. "___ Fables"
48. "Drat!"
51. Dog doc
53. Snick and ___
54. Female golfer who played in a pro men's tournament at age 14
58. Cookie with a filling
59. "You're absolutely right"
64. Paraphernalia
65. New ___ (57-Down, for one)
66. Google competitor
67. Mailed
68. "Bill & ___ Excellent Adventure"
69. With respect to

DOWN

1. Ending with spy or web
2. Doc org.
3. Place to put tips
4. Gun used in the Six-Day War
5. Gas in diner signs
6. Cries from the congregation
7. More eccentric
8. Low-calorie, in beer names
9. Barbara of "I Dream of Jeannie"
10. Lame excuse
11. Pledges
12. On again, as a lantern
13. Number after deux
18. "Sweet!"
21. Fee for a freighter
22. ___ brûlée
23. Aired again
24. Bitter
25. Life stories, for short
29. Will validation
31. Bit of salt
32. "___ bin ein Berliner"
34. Italian's "bye"
35. John who sang "Bennie and the Jets"
36. Run through a credit card machine
37. In need of a massage, maybe
39. Funeral ashes holder
41. Outcome of a 10–17 game
44. Detached
46. Partner in crime
47. End in ___ (come out even)
48. Urban pollutions
49. New staffer
50. Where a hurricane develops
52. Water pitchers
55. Potential atty.'s exam
56. Sled at the Winter Olympics
57. "Only Time" singer, 2001
60. Western treaty grp.
61. Channels 14+
62. Melted tar, e.g.
63. Opposite of vert.

by Damon J. Gulczynski

ACROSS

1 Delays no longer
5 Some intimate apparel
9 The Beatles' "___ Road"
14 Supper, e.g.
15 Per person
16 Kind of mark
17 "It was ___ mistake"
18 Urgent
19 Not rural
20 Coin composed of copper, nickel, zinc and manganese
23 Refuses
24 John, for short
25 Early afternoon hour
28 Pantheon members
31 Shrivel
33 Hair treatment that generally lasts three to six months
36 Mary Kay competitor
38 "Far out!"
39 Line-___ veto
40 Pro football team based in New Jersey
45 Catherine whose cow is said to have started the Great Chicago Fire
46 Actress Ward
47 Word before "rain," "heat" and "gloom of night" in a postal creed
48 "Take Me as ___"
50 Girlish laugh
55 Musical question posed by Alanis Morissette, as suggested by 20-, 33- and 40-Across
58 Lighter brand
61 ___ fixe (persistent thought)
62 Exploding star
63 Cook's wear
64 Go-getter
65 Kuwaiti pooh-bah
66 They may be durable
67 Donations to the needy
68 Foxx of "Sanford and Son"

DOWN

1 Stockpile
2 Anagrammatic cousin of Alice or Lacie
3 Add up
4 Czechs and Poles
5 Bureau locale
6 Speakeasy's worry
7 Prefix with phobia
8 Beach memento
9 Clear Scandinavian liquor
10 Victor in a duel with Hamilton
11 Short hairstyle
12 Second letter after epsilon
13 Tokyo dough
21 Mechanical whiz: Abbr.
22 Cemetery expanse
25 "___ what you think!"
26 "___ Only Just Begun"
27 Utah city
29 Like some turkey meat
30 Hosiery mishaps
32 Pipsqueak
33 Might
34 "Orinoco Flow" singer
35 Singer Brickell
36 Soon
37 Rider-propelled vehicle, for short
41 Prayers
42 TV host Seacrest
43 Capital on the Mediterranean
44 Hair removal product
49 Sacred peak in Greek myth
51 One who's toast
52 Knee-high, bearded figure
53 Spitting mad
54 Modern birthday greeting
55 Music device with earbuds
56 Elvis Presley or Marilyn Monroe
57 Burst (with)
58 Second in a series of sharp turns
59 Big Wall St. news
60 Con's opposite

by Katie Yeager

ACROSS

1 Rubberneck
5 Digital signal receiver
9 Bailout button
14 Down from the deck
15 16-Across's "La donna è mobile," e.g.
16 See 15-Across
17 16th-century Florentine food?
20 Show compassion
21 Nereid sister of Galatea
22 Stopper of things
25 Supermarket chain
28 Support staffer: Abbr.
32 Reason the tortoise won the race?
35 A ring bearer may go down it
37 Commonwealth country in Central America
38 Pennies
39 Clairvoyant's claim
41 Half of a 45 with more airplay
42 Turn toward the east
44 "Alas"
46 Baseballs, footballs and basketballs?
48 Shopping bag
49 Blacken
50 Like some sausages and Web sites
52 Air condition
54 Entree from the frozen food department
59 Freedom from the requirement of having long sleeves?
64 Thai or Chinese
65 Craving
66 Spree
67 Ice bucket accessory
68 Disgusting one
69 Queries

DOWN

1 Shirts and skirts
2 Salt's direction
3 Policy ___
4 River in a Best Picture title
5 Lays a claim (on)
6 Patient observers: Abbr.
7 Padre's sister
8 Dematerialize
9 Drawn
10 Baja boss
11 Time to remember
12 Mil. leader
13 Draw
18 Press coverage
19 Housemate, informally
23 Bundle in a barn
24 Comedian Yakov Smirnoff, by birth
25 Emphatic confirmation of action
26 Eye intently
27 Naval affirmative
28 Without profit
29 Guide for Hillary
30 ___ moment
31 Spud
33 Put one's feet up
34 Poet who wrote "Old Possum's Book of Practical Cats"
36 Ain't as it should be?
40 Part of PRNDL
43 Groove for a letter-shaped bolt
45 Ruby
47 Freak
51 Anonymous John
52 Farrah Fawcett's signature do
53 Rockies, e.g.: Abbr.
55 "Ciao!"
56 Old hands
57 "Don't worry about me"
58 Figs. like "a million or so"
59 Fink
60 Equal: Prefix
61 ___ and tonic
62 "Yo" man?
63 Ottoman V.I.P.

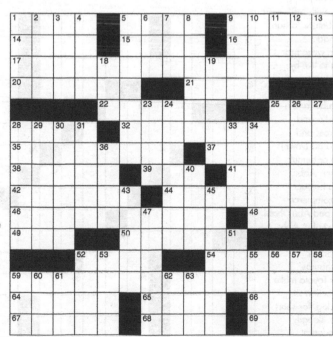

by Paula Gamache

ACROSS

1 French friends
5 Four: Prefix
10 "___ be a cold day in hell . . ."
14 Make over
15 Shake hands (on)
16 Heavy cart
17 1968 album by John Lennon and Yoko Ono
19 Land of the so-called "Troubles"
20 Fashion designer Perry
21 Classic muscle car
22 Men whom women can't trust
23 It's measured in amperes: Abbr.
26 What a wizard casts
28 Umpire's call at the start of an inning
32 Averts, with "off"
35 Word before Jordan or Canada
36 Kitchen wrap brand
38 Words to live by
39 Shah : Iran :: ___ : Russia
41 Boob tube (and a hint to 17- and 65-Across and 11- and 30-Down)
43 Bridge or tunnel designer: Abbr.
44 Santa's helpers
46 Cybercommerce
48 Dubai and Abu Dhabi are part of it: Abbr.
49 Oozed
51 2009 Super Bowl champs
53 Luxury Toyota make
55 Construction site watchdog, for short
56 Coffee, slangily
58 Succeeded at musical chairs
60 Bewildered
64 News item that often has a person's age in the headline
65 Polynesian-themed restaurant chain
68 "If all ___ fails . . ."
69 White-feathered wader
70 2.54 centimeters
71 Norman who created "All in the Family"
72 University officials
73 "A Death in the Family" author James

DOWN

1 Commedia dell'___
2 Whimper
3 Fox's "American ___"
4 Communist council
5 Contents of a La Brea pit
6 Silly Putty holder
7 Calc prerequisite
8 Landlords' due
9 "___ Fables"
10 "Goodness gracious!"
11 Courtroom
12 Cooking grease
13 Caustic compounds
18 The British ___
24 The "E" of Q.E.D.
25 Sneaky pitch
27 And so on: Abbr.
28 ___ Motel ("Psycho" setting)
29 Airplane seating request
30 Document checked at the border
31 They might be checkered
33 ___ Allan Poe
34 Sensitive spots
37 "Keen!"
40 Fast-firing firearm
42 Scores like 1-1 and 2-2
45 Reason for an R rating
47 "The Merry Widow" composer
50 Checked for fingerprints
52 Riga's land
54 "Beetle Bailey" boss
56 "Piano Man" performer Billy
57 Up to the task
59 "Gone with the Wind" plantation
61 Do lullabies, e.g.
62 Behold, to Brutus
63 Former Davis Cup captain Arthur
66 Cozy room
67 Visitors from Venus, say

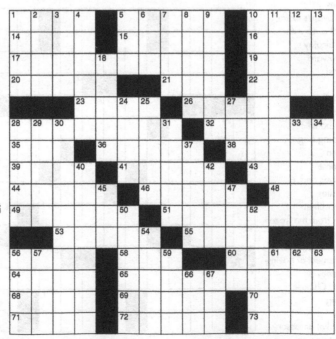

by Randall J. Hartman

ACROSS

1 Turkish ___
5 Dutch ___
10 Like horses' hooves
14 Bush not seen much nowadays
15 Toward the Arctic
16 Sioux City's locale
17 Lampblack
18 Measure of prevention or strength?
19 Superheroes battling the evil Magneto
20 Russian ___
22 Swiss ___
24 Now and again
25 Military pooh-bahs
26 Preceders of xis
27 Buck's tail?
28 Cap with a pompom
31 Semicircular building extension
34 Australian ___
35 American ___
36 Light wood
38 The Buckeyes, for short
39 Skirt
41 Italian ___
42 Canadian ___
44 Union agreements?
45 Golf peg
46 Scientologist Hubbard
47 Hill, in Haifa
49 Spanish verse
51 Operatic movement circa 1900
55 Danish ___
57 Portuguese ___
58 Very much
59 Appetite stimulant
61 Collector's suffix
62 Place to order a sandwich or espresso
63 Sturdy chiffon
64 Put out
65 Ivan or Feodor
66 French ___
67 Spanish ___

DOWN

1 Iraqi seaport
2 Going on
3 Lake catch
4 Crisis center connections
5 Govt. securities
6 Licks soundly
7 White-tailed eagle
8 Takeoff and landing overseers: Abbr.
9 Brandon Lee's last movie
10 Boxcars
11 Locale for a pioneer family
12 Is in the red
13 Hamlet, e.g.
21 Part of the Australian coat of arms
23 Outlander in Hawaii
25 Brand of razors and coffee makers
27 Burning issue
29 Fashion designer Gucci
30 Ladies of Versailles: Abbr.
31 Not much
32 Double time, for one
33 Convertible
34 Après-ski drink
37 Better trained
40 Slanderer
43 Tiny marcher
47 Kind of farmer
48 Leandro's partner in a Mancinelli opera
50 Prized fur
51 "Let's go, amigo!"
52 Hindu wise one
53 Bouncing off the walls
54 Speak before throngs
55 Agreement
56 "'Tis a pity"
57 Lisa with a "mystic smile"
60 Grande opening?

by John Underwood

84

ACROSS

1 ___ the Hutt of "Star Wars"
6 "Me, me, me" attitude
9 Parties where dresses are rarely seen
14 Key location
15 Works on the wall?
16 ^
17 Comment at the reptile exhibition?
19 Dog with an upturned tail
20 Online chuckle
21 Kisser
22 Underhanded
23 Joining alloy
25 Spread out
27 Where the Nobel Peace Prize is awarded
29 Daring actions
33 Put into effect
36 Terrier type
38 ___ fruit
39 New Mexico athlete
40 O. Henry specialty
41 Mop the floor with
42 From
43 Find awful
44 Wild time
45 Not taking sides
47 Prefix with meter
49 Crew
51 Depot purchase
55 Halve
58 Grow dim
60 English cathedral city
61 Hacienda brick
62 Bruin, Golden Bear or Wildcat?
64 Till now
65 Rumble in the Jungle victor
66 Orange box
67 Does in
68 Marked off
69 Conger catcher

DOWN

1 Bloodhounds have big ones
2 Sound before a blessing?
3 Ultimate aim
4 Baseball club
5 Bit of a limerick
6 Bloodhounds have big ones
7 Dozen dozen
8 Like some stocks, for short
9 Non-vector
10 Command to a photog?
11 "Celeste Aida," e.g.
12 Stan on the sax
13 Hotel visit
18 Weightlifter's maneuver
22 Weather caution for motorists
24 Horse vet?
26 Gym class
28 Ruby's victim
30 Prince of opera
31 What a private eye may eye
32 Something to build on
33 Spirited style
34 Plane part
35 "___ Ben Adhem" (Leigh Hunt poem)
37 Baby beaver
40 U follower
44 "Nova" subject
46 Grand Prix participants
48 Sight from Taormina
50 Low-lying wetland
52 ___ Atatürk, founder of modern Turkey
53 Please no end
54 Polk's predecessor
55 Stereo knob
56 Tiger Beat cover subject
57 Soft seat
59 Timothy Leary dropped it
62 Irene's counterpart in Roman myth
63 Pique condition?

by Richard Silvestri

ACROSS

1. Ballet bend
5. Stogie
10. "Kapow!"
14. Optimistic
15. Zee : English :: ___ : Greek
16. Seized vehicle
17. "Dies ___" (Latin hymn)
18. One of 24 for pure gold
19. Animals that might hear "gee" and "haw"
20. What a person in an emergency might have to make
23. Portuguese colony until 1999
24. Benedict XVI, e.g.
28. Snares
32. Poetic da-DUM, da-DUM, da-DUM, e.g.
33. Some glazed pottery
38. ___ de France
39. Philip who wrote "Goodbye, Columbus"
40. Joy's partner
41. Capital NNW of Copenhagen
42. Funnyman Philips
43. Any of the Jonas Brothers, e.g.
45. "Divine Comedy" writer
47. Attacked
48. Lord's Prayer phrase before "as it is in heaven"
51. Prefix with national or grain
55. Breakfast brand since 1928 that hints at the starts of 20-, 33- and 43-Across
59. Unilever swab
62. Poet T. S. ___
63. Funnyman Jay

64. Morales of "NYPD Blue"
65. The late Mrs. McCartney
66. School where Aldous Huxley taught George Orwell
67. "Stop it!"
68. Pricey seating areas
69. Ripped

DOWN

1. Light refractor
2. ___ Doone cookies
3. Sci-fi writer Asimov
4. Pirate costume feature
5. Pepsi alternative
6. Apple computer
7. Ex-Spice Girl Halliwell
8. Showing shock

9. 3:1 or 7:2, e.g.
10. Novelist Emily or Charlotte
11. ___ Luthor of "Superman"
12. Mimic
13. Tue. preceder
21. Uncool sort
22. "This round's ___"
25. Formal response to "Who's there?"
26. Guy
27. Air-conditioning gas
29. Dog food brand
30. Crook, in cop lingo
31. Does the sidestroke or butterfly
33. Doctrine
34. Like Jupiter, but not Zeus
35. Do penance
36. Together, to Toscanini
37. Take five

41. Rare birth occurrence
43. Gilpin of "Frasier"
44. Dog food brand
46. La Brea attraction
49. Immune system agent
50. Sun: Prefix
52. Deceive
53. Voice below alto
54. "Saying ___ thing, doing . . ."
56. Double-decker checker
57. Went on horseback
58. "Take ___ a sign"
59. Abbr. at the end of a proof
60. General on a Chinese menu
61. Writer Fleming

by David Kwong

ACROSS

1 God, with "one's"
6 Airport guesses, for short
10 Word after matinee or teen
14 Quick, like a cat
15 "Whip It" rock group
16 Zilch
17 Chewed the fat
18 Shootout shout
19 Cereal "for kids"
20 Umber or chocolate brown
23 Pre-K enrollee
24 Org. for boomers, now
25 Early 10th-century year
28 Military treatise by Sun Tzu
34 Bathroom dispenser refill
36 The Velvet Fog
37 Trademarked citrus
38 Thing in a sling
41 Party with techno music, perhaps
42 Friars Club event
44 Gave a makeover
46 Captain's "Listen up!"
49 Pig's pad
50 Gold medalist Lipinski
51 Profs' helpers
53 Sad, like 20-, 28- and 46-Across?
59 Shoot up
60 Year-end air
61 Built-up
63 Adviser, say
64 A person may have one of invincibility
65 Qaddafi's land
66 Suffer from sunburn
67 Lee of Marvel Comics
68 Big name in printers

DOWN

1 Hot Lips Houlihan's rank: Abbr.
2 Petri dish stuff
3 Fuzzy fruit
4 Give a seat to
5 Candy that makes your mouth burn
6 Ancient Icelandic work
7 U.S. Virgin Is., e.g.
8 PC user's self-image
9 "Who cares?"
10 Managing perfectly
11 "Rats!"
12 "Garfield" canine
13 Left Coast airport code
21 Body of cultural values
22 It's faster than a walk
25 Antique farm device
26 Myopic Mr. __

27 Acquired relative
29 Do lunch
30 To the left, at sea
31 Cylindrical sandwiches
32 W.W. II-era G.I., e.g.
33 Like an oboe's sound
35 Drier's need
39 Book before Esth.
40 Madonna title role
43 Flooring wood
45 In most cases
47 Concert locales
48 Were completely depleted
52 "Blondie" or "Cathy"
53 Cheese with a moldy rind
54 Hectored
55 Wife of Zeus
56 Pizazz
57 Falls back

58 "The Banana Boat Song" word
59 Watergate tape problem
62 Tandoor-baked bread

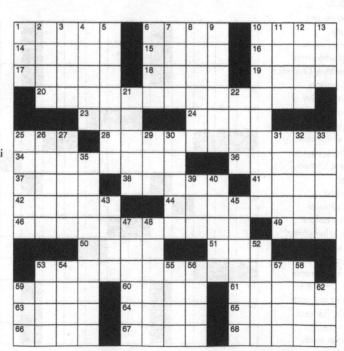

by Kristian House

ACROSS

1 Hits with bug spray
5 Jaguar, e.g.
8 With 61-Across, a possible title for this puzzle
13 It may be bright
14 Ex-politico with a Nobel and an Emmy
15 The Beatles produced it
16 New entrepreneur's need
17 Cadets' org.
18 English county on the North Sea
19 Home of the Sundance Film Festival
22 Dipstick coating
23 King, in Portugal
24 Debussy subject
25 Foofaraw
28 Corporate action that increases the par value of its stock
31 "And I ___ . . ."
33 Wordsmith's ref.
34 Sari-clad royal
35 Fencing move
36 Dickensian cry
37 Makes fun of, in a way
38 Right hand
39 Monk's title
40 Like gnats
41 Bone, for one
44 Grazed, e.g.
45 One of the Manning brothers
46 Noted convert to Islam in 1964
47 Semi part
50 1999 Melissa Joan Hart movie
53 Parting word
56 Poverty, pollution and such
57 Have ___ to one's head
58 Closet filler
59 Look out for?
60 "Quo Vadis" role
61 See 8-Across
62 Mosquito protection
63 Mushroomed

DOWN

1 Nada
2 First name in 1950s politics
3 ___ onion
4 Brought to ruin
5 Bug-building game
6 Pseudo-cultured
7 Shawnee chief at the Battle of Tippecanoe
8 Artists' boo-boos
9 Beanery fare
10 Favored bunch
11 "For shame!"
12 Cigarettes have it
14 Show sorrow
20 Minos's land
21 Ticked (off)
25 Word of woe
26 Awfully small
27 Porter's regretful "Miss"
28 Physician/ synonymist
29 Gads about
30 Plain English
31 Library sign
32 Excessive, as force
35 Clark's crush on "Smallville"
36 From Sucre, say
37 Battlefield shout
39 "The Persistence of Memory" painter
40 Most likely to sunburn
42 Off-season offerings
43 Shakespearean soliloquist
47 Hoops player
48 Like a clear sky
49 At this point
50 Animal on XING signs
51 Hamburg's river
52 Summoned, in a way
53 Subj. with unknowns
54 Go kaput
55 "___ pig's eye!"

by Susan Gelfand

ACROSS

1 Offspring of bucks and does
6 Tobacco mouthful
10 ___ slaw
14 Alaskan native
15 Top-notch
16 N.F.L. Hall-of-Famer Dickerson
17 Stretchable holder
19 Molten flow
20 "Delicious!"
21 Genre for "The Maltese Falcon"
22 Lose steam, with "out"
23 Loony
27 Stats in hockey and basketball
29 Endings with mountain and election
30 Western alliance, for short
31 Prefix with phobia
32 Get a move on
35 Strong family connections, idiomatically
40 Camera choice, in brief
41 French miss: Abbr.
42 Pretentiously styled
43 "That's a good one!"
44 OPEC units
47 Tax-free investment
51 Aids and ___
52 "___ 18" (Leon Uris novel)
53 Fed. property manager
56 Basis of a lawsuit
57 Tux go-with
60 Projecting edge on a roof
61 Sound heard with the phrase "Just like that!"
62 Country singer Tennessee ___ Ford
63 Suffix with poll or pun
64 Atoms with + or − symbols
65 Talks like Don Corleone

DOWN

1 50-acre homestead, maybe
2 Reunion attendee, for short
3 Internet guru
4 Heart
5 Dictation takers
6 Mountain retreats
7 Stockpile
8 The Beach Boys' "Barbara ___"
9 Thu. preceder
10 OK! magazine topics
11 Talk bombastically
12 Animate
13 Modern-day birthday greeting
18 Win by a wide margin
22 Ross who founded the Reform Party
24 Big melee
25 Kind of support offered by a 3-Down
26 Wife of Zeus
27 Aardvarks' fare
28 Wry comic Mort
31 Lunched, say
32 Armed thugs
33 Worldwide: Abbr.
34 Alternative to Häagen-Dazs
36 Apples on desktops
37 For grades 1–12
38 Part of a Three Stooges routine
39 1-Down building
43 One getting a single or a double, e.g.
44 Hoverers over sports stadiums
45 Well-suited
46 One guffawing
47 Chess endings
48 W.W. II Atlantic lurker
49 Chutzpah
50 Jordan's capital
54 Paper doll–making sound
55 Hot-weather quenchers
57 CBS forensic drama
58 Numero ___
59 Victoria's Secret purchase

by Alan Arbesfeld

ACROSS

1 Birthstone for most Scorpios
6 Sir's complement
10 Insignificant type
15 Friend in a sombrero
16 1970s–'80s Dodge
17 Ancient region with an architectural style named after it
18 Root of all Romance languages
19 Margin to maneuver
21 Strain to see over the top
23 [That makes me a little angry]
24 Hammer or tongs
25 Pants half
28 G.P.S. offering
31 River of Hades
34 Honeymooners' destination
36 Social finishes?
38 Bum
40 City God destroyed with fire and brimstone
41 Eat humble pie
45 Company newbie
46 Classic Jags
47 One's equal
48 "That's it for now!"
51 Hard throws to first base, say
53 Sound of bacon frying
54 Perform, as one's trade
55 Real pill
57 Line on a receipt
59 Be a street peddler
65 Toothless enemy
68 Terse bridge bid
69 Norwegian coast feature
70 Street that may be a U.S. highway
71 Milk dispenser
72 Mafia dons

73 Capital on a 69-Across
74 "Here's to . . . ," e.g.

DOWN

1 1 on the Mohs scale
2 Five-star Bradley
3 Hummus scooper-upper
4 Cause of some wrinkles
5 Land-use regulators
6 Like golf greens, frequently
7 Friend who's française
8 Unfocused dread
9 Filet ___
10 Haberdashery accessory
11 Slacker's bane
12 Musician Brian
13 Carnival locale

14 1989 Bond girl Bouvier
20 First in a string of 13 popes
22 Big name in lawn products
25 Part of L.P.G.A.
26 Wears away
27 Arcade fans
28 Fender bender, e.g.
29 Whenever your heart desires
30 ___ white
32 "Ouch!"
33 ___ 360
35 Hiker's snack
37 Musher's carrier
39 Preparing hash for G.I. Joe, say
42 They're spotted in tall grass
43 Wide shoe spec
44 U.S.M.C. noncoms
49 Politico Gingrich

50 One for whom Nome may be home
52 Walked to the door
56 Forum attire
58 Tic-tac-toe alternatives
59 Key to the city recipient, maybe
60 Singer Sedaka
61 Professzor Rubik
62 Stigma borne by Hester Prynne
63 Hydrocarbon suffixes
64 Type
65 Low-rank inits.
66 Steely Dan's stellar seller
67 Top 40 genre

by Stephen Edward Anderson

ACROSS

1 Base coat
7 "More than I need to know," in modern lingo
10 Turn over
14 U.S./Mexico border city
15 Games org.
16 Tiny bit
17 Is nuts for
18 Chart shape
19 Littlest sucker
20 Component of bronze
21 Pulitzer Prize entries
24 Big lug
25 Web-footed animal
26 Ride with runners
28 ___ Zion Church
29 Makes evolutionary changes
34 Brand of clothing or energy drink
36 Tickle
37 Stand that a speaker might take
39 Randomizing device
41 Burgers on the hoof
42 Meal on a blanket
43 Even chance
45 Old spy org.
46 Resistance units
49 Muhammad's pugilistic daughter
51 Some jazz
52 They may be served at the beach
58 ". . . ___ quit!"
59 ORD or LAX figs.
60 Above, to bards
61 Indian encountered by Columbus
63 When tripled, a 1970 war film
64 My ___, Vietnam
65 "___ Nacht" (German carol)
66 Boarding pass datum

67 Pro-___ (some tourneys)
68 Dissed verbally

DOWN

1 "___ Republic"
2 Michelin offering
3 Some ornamental barriers
4 Fruits de ___ (menu heading)
5 Scene of a fall
6 Sommelier's selection
7 One with the inside track at the track?
8 Like a towelette
9 Summer cooler
10 Singer Vikki
11 Place for a thimble
12 Ready to serve
13 Rescue crew, briefly

22 John's ode to Yoko
23 Make a father of
27 Spoils, with "on"
28 ___ Lingus
30 Prenatal test, for short
31 Party servers
32 Philosopher Lao-___
33 Sun. speech
35 Schoolmaster's rod
37 W.W. II transport: Abbr.
38 Arena where 37-Downs were used: Abbr.
39 Rope fiber
40 CD burners
42 Star in Ursa Minor
44 Radio no-no
47 It may need boosting
48 What 21- and 52-Across and 3- and 31-Down might be

50 Construction girder
52 Checks out thoroughly
53 Oklahoma tribe
54 Zhivago's love
55 Aspiring atty.'s exam
56 Bonny one
57 Mex. miss
62 Grafton's "___ for Alibi"

by Kelly Browder

ACROSS

1 Spooky
6 Walk with heavy steps
11 College transcript no.
14 What a cowboy may use while saying "Giddyup!"
15 Course to breeze through
16 Brit. resource for wordsmiths
17 Inspector Clouseau movie, with "The"
19 Hi-fi supply
20 "If I Had a Hammer" singer Lopez
21 Rye and whole wheat
23 Invent, as a phrase
24 TV host Philbin
27 Stats for sluggers
29 Air that makes you go [cough, cough]
30 Alert to danger
31 Martial arts actor Lee
32 Asian New Year
33 Draped Delhi dress
34 Start a Web session
35 Poet Gelett Burgess wrote that he never saw one
38 Bitterly pungent
41 Gentle rise and fall of the voice
42 Ghost's cry
45 Plodding journeys
46 Emperor who fiddled around?
47 Like the models in a swimsuit issue
48 Pie à la ___
49 Patients, to doctors
50 What you might catch a tiger by, in a saying
51 Pull out
53 Antelope with a hump and twisted horns

55 "How was ___ know?"
56 Lewis Carroll character who's late
60 Politico ___ Paul
61 Belly button
62 Public square
63 Unspecified amount
64 Take furtively
65 Rocker Bob with the Silver Bullet Band

DOWN

1 Parapsychology subject, briefly
2 Perfect example
3 Go wild
4 Annoying
5 Jock's channel
6 Number of sides in a decagon
7 Squealer
8 Rubbish holder
9 Fort ___, Fla.
10 Cut, as expenses
11 Edgar Allan Poe story, with "The"
12 Its brands include Frito-Lay and Tropicana
13 Commercials
18 Combat with fighter-bombers
22 Symbol by the phrase "You are here"
23 Chicago's winter hrs.
25 O.K. Corral gunslinger
26 Decorative gratings
28 One of 100 on the Hill: Abbr.
31 Ink stain
33 Soapy froth
35 Cheapskate
36 Yeats's homeland

37 Ninth-inning relief pitcher
38 Source of PIN money?
39 Salad cube
40 John Steinbeck book, with "The"
42 Hacky Sack, basically
43 Form rust, say
44 Popeye's Olive ___
46 Indigenous
47 Sty : hogs :: ___ : horses
49 George M. who composed "Over There"
52 Holds the title to
54 Swimmers' distances
55 Money for the senior yrs.
57 Afternoon social
58 Antlered animal
59 Black goo

by Lynn Lempel

92

ACROSS

1 Loss of heart
7 Mardi Gras wear
11 Go for it
14 "Seinfeld" woman
15 Prefix with potent
16 Go fast
17 Prison for soda jerks?
19 Simile center
20 When prompted
21 Proofer's mark
22 MapQuest suggestions: Abbr.
23 "What's Going On" singer Marvin
24 Prison for bishops?
26 La-la lead-in
28 Patches, as a fairway
29 Sweep's heap
32 Modern means of relaying jokes
36 Shut down
39 Prison for vintners?
42 Islamic equivalent of kosher
43 Bandleader Skinnay ___
44 Part of a journey
45 Lady of the Haus
47 10-digit no.
49 Prison for corny humorists?
54 Ayatollah's land
58 Has
59 Melt ingredient
60 Cartoon art genre
61 A fire sign
62 Prison for gardeners?
64 Doc with a tongue depressor, maybe
65 Creole cooking pod
66 "Good comeback!"
67 Draft org.
68 Call for
69 Slow movers

DOWN

1 Clear up, as a windshield
2 Massey of old films
3 Smart-mouthed
4 Stately dance in 3/4 time
5 It may be upped
6 Roll-call call
7 "Haystacks" artist Claude
8 More than enough
9 Shows derision
10 Thanksgiving guests, often
11 "Over and out"
12 Affected by 13- Down
13 Bakery supply
18 Infamous Amin
22 Its competitors may be thrown
24 Singer Michelle or Cass
25 Full of merriment
27 Slo-mo footage, perhaps
29 Oktoberfest "Oh!"
30 Doo-wop group ___ Na Na
31 Macramé ties
33 Census datum
34 Travel guide listing
35 Spy novelist Deighton
37 "Didn't I tell you?"
38 Fraction of a joule
40 Horses that produce milk
41 Nancy in France, e.g.
46 Slow on the ___
48 ___ franca
49 They may be punched
50 1936 Olympics star Jesse
51 Bizarre
52 Work, as dough
53 The "E" in 64-Across
55 Christina of "Monster"
56 Menotti title role
57 Spanish babies
60 Like most bathroom graffiti: Abbr.
62 Took the cake
63 "___ been real!"

by Jeffrey Wechsler

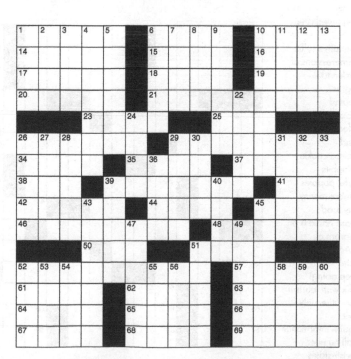

ACROSS

1 Revenue / Result
6 Many a holiday visitor / Bandit
10 Welcome, as a visitor / Try to make a date with
14 Comedian George
15 1980s Geena Davis sitcom
16 Locale for a seat of honor
17 1985 Kate Nelligan title role
18 Chickadee's perch
19 Up to the job
20 Condor's claw
21 College asset
23 Glean
25 Oldest U.S. civil liberties org.
26 At a lecture, say / Surpass in quality
29 Steel helmets with visors
34 Daughter of 28-Down
35 Genesis victim
37 Gawk
38 Priest's garb
39 Choice for a dog, as well as a hint to this puzzle's theme
41 Half a score
42 Has rolling in the aisles
44 Trick ending?
45 Gist
46 Lacking inflection
48 Sub / Excel
50 D.C. bigwig
51 False god
52 Grand Canyon material
57 Doritos dip
61 "Uh-huh"
62 What a surveyor surveys
63 Govt. security
64 ___ Bora, wild part of Afghanistan
65 The Box Tops' "___ Her in Church"
66 Painter's prop
67 Soon to get / Trying to get
68 Ushered / Showed the door
69 Attract / Protract

DOWN

1 Fjord / Bargain locale
2 Mixer
3 Autobahn auto
4 Holiday display
5 Periodicals not brought by a postal carrier
6 Foot part / Go beyond
7 White House adjunct
8 Parched
9 They may be covered and circled
10 Unwavering
11 Kemo ___
12 Brick baker
13 Map feature / Start
22 Watch location
24 ___ example
26 Arriving at the tail end / Survive
27 It has four strings
28 Brother of Rebecca, in the Bible
29 Some Muppet dolls
30 Burn balm
31 Consumed
32 Tire feature
33 Submitted, as an entry / Emitted
36 Honcho
39 Antilles, e.g.
40 ___ Major
43 Spouse's response
45 India's ___ Coast
47 Necessitate
49 Tried
51 Hit so as to make collapse / Win over
52 '60s protest / Skip, as a dance
53 From
54 Peter at the ivories
55 "It's either you ___"
56 Poverty
58 Marge's TV daughter
59 What Cain did to 35-Across
60 Tired / Total

by C. W. Stewart

ACROSS

1 What skunks do
6 Oared racing shell
11 Harley-Davidson, slangily
14 Domed domicile
15 Book after Daniel
16 One-spot
17 "Keep going!"
19 Born: Fr.
20 Workers just for the day
21 Edgar who painted dancers
23 "Sound off — one, two . . .," e.g.
26 Square cracker
28 ___ about (roughly)
29 Neighbor of an Azerbaijani
31 Cheap seat cover material
33 Pizazz
34 Cough medicine amt.
37 Superlative suffix
38 Do impressions of
41 Garden tool
42 "I agree"
43 Donated
44 Erupts
46 Coffee liqueur brand
50 Nabisco cookie
51 Bibliophile
53 Playful puppies
55 Mumbai money
56 Baby food (whose name is an anagram of 55-Across)
57 Hostel
58 "Keep going!"
64 Prefix with tourism
65 Decorative upholstery fabric
66 Acquire information
67 Small number
68 Peevish states
69 Letters before tees

DOWN

1 Use a stool
2 Store head: Abbr.
3 Bridge writer Culbertson
4 Scratch-off game, e.g.
5 Best Actress for "Two Women"
6 Woodworking tool
7 Gear teeth
8 Where Springsteen was born, in song
9 Floral necklace
10 Noncellular phones
11 "Keep going!"
12 Atlantic or Pacific
13 Fliers in V's
18 Village People hit whose title completes the line "It's fun to stay at the . . ."
22 Seventh Greek letter
23 Small flock
24 Licorice-tasting seed
25 "Keep going!"
26 Actress Ward
27 Course related to physiology: Abbr.
30 It might go from 0 to 60 minutes
32 Easily torn bands of tissue
35 Spreader of seeds
36 Mexican money
39 Papa's mate
40 "Terrible" czar
45 Popular chain of chicken restaurants
47 Dick was his running mate in '52 and '56
48 Hardens
49 Broadcasts
51 Succinct
52 ¹⁄₁₆ of a pound
54 "Positive thinker" Norman Vincent ___
56 Animal hide
59 Seeming eternity
60 7, to Caesar
61 "___ Rheingold"
62 Wrath
63 Coast Guard officer: Abbr.

by Betty Keller

ACROSS

1 Org. for boomers, now
5 Smooth-talking
9 Cause of something going up?
14 Iranian money
15 The last Mrs. Charlie Chaplin
16 London line
17 Food-stamping org.
18 Do a cashier's job
19 Tech callers
20 Attack helicopter
22 "___ Lay Dying"
23 Raptor's roost
24 Sister of Rachel
26 Snack machine inserts
29 Abode, informally
31 Do a cashier's job
33 Day-___ colors
34 "Just a ___" (1931 hit)
37 Director Kazan
38 Pick on, in a way
39 WWW bookmark
40 Often-joked-about professionals
42 Summer on the Seine
43 Ellington's "Prelude ___ Kiss"
44 Will-___-wisp
45 Walk unsteadily
47 U.S.N.A. grad
48 Portuguese king
49 Zeus, to the Romans
50 The Big Board, for short
52 Cornell or Pound
54 Make rhapsodic
58 Where to read about the 50-Across: Abbr.
60 In the altogether
62 Gaucho's rope
64 Baseball's Moises
65 "Holy cow!"
66 "Over the Rainbow" composer Harold
67 Lincoln's state: Abbr.
68 Sons of ___ (group promoting Irish heritage)
69 Far from faithful
70 Determination
71 Root beer brand

DOWN

1 Tourist mecca off Venezuela
2 Seating option
3 Weather forecaster's tool
4 Tenor Domingo
5 "Holy cow!"
6 Many subway trains
7 Blown away
8 Sure to bring in money
9 Pastel hue
10 Costner's "Tin Cup" co-star
11 Really steamed
12 Wilder's "___ Town"
13 Classic game console letters
21 Radio host Garrison
25 Buzz, bob or bangs
27 Select few
28 Unloaded?
30 Colonel Sanders facial feature
32 Appliance with a pilot
34 Word before "Morgen" or "Tag"
35 O. Henry literary device
36 See-through partition
37 Word that can follow each half of 20- and 60-Across and 11- and 36-Down
41 Super-duper
46 Stuck in traffic, say
49 Derek of "I, Claudius"
51 ___ Park, Colo.
53 Kaiser or czar
55 Director Kurosawa
56 Not so hot
57 Idyllic spots
59 Girl with the dog Spot
61 Quarterback Warner
62 Luftwaffe foe: Abbr.
63 Portfolio part, for short

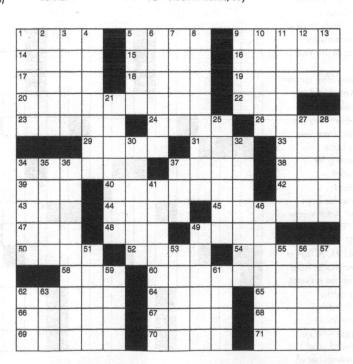

by Thomas Takaro

96

ACROSS

1 Ohio town called the Bicycle Capital of the Midwest
6 Sitcom father of Mearth
10 Longest-serving senator in U.S. history
14 Sing ___
15 "The ___ Love"
16 Be biased
17 Wedding flower girl, maybe
18 Librarian's imperative
19 It's below the elbow
20 *Bush cabinet member who resigned in 2006
23 Wall Street earnings abbr.
24 Monopoly token
25 ___ Grand
26 *Her "Rehab" won a Grammy for Song of the Year
31 Out
34 Leaves after dinner?
35 Actress Naldi of the silents
36 All day every day
39 Friend from way, way back
41 Opening for outside?
42 Spread
44 Places for hops
45 *Best Actor winner for "The Champ," 1931
49 First P.M. of Burma
50 Proto-matter from which the universe was made
51 Real ending?
54 *"Star Wars" actress who's a Harvard grad
58 New member of la familia

59 Simple quatrain form
60 Al-Qatif, for one
61 ___ Sea, outlet of the Amu Darya
62 Small songbirds
63 New Mexico county
64 Glowing
65 Old pump name
66 Livia, to Tiberius

DOWN

1 2005 #1 album for Coldplay
2 Poet who wrote "This is the way the world ends / Not with a bang but a whimper"
3 Incessantly
4 Ancient Peruvian
5 What some amusement park rides have

6 Rob of "Numb3rs"
7 A pint, typically, at a blood bank
8 Chew out
9 Restaurant offering that might come with a toy
10 1957 Fats Domino hit
11 Holler
12 Pretoria money
13 Strand material
21 Towel off
22 String after E
26 "No doubt!"
27 Prefix with liberal
28 180's
29 Factoid for fantasy baseball
30 "I'm all ___"
31 Fresh
32 "Livin' La Vida ___"
33 Worldwide: Abbr.

37 Kiss
38 "The Bells" writer
40 Stereotypically messy digs
43 "The Second Coming" poet
46 Tennis's Ivanovic
47 City on the Rio Grande
48 Want ad abbr.
51 "No more for me"
52 Congo, once
53 Artist James
54 "I, Claudius" figure
55 "Down with . . . !": Fr.
56 Relative of a stork
57 "Ciao"
58 Judging by their names, where the answers to the four starred clues might be found?

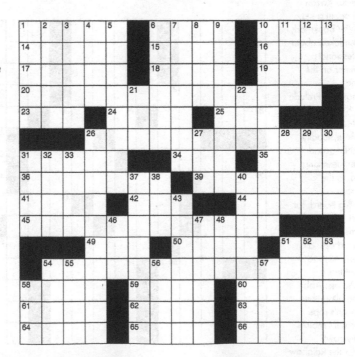

by Caleb Madison

Note: The answers to the eight starred clues all have something in common, each in a different way.

ACROSS
1 China's ___ Zedong
4 ___ and sciences
8 Wrist, elbow and ankle
14 Reach
16 Shook hands (on)
17 *Fraternity with a sweetheart of a song
18 *Drink that often comes with an umbrella
19 Afternoon socials
20 "My bad!"
22 Cold war foe, for short
23 Info on a W-2 form: Abbr.
24 *Like some socks
26 "Après ___ le déluge"
28 Ready for skinny-dipping
29 Rx signers
32 Bryn Mawr graduate
35 Cause of a clock change twice a yr.
36 Paint layer
37 *Smart aleck
39 *Salon supply in a bottle
41 "___ go bragh!"
42 Cold and blustery
44 Attach with Elmer's
45 Cul-de-___
46 "___ Was a Rollin' Stone"
47 "Bad" cholesterol, for short
48 *Good picnic forecast
51 Opposite of post-
54 "The Simpsons" girl
56 Lt. Kojak
57 Plenty
58 *Chocolaty ice cream dessert
60 *Second-generation senator from Indiana
62 Away from the coast
63 Faith
64 Insurance sellers

65 Exam given face-to-face
66 Snaky swimmer

DOWN
1 Sail holders
2 First sign of the zodiac
3 Hymn accompaniment
4 ___ Gardner, Mrs. Sinatra #2
5 Military info-gathering
6 Sierra Nevada resort lake
7 Grad student's income, often
8 Smucker's product
9 Track choice for Lionel trains
10 Like many St. Patrick's Day celebrants

11 Meshes
12 Rip
13 U.S. Star Wars program
15 AOL chitchat
21 "Be quiet!"
24 Queen's mate
25 Dangler on a dog collar
27 Broken mirror, to some
29 Small replica of the Spirit of St. Louis, e.g.
30 Harry Belafonte catchword
31 Brit's W.W. II gun
32 Fills with wonder
33 Franc : France :: ___ : Italy
34 Saintly glows
36 Gunk
38 Talk to persistently and with a big mouth

40 Badly
43 Purple Heart recipient
46 Lament
48 Network showing Capitol Hill proceedings
49 Cut off
50 Australian eucalyptus eater
52 Rolls-___ (car)
53 Jazzy Waters
54 Where inhaled air goes
55 No longer working
57 Lawyers' org.
58 ___ Farrow, Mrs. Sinatra #3
59 Bradley and Begley
61 Zilch

by Lynn Lempel

ACROSS

1 Comprehend
6 Contemptible
10 Shade of many a swimming pool basin
14 Surgeon's tool
15 Web addresses
16 Parts of a tea set
17 Sprightly
18 Politician's goal
19 Give the heave-ho
20 1940s hit radio show featuring the bartender Archie
23 Salad additive
24 Marveled audibly (at)
28 1939 James Joyce novel
33 Second-smallest state: Abbr.
34 Instrument held with two hands
35 Pakistani leader, 1977–88
36 1960s sitcom about a group of castaways
41 G.I. entertainers
42 X __ xylophone
43 Work unit
44 1946 Bing Crosby hit
49 Blog messages
50 Sculler's item
51 1960s sitcom set in a P.O.W. camp
59 On the briny
62 "Am __ late?"
63 __ cotta
64 Wimbledon surface
65 Head for
66 Jew traditionally dressed in a black coat and hat
67 Canned
68 Period of time
69 Solo

DOWN

1 Delighted
2 Prego competitor
3 "Yeah, right!"
4 "To thine own __ be true"
5 Victimize
6 Ado
7 Geographical datum
8 Czech, e.g., but not a Hungarian
9 Ferrara ruling family
10 Ad exhortation
11 Status __
12 Good times
13 Numbskull
21 Transgress
22 Kentucky Derby prize
25 Sand trap, e.g.
26 Barely making, with "out"
27 Defunct
28 Prison population
29 Needing a doctor's attention
30 "__ Fly Now" ("Rocky" theme)
31 Tummy muscles
32 "__ won't!"
33 Establishment with a revolving mirrored ball
36 Forrest __, 1994 Oscar-winning role
37 Schoolyard retort
38 Fed. property overseer
39 Publicize
40 Novelist Deighton
45 Available
46 "Already?"
47 "Rubbish!"
48 First name in soul
52 Play dates?
53 Surmounting
54 __ bene
55 Down-to-earth
56 Roughly
57 Land that's saluted in this puzzle
58 Marquis de __
59 Menu phrase
60 Instrument famously played by Bill Clinton on "The Arsenio Hall Show"
61 One catching a ram's eye

by Richard Chisholm

ACROSS

1 Parroting sorts
6 Stud on a stud farm
10 Good name, casually
13 Venue for some clowns
14 Word before city or child
15 Basis for some discrimination
16 Mystery desserts?
18 Thing to roll over, in brief
19 East ___, U.N. member since 2002
20 Central part
22 Oscar winner Sorvino
25 Acquired relative
27 Musical with the song "Mr. Mistoffelees"
28 Equal to, with "with"
30 O.K. to do
32 Orange feature
33 Bates's business, in film
35 Video shooter, for short
38 Direction from K.C. to Detroit
39 Stir up
41 ___-Ida (Tater Tots maker)
42 Top end of a scale
43 Miming dances
44 Visibly frightened
46 Bucky Beaver's toothpaste
48 High-hats
49 Soprano Gluck
51 Refrain syllables
54 "Spare me!," e.g.
55 Place for a lark
57 Winter coat feature
59 Diamond corner
60 Sculler's affliction?
65 Time of anticipation
66 First-rate
67 Many an art film
68 ___ judicata
69 Hebrides isle
70 Take as one's own

DOWN

1 Flight board abbr.
2 Samoan staple
3 Byrnes of TV's "77 Sunset Strip"
4 Reason for a long delay in getting approval, maybe
5 Arias, e.g.
6 Motorist's headache
7 Calligrapher's buy
8 Period of seven days without bathing?
9 Gaelic tongue
10 What the sky might do in an inebriate's dream?
11 Everglades denizen
12 Belfry sounds
14 Pic to click
17 Mideast V.I.P.
21 Zenith competitor
22 "Impression, Sunrise" painter
23 Cockamamie
24 Illustrations for a Poe poem?
26 Choir voices
29 Leader of the pack
31 Pick up bit by bit
33 Place for a crown
34 In vitro items
36 Mountain ridge
37 Group with a meeting of the minds?
40 Employment in Munchkinland?
45 Choir voice
47 Inflate, in a way
48 Spilled the beans
49 Honey-hued
50 Take a powder
52 Sitcom with the catchphrase "Kiss my grits!"
53 ___ sausage
56 Tolkien beasts
58 "Beowulf," e.g.
61 Modus operandi
62 Courtroom vow
63 Barely beat
64 The "all" in "Collect them all!"

by Robert A. Doll

100

ACROSS

1 Point the finger at
6 Impudent
10 Jail unit
14 Parts to play
15 One putting finishing touches on a cake
16 Light greenish blue
17 Worker for 15%, say
18 "Meet Me at the ___"
19 Japanese wrestling
20 Fix part of dinner with lettuce, carrots, peppers, etc.
22 Large part of a waiter's income
23 A.B.A. member: Abbr.
24 Game company behind Sonic the Hedgehog
26 Play a part
29 Go off like Mount St. Helens
31 Sailor's "Stop!"
35 Writer Harte
37 Put ___ good word for
38 Words cried before "No hands!"
39 Activity with bubbles
40 Retail giant selling dog food, birdcages and such
42 Knots
43 Islands west of Portugal
45 ___-Magnon man
46 Coup d'___
47 Church council
48 Food Network stars
50 "___ you ready?"
51 Take a 39-Across
53 Boneheads
55 ___ California
58 Prepare to camp
63 Minnesota's St. ___ College
64 What "video" means literally

65 Bit part
66 Sitarist Shankar
67 In tatters
68 Perrier competitor
69 Pesky flier
70 Lighted sign over a door
71 Bush's 2004 opponent

DOWN

1 Kid with frequent temper tantrums
2 Golden arches, for McDonald's
3 Pub draughts
4 High-I.Q. group
5 Billionaire's home
6 Petty
7 Environmental sci.
8 Meal
9 Swap
10 Participate on Election Day

11 Prefix with lateral
12 It's in your throat when you choke up
13 Vientiane's land
21 Bacon units
25 Fed. auditing agcy.
26 The P.L.O.'s Mahmoud ___
27 Touched in the head
28 Wyoming's ___ Range
30 Where watermelons grow
32 Japanese dog
33 Mascara mess
34 Important sense for a gourmet
36 Show childish anger
38 Sponge used in a 39-Across
41 Moon shape
44 Psychologist/writer LeShan

48 Longtime Comiskey Park team, informally
49 Sissy of "Carrie"
52 Ill will
54 Prevent, with "off"
55 Tennis's Bjorn
56 Astronaut Shepard or Bean
57 Coffee, slangily
59 Garr or Hatcher
60 Mideast bigwig
61 Close
62 Broadway honor

by Randy Sowell

ACROSS

1 Wrote an ode to
7 China's Chou En-___
10 Captain Hook's henchman
14 Cause of weird weather
15 Press worker's stain
16 Brighton bye-bye
17 Augments
18 Wine servers
20 Adolescent boy's growth
22 Recurring Woody Allen theme
23 Have a go at
24 What oil helps dissolve
25 "I Pity the Fool" star
26 Brother of Little Joe on '60s TV
27 "Jingle Bells" starter
31 Little green man
34 Soldier's period of service
36 Isaac's eldest
37 Cocoon occupants
38 Little green men, for short
39 Target competitor
40 Where a tab is inserted
41 Joan of the Blackhearts
42 "Biography" network, once
43 King Cole was a merry one
45 "Death in Venice" author Thomas
47 Demolition aid
48 "The Witches" director Nicolas
49 Some Super Bowl Sunday highlights
52 Africa's largest city
55 Bargains for leniency
57 Dukakis in 1988 and Dole in 1996
59 (0,0) on a graph
60 Reach a high
61 Grampa Simpson
62 They can be found in 20- and 55-Across and 10- and 26-Down
63 Lap dog, informally
64 Window units, briefly
65 Electrician's alloy

DOWN

1 Did an axel, e.g.
2 Tree with catkins
3 It's observed on Oct. 24
4 Wink in tiddlywinks, e.g.
5 Make king or queen
6 Goofball
7 "Hungarian Rhapsodies" composer
8 Animated bug film of 1998
9 Clanton at the O.K. Corral
10 Musial's nickname
11 Helgenberger of "CSI"
12 LAX postings
13 American League division
19 Some are declared
21 J. P. Morgan co.
25 Scratch
26 Dehydration may help bring this on
27 Housecleaning aid
28 "This ___ outrage!"
29 Source of a fragrant oil
30 "___ Nacht" (German words of parting)
31 Lhasa ___
32 Temporary calm
33 Popular MP3 player
35 Mel in Cooperstown
39 Emblem on the Australian coat of arms
41 Protrude
44 ___ about (circa)
46 "___ Fables"
48 Gift on Valentine's Day
49 Chilly
50 Make less chilly
51 Less loopy
52 Al who created Fearless Fosdick
53 Away from the wind
54 "Out of Africa" author Dinesen
55 "Fast Money" network
56 Dosage unit
58 Battery size

by Pancho Harrison

102

ACROSS

1 Tree trunk
5 Some HDTVs
9 Heartbreaker who's "back in town" in a 1980 Carly Simon hit
14 Feature of mesh fabrics
16 The Carolinas, e.g., to the French
17 Debugs computer programs, e.g.
19 Two of racing's Unsers
20 Neighbor of B.C.
21 San ___, Marin County
22 La ___ Tar Pits
23 Bird feeder fill
24 Responds to rashes
31 Like Papa Bear's porridge
32 Collect splinters, so to speak
33 Tuskegee's locale: Abbr.
34 Nutmeg State sch.
35 Ore suffix
36 "What ___" ("Ho-hum")
38 Rap sheet entries, for short
39 Messenger ___
40 Record label owned by Sony
41 Does some mending
45 Cellular construction
46 Overlook
47 One of the Leeward Islands
50 Hesitant sounds
51 Mexicali Mrs.
54 Lines up the sewing
57 Coral creation
58 Blood type historically considered the universal donor
59 Only beardless Disney dwarf
60 Have a knish, say
61 Orbiting telescope launcher

DOWN

1 Florida city, for short
2 Australian gem
3 "Sure, why not?!"
4 Business letter abbr.
5 Return to one's seat?
6 Quarter of Algiers
7 Batter's fig.
8 Ethiopia's Haile ___
9 Glitterati
10 Blah, blah, blah, for short
11 Satirist Mort
12 Skier's turn
13 Gas brand in Canada
15 Prestigious business school
18 Umiak passenger
22 Road, in the Rheinland
24 Speech spot
25 Tiramisu topper
26 Place to rule
27 Business sign abbr.
28 Like Siberian winters
29 Give a lift
30 Long tales
35 What oysters "R" during "R" months
36 Da Vinci or Michelangelo, to Romans
37 Wordsmith's ref.
39 Florenz Ziegfeld offering
40 Set a lofty goal
42 Raw material for Wrigley's, once
43 To a great degree
44 MapQuest offerings
47 Make ___ dash
48 Brussels-based alliance
49 'Vette roof option
51 Islamic sect
52 Amps up
53 On the main
55 ___-Cat (winter vehicle)
56 Doz. eggs, commonly

by Jerry E. Rosman

ACROSS

1 Side of a doorway
5 1928 Oscar winner Jannings
9 ___ and dangerous
14 Actor Morales
15 Western locale called the Biggest Little City in the World
16 Late hotel queen Helmsley
17 Small hotel room specification
20 Modern workout system
21 Fan sound
22 "Hel-l-lp!"
23 Capone and Pacino
25 Sticky stuff
27 1944 thriller with Fred MacMurray and Barbara Stanwyck
36 ___-bitty
37 Falco of "The Sopranos"
38 Ad ___ per aspera (Kansas' motto)
39 Former AT&T rival
40 Princess Diana's family name
42 Suffix with president
43 Eagle's nest
45 Trojan War hero
46 Years, in Latin
47 Baked dessert with lemon filling, maybe
50 Partner of long. in a G.P.S. location
51 Small pouch
52 "___ sells seashells by the seashore" (tongue twister)
54 Bulletin board fastener
58 Oliver's love in "As You Like It"
62 Serious heart surgery
65 Brink
66 Continental money

67 Author Morrison
68 Words to live by
69 TV's warrior princess
70 Former jets to J.F.K.

DOWN

1 Words said in fun
2 Where India is
3 Lion's hair
4 Chronic whiner
5 Before, poetically
6 Cat's plaint
7 1/12 of a foot
8 Graph points
9 Swiss peak
10 Deduces
11 Not stereo
12 Letter attachments: Abbr.
13 When the sun shines

18 Laze about
19 Impulse
24 Ooze
26 Poet Khayyám
27 Probe persistently
28 Stream critter
29 Wombs
30 Like a score of 10 for 10
31 Japanese fighter
32 Go bad, as teeth
33 Singer Turner's autobiography
34 Drug that calms the nerves, slangily
35 New Haven collegian
40 Actress Ward
41 Old flames
44 Start of a daily school recital
46 Opposite of refuses
48 "___, Brute?"

49 Bordering on pornographic
52 Litigant
53 Tortoise's race opponent
55 Peak
56 Word in many a Nancy Drew title
57 "Show Boat" composer Jerome
59 Neighbor of Vietnam
60 "Money ___ everything"
61 Sale tag caution
62 Shopping channel
63 Scarlet
64 Feathered neckwear

by Andrea Carla Michaels

ACROSS

1 Internet address starter
5 Shoe part
9 Shoe mark
14 Where Donegal Bay is
15 Declare frankly
16 "The Yankee Years" co-writer
17 Word after "ppd." on a sports page
18 Like a 1943 copper penny
19 Desilu co-founder
20 Bitter-tasting vegetable
23 Steps nonchalantly
24 Common commemorative items
28 Mobile's state: Abbr.
29 Garfield's foil
31 The Eiger, for one
32 "Young Indian brave" in a 1960 Johnny Preston #1 hit
36 Even up
37 Arguing loudly
38 Abbr. in a help wanted ad
39 Essen's region
40 "Kid-tested, mother-approved" cereal
41 Least acceptable amount
45 Prefix with tourism
46 Resistance units
47 Unit of RAM, for short
48 Actress Bullock
50 Morphine and codeine, for two
54 Country singer with a hit sitcom
57 Dwelt
60 ___ & Chandon Champagne
61 Village Voice award
62 Baja buddy

63 Munich Mrs.
64 Make out
65 More than a twitch
66 Macy's department
67 S&L offerings

DOWN

1 Rosemary and thyme
2 Princess' topper
3 The Dixie Chicks and the Dixie Cups
4 Strong liking
5 "The Human Comedy" novelist William
6 Cameo shapes
7 Actress Loughlin of "90210"
8 Vessel by a basin
9 Less likely to collapse
10 Jazzman Chick

11 Subject of a Keats ode
12 Monk's title
13 Shriner's topper
21 Colombian city
22 Samoan port
25 10-year-old Oscar winner O'Neal
26 Peace Nobelist Root
27 ___ whale
29 Slender woodwinds
30 Consider
32 Landscapers' tools
33 City in New York's Mohawk Valley
34 "Frost/___," 2008 nominee for Best Picture
35 Listerine target
39 Tubular pasta
41 Yawn inducer
42 Melville's obsessed whaler

43 Driving force
44 Deutschland denial
49 Bottom-of-the-barrel stuff
50 Great blue expanse
51 River of Rome
52 Author Jong
53 Is in the market for
55 Like most car radios
56 Oliver Twist's request
57 ___ Cruces, N.M.
58 Handful for a baby sitter
59 Itinerary word

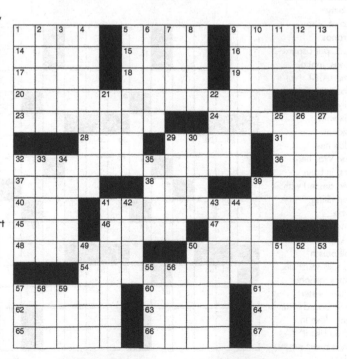

by Allan E. Parrish

105

ACROSS

1 Frog-dissecting class: Abbr.
5 "Ship of Fools" painter
10 Riot queller
14 Pink, maybe
15 Lawn care brand
16 "Such a pity"
17 Slate, e.g.
18 Where was the Battle of Bunker Hill fought?
20 Makes invalid
22 California Indian tribe: Var.
23 Seminary teaching
24 Drain
25 Cousin of a cat's-eye
29 What animal does a bulldogger throw?
30 Drop ___ (moon)
32 Soprano Gluck
33 Get copy right
35 Money
37 In what country are Panama hats made?
41 What is George Eliot's given name?
42 It'll keep the home fires burning
43 Queens's ___ Stadium
44 Seed cover
45 Golfer Ballesteros
47 From what animals do we get catgut?
52 Smallest
54 Soft shoe, briefly
55 Part of São Paulo
56 Column style
58 Putting up the greatest affront
59 In what country are Chinese gooseberries produced?
63 Times to call, in some want ads
64 Unoccupied
65 Deejay's interest, typically
66 Port opener?
67 Family dogs, for short
68 Very funny happenings
69 The "I" in M.I.T.: Abbr.

DOWN

1 Challah and baguettes
2 "You are so!" preceder
3 What color is the black box in a commercial jet?
4 Pea, for one
5 Short cuts
6 Bruins' retired "4"
7 What is actor Stewart Granger's family name?
8 For next to nothing, in slang
9 Brick carriers
10 Reddish brown
11 Clay, today
12 "Silent" prez
13 Adult ed. class, often
19 ___ Na Na
21 Rio Grande port
24 Recipe verb
26 "M*A*S*H" star
27 Eliot Ness and others
28 Bring home
31 The California gull is the state bird of which state?
34 For what animals are the Canary Islands named?
36 1974 Mocedades hit
37 Not différent
38 ___ package
39 Former Voice of America org.
40 Nobody too big or too small, on a sign
41 Fraction of a tick: Abbr.
43 What kind of fruit is an alligator pear?
46 Actor Estevez
48 Cab Calloway phrase
49 How many colleges are in the Big Ten?
50 Ford failures
51 Take care of a neighbor's dog, say
53 Piggy
57 He wrote "If called by a panther, / Don't anther"
58 Nutritional amts.
59 Cowboys' org.
60 Cold war ___
61 Site for a site
62 Site for a site

by Ed Stein and Paula Gamache

ACROSS
1 Iditarod vehicle
5 Money for the poor
9 In a stupor
14 Skunk ___ Le Pew
15 Jacob's wife
16 President sworn in on Lincoln's Bible
17 They can be stroked or bruised
18 "Othello" character who says "Who steals my purse steals trash"
19 Bearer of gold, frankincense or 66-Across
20 Speaking with lofty language
23 Cunning
24 "Do ___ others . . ."
25 Riddle
29 Ginger ___ (Canada Dry product)
30 Droop
31 ___ Luthor of "Superman"
32 Withholding nothing
37 Jazz's Fitzgerald
38 October 31 shout
39 Luau garlands
40 What a fresh ad campaign helps combat
45 History segment
46 Auditor's org.
47 Like carrots that crunch
48 Calm
50 Campbell's product
52 Damage
55 Holder of the first-in-the-nation presidential primary
58 "Dancing With the Stars" airer
61 Help in crime
62 Tolkien creatures
63 One getting one-on-one instruction
64 Egg on

65 Sainted fifth-century pope
66 Gift brought to Bethlehem
67 Pb, in chemistry
68 Its cycle is indicated by the starts of 20-, 32-, 40- and 55-Across

DOWN
1 Shoots, as lava
2 Permissible
3 Strong bond
4 Arnaz of "I Love Lucy"
5 Like celestial bodies exhibiting syzygy
6 Pounced (on)
7 Nearsighted Mr. of cartoons
8 What a cobbler works on

9 Santo ___, Caribbean capital
10 Beaded counters
11 Zig's partner
12 Cousin of an ostrich
13 Prosecutors, briefly
21 ___ and void
22 Blue-winged duck
26 3-Down and others
27 Earn
28 x and y, on a graph
29 Jai ___
30 Sean Connery, nationally speaking
32 Airborne signal
33 Like a bone from the elbow to the wrist
34 Bird seen in hieroglyphics
35 Bush 43, to Bush 41
36 Large amount
37 Rams' mates

41 Ancient Assyrian capital
42 Sprouted
43 Blew, as a volcano
44 Notorious B.I.G. releases
49 Key in
50 Buffalo hockey player
51 "Phi, chi, psi" follower
52 Actor Sal of "Exodus"
53 "Star Wars" droid
54 Plant exudation
56 Lug
57 Captain's place
58 Dispenser of 20s
59 Totally accept, as an idea
60 Midpoint: Abbr.

by Dustin Foley

ACROSS

1 Pat down
6 Lead character on "Saved by the Bell"
10 On a cruise
14 Neopagan belief
15 Second word of many fairy tales
16 Extremist sect
17 Red Sox Hall-of-Famer Bobby
18 ___ Strauss jeans
19 Spelunker's hangout
20 Valuable discoveries
23 Prevailed
24 Most enlightened
25 Cry while holding a bag
31 Exploding stars
32 Loud chuckles
33 Married mlle.
36 Sch. on the bank of the Rio Grande
37 East ___ (nation since 2002)
38 Billy who sang "We Didn't Start the Fire"
39 Lean-___
40 Ebbed
41 The time it takes mountains to rise
42 Proven to work
44 Cirque du ___
47 Diplomat's bldg.
48 Semi
54 Impulsive
55 Home of Città del Vaticano
56 Less common
58 Letter-routing abbr.
59 Actor McGregor
60 Brilliant display
61 South-of-the-border currency
62 "Well, gosh darn!"
63 Timetables, informally

DOWN

1 Subject line starter on many an e-mail joke
2 Hilarious act
3 Cake decorator
4 Twist-off bottle top
5 Word derived from Japanese for "empty orchestra"
6 Last letter of a pilot's alphabet
7 Imitator
8 Sheltered inlet
9 Sweaters and such
10 Approach aggressively
11 Debonair
12 Dwellers in Middle-earth
13 "This is only ___"
21 ___-cone
22 Narrow inlets
25 Letter-shaped fastener
26 ___-Rooter
27 Currier and ___
28 Riesling wines are produced in its valley
29 Having dams at various locations, as a river
30 Spinoff of "The Mary Tyler Moore Show"
33 What boats may do in an inlet
34 File, Edit or Help
35 "That's something ___"
37 Made to order, as a suit
38 Not just dark
40 Habeas corpus, for one
41 Looks up to
42 Electronic dance genre
43 Teacher's union: Abbr.
44 Amusement park ride feature
45 Hold forth
46 Endures
49 Prime seating spot
50 Untouchable, e.g.
51 "You ___?"
52 Writer ___ Stanley Gardner
53 Go over Time?
57 Football blockers: Abbr.

by Joon Pahk

108

ACROSS
1 Venetian who explored for England in the 15th century
6 Paints gently
10 Mattress filler during a recession, maybe
14 Last Oldsmobile car
15 Palindromic magazine name
16 "A pity"
17 Tail-less Old World mammal
18 Land of the descendants of 67-Across
19 "Step right up!"
20 An Olympic swimmer needs a big one
23 50+ org.
24 Royal family
28 Less than 1%
31 It may be over a window
35 Tricks
37 Not so common
38 The Greatest
39 Son of, in Arab names
40 Akihito's wife, e.g.
42 Rebelling Turner
43 __ pooped to pop
44 Shire of "Rocky"
45 Treaty signing
47 Sound practical judgment
50 After 2004, the only way to buy a 14-Across
51 Slander
52 Modern way to put out an album
54 Fateful event for the Titanic
61 Diamond group
64 Runner in Pamplona
65 Like spoken n's
66 It turns a hundred into a thousand
67 Jacob's twin
68 Makes like the Cheshire Cat

69 Element that can precede the starts of 20-, 31-, 47- and 54-Across
70 Where the crew chows down
71 "Poor Richard's Almanack" bit

DOWN
1 Give a ring
2 Baseball's Felipe or Jesus
3 Capital of Switzerland
4 Art form that commonly depicts a swan
5 Puccini opera
6 Group with the 1968 hit "Hush"
7 2006 Emmy winner for "The West Wing"
8 Congressional Black Caucus, e.g.
9 Rest stop sight
10 Echo location
11 Stout, e.g.
12 "Harlem Nocturne" instrument
13 1940s–'50s White House inits.
21 Part of a circle
22 Common companion of a dry throat
25 Astronomical discovery of 1781
26 Grief relief
27 Ready to be typeset
28 Paul Revere and others
29 Big bang
30 Turn a deaf ear to
32 __ to go
33 Spying against one's own country, say
34 He ran to succeed 13-Down: Abbr.
36 Et __
41 More, on Mallorca
46 Author Kipling
48 Biblical strongman
49 Part of S.A.S.E.: Abbr.
53 Line dance
55 Hot pair
56 A teaspoonful, maybe
57 Reconstruction and the Roaring Twenties
58 Indian's home
59 Club familiars
60 End of a warning
61 Gun produced by Israel Military Industries
62 La Méditerranée, e.g.
63 Whiz

by Joey Weissbrot

ACROSS

1 Best-selling computer game of the 1990s
5 Players in a play
9 Unwanted e-mail
13 Helicopter blade
15 "___ your thirst" (former Sprite slogan)
16 Therefore
17 Myanmar, once
18 Al Capone, for one
20 Mentalist Geller
21 Little devil
23 Breadth
24 Not heeding danger
27 Apartment that's owned, not leased
28 Nick at ___
29 Computer whiz
32 ___ Antonio, Tex.
33 Jobs at Apple
35 Corridors
37 Widespread Internet prank involving a bait-and-switch link to a music video
41 Reason for engine trouble, perhaps
42 Christmas carols
45 ___ and eggs
48 Metal that gave its name to a shade of blue
51 Writer Harte
52 Caribbean vacation spot
54 Mick Jagger or Bruce Springsteen
56 Prayer beads
58 Parisian "yes"
59 Studio that made "Notorious"
60 Packs for bikers and hikers
63 Young pigeon
65 52-Across, e.g.
66 Cry while careering downhill
67 Bulrush, e.g.
68 Fortuneteller
69 Stop or Do Not Pass
70 Almost-failing grades

DOWN

1 Owner of the Springfield Nuclear Power Plant on "The Simpsons"
2 Shout in tag
3 Less forgiving
4 ___ Sawyer
5 Body in a whodunit
6 "The ___ Daba Honeymoon"
7 Fraction of a min.
8 Little fella
9 Fight that might include fisticuffs
10 Prettifies oneself, as in a mirror
11 Order of business at a meeting
12 "When it rains, it pours" salt brand
14 Train travel
19 Be great at
22 Encountered
25 Bandleader Eubanks of "The Jay Leno Show"
26 Learned one
30 "2001" computer
31 Running a temperature, say
34 High-m.p.g. vehicles
36 Hoity-toity sorts
38 Hootchy-___
39 "Spare" part of the body
40 She says "The lady doth protest too much, methinks" in "Hamlet"
43 Problem with pipes
44 Disco lights
45 Joel Chandler ___, creator of Uncle Remus
46 Excite
47 What a bodybuilder builds
49 Undo, as laces
50 Fort Worth sch.
53 Cake maker
55 Smooch
57 Deviations of a ship's course
61 "The Sweetheart of Sigma ___"
62 What's tapped at a beer bust
64 Letters at the end of a proof

by Natan Last

ACROSS

1 Go 50 in a 30-m.p.h. zone, e.g.
6 Joyful tune
10 Enthusiasm
14 Similar
15 "Are you ___ out?"
16 Utah ski resort
17 1985 Glenn Close/Jeff Bridges thriller
19 Saint Barthélemy et d'autres
20 German's "Dear me!"
21 Mail service made obsolete by the transcontinental telegraph
23 Fish stew containers
25 Slowly, in music
26 Most Little Leaguers
27 Hay unit
30 Hardly a little angel
32 Simple swimming stroke
37 In a Kinks hit s/he "walked like a woman and talked like a man"
38 Waiters' handouts
39 Mob scene
40 Widening in a highway, maybe
42 Lenin's "What ___ Be Done?"
43 River of Spain
44 Eisenhower and Turner
46 "When You Wish Upon ___"
50 Groveled
53 1970s Robert Young TV role
57 "Gloria in excelsis ___"
58 Farm team
59 What the long Across answers with circles have
61 Go here and there
62 Actress Hathaway
63 "Evil ___" (comics series)
64 Oklahoma city
65 Bat, ball, glove, etc.
66 Number of hills in Roma

DOWN

1 Pat of "Wheel of Fortune"
2 Come in second
3 It's last to be sunk
4 Heart test readout: Abbr.
5 Very much
6 Property claims
7 Four-time Harrison Ford film role
8 Second-level seating
9 Fearsome display at a natural history museum
10 Congo's name before 1997
11 TV's DeGeneres
12 Mushroom producer, for short
13 Rodeo rope
18 Bucks' partners
22 Appeal
24 General Mills brand
27 "Bedtime for ___" (Reagan film)
28 Contents of the Spanish Main
29 8-track alternatives
30 Deli sandwich, for short
31 Kanga's baby
32 Honeybunch
33 Like raisins vis-à-vis grapes
34 Andrei Sakharov in the Soviet era, e.g.
35 Film studio locale
36 W.W. II command
38 World Series org.
41 Where Simón Bolívar was once president
44 The Beatles' "Let ___"
45 Economist John Maynard ___
46 Love, Italian-style
47 The "S" in WASP
48 Rome's ___ Fountain
49 Pimply
50 Tree with catkins
51 Send, as payment
52 "We're off ___ the Wizard . . ."
54 Catch and throw back, as fly balls
55 Burgundy or Bordeaux
56 "The Simpsons" teacher who is called Mrs. K
60 Test for Ph.D. wannabes

by Barry Boone

ACROSS

1 Booker T.'s bandmates in '60s R&B
4 San Diego Zoo attractions
10 [fizzle]
14 "Can't Get It Out of My Head" grp.
15 "Peter and the Wolf" musician
16 View from Buffalo
17 Have surgery
20 Great time
21 Actress Polo of "Meet the Parents"
22 RR stop
23 ___ David
24 With 37- and 50-Across, privileged
26 Colorful glacier layer
29 Bubble contents
30 Family girl
31 Family girl
34 Dolt
37 See 24-Across
41 Co. acquired by Verizon in 2006
42 Sturdy building material
43 Court figs.
45 D.C. influence wielder
48 Designer's starting point
50 See 24-Across
55 "Keep ___ alive!"
56 Geisha's accessory
57 Diamond legend, with "the"
58 "Bowling for Columbine" documentarian
60 "Gimme!"
64 Mine, in Marseille
65 ___ Palace, French presidential residence
66 Seventh in a series of 24
67 It may be caught in a trap
68 Sure
69 Rogers who was elected twice to the Country Music Hall of Fame

DOWN

1 Sister in "Little Women"
2 Doctrine that de-emphasizes regional interests
3 Barry White's genre
4 Some marine herds
5 Help in a bad way
6 ___'easter
7 "Likewise"
8 One of the 12 tribes of Israel
9 Chest protectors
10 Slammer
11 Bill passed many times on the Hill, formerly
12 It may be taken in court, with "the"
13 Pop/R&B singer ___ Marie
18 Kitty's pickup point
19 Fuzzy fruit
23 "Numb3rs" network
24 They may come in a round
25 Modern locale of ancient Persepolis
27 Accts. payable receipt
28 French bus. firm
32 Winter Minn. hrs.
33 Pleistocene, e.g.
35 Fries, often
36 Began paying attention
38 They may be licked or smacked
39 "Vas ___ Vas" (former derivative Spanish-language game show)
40 Wine: Prefix
44 Geneviève, e.g.: Abbr.
46 Prefix with dextrous
47 Actress Phyllis of "I Was a Teenage Frankenstein"
49 Comrade of Mao
50 Butcher's discards
51 Feminist Wolf who wrote "The Beauty Myth"
52 Bankrupt company in 2002 headlines
53 Curved fastener
54 Milkman of musical fame
58 Talking horse of old TV
59 Mind
61 Hobbyist's purchase
62 Spanish "that"
63 "That's great news!"

by Michael Vuolo

112

ACROSS

1 Knights' competition
6 Baby kangaroo
10 Kid around
14 Winfrey who said "I still have my feet on the ground, I just wear better shoes"
15 Feminine suffix
16 Length × width, for a rectangle
17 Brother outlaw in the Wild West
19 Spick-and-span
20 Suffix with pay
21 "___ happy returns"
22 Imbeciles
24 Ones with caws for alarm?
25 Some boxing wins, for short
26 Humiliate
28 Cause for a mistrial
32 Not taut
33 "Tell ___ lies"
34 Prime draft status
35 Googly-eyed Muppet
36 Retail clothing giant . . . or a description of 17- and 54-Across and 10- and 24- Down?
37 Color for baby girls, traditionally
38 L.B.J. son-in-law Charles
39 Things inflated with hot air?
40 Cabalists' plans
41 Mexican beans
43 Makes progress
44 Up to the task
45 19th-century educator Horace
46 Politico Milk of "Milk"
49 Bo : Obama :: ___ : Roosevelt
50 "___ Baba and the 40 Thieves"
53 Jai ___
54 White Sox outfielder nicknamed "Shoeless"
57 Injured
58 Choir voice
59 Discover by chance
60 Home of Iowa State University
61 Back end
62 Midterms and finals

DOWN

1 "___ left his home in Tucson, Arizona" (Beatles lyric)
2 Autobahn auto
3 With 45-Down, home of the Big Dipper
4 Carrier to Copenhagen
5 1994 Jim Carrey film
6 Levi's, e.g.
7 "Time Is ___ Side" (Rolling Stones hit)
8 Opposite of WSW
9 "So you've said"
10 "Me and Bobby McGee" singer, 1971
11 Nabisco cookie
12 Chair or sofa
13 Bowlers that don't bowl
18 "The Gong Show" panelist ___ P. Morgan
23 Hound
24 Longtime New York senator for whom a center is named
25 iPod downloads
26 "It's ___ nothing"
27 Thumper's "deer friend"
28 Give a ___ welcome
29 The "U" in A.C.L.U.
30 Payments to landlords
31 Talks, talks, talks
32 Feudal worker
33 Fibber of old radio
36 Smucker's container
40 Flair
42 U.K. award
43 Black-tie affair
45 See 3-Down
46 "That's rich!"
47 Homecoming attendee, in brief
48 Once in a blue moon
49 Greek cheese
50 Dashiell Hammett hound
51 Tapestry device
52 Places to stay the night
55 Bullring cheer
56 Spherical breakfast cereal

by Randall J. Hartman

ACROSS

1 Soft or crunchy snack
5 Like a 52-Across
10 Start of an incantation
14 The "A" in Chester A. Arthur
15 Rudely assertive
16 When repeated, Road Runner's call
17 1908 Cubs player and position
20 How fame comes, sometimes
21 Friars Club event
22 The Braves, on a scoreboard
23 "Pants on fire" person
25 1908 Cubs player and position
33 Chutzpah
34 Put an edge on
35 Hydrotherapy locale
36 "How sweet ___!"
37 Barbers' touch-ups
39 Polish's partner
40 U. of Miami's athletic org.
41 Baseball analyst Hershiser
42 Command to an attack dog
43 1908 Cubs player and position
47 Salt Lake City athletes
48 Ike's W.W. II command
49 "Yes we can" sloganeer
52 2006 Ken Jennings book . . . or the author himself
57 What 17-, 25- and 43-Across were, famously
60 Virginia ___ (noted 1587 birth)
61 The Dapper Don
62 Fountain order
63 Polaris or Sirius
64 Jimmy of the Daily Planet
65 They're splitsville

DOWN

1 "Toodles"
2 Touched down
3 Water-to-wine site
4 Peeling potatoes, stereotypically
5 Mast extensions
6 Bodyguard's asset
7 Only African-American male to win Wimbledon
8 P, on a fraternity house
9 Norse war god
10 Work like paper towels
11 Software test version
12 Vintage autos
13 Date with an M.D.
18 Clear, as a tape
19 The "t" in Nafta
23 Machine with a shuttle
24 Rustic lodgings
25 1946 high-tech wonder
26 Climbing plant with pealike flowers
27 Novelist Jong
28 Homes on wheels, in brief
29 Hot dog topper
30 Humane org. since 1866
31 Black-clad and white-clad Mad adversaries
32 Wonderland cake phrase
37 Logic diagram
38 Flag tossers, for short
39 Bro or sis
41 Of base 8
42 Showing no emotion
44 "Sorry, Wrong ___"
45 Add a star to, say
46 Not leave the house
49 They may be stacked against you
50 Dinghy, e.g.
51 Surrounding glow
52 Nonkosher diner offerings
53 Iditarod terminus
54 Huge-screen format
55 Up to it
56 Hotel room roll-ins
58 Part of Freud's "psychic apparatus"
59 Vote seeker, for short

by Ronald J. and Nancy J. Byron

114

When this puzzle is done, the nine circles will contain the letters A through I. Connect them with a line, in alphabetical order, and you will form an illustration of the puzzle's theme.

ACROSS

1 A Morse "I" consists of two
5 Penultimate fairy tale word
9 Deadly snake
14 "Climb ___ Mountain"
15 Long skirt
16 Break point
17 With 59-Across, A-B-C-A in the illustration
18 Ship in "Pirates of the Caribbean"
20 Stop ___ dime
21 Half of a mountaineering expedition
22 Dressed like a certain keg party attendee
24 Prefix with lateral
25 F-G
29 Ship's christening, e.g.
30 C-D
31 "___ expert, but . . ."
32 Certain California wines
34 Pirating
36 "Top Hat" dancer
39 Does some electrical work on
40 Counterpart of un ángel
41 Santa-tracking org.
42 End in ___
43 A-B
45 Send, as payment
49 E-F-G-H-E
50 Part of U.C.L.A.
51 Brainstorm
52 People in fierce snowball fights
54 Yearbook sect.
55 Ship to the New World
59 See 17-Across
60 Ancient theater
61 Makeup of some little balls

62 Response to a charge
63 Stethoscope users, at times
64 Away from the wind
65 Lava lamps and pet rocks, once

DOWN

1 Bump down but keep on
2 Chekhov play or its antihero
3 "M*A*S*H" procedure
4 Lexicographical abbr.
5 Incorporate, as a YouTube video into a Web site
6 Actor Kilmer and others
7 Horse-race bets on win and place
8 Kitchen gadgets

9 Hook or Cook: Abbr.
10 Tribute with feet
11 Deadly snake
12 1921 play that introduced the word "robot"
13 One of the oceans: Abbr.
19 One who may put you in stitches?
21 Part of a larger picture
23 Poe's "___ Lee"
25 "Don't Go Breaking My Heart" duettist, 1976
26 Mideast V.I.P.
27 Cousin of -trix
28 Old shipbuilding needs
30 Writer Rita ___ Brown
33 Leak on a ship, e.g.

35 Tournament wrap-up
36 Wife of Esau
37 In ___ (as found)
38 Following detective
39 CD-___
41 It may be flared
44 "Yowie, zowie!"
46 "Mississippi ___" (1992 film)
47 Words of resignation
48 Magnetic induction units
51 Livid
52 D- reviews
53 Aachen article
55 ___ sauce
56 Suffix with many fruit names
57 Minus: Abbr.
58 Dress (up)
59 Number on a bottle at the beach

by Daniel A. Finan

ACROSS

1 Part of a Halloween costume
5 Rich soil component
10 Get an ___ effort
14 "Do ___ others as . . ."
15 Not appropriate
16 Duo plus one
17 Mark left from an injury
18 Refuse a request
19 Detained
20 Separate grains from wheat, e.g.
22 Valentine candy message
24 Animated TV character whose best friend is Boots
28 Suffix with access
29 Young dog or seal
30 China's Mao ___-tung
31 ___ Jima
32 Casey of "American Top 40"
34 Main port of Yemen
35 2008 campaign personality
40 Like paintings and some juries
41 As a result
42 Fruity cooler
43 Animal pouch
46 Plane takeoff guess: Abbr.
47 Chicken ___ king
50 Norman Rockwell painting subject of W.W. II
54 Fix permanently, as an interest rate
55 Helmet from W.W. I or W.W. II
56 "Beauty ___ the eye . . ."
58 Semiconductor giant
60 Idiot
61 Tenth: Prefix
62 Hospital attendant
63 Kuwaiti leader
64 Business V.I.P.
65 Velocity
66 Say "No, I didn't"

DOWN

1 High-priority item
2 Katie Couric, for one
3 Like the night sky
4 Seoul's home
5 Top-secret
6 Italian article
7 Answer that's between yes and no
8 Coming immediately after, as on TV
9 Leaves in a huff, with "out"
10 Prefix with -centric
11 Something for nothing, as what a hitchhiker seeks
12 OPEC product
13 Fishing pole
21 March 17 honoree, for short
23 ___ de France
25 Sword of sport
26 Fancy pitcher
27 Politico ___ Paul
32 Beer blast centerpiece
33 Measure of a car's 65-Across: Abbr.
34 Lincoln, informally
35 Cousin of karate
36 Minimum pizza order
37 Lusty look
38 Like the Beatles' White Album
39 The year 1406
40 Part of a guffaw
43 1/60 of a min.
44 Diet doctor
45 "Don't let it get you down!"
47 Comfortable (with)
48 Go right at it, as work
49 Vein's counterpart
51 Kind of column, in architecture
52 ___ nous (between us)
53 Kaput
56 Suffix with chlor-
57 It sells in advertising, they say
59 180° from WNW

by Joe Krozel

116

ACROSS

1 They put the frosting on the cake
6 Grant's is in New York
10 ___ as a post
14 Pacific archipelago nation
15 "Young Frankenstein" role
16 Golden State sch.
17 Fix the hair just so, say
18 Bind with a band
19 Actress Singer of "Footloose"
20 ___ as an arrow
22 Jug capacity
24 ___ as a pin
25 ___ as a fox
26 ___ as an ox
29 Outlaw Barrow
30 "Bingo!"
31 Newton's Black Panther Party co-founder
33 Barbecue remnants
37 ___ as an owl
39 Command to a dog
41 ___ as a dog
42 Some chips, maybe
44 Less loony
46 4 on a telephone
47 Bottom dog
49 Some chips
51 Theme of this puzzle
54 Eric who played 2003's Hulk
55 Like, with "with"
56 ___ as an eel
60 Chowderheads
61 Sparkling wine locale
63 Indoor trees may grow in them
64 Words after "woe"
65 One end of a hammer
66 ___ as a judge
67 ___ as a doornail
68 ___ as a diamond
69 The way things are going

DOWN

1 AOL and others
2 Auto denter in a supermarket parking lot
3 Leader in a robe
4 Italian cheese
5 Latin for 37-Across
6 ___ as a drum
7 Doing the job
8 Apartment bldg. V.I.P.
9 The Joker in Batman movies, e.g.
10 Tedium
11 Gastroenteritis cause, maybe
12 Baseball All-Star every year from 1955 to 1975
13 Impulsive indulgence
21 Light green plums
23 Lawrence Welk's "one"/"two" connector
25 ___ as a whistle
26 Fellers in the woods?
27 ___ as a rail
28 Literally, "scraped"
29 ___ as a bell
32 Cathedral recesses
34 ___ as a kite
35 Repetitive reply
36 Nordic runners
38 Overshadowed
40 Alaskan peninsula where Seward is located
43 Nut for caffeine?
45 Told to in order to get an opinion
48 Angelic figure
50 Prisoner's opposite
51 ___ as a rock
52 Busy
53 Volcanic buildup
54 ___ as a bat
56 Suffix with pun
57 Kathryn of "Law & Order: Criminal Intent"
58 It means nothing to Sarkozy
59 Area within a picket fence, say
62 Pirate's realm

by Matt Ginsberg

ACROSS

1 *Start of a 38-Across
5 "The Good Earth" heroine
9 So last year
14 ___ about
15 *Small part of a spork
16 Recyclable item
17 Prayer wheel user
18 *Musical quality
19 Strike down
20 Cockpit announcements, briefly
21 Millstone
22 *Made tracks
23 Strength
25 Cord unit
27 Good name for an investment adviser?
29 Permanently attached, in zoology
32 Early MP3-sharing Web site
35 *Teed off
37 Up-to-date
38 Hint to the word ladder in the answers to the starred clues
43 ". . . and that's final!"
44 *Put into piles
45 Canal site, maybe
47 Showing irritation
52 Last in a series
53 Toxic pollutant, for short
55 Sweet, in Italy
56 *Locale in a western
59 Many Christmas ornaments
62 Holly
63 Crossword maker or editor, at times
64 *It may precede a stroke
65 Rat Pack nickname
66 Dirección sailed by Columbus
67 *Ax

68 Change components, often
69 Dag Hammarskjöld, for one
70 Some cameras, for short
71 *End of a 38-Across

DOWN

1 At minimum
2 How baseball games rarely end
3 Kind of land
4 Undoes
5 Camp Swampy dog
6 Symbol of courage
7 Undo
8 "Kinsey" star, 2004
9 Orkin victim
10 Survivalist's stockpile
11 Full of energy
12 "The Way of Perfection" writer
13 Word after red or dead
24 Solomon's asset
26 In profusion
28 Pseudo-cultured
30 Stockpile
31 Muff one
33 Like some men's hair
34 Nasdaq buy: Abbr.
36 Wynn and Harris
38 Quick drive
39 Tried out at an Air Force base
40 Theater for niche audiences
41 Medical research org.
42 Doo-___
46 Shows scorn
48 Lacking
49 "Fighting" athletes
50 Part of an act, perhaps
51 Simple sugar
54 Range setting
57 On Soc. Sec., say
58 Trap, in a way
60 Winter exclamation
61 Goes with
63 Orgs. with "Inc." in their names

by Barry C. Silk

ACROSS

1 In ___ land (daydreaming)
5 Boeing products
9 Path around the earth
14 Greek vowels
15 Elvis Presley's middle name
16 Battery brand
17 Succumbing to second thoughts
20 Beatnik's "Got it!"
21 "Salut!," in Scandinavia
22 Concorde, in brief
23 Performed prior to the main act
25 What it takes to tango
26 "That's all ___ wrote"
27 Neither's partner
28 Billiard sticks
31 One still in the game, in poker
33 Submit, as homework
35 Low digits
36 Succumbing to second thoughts
40 Mare's newborn
41 Colbert ___ (Comedy Central show audience)
42 Blunders
45 978-0060935443, for Roget's Thesaurus
46 U.K. record label
49 Genetic material
50 Hunky-dory
52 Sailor
54 ___ and downs
55 How Santa dresses, mostly
58 Anatomical passages
59 Succumbing to second thoughts
62 Start of the Spanish calendar
63 Biblical captain for 40 days and 40 nights
64 Golden ___ (senior citizen)

65 Two-door or four-door car
66 Friend in war
67 Unfreeze

DOWN

1 Veterans' group, informally
2 Returning to the previous speed, in music
3 Agitated state
4 Actor/brother Sean or Mackenzie
5 Dutch painter Steen
6 Energy units
7 Tick-___
8 High-hatter
9 Fewer than 100 shares
10 Fight adjudicator, for short
11 "Gesundheit!"

12 Arctic covering
13 Walks unsteadily
18 Drug used to treat poisoning
19 Statutes
24 Easy two-pointer in basketball
29 Genesis garden
30 Mount ___, where the Commandments were given to Moses
32 Loads
33 Largest city on the island of Hawaii
34 Tiny criticisms
36 Dixie bread
37 Pestered
38 Writing points
39 Entered
40 Old schoolmasters' sticks
43 Ruin, as one's parade
44 Any one of the Top 40

46 Come out
47 ___ Comics, home of Spider-Man and the Fantastic Four
48 Add with a caret, e.g.
51 Swedish coin
53 Starting group of athletes
56 Certain alkene
57 Order to the person holding the deck of cards
60 Author Levin
61 Not camera-ready?

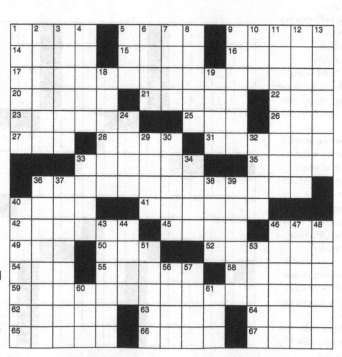

by Mark Milhet

ACROSS

1 Cheney's successor as vice president
6 Prize in the ad biz
10 ___ irregular basis
14 Hersey's "A Bell for ___"
15 Prefix with nautical
16 Count (on)
17 Decide against reorganizing the pet store?
20 Mediterranean tree
21 Geog. or geol.
22 Stagehands' items
23 Picked out of a lineup
25 Ankle-related
28 Announcement from a cockpit, for short
30 Doughnut-shaped
32 Very chocolaty, say
33 Finish shooting a movie
34 Bathroom fixture
36 Break in the day
37 Cousin of beige
38 Conversation-filled places in a restaurant?
42 Oscar winner Winslet
43 ___ Aviv, Israel
44 Evil computer in "2001"
45 Mother of Horus
46 Sign of the future
48 Come up again and again
52 Computer connection choice
53 Massless particle
55 A MS. might come back in it
56 Make a connection with
58 "Au Revoir, ___ Enfants"
60 Pre-___ (undergrad study)
61 What chicks have?
65 "Deutschland ___ Alles"
66 "Windows to the soul"
67 Amazingly coincidental
68 Zero
69 Certain conifers
70 "The Devil Wears ___"

DOWN

1 Mismatch
2 Musical whose opening song is "All the Dearly Beloved"
3 What a flashing red light may indicate
4 Suffix with differ
5 Jules et Jim, par exemple
6 Expensive eggs
7 Washington and ___ University
8 Certain savings plan, for short
9 Sound from a 38-Down
10 Very small pasta
11 Pacific Northwest tribe
12 Baseball V.I.P.'s
13 Comedian Louis
18 When Canada celebrates Thanksgiving: Abbr.
19 Web address
24 Airheads
26 Hair curl
27 Nonsense singing
29 Clerk on "The Simpsons"
31 Since, slangily
33 "Citizen Kane" director
35 Nestlé candy
38 Low-pitched instrument
39 Availed oneself of
40 Whom Marlin sought in a 2003 film
41 Tavern
42 Young goat
47 Amazingly enough
49 Cell phone feature, often
50 Computer handle
51 Sudan/Saudi Arabia separator
53 Sch. group
54 Largest U.S. labor union: Abbr.
57 Old Testament book
59 Dance lesson
61 Enjoyment
62 Hide the gray, say
63 Many's opposite
64 "How Stella Got ___ Groove Back"

by Trip Payne

120

ACROSS
1 No. crunchers
5 Haute cuisine it's not
9 Places for links
14 Rope material
15 Audiophile's concern
16 Of service
17 307 for Wyoming and 907 for Alaska
19 El Líder of Argentina
20 Not paying immediately at the bar
22 100 or so, e.g.: Abbr.
23 Use a prie-dieu
24 Adoptee in Genesis
26 2002 Adam Sandler title role
29 Building beams
30 Through the uprights
31 Hams it up
34 "Whew!"
35 Google search need . . . or a hint to the ends of 20- and 49-Across and 11- and 28-Down
38 Satisfied sound
39 Like drinks with umbrellas
41 Fraternal letters
42 Sax type
43 "A diamond is forever" sloganeer
46 Lower oneself
47 Deduces, with "out"
48 Pewter component
49 Go ballistic
54 "Socrate" composer Erik
56 1978 Cheech & Chong movie
57 "It's the end of ___"
58 "Holy ___!"
59 Line of rotation
60 Less typical
61 Morel morsel
62 Duma dissent

DOWN
1 Burn on the grill
2 Machu Picchu's land
3 "You said it!"
4 Punished with a wooden spoon, say
5 Like Cheech & Chong, typically
6 41-Across meeting places
7 Center Shaq
8 Annoying type
9 China's place
10 Beehive State native
11 Apartment building feature
12 Dental hygienist's advice
13 In the mail
18 Cannes film
21 ___ Alert (abduction bulletin)
25 Majorca Mrs.
26 Those in charge: Abbr.
27 Crowd sound
28 Road sign warning
29 1961 Literature Nobelist Andric
31 Harry Potter's pet Hedwig, e.g.
32 Hammer-wielding god
33 "___ All That" (Freddie Prinze Jr. film)
35 Cordelia's father
36 Low-budget prefix
37 Yevtushenko's "Babi ___"
40 Louvre pyramid architect
41 Reception toast giver
43 Easily managed
44 Penn, to Pennsylvania
45 Uncle ___ rice
46 Paul Anka #1 hit
47 Greyhound stop
48 Autocrat until 1917
50 Bottom lines
51 Classic Manhattan theater
52 Dust Bowl migrant
53 For fear that
55 Ill temper

by Michael Callaway Barnhart

ACROSS

1 Africa's ___ Victoria
5 Rope material
9 Letter after beta
14 ___ of March
15 Theater award
16 Bird-related
17 1971 Tom Jones hit
19 Appealingly piquant
20 Photocopier cartridge contents
21 Weeper of Greek myth
23 Perfumery emanations
25 Hot sauce brand
30 1972 Carly Simon hit
33 Items on which baseball insignia appear
37 Opposite of post-
38 Seasons or deices
39 Have ___ (be connected)
40 Bergen dummy Mortimer
43 Words of understanding
44 Windshield flip-down
46 Geese formation shape
47 Finishing 11th out of 11, e.g.
48 1966 Monkees hit
52 Photographers, informally
53 Parish leader
58 ___ chip, which might be topped with 19-Across 27-Down dip
61 Still kicking
62 ___ the Hutt of "Star Wars"
66 1962 Crystals hit
68 Martian or Venusian
69 ___ May Clampett of "The Beverly Hillbillies"
70 Suffix with concession
71 Poet Stephen Vincent ___
72 Gin flavoring
73 London art gallery

DOWN

1 Rosters
2 Kind of committee
3 New Hampshire college town
4 Krupp Works city
5 Christmas or Thanksgiving: Abbr.
6 Abba of Israel
7 Longish skirt
8 Mescaline-yielding cactus
9 Garden pavilions
10 N.Y.C.'s Park or Lex
11 Prefix with place or print
12 Yoga class surface
13 "___ takers?"
18 Pseudo-stylish
22 English majors' degs.
24 Absorbs, with "up"
26 Be of use
27 Tex-Mex preparation
28 Uses as a reference
29 Beginning stage
31 Makeshift vote receptacle
32 Superman portrayer Christopher
33 Be nitpicky
34 Japanese cartoon art
35 Native of the Leaning Tower city
36 Nose-in-the-air sorts
41 Minister's nickname
42 Animal that may be caught in the headlights
45 Carpet leftover
49 Meadow
50 Rainfall units
51 Derrière
54 Golf shoe gripper
55 Fibula's neighbor
56 Plain to see
57 C.S.A. general
59 Satan's domain
60 Norway's capital
62 Sharp left or right, in the ring
63 Ginger ___
64 Bargain basement container
65 Quilting party
67 Sailor's assent

by Fred Piscop

122

ACROSS
1 Get some sun
4 Blow one's stack
9 Kid-lit pachyderm
14 Naked ___ jaybird
15 Sine, cosine or tangent
16 Tourist mecca off the coast of Venezuela
17 "Beat swords into plowshares"
20 Way off
21 Parasol's offering
22 Cathedral area
23 Grazed, say
25 Silver of the silver screen
27 "Ignore the red, white and blue"
35 Marx Brothers-like
36 Meat favored by Sarah Palin
37 With 44-Across, a traditional Catholic prayer
39 Ring decisions, for short
40 Chuck who sang "Maybellene"
41 Petty quarrel
42 Moray, for one
43 "Peachy keen!"
44 See 37-Across
45 "Oust from practice, then interrogate"
48 Take steps
49 The "A" in MoMA
50 Shi'ite leader
53 Typical John Wayne film
57 Stir up
61 "Scatter while fleeing"
64 Neptune's realm
65 Word before city or tube
66 Etiquette guru Vanderbilt
67 Smallest possible
68 Has to have
69 Masseur's place

DOWN
1 Bit of verbal trumpeting
2 "A likely story"
3 Shuttle org.
4 Pull a boner
5 Any of several Egyptian kings
6 Six-sided state
7 ___ colada
8 Rocker Rundgren
9 Ovine sound
10 Giorgio of fashion
11 Fist ___ (modern greeting)
12 Lincoln and others
13 Like proverbial hen's teeth
18 A Musketeer
19 Rejection of church dogma
24 Behavioral quirk
26 Rich rock
27 Palm fruit
28 Put one's John Hancock on
29 Vodka brand, informally
30 Makeup mishap
31 Main artery
32 Mental midget
33 Blue Grotto's isle
34 To no ___
38 List-ending abbr.
40 Bang, as a drum
41 "No Exit" dramatist
43 "30 Rock" network
44 Dugout V.I.P.: Abbr.
46 Rio dances
47 Moved like a hummingbird
50 Miley Cyrus, to teens
51 Owls' prey
52 Where pirates go
54 Score after deuce
55 Mute, with "down"
56 Feminine suffix
58 Portfolio holdings, briefly
59 Sugar unit
60 One-named New Age singer
62 Tiny colonist
63 Four-baggers: Abbr.

by Wayne and P. K. King

ACROSS

1 Windy City team
5 "Me, me, me" sort
9 Like a teddy bear
14 Summer Games org.
15 Radiate
16 Steinbeck migrants
17 Certain mortgage, briefly
18 All over
19 Successfully defend
20 Spicy bar fare
23 Turns, in a way
24 It may have orchids or plumerias
25 Ceremonial utterance
28 Yellow
32 Author Ferber
36 Kiltie's turndown
37 Wipe out
38 Cape Cod town
40 Baseball bigwigs, for short
42 Largish combo
43 Lacking melanin
45 Where It.'s at
47 "Dear" ones
48 Game to 11 points
51 Milk source
52 Crew leader
53 Place for pampering
58 Easy preparation instruction . . . or a hint to the starts of 20-, 28- and 48-Across
61 Big cheese
64 Form of silica
65 Group of thousands, maybe
66 Muscat native
67 Comstock's find
68 Scoreboard tally
69 One, for one
70 Sail support
71 2004 Brad Pitt film

DOWN

1 Cuts back
2 Finish off
3 Super, in showbiz
4 "Futurama" genre
5 Buys and sells
6 "___ expert, but . . ."
7 Op-ed's offering
8 Freely
9 Pardoned
10 Luau strings
11 Mail aid
12 Zuider ___
13 Fashion monogram
21 Tide competitor
22 Frau's "forget it"
25 Certain Oriental rug maker
26 Ward off
27 "Golden Boy" playwright
29 Internet annoyance
30 Red Sea land
31 They may clash
32 Les ___-Unis
33 1964 Tony Randall title role
34 Having a rough knotted surface
35 Seed covering
39 18 inches, give or take
41 Radiation source
44 Siouan speakers
46 "Batman" villain, with "the"
49 Sings the praises of
50 Go back and forth in the woods?
54 America's Cup entrant
55 Flight part
56 Green topping
57 Too-too
58 Mitchell who wrote and sang "Chelsea Morning"
59 Per unit
60 Jean Arp's movement
61 Signal at Christie's
62 "___ losing it?"
63 Avocation, slangily

by Nancy Kavanaugh

124

ACROSS

1. "___ or charge?"
5. Winger or Messing
10. Suffix with song or slug
14. Rights org.
15. Go inside
16. Parisian girlfriend
17. Graham cracker pie shell
19. Binges
20. Poster paints
21. President who followed Harry
23. AOL or MSN: Abbr.
24. 18-wheeler
25. Exhausted
26. Spider or worm
31. Delights in
34. Molecule part
35. Tint
36. Bog material
37. Freezer cubes
38. Spreadsheet contents
39. Bond creator Fleming
40. Lois of the Daily Planet
42. Pan-fries
44. Lending crisis
47. ___ I.R.A. (savings plan for old age)
48. Tippler
49. Engineering sch. in Troy, N.Y.
52. Fruit for a monkey
55. Common burger topper
57. All in a twitter
58. Cajun seafood dish
60. Make over
61. Friend of Fran and Ollie
62. At the peak of
63. Garden of ___
64. Exorbitant
65. "Hey, you!"

DOWN

1. Prickly plants
2. Real estate units
3. Batter's dry spell
4. Camel feature
5. Criticizes openly
6. Infuriate
7. A/C measures
8. Hi-___ monitor
9. Style of the 1920s and '30s
10. Tex-Mex treat
11. Online 'zine
12. Sound of relief
13. Try out
18. Fruit on a bush
22. Toasty
25. Computer memory measure
26. Foldaway bed
27. Harness racer
28. One of the five W's
29. Minstrel's instrument
30. Votes opposite the nays
31. The "Odyssey" or "Beowulf"
32. Close by
33. Tarzan's love
37. Ruler division
38. "Well, that's obvious!"
40. Cowardly resident of Oz
41. Blitzes
42. Year-round Alp topper
43. Cast member
45. Fire-breathing beast
46. Functional
49. Mob scenes
50. Collared pullovers
51. Bumbling
52. Like Mother Hubbard's cupboard
53. Ripened
54. Bump on a branch
55. Autumn tool
56. Twice-a-month tide
59. Dirt road feature

by Billie Truitt

ACROSS

1 Industry honcho
5 "Do the ___!"
9 Suffix with beer or fun
13 Move, in Realtor lingo
14 XM ___
15 In the old days
16 Lunchbox dessert item
17 Jump for joy
18 "The Good Earth" heroine
19 Tom Collins or Rob Roy
21 Turkic people
23 Grass bought in rolls
24 End of an exhaust system
26 Beehive State athlete
29 Guitar pioneer Paul
31 Paddler's target
32 Unrealistic idea
35 Hold back, as a news story
39 Salon sound
40 In a foxy fashion
42 "Uh-uh"
43 Regatta entry
45 1992 U.S. Olympic hoopsters, with "the"
47 Peseta's replacement
49 La-la lead-in
50 ___-mo
51 Basketball or baseball
55 Ike's monogram
57 Tangle in a net: Var.
58 Fighting rooster
63 Hair removal brand
64 Take forcibly, old-style
66 Tom Wolfe novel "___ in Full"
67 Bigger than mega-
68 Elizabeth of cosmetics
69 After-beach wear
70 Supersecure airline
71 Name on toy fuel trucks
72 Two caplets, say

DOWN

1 Swamp menace, for short
2 Total loser
3 Guinness or Waugh
4 Corner pieces, in chess
5 Ankle-length dress
6 X-rated
7 Up to, in ads
8 Real babe
9 Evidence washed away by the tide
10 China's Zhou ___
11 Bluff formed by a fault
12 In need of a rubdown
14 Blogger's audience
20 Ratted (on)
22 "Sad to say . . ."
25 Decorative band
26 "___-daisy!"
27 Fey of "30 Rock"
28 Huge in scope
30 Only now and then
33 Short-lived
34 Firth of Clyde town
36 The "ten" in "hang ten"
37 Stone for many Libras
38 Nautilus skipper
41 Landscaper's crew
44 Harbor workhorses
46 Showed up in time for
48 Gung-ho
51 Trace of color
52 Messages that may contain emoticons
53 Old computer
54 "Zounds!"
56 Paperless birthday greeting
59 Birds, collectively
60 1847 Melville work
61 Some urban rides
62 "Trick" body part
65 Before, to a bard

by Damon J. Gulczynski

126

ACROSS

1 Actor Assante
7 Imprison
12 Mil. rank
15 Oregonian
16 Frost lines
17 Netscape acquirer
18 Entrance requirement, maybe
20 Meter-candle
21 Barack Obama, 2005–08, e.g.
23 Part of Santa's bagful
24 ___ Enterprise
25 1950s White House resident
27 Rookie's superstition
32 Skier's wish
34 Archaeological find
35 "Just kidding!"
36 Texas city . . . and a hint to the starts of 21-, 27-, 45- and 56-Across
42 ___-wop
43 Bum ___
44 To be, to Brutus
45 Subsidiary member of a firm
51 Blockage remover
52 Actress ___ Ling of "The Crow"
53 Fool
56 Some restaurant and pharmacy lures
62 Feel awful
63 French Academy's 40 members
64 Classic British two-seaters
65 Vapid
66 Ogle
67 Like Dvořák's "Serenade for Strings"
68 Philosopher Kierkegaard
69 Gauge

DOWN

1 Toward the stern
2 Not an original
3 "Ahoy, ___!"
4 Company with the stock symbol CAR
5 Belg. neighbor
6 Solicit, as business
7 Still
8 Subway Series participant
9 "Desperate Housewives" role
10 Part of PTA: Abbr.
11 Bring back to domestication
12 Gold-colored horses
13 Multipurpose, somehow
14 160, to Caesar
19 Place for a gauge, informally
22 Persian for "crown"
26 Bus. card info
27 Tijuana tanner
28 Pooh pal
29 High school dept.
30 Little bit
31 Messenger ___
32 Half-salute
33 Only you
37 Make a clanger
38 Clothing retailer since 1969
39 Air monitor, for short
40 Shirt to wear with shorts
41 Mideast land: Abbr.
42 CD players
46 Days ___
47 Ear inflammation
48 Ones who drive people home?
49 Australian island: Abbr.
50 San ___, Christmas figure in Italy
53 Entrap
54 World record?
55 Attention getters
57 [Gasp!]
58 Tail end
59 Sup
60 Tram loads
61 Shoshone speakers
62 Ennemi's opposite

by Ashish Vengsarkar

ACROSS

1 Home (in on)
5 Arrow shooters
9 Hunk
13 Lumberjacks' tools
14 Margarine
15 Uneaten part of an apple
16 Small milk carton capacity
17 Ken of "thirtysomething"
18 Eager
19 1989 Sally Field/ Dolly Parton/Shirley MacLaine movie
22 Hold up
23 Hunk
24 Foresail
27 "Here's to you!" and others
29 Old Pontiac
32 Electrical device for foreign travelers
34 "Git!"
35 2000 Martin Lawrence movie
39 Swamps
40 Cork
41 Novelist Tan
42 Seeks blindly
45 ___ Lanka
46 With 51-Down, John Ashcroft's predecessor as attorney general
48 Legal matter
50 1992 Alec Baldwin/ Meg Ryan film
56 Not imaginary
57 Jai ___
58 "To Live and Die ___"
59 The "A" in A.D.
60 Lunkhead
61 Santa's landing place
62 Part of M.V.P.
63 Pitch
64 Thing hidden in each of the movie names in this puzzle

DOWN

1 Microwaves
2 Stage direction after an actor's last line
3 Philosopher Descartes
4 Blender maker
5 Classic John Lee Hooker song of 1962
6 Earthenware pot
7 Puts on a scale
8 One of Shakespeare's begins "Shall I compare thee to a summer's day?"
9 Milan's La ___
10 Some trophies
11 Diva's number
12 They have headboards and footboards
20 Game with a $100 million prize, maybe
21 Meditation syllables
24 "Star Wars" villain ___ the Hutt
25 "Knock it off" or "get it on," e.g.
26 Hip-hop wear
28 One of an octopus's octet
30 Police stunner
31 Onetime "S.N.L." player Cheri
33 Evenings, briefly
34 Soak (up)
36 Egyptian cobra
37 Shots taken by some athletes
38 Old Testament prophet
42 Bearded beast
43 Edit
44 Verdi hero married to Desdemona
47 Apportion
49 Mini or tutu
50 Nanny's vehicle
51 See 46-Across
52 New Mexico resort
53 "Are you ___ out?"
54 Gin flavoring
55 Not out

by Peter A. Collins

128

ACROSS

1 With 67-Across, an appropriate title for this puzzle?
5 Second of two sections
10 Beaver's project
13 Competed in a regatta
15 Formal answer to "Who's at the door?"
16 Vein contents
17 Where to learn a vocation
19 Earl Grey, for one
20 Set as a price
21 Ornery sort
22 Fictional salesman Willy
24 "Remington ___" of 1980s TV
26 "Who's the Boss?" co-star
28 Basis for a moneyless economy
33 When repeated, exuberant student's cry
36 Put pen to paper
37 Vitamin bottle info, for short
38 Go across
39 Artemis' Roman counterpart
40 "Veni, ___, vici"
41 Intraoffice PC hookup
42 Stately home
43 When some morning news programs begin
44 Two dollars per pound, say
47 Radiohead singer Thom
48 Yanni's music genre
52 Got a C, say
54 Drink with sushi
56 Drink with Christmas cookies
57 Palme ___ (Cannes prize)
58 "On/off" surrounder
62 Completely impress
63 Torpedo launcher
64 Emma of "Dynasty"
65 Go off course
66 Guilty feelings, e.g.
67 See 1-Across

DOWN

1 Spanish counterparts of mlles.
2 Beat in a match
3 Open-eyed
4 ___ Xing
5 Snaps
6 Sports players: Abbr.
7 Carnaval city
8 General on a Chinese menu
9 TV's Science Guy
10 Early printer type
11 Realm
12 Intend
14 Remove the nails from, as a cat
18 Plaintiff
23 Parts of lbs.
25 Black, in verse
26 One who goes on and on
27 Nick and Nora's pooch
29 Sudden, sharp pain
30 Render blank, as a floppy disk
31 Old Norse work
32 Incapacitate
33 Tropical vacation spot
34 Title planet in a 2001 Kevin Spacey movie
35 Character who first appeared in "The Secret of the Old Clock"
39 Like dungeons, typically
40 Feature of a house in the hills
42 Annotates, as a manuscript
43 Soaks in hot water, as 19-Across
45 "Yoo-___!"
46 Egyptian cross
49 "What's in ___?"
50 "Dunno"
51 Discharge
52 "It's now or never" time
53 Home of the Hawkeyes of the Big Ten
54 How some people go to a party
55 Romans preceder
59 Org. for heavyweights
60 Chloride, for one
61 On the ___ (fleeing)

by Mike Nothnagel

ACROSS

1. One-two part
4. Cattle-herding breed
9. Playground retort
14. Draft pick?
15. Keats title starter
16. Stands at wakes
17. Diam. × π
18. Get on
19. Daisy type
20. Words of encouragement to a Brit?
23. Up to
24. Abu Dhabi's fed.
25. Little jerks
28. "Hey, over here!"
29. Group of dancing Brits?
32. One way to think
34. Dark horse's win
35. Eggs Benedict need
38. With 30-Down, kind of clause
39. Aramis, to Athos
41. Causes for stadium cheers, for short
42. Extract with a solvent
44. Give off
46. British smart alecks?
49. Favor one side, perhaps
53. Dresden denial
54. Sail through
55. Wedding memento
56. Sleep like a Brit?
60. When doubled, a wolf's call
62. Turbine part
63. Sacha Baron Cohen character ___ G
64. On ___ (hot)
65. Money in la banque
66. Net judge's call
67. iPhone display unit
68. Piece in the game of go
69. Method: Abbr.

DOWN

1. Hike, as a price
2. Vulcans and Romulans
3. Left Bank toppers
4. Computer language in Y2K news
5. Take too much of, briefly
6. True-to-life
7. Bout
8. Clad like some Halloween paraders
9. Bernstein/Sondheim's "___ Like That"
10. Have a tussle
11. Hardest to see, perhaps
12. Direct conclusion?
13. Sugar suffix
21. Hummus holder
22. "The Crying Game" Oscar nominee
26. Like some actors going on stage
27. Things some designers design
29. Friday, notably
30. See 38-Across
31. British pound, informally
33. Leopold's partner in a sensational 1924 trial
35. Rough-___ (unfinished)
36. Get caught in ___
37. It may have a spinning ballerina
39. Pink-slip
40. Lambda followers
43. Like a solid argument
44. Just manages
45. Monarch crowned in 1558: Abbr.
47. Geneva's ___ Léman
48. Earth tones
50. Worthy principles
51. This-and-that concert performance
52. Puts forth
55. Chapter's partner
57. Seven-foot, say
58. Other, in Oaxaca
59. Provide with a rear view?
60. Chance, poetically
61. Ocean State sch.

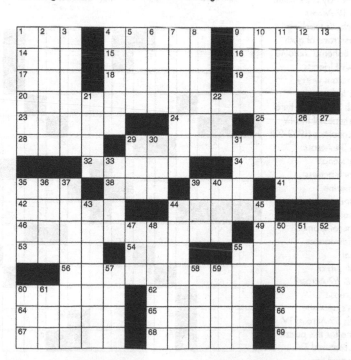

by Corey Rubin

ACROSS

1 With 66-Across, first in a series of five TV personalities (1954–57)
6 With 65-Across, second in a series of five TV personalities (1957–62)
10 "Think" sloganeer
13 Dropped flies and bad throws, in baseball
15 Sheltered from the wind
16 Teachers' org.
17 Fifth in a series of five TV personalities (2009–2010)
19 With 22-Across, fourth in a series of five TV personalities (1992–2009)
20 Football six-pointers, for short
21 Since way back when
22 See 19-Across
23 Teacher's teaching
24 Norse race of gods
25 "La Bohème" heroine
28 Closest friends
30 Free from worry
33 Two halved
34 With 35-Across, third in a series of five TV personalities (1962–92)
35 See 34-Across
40 Scot's cap
42 French actress Catherine
43 Despise
48 Minor hang-up
49 Unaccompanied performances
50 Taunt
53 Desk job at 58 & 59-Across?
54 Decrease
55 Con's opposite
58 With 59-Across, TV home for this puzzle's five featured TV personalities
59 See 58-Across

61 Suffix with ball
62 Opening stake
63 Prompt
64 Telephone book info: Abbr.
65 See 6-Across
66 See 1-Across

DOWN

1 Religious offshoot
2 Trampled
3 Sea eagles
4 U.S. broadcaster overseas
5 Bert's "Sesame Street" pal
6 Tech talk, e.g.
7 Not consistent with, as a way of thinking
8 Middling grades
9 Author Follett
10 How quips are delivered

11 Close-fitting cap
12 City hall leaders
14 Daughters' counterparts
18 Bandleader Count ___
22 Good place to have a cow?
23 Property claim
24 "He doesn't have ___ bone in his body"
25 Not minor: Abbr.
26 "How was ___ know?"
27 Speed limit abbr.
29 Early film director Thomas H. ___
31 "Nay" sayers
32 Shade of blue
36 Observe the Sabbath
37 The Sabbath, to Christians: Abbr.
38 Eggs in a lab
39 Less than zero: Abbr.

41 Purplish tint
42 Clear of defects, as software
43 Actor Kutcher
44 [Sob!]
45 Twins Mary-Kate and Ashley
46 Bon ___ (clever remark)
47 Neater
51 Bounce back, as sound
52 Insurance provider since 1850
54 Jaffe or Barrett
55 Grammy-winning Collins
56 All roads lead to this, they say
57 Wilson of "Zoolander"
59 Strike lightly
60 Letters on a Cardinals cap

by John Farmer

ACROSS

1 Recorder input: Abbr.
4 "Beloved" author Morrison
8 Run through
14 All __ day's work
15 "What __ for Love" ("A Chorus Line" song)
16 Setting for C. S. Lewis's "The Lion, the Witch and the Wardrobe"
17 Mountain shelter
19 Travels like a flying squirrel
20 Parched
21 Time off, to a sailor
23 Optometrist's concern
25 Poet Khayyám
26 Lawman Wyatt
28 Disfigure
29 Sound from a terrier
32 Endangered feline
36 Name before Cool or Camel
37 Office setting?
38 "Holy Toledo!"
39 Spring time: Abbr.
40 Supped
41 "Arabesque" actress, 1966
46 Lad
47 Rainbow component
48 Surmounting
49 Elusive Himalayan creature
50 99 and 86, on "Get Smart"
54 Highway posting
59 Like Hotspur's horse in "King Henry IV, Part I"
60 Where Hudson Bay is
61 Where rupees are spent
63 The Carnegie of Carnegie Mellon University
64 Dorothy __ of "The Wizard of Oz"
65 Apostrophized preposition
66 Abbr. preceding multiple surnames
67 Places for play things?
68 TV staple for over 30 years (and a hint to 17-, 21-, 32-, 41-, 54- and 61-Across)

DOWN

1 "Divine" showbiz nickname
2 One way to sing
3 Egypt's capital
4 Spanish uncle
5 "Most likely . . ."
6 Near
7 Prefix with logical
8 Former heavyweight champion Johansson
9 Duck type
10 Snoop
11 Shave __ haircut
12 Schreiber of the "Scream" films
13 Leisure
18 Cartoon skunk Pepé __
22 Birthplace of Elie Wiesel
24 Suffix with different
27 Italian archaeological locale
29 Cracked open
30 Lariat
31 Bit of green in a floral display
32 Try
33 Alliance since '49
34 Do as told
35 Cry of disbelief
41 Cat or dog, especially in the spring
42 Jesse James and gang
43 Cocked
44 What an andiron holds
45 Wagner composition
49 Sentence units
51 They're verboten
52 Spoken for
53 Complicated situation
54 Hustle
55 Glazier's sheet
56 Extremities
57 In-box fill: Abbr.
58 "Dies __" (hymn)
62 "__ Liaisons Dangereuses"

by Patrick Blindauer

132

ACROSS
1 Like some fevers
9 Title role for Ben Kingsley
15 Tiny, as a town
16 It's north of the Strait of Gibraltar
17 Some long flights
18 Teeming, as with bees
19 Fabric amts.
20 Letter sign-off
22 Diminutive endings
23 Restaurateur Toots
25 Stewart and Lovitz
27 Florida theme park
29 X-rated stuff
30 Garment line
33 "___ Gold" (Fonda film)
34 Banned apple spray
35 Actress Rogers
36 What this puzzle's perimeter contains abbreviations for
39 "Must've been something ___"
40 Visa alternative, for short
41 Early Mexican
42 Chemical in Drano
43 Make a snarling sound
44 In pursuit of
45 Hockey's Jaromir ___
46 Eau, across the Pyrenees
47 Dealer's wear
50 Wile E. Coyote's supplier
52 It's measured in minutes
55 Class clown's doings
57 Winter warmer
60 Farsi speakers
61 Summer cooler
62 Drink of the gods
63 Retired Mach I breaker

DOWN
1 When repeated, a Billy Idol hit
2 Give ___ to (approve)
3 Monocle part
4 Sounds from a hot tub
5 Hogwash
6 2004 Will Smith film
7 "___ your instructions . . ."
8 More, in a saying
9 1970s–'80s supermodel Carangi
10 Playing hooky
11 Colorful salamanders
12 "Curses!"
13 Bring on board
14 Pet food brand
21 Discount apparel chain
23 Part of a shoot
24 Parasite's home
26 Sharer's pronoun
27 Former QB John
28 Former QB Rodney
29 More artful
30 Blackjack player's request
31 Mideast bigwig: Var.
32 Like items in a junk drawer: Abbr.
33 Gas, e.g.: Abbr.
34 Eritrea's capital
35 Mediterranean land
37 Yin's counterpart
38 Vegan's protein source
43 Deadhead icon
44 What many fifth graders have reached
45 Like some tax returns
46 BP gas brand
47 Self-absorbed
48 Concerning
49 Opposite of legato, in mus.
51 In vogue
52 Big name in desktop computers
53 Map line
54 Showed up
56 Ukr., once, e.g.
58 New Deal inits.
59 Conquistador's prize

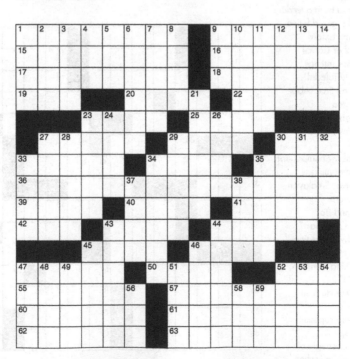

by Samuel A. Donaldson

ACROSS

1 See 1-Down
5 Manages
10 Indolent
14 Wheel turner
15 Cognizant
16 Suffix with buck
17 "Out, damned ___!"
18 Perry Mason's secretary ___ Street
19 "Thumbnail" writings
20 What a broken-down car may get
21 Thick growth of trees
23 Former Ford compacts
25 Simian
26 Burden
27 Bullfighter
32 W.W. II-ending weapon, for short
34 Diamond or sapphire
35 Work ___ sweat
36 Actor Gyllenhaal of "Brokeback Mountain"
37 Four-bagger
38 Despot Idi ___
39 Bauxite or galena
40 Much of afternoon TV
41 Subsided
42 Voice between tenor and bass
44 Dispatched, as a dragon
45 1980s TV's "Emerald Point ___"
46 Old indoor light source
49 It's more than 90 degrees
54 Three on a sundial
55 Actress Loughlin of "Full House"
56 Harsh light
57 Sicilian peak

58 Door to the outside
59 Like certain cereals
60 Explorer Ponce de ___
61 Gold's and others
62 Seize (from)
63 Words of approximation

DOWN

1 With 1-Across, Coke vs. Pepsi competition, e.g.
2 Montreal baseballers, 1969–2004
3 Crockpot
4 Asian holiday
5 West Point students
6 Country singer Buck
7 Buddies
8 Writer ___ Stanley Gardner
9 Mariner

10 ___ tar pits
11 1997 Indy 500 winner ___ Luyendyk
12 Menageries
13 Dennis ___ and the Classics IV (1960s–'70s group)
21 Beat badly
22 German-made car since 1899
24 "This round's ___"
27 Home of Arizona State University
28 Has debts
29 Tray transporter
30 "The Andy Griffith Show" boy
31 Author Ayn
32 Do ___ on (work over)
33 Theda of early films
34 ___ of Arc

37 Lockup
38 Cain's victim
40 Depots: Abbr.
41 Women's magazine founded in France
43 Eskimos
44 Like 33-Down's films
46 Really mean people
47 Mythical king of Crete
48 Instrument for Rachmaninoff
49 Designer Cassini
50 Hardly streamlined, as a car
51 Fit
52 Banned orchard spray
53 ___ Dogg of R&B/hip-hop
57 "Do Ya" group, for short

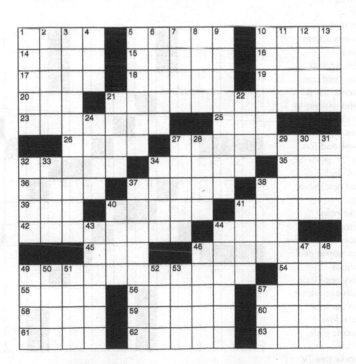

by Randy Sowell

134

ACROSS

1 Breezes through
5 Andrews and Edwards, for two: Abbr.
9 Wall supports
14 Blockhead
15 Zoo barrier
16 One getting one-on-one help
17 *Movie starring a cross-dressing John Travolta
19 Having a lot to lose?
20 In base 8
21 *Big writing assignment
23 Enjoyed Bazooka, e.g.
25 Carillon sounds
26 Lowly worker
28 ". . . ___ thousand times . . ."
29 Step up from dial-up
32 Not at rest
36 Driver's license feature
38 Lab container
39 Word that can precede the starts of the answers to the eight starred clues
42 Lowell and Tan
43 The "A" in WASP
45 Is on deck
47 Most apts. have them
48 Strike caller
51 Wizard's stick
52 Places to serve slop
54 Flea market deal, perhaps
58 *Very easy tasks
62 Unable to retreat, as an animal
63 Fine fiddle
64 *Electric Slide, for one
66 Introductory TV episode
67 Author Bagnold
68 Not e'en once
69 Idyllic places
70 B'way booth in Times Square
71 Temperance supporters

DOWN

1 Like some committees
2 Alternative to first-class
3 Cream of the crop
4 *Nonbinding vote
5 Sound booster at a concert
6 Siege site
7 Called to a lamb, say
8 "Sophie's Choice" author
9 *Like a band-aid solution
10 Instruments in military bands
11 Lone Star State sch.
12 Dis and dis
13 Palm reader, e.g.
18 Winter driving hazard
22 6 on a telephone
24 The Everly Brothers' "All I Have to ___ Dream"
27 Japanese drama
29 Capitol feature
30 River of Hades
31 Not grasping the material, say
32 Lendl of tennis
33 Padre's boy
34 Rack purchases, briefly
35 Yuletide quaff
37 *Heels-over-head feat
40 Column crosser
41 Sign of sorrow
44 *Defeats mentally
46 Golf's Slammin' Sammy
49 Actress Farrow
50 Bit of shotgun shot
52 Determined to achieve
53 Long-bodied lizard
55 One of the Yokums
56 Cagney's TV partner
57 Close watchers
58 New Jersey's ___ May
59 In the thick of
60 Curly cabbage
61 Fit of pique
65 Publishers' hirees: Abbr.

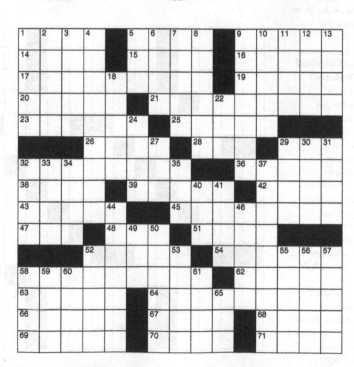

by Steve Dobis

135

ACROSS
1 This and that
6 Locale of famous playing fields
10 Start of the 13th century
14 Top of some forms
15 Whole lot
16 Obsessed mariner
17 Encyclopedia volume
18 Element number 55-Across
20 Bygone compact
21 Go carefully (over)
22 Dryer remains
23 Atlanta Brave who wore the number 55-Across
26 Done in
28 Halloween candy
29 Justification
30 Promising
34 Chemical suffix
35 President number 55-Across
38 It's a wrap
40 Cousin of a camel
41 Turn "this" into "_ .... ," e.g.
44 Earl Grey holder
48 Prefix with -hedron
49 Feb. 7, 2010, the date of this event's number 55-Across
52 Group of courses
53 Times in want ads
54 Cell material
55 See 18-, 23-, 35- and 49-Across
57 Steamy
59 Lake ___, discovery of Louis Jolliet
60 Lord over
61 Senseless
62 Absolutely
63 Melodramatic cry
64 Fireplace tool

DOWN
1 Snub
2 Musical liability
3 Brought to ruin
4 Charge
5 Transmit electronically
6 Calculator message
7 Bullish beginning?
8 A lot
9 Nonacademic degree
10 Capital founded by Spanish invaders, 1571
11 Sight from Taiwan
12 Admonishment
13 ThinkPad developer
19 If not
21 Music section
24 "American Idol" judge DioGuardi
25 Suffix with liquid
27 Santa Fe-to-Colo. Spr. direction
29 Sale sweeteners
31 Euro predecessor
32 Abbr. on a blotter
33 Truck scale unit
35 Study of Louis Pasteur
36 Stellar server
37 Old Dead Sea kingdom
38 Red or black, at a gaming table
39 Bar request
42 Held the floor
43 Tony winner Tyne
45 Apollo astronaut Frank
46 Deck cover
47 Forest clearings
49 1988 Olympics host
50 Palate part
51 Shimon of Israel
55 Ness, for one
56 Term of address in a monastery
57 Any of the Billboard Top 40
58 Game with Skip cards

by Richard Silvestri

136

ACROSS

1 Trap
6 Actress Stapleton of "All in the Family"
10 Way off
14 "The Goose That Laid the Golden Eggs" writer
15 The Bruins of the N.C.A.A.
16 ___ Valley, Calif.
17 "Portnoy's Complaint" author
19 Quick cut
20 Word after Web or camp
21 Geological stretch
22 Hosiery hue
23 Founder of the Christian Broadcasting Network
27 What oil cleanups clean up
30 Make ashamed
31 Silver or platinum
32 Italian and French bread?
34 Escape
37 "Duck soup!"
38 Promoters . . . or a description of 17-, 23-, 46- and 57-Across?
39 It may hold back the sea
40 Flight info
41 Twists out of shape
42 Russian revolutionary with a goatee
43 Old office note taker
45 Bank (on)
46 "Le Déjeuner des Canotiers" painter
50 Billy Crystal or Whoopi Goldberg for the Oscars, often
51 Perjure oneself
52 Currier's partner in lithography

56 "Phooey!"
57 He didn't really cry "The British are coming!"
60 Matured
61 Ferris wheel or bumper cars
62 Three wishes granter
63 Tennis do-overs
64 Poetical tributes
65 Willow for wicker

DOWN

1 Drains
2 Classic soft drink
3 With 41-Down, seemingly
4 Be a wizard or an elf, say, in Dungeons & Dragons
5 Prefix with center
6 One of 12 at a trial
7 Commercial prefix with Lodge

8 Computer key abbr.
9 "I'll pass"
10 Stock, bank deposits, real estate, etc.
11 Where winners are often photographed
12 Friend in a sombrero
13 Mature
18 No ___ Allowed (motel sign)
22 They're worn under blouses
24 The works
25 Reveals
26 Deep black
27 "Peter Pan" pirate
28 Mulching matter
29 "Mum's the word!"
32 Misplay, e.g.
33 Official behind a catcher
35 Related (to)

36 Repair
38 Window section
39 Takes away from, with "of"
41 See 3-Down
42 Luau gift
44 Stock analysts study them
45 Activist
46 Piano part
47 Concern of 38-Across
48 Escape from
49 "Frasier" character
53 Start of Caesar's boast
54 Buffalo's county
55 Clairvoyant
57 Golf lesson provider
58 Relief
59 Kind of trip for the conceited

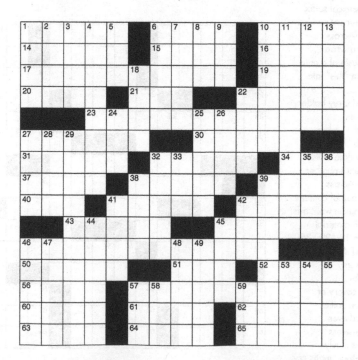

by John Dunn

ACROSS

1 Leave in a hurry
7 Toothed tools
11 Where a truck driver sits
14 Swingline item
15 Field yield
16 Corrida cheer
17 *Impervious to picking, as a lock
19 Telecom giant acquired by Verizon
20 Legal ending
21 Leisure
22 Air apparent?
23 "Liquid diet" devotee
25 *Engraver's surface
28 Piled carelessly
30 Superlative suffix
31 Seized vehicle
32 High-rise apartment garden site
36 *Motto of the U.S. Coast Guard
40 Playful kissing
41 Middle-earth creatures
43 Catherine, the last wife of Henry VIII
45 Nestles
47 *Routine-bound bureaucrat
51 Online communications, for short
52 Notable times
53 Start the kitty
54 Tibetan beast
56 Rocker Ocasek
57 *Countries with big militaries
61 Part of a tuba's sound
62 Vietnam's continent
63 Naturally illuminated
64 Petal plucker's pronoun
65 Remain undecided
66 Compliment heard in the dress department

DOWN

1 Q–U connection
2 Hagen of Broadway
3 Camp clothing identifier
4 Antonyms: Abbr.
5 Lamb's coat
6 Not agin
7 Bit of fabric
8 Got out of bed
9 Affection seeker
10 Tanning lotion letters
11 """"
12 "Little Women" author
13 It's darker than cream
18 Jalapeños and chilies
22 Rained pellets
23 Knight's title
24 Bills in tills
26 Hall's singing partner

27 Type size
29 Men of La Mancha
33 Sch. in Troy, N.Y.
34 Owner of a brand?
35 Debate the pros and cons
37 Sign of a contented cat
38 Improbable
39 Flower holder
42 Deflation sound
43 Persona non grata
44 Geronimo's tribe
46 Recover from a soaking
47 Those "walking" through the answers to the starred clues
48 YouTube button
49 Remove, as a corsage
50 Lieu

55 Barley beards
57 Knucklehead
58 Letter before omega
59 ___ Grande
60 "The ___ Erwin Show" of 1950s TV

by Paula Gamache

138

ACROSS

1 Sub for
6 Jungfrau or Eiger
9 Campaign against Troy, e.g.
14 Word after "thou"
15 Lighter maker
16 Bow, the "It Girl"
17 "Rikki-___-Tavi"
18 Mid 10th-century year
19 Tiny bits
20 Feature of a Las Vegas "bandit"
22 April 1 cigar sound
24 George Harrison's "___ It a Pity"
25 Do a Sherpa's work
27 24-line verse form
29 Toy on a layout
32 Water cannon target
33 Patch up
34 Nutrition label units
36 Branded beast
38 Lard holder
39 Kiltie's instrument
44 Huskies' sch.
46 Thing depicted by this puzzle's circled letters
47 "Night" novelist
51 Jet fuel component
54 Software buyer, usually
56 Kidney-related
57 "That was ___ . . ."
58 Tool at Henley
60 It beats the alternative, in a saying
63 Radio letter after sierra
65 Here-there link
67 Like porridge
68 Like SEALs
69 "That's not fair!"
70 Blast from the past
71 Architectural Digest topic
72 Pay stub abbr.
73 Items in a 46-Across, often

DOWN

1 Concerning
2 Place for a Vandyke
3 "Bye, now"
4 High-pH
5 Add while cooking
6 Multiple-choice choices
7 Life's partner
8 Place for a programming class, perhaps
9 Poli ___
10 Philippine seaport
11 Bothers no end
12 Starbucks size
13 Egg roll time
21 Ruler divs.
23 Old-time schoolteacher
26 "I ___ differ"
28 Daffy Duck trademark
29 One might pass for these, briefly
30 One down in the dumps?
31 Magician's prop
35 Daisy Mae's guy
37 Wishes undone
40 "Meet you then!"
41 Church dignitaries
42 Dark time, to a bard
43 Drop in on
45 '63 Liz Taylor role
47 Licked, e.g.
48 Yoga instructor's direction
49 Like paradise
50 Serenaded
52 Flying Cloud automaker
53 Like the art in some exhibits
55 Told in order to get a quick opinion
59 Cheer (for)
61 Heroic deed
62 Docs who might treat sinusitis
64 Key contraction
66 Axle, e.g.

by Peter A. Collins and Joe Krozel

ACROSS

1 King Kong, e.g.
4 Trailer's connection to a car
9 Highly skilled
14 Where IV's may be administered
15 Japanese automaker
16 Theatrical medley
17 Emphatic south-of-the-border assent
19 Lessen
20 Comet, say, to the impressionable
21 Mocking remark
22 After-dinner candies
23 Central American canal locale
25 In great shape
26 Beginning piano student's exercise
33 Feeds, as pigs
37 Thing to hum or whistle
38 Neural transmitter
39 Vagrant
40 Test answer you have a 50/50 chance of guessing right
41 Nevada gambling mecca
42 Demon's doing
43 Nobelist Wiesel
44 Just sits around
45 Parting words
48 Finish
49 Prickly plant
54 No longer fashionable
57 Killer whale
60 United ___ Emirates
61 A-list
62 Wind that cools a beach
64 Aviator ___ Post
65 Word said upon answering a phone
66 Suffix with rocket or racket
67 Shop
68 Woody or Gracie
69 Banned bug spray

DOWN

1 See 8-Down
2 ___ donna (vain sort)
3 Ruhr Valley city
4 Contains
5 Winter river obstruction
6 Bluefin, for one
7 Wheat or soybeans
8 Loser to a tortoise, in a fable by 1-Down
9 Fragrance named for a Musketeer
10 Quick, cashless way to pay for things
11 "___ Almighty" (2007 movie)
12 Miniature golf shot
13 Gadgets not needed in miniature golf
18 "___ pig's eye!"
24 Roast hosts, for short
25 Costing nothing
27 The Beatles' "Any Time ___"
28 Roberts of "Erin Brockovich"
29 Beginning
30 Rink leap
31 The ___ Ranger
32 Outfielder Slaughter in the Baseball Hall of Fame
33 Kenny Rogers's "___ a Mystery"
34 Zero, in tennis
35 Village Voice award
36 Leisure suit fabric
40 Hatfield/McCoy affair
44 Ill temper
46 Cyclops feature
47 Give power to
50 ___ kwon do
51 Cornered
52 Vegged out
53 Roger with a thumbs-up or thumbs-down
54 Sunday seats
55 Touched down
56 Storage for forage
57 Workplace watchdog org.
58 Irish dance
59 Do some telemarketing
63 "Apollo 13" director Howard

by Fred Piscop

140

ACROSS

1 Place for an oath
6 It's bugled on a base
10 Elevs.
14 Electron tube with two elements
15 Loads
16 Asia's shrunken ___ Sea
17 "Sharp Dressed Man" band
18 1970 Kinks song
19 TV explorer of note
20 Slapstick puppet show
23 Didn't bother
26 Guthrie at Woodstock
27 Baseball's Young and others
28 The Monkees' "___ Believer"
29 Kind of tide
31 Impress permanently
33 "I'm ready for anything!"
37 Centers of circles
40 Room at the top of stairs
41 Mideast fed.
42 Tacitus or Tiberius
43 Not a mainstream religion
44 Go get some shuteye
46 Prefix with pad
48 Mermaid's realm
49 Mail carrier's assignment: Abbr.
50 State of shock
52 Custard ingredients
55 Drink said to prolong life
57 Yuletide tune
60 Mercury or Saturn
61 Wise to
62 da-DUM, da-DUM, da-DUM
66 Tied
67 Je ne sais ___
68 Like redheads' tempers, supposedly
69 Villain in 2009's "Star Trek"
70 Bygone barrier breakers
71 Mystery writer's award

DOWN

1 Carpenter's tool with a curved blade
2 Eight-times-married Taylor
3 Tyke
4 Take on
5 Form of government Plato wrote about
6 Baby powder ingredient
7 Lei giver's greeting
8 ___ opposites
9 Co-creator of the Fantastic Four
10 Journey to Mecca
11 He said "Here's to our wives and girlfriends . . . may they never meet!"
12 Arriving after the bell, say
13 Wows at a comedy club
21 Classic brand of hair remover
22 E, in Morse code
23 Simpson and Kudrow
24 Ham it up
25 Magazine staffer
30 It has many needles
32 Bus. honchos
34 Toy you might enjoy while running
35 Basis for a Quaker cereal
36 Citi Field team
38 They have many needles
39 Worker on a comic book
42 Actuality
44 140 and up, say
45 Cad
47 Tennis umpire's cry
50 Some Madison Ave. workers
51 Drive drunkenly, perhaps
53 The "Homo" in "Homo sapiens"
54 "Tell me"
56 "In case you didn't hear me the first time . . ."
58 Casino game with Ping-Pong-like balls
59 Spanish liqueur
63 Computer unit, informally
64 Cup holder?
65 Leb. neighbor

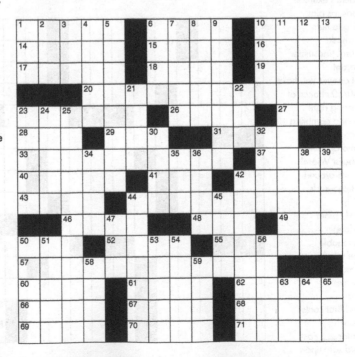

by Caleb Madison

ACROSS

1 "60 Minutes" correspondent starting in 1991
6 It may be run up
9 Hunky-dory
12 More delicate
14 "I don't believe this!"
15 Many-armed org.?
16 Talking like a junkie?
18 Be discordant
19 Rock's David Lee ___
20 Canapé topper
21 "The Hot Zone" virus
23 Agnostic's display?
26 Vanessa Williams/ Brian McKnight duet
29 Be nosy
30 Sunbathing at Ipanema, e.g.?
34 Plaza locale: Abbr.
37 Suffix with psych-
38 With 22-Down, recliner brand
39 ___-dieu
40 Widower of Maude on "The Simpsons"
41 Rink jewelry?
45 Female whale
46 E-mails from Nigerian princes, e.g.
47 Letter carrier's uniform?
53 The 40 of a "back 40"
54 Targets of a Moe Howard poke
55 ___ operandi (methods)
59 Cote call
60 Promote one's business, maybe . . . or a hint to 16-, 23-, 30-, 41- and 47-Across
63 Barrister's abbr.
64 Group with a Grand Lodge in Chicago

65 "Fiddler on the Roof" setting
66 Wahine's offering
67 Indian novelist Raja ___
68 Tanning element

DOWN

1 Baghdad's ___ City
2 Newbie: Var.
3 Stuck, after "in"
4 Buccaneers' place
5 Set the tempo
6 Fence supplier
7 Mayo is part of it
8 Parched
9 Pear variety
10 Name in dental hygiene
11 Unit of purity
13 Fencing thrust: Var.
14 Uniformed comics dog

17 Call from a farm field
22 See 38-Across
24 Blazin' Blueberry drink brand
25 Just right
26 Scientology's ___ Hubbard
27 Chantilly's department
28 Tear up, so to speak
31 Off one's feed
32 Batman after Michael
33 Suffix with final
34 Fare "for kids"
35 ___ tar (baseball team supply)
36 Things to tap
39 Device with a flat panel
41 Whoop it up
42 Part of M.Y.O.B.
43 What "Rh" may stand for

44 A.L. East team, on scoreboards
45 A.L. Central team, on scoreboards
47 Normand of old movies
48 Make ___ for (support)
49 Operation ___ Freedom
50 Gordon ___ ("Wall Street" role)
51 Shoemakers' supplies
52 Flying Cloud of 1927–36
56 Lollapalooza
57 What's spread on a spreadsheet
58 Way to stand by
61 Tuskegee U. locale
62 Day after so-called "hump day": Abbr.

by Corey Rubin

142

ACROSS

1 Prom night transportation
5 Jack who once hosted "The Tonight Show"
9 Bring upon oneself
14 "Green" sci.
15 "___ upon a time . . ."
16 Drunkard
17 Seven or eight hours, typically
20 Furtively
21 When repeated, sound of disapproval
22 James who wrote "A Death in the Family"
23 Early delivery in the delivery room
27 "Hey, way to go!"
30 Kristofferson of music
31 Columbus Day mo.
32 Moon's path
33 Salon sound
34 Chop ___
35 Inventor's goal
38 180-degree turns, in slang
39 Removes a squeak from
40 Where 43-Across run free
41 Super Bowl stats
42 Do nothing and like it
43 Mustangs, e.g.
44 Did nothing
46 Rock's ___ the Hoople
47 Drunk motorist's offense, briefly
48 Brainy bunch
52 They rarely see the light of day
56 Martini garnish
57 "___ I say, not . . ."
58 Neither fem. nor masc.
59 A little drunk
60 Igor, to Dr. Frankenstein: Abbr.
61 Equipment at Vail

DOWN

1 Plastic block brand
2 Pic you can click
3 Not worth debating, as a point
4 Things that die hard
5 Self-confident, as a pageant contestant
6 Journalistic slant
7 Sore all over
8 Like Gen. Colin Powell: Abbr.
9 Topics of debate
10 Nick of "48 HRS."
11 Pool player's stick
12 Take advantage of
13 Dem.'s opponent
18 Make null and void
19 Prepares to streak
23 Fuel-efficient Toyota
24 Expresses great sorrow
25 Freezing period
26 Classic Jaguars
27 "Forget the excuses!"
28 Frozen potato brand
29 Diagnostic that entails sticking the forearm with a needle
30 Small, rounded hill
33 "Say cheese!"
34 Bravura performances
36 Dormmate
37 X-rated
42 Hardly ostentatious
43 "Really and truly"
45 Modern viewing options, for short
46 Flat-topped Southwestern hills
48 Old Pontiac muscle cars
49 Hide-and-___
50 Decorative needle case
51 Former fast fliers
52 Automaton, for short
53 Yeller in the Yale Bowl
54 Not guzzle
55 BlackBerry or iPhone, briefly

by Paula Gamache

ACROSS

1 Senate page, e.g.
5 Island neighbor of Tonga and Tuvalu
9 Places of interest?
14 Sea dog's libation
15 North African port
16 "Take this job and shove it!"
17 *Informal greeting
19 Like undercooked eggs
20 New wing
21 Credit union's activity
23 It may be stacked or cut
26 Knock over, so to speak
27 "Eureka!"
30 *At times
36 PC video gear, for short
38 Take it on the ___
39 Lion-colored
40 Exercise in pronunciation . . . like the first words of the answers to the starred clues
44 Scout's mission, for short
45 Hide-hair link
46 One of TV's Mavericks
47 *One not using the company cafeteria, maybe
51 U.F.O. crew
52 Fall back
53 Stone for many Libras
55 Mocks
59 Were in accord
63 PC-less Internet hookup, once
64 *Bay Area concert venue
67 More than sore
68 Newton or ohm
69 Liniment target
70 Fan mags
71 Sonic the Hedgehog's company
72 Black belt's blow

DOWN

1 Ottoman Empire V.I.P.
2 Hotel room amenity
3 Elevator direction half the time
4 Prodded, with "on"
5 "Friend or ___?"
6 Org. with a code
7 One corner of a Monopoly board
8 Worker for free, often
9 Small pool site in a yard
10 Here, in Honduras
11 Former Georgia senator Sam
12 Piece moved in castling
13 Pig's home
18 Plow team
22 Affirmative action
24 Revolver inventor
25 "The Bridge on the River ___"
27 Sharp-tongued
28 More vigorous
29 BP gas brand
31 In the midst of
32 Clothing
33 Clued in
34 Boxed-off map section
35 Kremlin denials
37 Garbage hauler
41 Rattles
42 Scrapped, as a mission
43 Get ready for an exam
48 Small ammo
49 Device you can count on
50 Big Indian
54 Pale shade of violet
55 Ryan of "Boston Public"
56 Israel's Abba
57 Suffix with kitchen or room
58 TV color adjustment
60 "Goldberg Variations" composer
61 Tunnel effect
62 Hard to fathom
63 1978 Diana Ross musical, with "The"
65 Halloween wear
66 Education-conscious org.

by Steve Dobis

144

ACROSS

1 City SW of Syracuse
7 Ripoff
11 First word of 10-/25-Down's "Billie Jean"
14 Richie who wrote "We Are the World" with 10-/25-Down
15 1982 blockbuster by 10-/25-Down
17 Moviegoer's chocolate bite
18 More honest
19 Kind of cheese
21 Its symbol is omega
22 Right away
24 Trek to Mecca
26 Zero
30 Give the slip to
32 1991 hit album by 10-/25-Down
35 "Yum!"
37 Air-conditioned
38 Dir. from Gary, Ind., to Sault Ste. Marie
39 Grates on
40 "Don't you ___ for no favors" (42-Down lyric on 32-Across)
42 Joan of rock
43 Middle of the second century
44 Ziegfeld and others
45 Deluges
47 Nickname for 10-/25-Down
50 Romeo's love?
51 Popeye creator Elzie ___
52 Zero
54 Old spy grp.
55 Vitality
57 Juan's uncle?
59 Skin cream ingredient
64 Less than wholesale
67 Vocal style of 10-/25-Down, at times
68 First record label of 10-/25-Down

69 "Farewell"
70 Stink up the joint
71 Small piano

DOWN

1 Some urban rails
2 Writer ___ Yutang
3 Classic part of a 10-/25-Down stage act
4 Atahualpa, for one
5 Gets to
6 Greek leader?
7 City grid: Abbr.
8 ___-Town (Midwest hub)
9 River under the Ponte Vecchio
10 With 25-Down, this puzzle's honoree
11 Certain camera, for short
12 Laugh syllable

13 Miss the mark
16 Ring-tailed primate
20 Quirky
22 Old fast-food chain
23 Be positioned above
25 See 10-Down
27 Song on 32-Across
28 Bird dogs, say
29 Flies over Africa?
31 Bad-mouth
33 Jean Valjean, e.g.
34 Takes off
36 Either 50 of 50/50
41 Appeasement
42 First song on 32-Across
44 With 10-Down, 1975 album by 10-/25-Down
46 Handheld device
48 Goggles
49 Bit of wordplay
53 Rich soils

56 Rose family member
58 Play starter
59 Vance in Okla., e.g.
60 Minstrel's song
61 Arena cry
62 Itinerary part: Abbr.
63 Just dandy
65 Riksdag locale: Abbr.
66 Cable channel with the slogan "We Know Drama"

by David J. Kahn

ACROSS

1 Fruit often cut into balls
6 ___ Disney Pictures
10 Actress Thompson of "Howards End"
14 Give off, as charm
15 Song for a diva
16 The North and the South, in the Civil War
17 Company-paid medical and dental coverage, college tuition, etc.
20 Controversial substance in baseball news
21 Reduce to mush
22 "___ look like a mind reader?"
24 Most like Solomon
25 Upholstered piece
30 Dorothy, to Em
32 Not so congenial
33 Poet ___ St. Vincent Millay
34 Tanning lotion abbr.
37 A sot he's not
41 Tissue layer
42 "This will ___ further!"
43 Artful deception
44 Factory
46 Pattern on a pinto horse
47 Angora goat's fleece
50 ___ Lanka
52 Ward off
53 Ireland's hue
59 Bit of attire for a business interview, maybe
63 Bowlful accompanying teriyaki
64 A slave to opera?
65 Superior to
66 Pindaric pieces
67 Hosiery spoiler
68 Identified

DOWN

1 Diner on "Alice"
2 Emergency door sign
3 Garage job, for short
4 Baltic Sea feeder
5 Wolfe of whodunits
6 Hard-to-find guy in children's books
7 Wall St. whiz
8 Tell a whopper
9 Get some sun
10 Pour forth
11 Wavy pattern on fabric
12 Apportions, with "out"
13 Liability's opposite
18 Capitol Hill helper
19 Cast-of-thousands movie
23 Hits the tab key, say
24 Grow tiresome
25 Nincompoop
26 Environmental sci.
27 Neat
28 ___ time (golf course slot)
29 Blow it
31 ___-European languages
33 School attended by princes
34 Burlesque bit
35 ___-mell
36 Gratis
38 Petri dish gel
39 "Here ___ again"
40 Macadamia, for one
44 Breaks down grammatically
45 Lo-fat
46 Actress Rogers who was once married to Tom Cruise
47 PC shortcut
48 Egg-shaped
49 "It follows that . . ."
51 Put a new price on
54 Politico Bayh
55 McEntire of country music
56 Molecule building block
57 Not prerecorded
58 Monopoly card
60 ___ Tafari (Haile Selassie)
61 Beaujolais or Chablis
62 Critic ___ Louise Huxtable

by Fred Piscop

146

ACROSS

1 500 sheets
5 Cuts down
10 Panty raid prize
13 It takes a hammering
15 Roundup rope
16 It might make a ewe turn
17 Late-arriving TV detective?
19 Puppy's bark
20 Nimble circus performer
21 Short-term govt. securities
23 Like a wallflower
24 Alpha's counterpart
27 Lesser-used PC key
28 Late-arriving actor of old?
32 Classroom jottings
35 Home for Adam and Eve
36 Campus e-mail letters?
37 Verve
38 Former U.N. head Kofi ___
40 Fish with only minute fins
41 Harrison of "My Fair Lady"
42 Work monotonously
43 Like some needs
44 Late-arriving singer/ actress of old?
48 ___ of Good Feelings
49 Parcel out
50 Blackball
53 Knack
56 Region of pre-Roman Italy
58 ___ Lilly & Co.
59 Late-arriving disco singer?
62 "Act your ___!"
63 Many Conan O'Brien lines
64 Down the hatch
65 U.K. fliers
66 Word next to an arrow in a maze
67 Screen star Lamarr

DOWN

1 Indian royalty
2 Tennyson title hero ___ Arden
3 New York's ___ Fisher Hall
4 Kind of soup at a Japanese restaurant
5 Having decorative grooves
6 Obstacle for a barber
7 Source of a hippie's high
8 Exam for A.B.A.-approved schools
9 Protein-rich legume
10 "A little dab'll do ya" brand
11 Complain bitterly
12 Concert blasters
14 Feats for Hercules
18 Docile
22 AOL, for one
25 Monster defeated by Beowulf
26 Slave entombed with Radames
28 Swamp
29 100 years: Abbr.
30 Just loafing
31 The hots
32 Jock's counterpart
33 Margarine
34 Government's gift to I.R.S. filers
38 Drink from a stein
39 Star of changing brightness
40 Official lang. of Guyana
42 Manners
43 Erroneous
45 Fury
46 Atlanta Braves' div.
47 Tiny bit
50 "Et tu, ___?"
51 Got ready to shoot
52 Kids' caretaker
53 Shred
54 Sea lettuce, e.g.
55 Talk up
57 One of the Four Corners states
60 Actress Peeples
61 "Car Talk" airer

by Lynn Lempel

Note: When completed, this puzzle grid will contain an unusual feature that appears nine times. Can you find it?

ACROSS

1 Steal from
4 Go on a jag
9 "Beat it!"
14 "O Henry, ___ thine eyes!": Shak.
15 "In an ___ world . . ."
16 Boorish
17 Spell-off
18 Just learning about
19 "I've ___ up to here!"
20 Make arable, perhaps
22 Ants, archaically
23 Acts the shrew
24 ___ Penh, Cambodia: Var.
25 Is compassionate
30 Half a flock, maybe
34 Sisters' org.
35 Dues payer
36 Hindu god
37 What a cow chews
38 Style of truck with a vertical front
40 Mule of song
41 "101 ___ for a Dead Cat" (1981 best seller)
43 Multi-act shows
44 "The Closer" cable channel
45 1978 Yankees hero Bucky
46 Remains of a felling
48 "So satisfying!" sounds
50 Louis XIV, Louis XVI et al.
52 Deep divides
55 Bacardi concoction, perhaps
59 "___ lost his mind?"
60 Yam or taro
61 Fish-to-be
62 Pale with fright
63 Ohm's symbol
64 "A Chorus Line" song
65 Casts off
66 Alternative to roll-on
67 Bard's nightfall

DOWN

1 Batcave figure
2 Diva's workplace
3 Place for a pilsner
4 Cherry variety
5 "Aha!" elicitor
6 "Winning the Future" author Gingrich
7 Event receipts
8 "Xanadu" band, for short
9 Dorky sort
10 Pulled an all-nighter
11 Like cutting in line, e.g.
12 Mine opening
13 "Amazin'" team
21 Mag. copy
22 Followers of appetizers
24 Sneak peek, informally
26 ___ Theaters (national cinema chain)

27 Fireplace floors
28 Fireplace remains
29 Higher-ranking than
31 Louisiana city named for the fifth U.S. president
32 Big name in women's apparel since 1949
33 Margarita glass rim coating
34 Gulf war missile
39 Run after Q
42 Squirreled away
47 Montevideo's land: Abbr.
49 Church chorus
51 Unwashed hair may have it
52 Cartoonist Addams
53 "Slung" dish
54 Arthur who wrote "A Hard Road to Glory"
55 Beef cut

56 Super, slangily
57 Prefix with vitamins
58 Do penance, say
60 How-___ (do-it-yourself books)

by Tim Wescott

148

ACROSS

1. Chicago's ___ Planetarium
6. Country singer Brooks
11. Opposite of dis
14. Like oil directly from a well
15. Hilo hello
16. Aussie hopper
17. Ditch digging, e.g.
19. Little Rock's home: Abbr.
20. Yolk's site
21. City name before Heat or Vice
22. "Inferno" writer
24. Money borrowed from a friend, e.g.
26. Fleet
29. Bald person's purchase
30. Serve, as tea
31. "Airplane!" or "Spaceballs"
34. Flow back
37. The Dalai Lama, e.g.
41. At any time, to a poet
42. Six ___ a-laying (gift in a Christmas song)
43. Silent screen star Naldi
44. Reverse of WSW
45. Acid blocker sold over the counter
47. Slash symbol, e.g.
53. Helicopter part
54. Hotelier Helmsley
55. Address for an overseas G.I.
58. Wonderment
59. Comfily ready to sleep . . . or a hint to 17-, 24-, 37- and 47-Across
62. Moms
63. One of the Judds
64. Ryan of "The Beverly Hillbillies"
65. Tidbit for an aardvark
66. Lugs
67. Homes for 65-Acrosses

DOWN

1. Pinnacle
2. Wet blanket
3. Aqua-___
4. Univ. e-mail ending
5. Cleaned out, as with a pipe cleaner
6. Black-tie affairs
7. "Remember the ___!" (rallying cry of 1836)
8. Harbinger of spring
9. Even if, informally
10. What a serf led
11. Clog-busting brand
12. Main artery
13. Thimble or shoe, in Monopoly
18. Franc : France :: ___ : Italy
23. 2x + 5 = 15 subj.
24. Last name of Henry VIII's last
25. M.P.'s quarry
26. Cathedral recess
27. Hillbilly's belt
28. John who founded the Sierra Club
31. Take to court
32. Dads
33. Shout after a bull charges
34. Blue-pencil
35. Gamma preceder
36. Bric-a-___
38. Unaware
39. Many a driver's ed student
40. First name of Henry VIII's second
44. Self-esteem
45. Next-to-last element alphabetically
46. ___ Skywalker of "Star Wars"
47. Comedy's counterpart
48. Cedar Rapids native
49. Event that could be seen as far away as Las Vegas in the '50s
50. Mete out
51. "I'll do it!"
52. 1930s–'40s heavyweight champ Joe
55. Fruit drinks
56. Pub serving
57. Small bills
60. Thai neighbor
61. Before, poetically

by C. W. Stewart

ACROSS

1 Partner of punishment
6 John Irving title character
10 Leftovers from threshing
15 Dwelling section whose name comes from the Arabic for "forbidden place"
16 Kind of exam
17 Oscar winner Berry
18 Dickens novel with the 56-Across as its backdrop
21 Not an elective: Abbr.
22 Like hen's teeth
23 Features of the Sierras
24 Venue
25 Nickelodeon explorer
27 Declaration attributed to Marie Antoinette just before the 56-Across
33 Oyster eater in a Lewis Carroll verse
34 Fraternal group
35 Stale Italian bread?
37 "___ Irish Rose"
38 Catch sight of
39 Miserly Marner
40 ___ Pahlevi, last shah of Iran
41 Launder
42 Without profit
43 Song of the 56-Across
46 Butter slices
47 Indian tourist mecca
48 109, famously
52 "Yikes!"
53 To's opposite
56 Event that began in 1789
60 Play caller
61 "Milk's favorite cookie," in commercials
62 Unguent
63 Binge
64 Volunteer State: Abbr.
65 Grove constituents

DOWN

1 Scorch
2 Assign stars to, say
3 With 33-Down, topic in the 2008 presidential campaign
4 ___ B or ___ C of the Spice Girls
5 Retired
6 Get out of jail
7 Johnson of "Laugh-In"
8 Unprocessed
9 Negotiating partner of Isr.
10 Sarkozy's presidential predecessor
11 Loathe
12 Landed
13 Leave, as out of fear
14 Admit, with "up"
19 Solemn promises
20 Vehicles on the links
24 Dam site
25 Oracle site
26 Like some chardonnays
27 Arista or Motown
28 "My Fair Lady" role
29 Tinkers (with)
30 Singer Keys
31 Drug units
32 Wipe out
33 See 3-Down
36 Superlative suffix
38 Big ___ Conference
39 Hoagy Carmichael classic
41 Anger
42 Like some pond life
44 Geronimo, e.g.
45 Middle of an atoll
48 Gomer Pyle and platoonmates, by rank: Abbr.
49 Classic Vegas hotel, with "the"
50 Winnie-the-Pooh, for one
51 On a single occasion
52 Tied up
53 Manicurist's tool
54 Wander
55 Change for a five
57 Spoil
58 "Able was I ___ I saw Elba"
59 La Brea goo

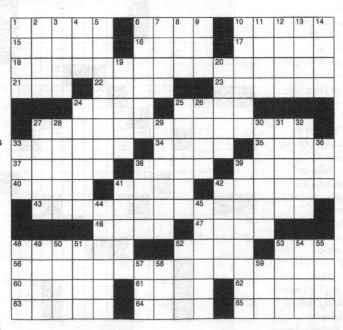

by Donna S. Levin

150

ACROSS

1 It may be hand-picked
6 Not express
11 "The word"
14 Deep blue
15 Earthy tone
16 Brian who produced or co-produced seven U2 albums
17 Feeling of nonfulfillment
19 "Wait Wait . . . Don't Tell Me!" network
20 Went for, at an auction
21 Playing marbles
23 Case of bad spelling?
24 Frequent home acquisition
26 Fill in for
29 Big __
30 Friend of Falstaff
31 Szyslak of Springfield
32 "Come on, pack your stuff . . . !"
35 Signs
38 Statement about 17-, 24-, 49- and 59-Across
41 "Baseball Tonight" network
42 Hall-of-Fame QB/ kicker George
43 With 45-Down, "Trust No One" series
44 Fandango offerings, slangily
46 "__ Dalloway"
47 Arterial implant
49 Burgers and fries, often
52 Orch. section
53 Aggrieved person's cry, maybe
54 Bill & __ Gates Foundation
58 "My Big Fat Greek Wedding" actress Vardalos
59 Item that may have a date stamp

62 Comprehended
63 Like 36 piano keys
64 Original Thanksgiving fare
65 Cosine of 2 pi
66 Where Moses received the Law
67 Kingly title in Spanish

DOWN

1 Big Broadway hit
2 It might be a lot
3 Neither masc. nor fem.
4 Violinist Heifetz
5 Surreptitiously
6 Whites or darks, say
7 Mo. of Indigenous Peoples Day
8 Christogram part
9 Bellowing
10 Extent
11 Internal memo?

12 Let off the hook?
13 Robert who won a Tony for "How to Succeed in Business Without Really Trying"
18 Kingly title in Latin
22 Another time
24 Colonel suspected of murder
25 Hearts, e.g.
26 French girlfriend
27 Barracks lineup
28 Maybe takes one risk too many
29 Sailor's patron
33 Recede
34 Rubber-stamped
36 Former baseball commissioner Bowie
37 "Leave it in" mark
39 "Clear Light of Day" author Desai

40 Town near New London, Conn.
45 See 43-Across
48 Like "Survivor" councils
49 Bat used for fielding practice
50 Chloride or carbonate
51 Graceful African antelope
52 Homily: Abbr.
54 Polite request for permission
55 Hard-boiled, in a way
56 Nod off
57 "The House Without __" (first Charlie Chan mystery)
60 __ mot
61 Uracil-containing macromolecule

by Joon Pahk

ACROSS

1 "Uncle ___ Cabin"
5 Witches' faces have them
10 ___ vu
14 "Put a sock ___!"
15 Writer T. S. or George
16 Midterm, e.g.
17 Sicilian spewer
18 Former British P.M. Tony
19 Surprisingly lively for one's age
20 What the love of money is, they say
23 Lop off, as branches
24 RR depot
25 "The Lord of the Rings" enemy
28 "So long!"
31 Ninth-inning pitcher
33 Squealer
36 Stop a prevailing trend
38 Gillette razor
40 "I'll take that as ___"
41 30-second spot, e.g.
42 Quickly turn the pages of
47 That: Sp.
48 Mexican revolutionary ___ Villa
49 Check the fit of, as a dress
51 "___ Pinafore"
52 Hospital trauma ctrs.
54 "Oh, bushwa!"
57 Factory supervisors . . . or a hint to the starts of 20-, 36- and 42-Across
62 Old woman's home in a nursery rhyme
64 "Fear of Flying" writer Jong
65 Marco Polo crossed it
66 Simplicity
67 Contract conditions
68 Sore, with "off"

69 Arduous journey
70 Like Georgia Brown of song
71 "Put a tiger in your tank" brand

DOWN

1 It may hang out in a sports stadium
2 First in the rankings
3 17-year-old, legally
4 Condition of affairs
5 Duck features
6 ___ breve (2/2 time in music)
7 Iranian money
8 Works long and hard
9 Seventh inning ritual
10 Arnaz of "I Love Lucy"
11 Nitroglycerin or dynamite
12 Cookie holder
13 "The Joy Luck Club" writer Tan
21 George Washingtons
22 Low-lying area
26 ___ a beet
27 Belief
29 Vintage designation
30 "I ___ amused!"
32 Hall-of-Famer Me!
33 Alice's mate on "The Honeymooners"
34 First string
35 Make lemons into melons, e.g.?
37 Go from gig to gig
39 Steelers' grp.
43 Ellington's "Take ___ Train"
44 Big stingers
45 One who mounts and dismounts a horse
46 Georgetown athlete
50 Nullify

53 Spread, as seed
55 Go-aheads
56 Great Lakes Indians
58 Cousin of an onion
59 Bog
60 Summit
61 Lead-in to masochism
62 Filming site
63 Part of 33-Down's laugh

by Pancho Harrison

152

ACROSS

1 Almost half of U.S. immigrants in 1840
6 Male tabbies
10 O.K. Corral figure
14 Actress Thomas
15 Smell ___ (be suspicious)
16 Console used with the game Halo
17 Like stadiums after touchdowns
18 Places to put briefs
20 New York Times headline of 7/21/69
22 Letters that please angels
23 Clumsy boat
24 Hoagy Carmichael lyric "___ lazy river . . ."
25 1988 Dennis Quaid/Meg Ryan movie
28 Subject of a photo beneath 20-Across
32 La ___ vita
33 Old-time Norwegian skating sensation
34 Soprano ___ Te Kanawa
37 Loses traction
40 D-Day vessels
41 Desktop symbols
43 The Dapper Don
45 With 55-Across, message left by 28-Across for future explorers
49 Peeve
50 Geom. prerequisite
51 "Aladdin" hero
52 Little Red Book writer
55 See 45-Across
59 Even more certain: Lat.
61 Diacritical squiggle
62 Sight in the Arctic Ocean
63 When morning ends
64 "Silas Marner" author

65 Whirling water
66 Anglo-Saxon laborer
67 Opportunities, metaphorically

DOWN

1 Mosque leaders
2 Less common
3 Like some patches
4 Cabbage dish
5 Whom Hamlet calls "A man that Fortune's buffets and rewards / Hast ta'en with equal thanks"
6 Sass, with "to"
7 McFlurry flavor
8 Large wine bottle
9 They may come in sheets
10 ___ 67 (onetime Montreal event)
11 Forsakes

12 Reel's partner
13 Stores for G.I.'s
19 Reluctant
21 Respites
26 Handling the matter
27 Matures
29 Minneapolis suburb
30 Have the throne
31 Archaeologist's find
34 Fuzzy fruit
35 Cupcake finisher
36 1970s James Garner TV title role
38 Pleasure-associated neurotransmitter
39 Inscribed pillar
42 Natty
44 Not pure
46 Julia's "Seinfeld" role
47 Inuit homes
48 Estevez of the Brat Pack

53 Choice words
54 "Waiting for Lefty" playwright
56 Bacchanalian revelry
57 "Dianetics" author ___ Hubbard
58 D.E.A. seizure, maybe
59 The Rail Splitter
60 G-man

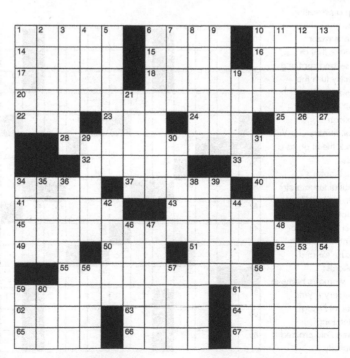

by Donna S. Levin

ACROSS

1 It's found in chambers
5 Moves quickly
10 It was dropped in the '60s
14 Just watch TV, say
15 Historic San Francisco theater, with "the"
16 Dame ___ Everage (Barry Humphries character)
17 Olympic boxing gold medalist of 1964
19 It may be down at the heel
20 For the nonce
21 Was in a no-win situation?
23 Under the table
24 King in "Jesus Christ Superstar"
25 Hero of Super Bowl III
27 Run out of gas, say
29 Tooth trouble
30 47th U.S. vice president
35 Cheri of "Scary Movie"
38 Abrasive soap brand
39 While away, as time
42 Trampled (on)
43 Wipe
45 Oscar winner of 1990
47 Pockets of dough?
50 Light hair color
51 Singer on day three of 1969's Woodstock
54 Handy
59 Scand. land
60 "No, mein Herr"
61 Egyptian god with the head of a jackal
62 "'Tis a pity"
64 School cafeteria fare . . . and a hint to this puzzle's theme
66 Commend, as for outstanding service
67 More sick, in dialect
68 Bibliophile's suffix
69 Archie or Veronica
70 Winter Palace figures
71 Canine order

DOWN

1 Jewish leader?
2 Roger who played the same role seven times
3 Paramount
4 "___ the races!"
5 Disney World transport
6 Cartoonist Chast
7 Nitrous ___
8 Steering system component
9 Composed
10 1950s political inits.
11 Sound system staples
12 Indigenous Canadian
13 Title before Sidious or Maul
18 ___-wip
22 Steve Martin's birthplace
25 Cherokee, for one
26 Certain finish
28 Bouncers check them, briefly
30 Cheer for a matador
31 Candy holder
32 Disappear
33 Meat-and-potatoes
34 Three-time Keanu Reeves character
36 "Arabian Nights" bird
37 Uganda's ___ Amin
40 By
41 Wedding reception hirees
44 Neighbor of Slough
46 Like the 28-Down of underage drinkers
48 Gets 100 on a test
49 Learned things
51 Pass
52 Half of Brangelina
53 ___ Gay (W.W. II bomber)
55 Some apples
56 W.W. II menace
57 ___ College, north of Albany, N.Y.
58 Lamb piece
61 Loan figs.
63 Committee member, maybe: Abbr.
65 Word in a price

by Patrick Blindauer

154

ACROSS
1 Bogged down
6 Sword handles
11 ___-Magnon man
14 High-speed train from Boston to Washington
15 Stand in a queue for, say
16 Drink with Grabbin' Grape and Smashin' Wild Berry flavors
17 College professor's mantra
20 Splenda rival
21 Short-sheeting a bed, TP'ing a house, etc.
22 2K race, e.g.
25 Bloodhound's trail
27 Yoko of "Double Fantasy"
28 Uganda's ___ Amin
30 As, chemically
34 G.P.S. offering: Abbr.
35 Highway entrances and exits, typically
37 "First, ___ harm" (medical axiom)
38 Highly collectible illustrator
42 Kuwaiti chief
43 ___ orange
44 The upper Midwest's ___ Canals
45 Hits the hay
48 Stimpy's cartoon pal
49 Ernie of golf fame
50 Penny vis-à-vis a dime
52 Gird oneself
54 Finisher of pottery or cakes
57 ___ note (dictionary bit)
59 Lafayette or Orleans
64 Bed-and-breakfast
65 Dazzling effect
66 Dull, in poetry
67 "Wanna ___?"
68 What light bulbs and bootblacks do
69 English nobles

DOWN
1 Atlas page
2 Critical hosp. area
3 Yank's foe in the Civil War
4 Aunt from "Oklahoma!"
5 Rum and lime juice drink
6 LOL, out loud
7 Mil. truants
8 Distant
9 One leaving cash on the table?
10 Backs of boats
11 It might be cut by an uppercut
12 Jeopardy
13 Adolph who was chief of The New York Times from 1896 to 1935
18 Dairy Queen order
19 Deemed not suitable for kids
22 Previous
23 Wild
24 1944 Jean-Paul Sartre play
26 One of the Wise Men
29 "Please help me with directions"
31 Boom, zoom and vroom
32 Cushiony part of a shoe
33 Matt Lauer or Meredith Vieira for "Today"
36 They have precincts: Abbr.
39 Nancy's 56-Down in the comics
40 Feature of a May-December romance
41 Deserter
46 ___ Peanut Butter Cups
47 Fortify with vitamins, e.g.
51 Style of Chinese cuisine
53 ___ incognita
54 Fast-talking
55 Unaccompanied
56 See 39-Down
58 Completely fill
60 Rope-a-dope boxer
61 Suffix with cash
62 "My gal" of song
63 60-min. periods

by Allan E. Parrish

ACROSS

1 Tight-lipped
4 "Stat!"
8 Seven-up and crazy eights
13 Lennon's second wife
14 June of "Monster-in-Law"
16 Disco-era suffix
17 "Sure thing"
20 Note in an E major scale
21 Word before sheet or music
22 Loughlin of "90210"
23 Bygone despot
25 Outfielder's asset
28 "Chances are good"
33 "___ Said" (Neil Diamond hit)
34 ___ Lama
35 "It could go either way"
41 Like dessert wines
42 Water co., e.g.
43 "Doubtful"
50 Turned on
51 Studio constructions
52 Close by
53 Gitmo mil. branch
54 Counselor's clients, perhaps
56 "Forget it!"
62 Perfect
63 Fluctuates wildly
64 Ill temper
65 Apt to pout
66 Had a bawl
67 Ballpark fig.

DOWN

1 "The Jungle Book" hero
2 Oneness
3 Insect monster of Japanese film
4 Get an ___ effort
5 Borscht, e.g.
6 Amazon ___ (aggressive insect)
7 "Stat!"
8 Shocked reaction
9 F.B.I. worker: Abbr.
10 "You don't mean ME?!"
11 Self-esteem
12 Sequel title starter, sometimes
15 Surrounding glows
18 Precipitation that may be the size of golf balls
19 Banjoist Scruggs
23 The so-called fourth dimension
24 Attire on the slopes
25 Melville's obsessed captain
26 Thing to play
27 Haunted house sound
29 More than deceive
30 Put down
31 Pastoral poems
32 God, in Roma
35 AOL alternative
36 Whom an M.P. hunts
37 Hulking Himalayan of legend
38 Asteroid area, e.g.
39 Range units: Abbr.
40 Bailed-out co. in the news
44 ___ buco
45 "South Park" boy
46 "Movin' ___" ("The Jeffersons" theme)
47 Cheech or Chong persona
48 Gawking sorts
49 Where one might see "OMG" or "TTYL"
53 Hideous
54 Dojo blow
55 Brewery dryer
56 Deadeye's skill
57 Words said after ". . . so help you God?"
58 Keanu's "The Matrix" role
59 Wee bit
60 "Stat!"
61 Floor vote

by Tony Orbach

156

ACROSS

1 Clinks
6 Way out
10 Baseball star in Senate steroid hearings
14 Sheltered water
15 Repetitive routine
16 It may be pumped
17 Argue forcibly
20 South American cruise stop
21 Finish lacing up
22 ___ fly (run producer)
25 Catch red-handed
27 Royal Navy drink of old
28 Pesticide spreader, e.g.
32 Brian of ambient music
35 Prefix with sphere
36 Arthurian times, say
37 Name in 2001 bankruptcy news
39 Knoxville sch.
41 Grizzlies' org.
42 "Call it!" call
43 Lehmann of opera
44 Damage, so to speak
46 Con man?
47 Chaotic place
48 Terse
51 "Don't ___ me, bro!"
53 Dark half of a Chinese circle
54 G.P.S. heading
55 Like a Möbius strip
59 Class with the periodic table on the wall, often: Abbr.
61 Where Olaf I or Olaf II sat
66 "___ la Douce" (1963 film)
67 Fish-eating raptor
68 Moves gingerly
69 Cold war propaganda disseminator
70 Rink fake
71 Like Yogi Berra, physically

DOWN

1 Huck's raftmate
2 Bibliophile's suffix
3 Sort
4 Lounge lizard's look
5 Discolorations
6 Works in a gallery
7 Snow structure
8 Yours, in Tours
9 Bridge no-no
10 2007 Michael Moore documentary
11 Juicer remnants
12 Eh
13 Work without ___ (be daring)
18 Needing a rinse
19 "La Bohème" setting
22 Charles who created Peppermint Patty
23 "Am not!" response
24 Shake hands
26 It's most useful when it's broken
29 Blood drive donation
30 Shady retreat
31 Like bread dough or beer
33 Actor Nick and family
34 Like some football kicks
38 Tandoor-baked bread
40 Storied monster, informally
45 Dance for Chubby Checker
49 Counterbalanced, as bets
50 What some races are won by
52 ___ the custom (traditionally)
55 "Get ___!" ("Stop procrastinating!")
56 "The Thin Man" detective
57 Mayo's land
58 Dungeonlike
60 Modern home of ancient Ur
62 Alumna bio word
63 Columbus sch.
64 Teachers' org.
65 1970s self-improvement program

by Tim Wescott

ACROSS

1 Going for broke, as a poker player
6 Goatee, for one
11 Corp.'s head money person
14 Sarge's superior
15 ___-Detoo of "Star Wars"
16 Flight board abbr.
17 Campus/off-campus community, collectively
19 Bone that's part of a "cage"
20 iPhone downloads
21 Composer Stravinsky
22 Peru's peaks
24 Majority Muslim in Iran
26 Declaration that may be followed by "So sue me"
27 Confederate flag
31 Roasting rods
34 Med. group
35 Place for ChapStick
36 Charged particle
37 John Lennon's lady
41 Environmentalist's prefix
42 "Believe It or ___!"
43 Daisy ___ of "Li'l Abner"
44 Hat for a military specialist
46 Extreme pessimism
51 Job for a roadside assistance worker
52 Tater Tots maker
55 No longer vivid
56 ___ bene
58 Oompah band instrument
60 Lincoln, the Rail-Splitter
61 Damage from ordinary use
64 ___ de France
65 Where a wedding march ends

66 River mouth feature
67 Dem.'s foe
68 Triangular road sign
69 1950s Ford flop

DOWN

1 Resort near Snowbird
2 Figure skating figures
3 Boast of some shampoos
4 "No use arguing with me"
5 PBS funder
6 Nag to death
7 As a result
8 Suffix with origin
9 Part of an airplane seat assignment
10 Disney's ___ Duck
11 Seller of coupes and sedans
12 Chinese side dish
13 Heavenly bodies

18 Old-time actress Talbot or Naldi
23 Penpoint
25 Teeny, informally
26 Listen ___ (hear via eavesdropping)
28 Protected, as the feet
29 "I love," in Latin
30 Parking space
31 Perform on "American Idol," e.g.
32 Place to "rack 'em up"
33 Unable to dig oneself out
38 Muscat's land
39 It's north of Okla.
40 Melancholy instrument
45 Sent out, as rays
47 Fall behind financially
48 Chicago alternative to O'Hare
49 Senile sort
50 Algerian port

53 Face-offs with guns or swords
54 Lessen
55 Without a cloud in the sky
56 ___ the Great of children's literature
57 Grueling grilling
59 Asia's shrunken ___ Sea
62 "The Book of ___" (2010 film)
63 Ike's monogram

by Nancy Salomon

158

ACROSS

1 Establishments with mirrored balls
7 Snacked
10 In a state of 10-Down
14 Involve
15 South of South America
16 Help the dishwasher, perhaps
17 In a precise manner
18 It's directly below V-B-N-M
20 Turn in many a children's game
21 Relative of a raccoon
22 Bark beetle's habitat
23 Highway safety marker
27 Caballer's need
28 No ___ sight
32 Away from home
35 Unwelcome financial exams
39 French river or department
40 Punch in the mouth, slangily
43 Westernmost of the Aleutians
44 Alice's best friend on "The Honeymooners"
45 Honor society letter
46 "___ never believe this!"
48 "___ first you don't succeed . . ."
50 Homecoming display
56 Pompous fool
59 Cut down
60 Cuts down
62 Cold treat that can precede the last word of 18-, 23-, 40- or 50-Across
64 Menu selection
66 Not dry
67 Full house sign
68 Pig, when rummaging for truffles
69 Diva's delivery
70 Newspaper staffers, in brief
71 Fleet of warships

DOWN

1 Rooms with recliners
2 All thumbs
3 Flight segment
4 Forty winks
5 Olive product
6 Tricky
7 Part of P.G.A.: Abbr.
8 Rapper ___ Shakur
9 Sister of Clio
10 Feeling when you're 10-Across
11 Taunt
12 Birthstone for most Libras
13 Start, as of an idea
19 French filmdom
21 Remnant of a burned coal
24 Verbal brickbats
25 Tennis "misstep"
26 Plenty, to a poet
29 Icicle feature
30 Narrow winning margin
31 Classic soda pop
32 Give the go-ahead
33 "Do ___ others . . ."
34 South African Peace Nobelist, 1984
36 "It ___" (reply to "Who's there?")
37 Prepared for takeoff
38 [Well, see if I care!]
41 Late actor Robert of "I Spy"
42 Give out cards
47 Bert of "The Wizard of Oz"
49 Indian percussion
51 Witherspoon of "Legally Blonde"
52 Cy Young, e.g.
53 Visual sales pitches
54 Line from the heart
55 Tammany Hall "boss"
56 Elton John/Tim Rice musical
57 Mark for life
58 Place for a cab
61 It's repeated after "Que" in song
63 Tax preparer, for short
64 Diamond stat
65 Neither's partner

by Sarah Keller

ACROSS

1 Prefix with lateral
5 Frame side
9 Was in the arms of Morpheus
14 Ward who played Robin
15 Baseball family name
16 Conductors' platforms
17 Wait
18 Symbol of uncommunicativeness
19 Hockey no-no
20 One who plunders boatloads of jack-o'-lanterns?
23 Published
24 Zilch
25 Pet store offering
29 Pick-me-up
31 ___-devil
34 One way to read
35 Shook out of dreamland
36 In among
37 First-rate chastisement?
40 Tree of Life locale
41 Destination for a ferry from Livorno
42 Get stuffed
43 Words from the Rev.
44 One may be in waiting
45 Ship of fuels
46 "The tongue of the mind": Cervantes
47 Stage design
48 Nickname for an unpredictable Communist?
55 Family
56 Skyrocket
57 Love of Spain
59 Preceding on the page
60 "I'm off!"
61 Egypt's third-largest city
62 Arab League member
63 Yoked pair
64 What ". . . . . . ." means to a typesetter

DOWN

1 A drop in the ocean?
2 Will Rogers specialty
3 Official language of Pakistan
4 News clipping
5 Follower who does the dirty work
6 Bushed
7 Sound stressed, maybe
8 Traffic slower
9 Ghost
10 Neighborhood pub
11 Ready for release
12 Tar source
13 It's game
21 Fall preceder
22 Draw a conclusion
25 Krypton and others
26 Not get caught by
27 Rodeo specialist
28 Use as fuel
29 Hotel area
30 Furniture chain
31 Show of smugness
32 Pivotal point
33 Trimming tool
35 Ironworker's union?
36 Loads
38 Had in view
39 Banded gemstone
44 Heavy
45 Home of the Azadi Tower
46 Establish as fact
47 Union member
48 Hamburg's river
49 Leeway
50 Part of an analogy
51 Sweet-talk
52 Car wash gear
53 Shoot out
54 Snooze
55 Dark horse
58 Chinese calendar animal . . . or the key to this puzzle's theme

by Richard Silvestri

ACROSS

1 As a result
5 Handed (out)
10 Furry creature allied with Luke Skywalker and the Jedi knights
14 ___ of students
15 Deadly virus
16 Caster of spells
17 "My deepest apologies"
20 They go into overtime
21 Coffee orders with foamy tops
22 Actress Gardner and others
23 Deceptive talk, in slang
24 Soup ingredient from a pod
27 Worker's pay
28 Car navigational aid, for short
31 Had home cooking
32 Place for the words "Miss USA"
33 Margarita garnish
34 "No idea"
37 Actor's pursuit
38 Elvis ___ Presley
39 Emmy category
40 Opposite of NNW
41 Federal agent investigating taxes, informally
42 Pop maker in a nursery rhyme
43 Witches' ___
44 Sound gravelly
45 Nixed by Nixon, e.g.
48 Diversions . . . as hinted at by the ends of 17-, 34- and 52-Across
52 "Let's take that gamble"
54 And others: Abbr.
55 "Live Free ___" (New Hampshire motto)
56 Quadri- times two

57 "Star ___," biggest movie of 1977
58 Mexican dollars
59 Having everything in its place

DOWN

1 Cut and paste, say
2 Notes after do
3 Golden ___ Bridge
4 So-called universal donor blood
5 Skin-related
6 Theater awards
7 Arcing shots
8 90-degree turn
9 Vampire's undoing
10 Act with great feeling
11 Witch's blemish
12 Meanie
13 Frequently misplaced items

18 Large gully
19 Put money in the bank
23 Golden Fleece pursuer
24 Hideouts
25 Set of guiding beliefs
26 Author Zora ___ Hurston
27 Car with a big carrying capacity, informally
28 Lavish parties
29 Feather in one's cap
30 Super bargain
32 Scarecrow stuffing
33 Recycled metal
35 Try to impress in a conversation, say
36 "___ Fideles"
41 BlackBerry rival
42 Bathes
43 Plays tenpins

44 3:5, e.g.
45 It's afforded by a scenic overlook
46 Jazzy James
47 Peter the Great, for one
48 Highest degrees
49 They're often double-clicked
50 "Cómo ___ usted?"
51 32-card game
53 III in modern Rome

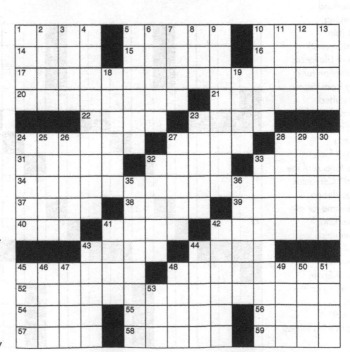

by Ian Livengood

ACROSS

1 Biblical strongman
7 Two cents' worth
10 Anti-D.U.I. org.
14 Climber's chopper
15 Sports org. with a tour
16 Skin care brand
17 Place to freshen up
19 Rock legend Hendrix
20 Display of grandeur
21 French-speaking African nation
22 Sport involving a chute
25 "Unforgettable" duettist Cole
31 Caen's river
32 Like clocks with hands
33 Tot's repeated questions
34 ID with two hyphens
37 Britney Spears's debut hit
40 Early Beatle Sutcliffe
41 Fully convinced
42 Joins
43 Hatcher with a Golden Globe
44 Disassembles, as a model airplane
45 Elite military group
49 On one's toes
50 Treatment with carbon dioxide
57 Prefix with star or bucks
58 Classic Miles Davis album . . . or a hint to the start of 17-, 22-, 37- or 45-Across
60 "___ Almighty" (Steve Carell movie)
61 Tattooist's supply
62 Characteristics
63 Bumper blemish
64 "Pick a card, ___ card"
65 Most achy

DOWN

1 Nurses, at the bar
2 Rent-___ (private security guard)
3 Whimper like a baby
4 One-named Nigerian songstress
5 Paul Bunyan's Babe and others
6 Dorky sort
7 Hybrid utensil
8 Way back when
9 Sweet potato
10 Desert with Joshua trees
11 Suspect's story
12 Friend of Pythias
13 Flopping at a comedy club
18 Ascended
21 Root used in some energy drinks
23 Start of a pirate's chant
24 Practice go-round
25 Catches, as a perp
26 Med school subj.
27 Forbidden-sounding perfume
28 Prince ___ Khan
29 Least strict
30 Pay no heed to
33 Subj. of a U.N. inspection, maybe
34 In ___ (as placed)
35 "Peter Pan" pirate
36 Loch ___ monster
38 Director Kazan
39 Up to, in ads
43 Iron-fisted boss
44 ___ car dealer
45 Identified
46 Tylenol alternative
47 Lacking meat, eggs, dairy, etc.
48 Like Abe Lincoln, physiologically
51 Goes bad
52 Early Jesse Jackson hairdo
53 Way up the slope
54 Netman Nastase
55 Contract loopholes, e.g.
56 Digs of twigs
58 Spectra automaker
59 B&B, e.g.

by Alex Boisvert

162

ACROSS

1 Painter's primer
6 Mex. miss
10 Big Apple neighborhood west of the East Village
14 English novelist Canetti who wrote "Crowds and Power"
15 Thing to look under
16 Privy to
17 Dear
20 Actress Thompson
21 When la Tour Eiffel lights up
22 Rock band with a lightning bolt in its logo
23 What children should be, so the saying goes
27 Electees
28 Mount in the Bible
29 "___ the last rose of summer" (start of a Thomas Moore poem)
30 ___ the day
31 Head out on the ranch?
33 Korean money
34 What Justin Timberlake's "bringin' back," in a song
35 Home of the Ivy League
39 Director Preminger
42 Palindromic exclamation
43 Many sand castle molds
47 Not con
48 Take to court
49 Carmaker whose name means "arise out of Asia"
51 ___ Mustard
52 It's a relief in Athens
56 Princess with a blaster
57 "That's big news, dude!"
58 Sentence segment: Abbr.
59 Likely to change everything
62 Baseball's Moises
63 Like lemonade sans sugar
64 Oscar-winning "Tootsie" actress
65 Cold war news source
66 Canine command
67 Comedian Wanda

DOWN

1 Book that spans 2,369 years
2 Gold or silver, but not bronze
3 Like the cats in "Lady and the Tramp"
4 Clear kitchen wrap
5 Sunrise direction in Berlin
6 Hoot and holler
7 1998 De Niro film
8 In direct competition
9 Google moneymakers
10 Lisa Simpson, to Patty or Selma
11 How one might go bungee jumping
12 Receptacle for Voldemort's soul in Harry Potter
13 Que. neighbor
18 Burden
19 Derisive laughs
24 Prefix with -meter
25 Fey of "30 Rock"
26 Susan of "L.A. Law"
32 Musician Brian
33 ". . . that's ___!"
34 Where to catch a bullet?: Abbr.
36 Player/preyer
37 "And after that?"
38 Exchange jabs or gibes
39 Right to left, e.g.: Abbr.
40 Light refrain
41 Stars in a ring
44 Place to see a flying camel
45 Drop down one's throat?
46 Big busting tools
48 Persian monarch
49 Full of difficulties
50 "___ first you . . ."
53 "___ Andronicus"
54 John who wrote "Appointment in Samarra"
55 Start of an appeal
59 Drop down one's throat
60 Urban grid: Abbr.
61 Chi-town trains

by Jonah Kagan

ACROSS

1 Noisy bird
6 "___ the night before . . ."
10 Exhilaration
14 Ninth planet no more
15 Days of King Arthur's Round Table, e.g.
16 Any brother in "Animal Crackers"
17 Broadway lyricist/composer who wrote "I Can Get It for You Wholesale"
19 Amo, amas, ___
20 Opposite of melted
21 Make ___ for (advocate)
22 California wine county
26 Whoop
28 Buddhist sect
29 Gas log fuel
31 Certify (to)
33 Virginia-born Pulitzer Prize novelist of 1942
36 Actress Cannon
37 Three ___ match
38 "Anybody home? . . . home? . . . home? . . ."
42 "God Bless America" composer
47 Drink that might come with a mint leaf
50 Japanese site of the 1972 Winter Olympics
51 Lon ___ of Cambodia
52 Greek portico
55 "You said it, ___!"
56 Elite roster
58 Cook, as steaks in an oven
60 Indy 500, e.g.
61 "The Call of the Wild" author
66 Chief Norse god
67 The "A" in U.S.A.: Abbr.
68 Seeing Eye dog, e.g.
69 Light bulb unit
70 Nothing, in Juárez
71 Pegasus, e.g.

DOWN

1 Speedometer reading : Abbr.
2 ___ carte
3 Dog prone to biting
4 From ___ Z
5 One who changes form during a full moon
6 Beginner
7 Mentally unclear
8 French military force
9 Go out with
10 Auto financing inits.
11 Childbirth training method
12 Undoes pencil marks
13 Scope
18 Sturm und ___
21 Kind of sax
22 Hurried
23 Paris suburb
24 Theme song of bandleader Vincent Lopez
25 Gift-giver's urging
27 Fall behind
30 "The Time Machine" people
32 Dweebs
34 The Beach Boys' "Barbara ___"
35 Is low around the waist, as pants
39 Blood circulation problem
40 Put on the payroll
41 ___ off (light switch options)
43 Remainder
44 Industrial container
45 Pesto seasoning
46 Ends of some novels
47 Lined up
48 Piña ___
49 Bring out
53 First president born in Hawaii
54 Followed a curved path
57 E-mail folder
59 Gumbo pod
61 First mo.
62 Hickory ___
63 What immortals never do
64 Shelley's "___ to the West Wind"
65 ___ Flanders of "The Simpsons"

by Randy Sowell

164

ACROSS

1 "What did Delaware?" "I don't know, but ___" (old joke)
7 "I ___ bored!"
11 Score components: Abbr.
14 Decorate flamboyantly, in slang
15 Simon ___
16 Noisy fight
17 King who was the son of Pepin the Short
19 "___ Rocker" (Springsteen song)
20 Electron's path
21 River that ends at Cairo
22 Cinematographer Nykvist
23 Post-copyright status
26 Sister of Snow White
29 Smack hard
30 Intuition, maybe: Abbr.
31 Darkens
34 Big name in vacuums
37 La Choy product
41 Russian country house
42 F.B.I. guys
43 Ming of the N.B.A.
44 Puts away plates
46 French carmaker
49 Easternmost U.S. capital
53 Graph paper pattern
54 Food thickener
55 For face value
59 Cabinet dept. overseeing farm interests
60 Fancy equine coif
62 No. on a calling card
63 Zealous
64 Not polished
65 Pothook shape
66 Till compartment
67 Like Dracula

DOWN

1 Classic record label for the Bee Gees and Cream
2 Bert who played a cowardly lion
3 Emirate dweller
4 Indicator of rank
5 Civilization, to Freud
6 Distant cousin of humans
7 Sapporo competitor
8 ___ Johnson
9 Church councils
10 Sugar suffix
11 Philip Marlowe or Sam Spade
12 Actress Marisa
13 Ex-Steeler Lynn
18 Crown ___
22 Unctuous flattery
24 "Venerable" monk
25 "Geez! That stings!"
26 Shipping dept. stamp
27 Dept. of Labor arm
28 Scary, Baby, Ginger, Posh and Sporty
32 Year McKinley was elected to a second term
33 First American in space
35 "Gotta go!"
36 Muscle malady
38 Hot: Fr.
39 Kit ___ (candy bars)
40 "Dedicated to the ___ Love"
45 Excessively fast
47 Japanese eel and rice dish
48 Lose patience and then some
49 Ornamental quartz
50 Earnestly recommends
51 "To repeat . . ."
52 Dust busters
56 Peel
57 Jug handle, in archaeology
58 Stalk in a marsh
60 Face the pitcher
61 Old French coin

by Paula Gamache

ACROSS

1 Resell quickly, as a house
5 No longer insure
9 Native to
13 Passed-down stories
14 Voodoo accessories
16 Flintstones' pet
17 Scary figure
18 Conclude
19 Med school subj.
20 Garden intruders
22 Denver's ___ University
24 Command to Rex
25 Ones flying in formation
27 Driveway applications
29 Rigel or Spica
32 Thérèse, for one: Abbr.
33 Pioneer in instant messaging
34 Protection: Var.
36 Himalayan legends
40 Easy way of pulling in . . . and a hint to the six circled words
44 2005 documentary subtitled "The Smartest Guys in the Room"
45 Orderly
46 Word for word?
47 U.S. Dept. of Justice raiders
49 Items for urban dog-walkers
52 Toga go-withs
56 Pound and others
57 "What ___ the chances?"
58 Day spa facial procedures
60 "___ the Sheriff" (Eric Clapton hit)
63 Watch from a hidden position
65 Half of a giant 1999 merger
67 ___-shanter

68 International shoe company
69 Skit collection
70 Composer Khachaturian
71 Lucy's love
72 Counterparts of dahs
73 Belgrade native

DOWN

1 Rap component, to a rapper
2 Special seating area
3 Asymmetric
4 River with its source in the Appalachians
5 Onetime White House monogram
6 Liberal pundit with a conservative father
7 Shoppe modifier
8 Cord ends
9 Rx overseer
10 Dishwasher cycle
11 Broadcasting
12 Big name in applesauce
15 Black and white Mad magazine figures
21 Paris possessive
23 Woodland reveler of myth
26 British submachine gun
28 Welsh national emblem
29 Wished
30 Pork cut
31 Stirs up
35 Visits la-la land
37 Vacation plan
38 "___ out?" (question to a pet)
39 Some cops: Abbr.
41 Prod
42 Ready for use
43 One-volume encyclopedia range
48 Topps competitor
50 ". . . ___ quit!"
51 Olive Garden dishes
52 Garden dish
53 As ___ (usually)
54 Willy Wonka Candy Company brand
55 Determined the gender of
59 M years before the Battle of Hastings
61 Epps or Sharif
62 Mausoleum
64 Decorative pond fish
66 Super ___ (1980s–'90s game console)

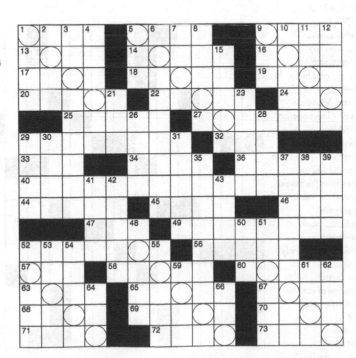

by Peter A. Collins

ACROSS

1 Navajo's neighbor in Arizona
5 Edinburgh native
9 Defect
13 Racetrack shapes
15 Many millennia
16 Parks who received the Presidential Medal of Freedom
17 Tendon
18 Common advice to travelers
20 Terminus
21 Seed with a licoricelike flavor
23 Beginning
24 Race that finishes in a tie
26 Warm embrace
27 Worms, to a fisherman
28 Early Fords that "put America on wheels"
32 Say "C-A-T" or "D-O-G," e.g.
34 Boathouse gear
36 "___ don't say!"
37 Doing something risky . . . or a hint to the last words of 18-, 24-, 49- and 58-Across
41 Avis or Alamo offering
42 Misfortunes
43 Uncles' mates
44 Being risked, as in a bet
47 Cassini of fashion
48 Cubes from the freezer
49 Bygone love interest
53 Digging tool
56 Weak-___ (easily intimidated)
57 Candlemaking supply
58 "Omigosh!"
60 Oven brand
62 Language of Pakistan
63 What Yale became in 1969
64 Hayseed
65 Vault (over)
66 "The ___ the limit"
67 Crème de la crème

DOWN

1 Cleaned with water, as a sidewalk
2 Sheeplike
3 Adorable zoo critters from China
4 Suffix with percent
5 Tone of many old photos
6 Where a hurricane makes landfall
7 ___ in a blue moon
8 "For shame!"
9 Outer edge
10 Hearth contents
11 U.S. tennis legend on a 37¢. stamp
12 The "W" of kWh
14 Widespread language of East Africa
19 Earsplitting
22 Ping-Pong table divider

25 Tyne of "Cagney & Lacey"
26 Party giver
28 CT scan alternatives
29 Suffering from insomnia
30 Wrong that's adjudicated in court
31 Takes to court
32 Org. for cat and dog lovers
33 Builder's map
34 Look at lustfully
35 Hole-making tool
38 Athletics brand with a swoosh
39 9:00 a.m. to 12:30 p.m., say, for a worker
40 Gasoline or peat
45 Neaten
46 Unreturned tennis serves
47 Keats's "___ to Psyche"
49 Not sharp or flat

50 Textile city of north-central England
51 Grooms comb them
52 Praise mightily
53 Place for a bar mitzvah service
54 Skin opening
55 Alan of "M*A*S*H"
56 Nutcase
59 Introducers of a show's acts, e.g.
61 "The Godfather" crowd, with "the"

by Lynn Lempel

ACROSS

1 Tiny
7 End of a Shakespeare play
11 MP3 holders
14 Artist Diego
15 One who talks only about himself, say
16 Egg layer
17 Genesis duo
19 Historical time
20 Fish-fowl connector
21 It's found on a nightstand
23 ___-Wan with the Force
26 Chum
28 "Enough!"
29 Certain mustache shape
33 Not great, but not awful either
34 TV part
35 Computer capacity, informally
38 Means of staying toasty at night
43 Yankee nickname starting in 2004
44 Control, as expenses
46 Treated, as a sprained ankle
50 American symbol
52 "Let's play!"
55 Major coll. fraternity
56 Sunburned
57 Made possible
59 "___ moment!" ("Don't rush me!")
61 French pronoun
62 Street weapon . . . or a hint to the circled letters in this puzzle
68 Under the weather
69 Bond girl Kurylenko
70 Spotted feline
71 Profs.' helpers
72 Wall Street inits.
73 Darcy's Pemberley, e.g., in "Pride and Prejudice"

DOWN

1 Parabola, e.g.
2 ___ Maria
3 Prefix with duct
4 Target audience of Details magazine
5 Country with a Guardian Council
6 One use of a Swiss Army knife
7 Lawyers' org.
8 Ty with batting titles
9 Sequoias, e.g.
10 Open grassland
11 Penny-pincher, slangily
12 Skin layer
13 Wake with a start
18 Blah
22 ___ Lonely Boys (rock band)
23 Cries of surprise
24 "The Well-Tempered Clavier" composer
25 Memo starter
27 Greek L's
30 Org. monitoring narcotics smuggling
31 "___ thousand flowers bloom"
32 Bible study: Abbr.
36 Tool you can lean on
37 Snick's partner
39 When you entered this world: Abbr.
40 Seoul-based automaker
41 Hwy. planner
42 10-point Q, e.g.
45 Actor Beatty
46 "That's clear"
47 Kind of oil
48 Contacts via the Net
49 Girl with a coming-out party
51 Secular
53 Johnny who used to cry "Come on down!"
54 As of late
58 Shovels
60 Rudimentary education
63 ___ Bo
64 Redo, in tennis
65 ___ mode
66 Half of a colon
67 Summer on the Seine

by Oliver Hill

ACROSS

1 Appetite arouser
6 Show appreciation, in a way
10 Busyness
13 Reporting to
14 "Gladiator" setting
15 Groucho's cigar, e.g.
16 Attila, for one?
18 First-rate stand-up comic
19 Bird sounds
20 Neck and neck
21 Is tiresome
22 How some things are set
24 When said three times, a dance
25 Cowardly boxer?
31 Voice opposition
35 Food with lots of fiber
36 North Carolina's ___ University
37 Jefferson's religious belief
39 "L' ___ c'est moi"
40 Like a photon
42 Herders' tools
43 Where to find a genie?
46 Colony worker
47 Polite reply that may be accompanied by eye-rolling
52 The Destroyer, in Hinduism
55 Relative of Bowser
57 Concerning
58 Trek
59 Holders of some pipe joints?
61 Start the bidding
62 Middling
63 Nimbi
64 Carry-on checkers: Abbr.
65 Bit of laughter
66 Teapot part . . . or a two-word hint to 16-, 25-, 43- and 59-Across

DOWN

1 Early counters
2 Military drone's job, for short
3 Spreads in bars
4 Like towelettes, typically
5 Barley bristle
6 Lily-livered
7 Prospector's strike
8 Word of agreement
9 A pop
10 "Habanera" from "Carmen" is one
11 "Let's Make a Deal" choice
12 Stops waffling
15 Flock leader
17 Caesar's "I came"
21 Taylor or Tyler
23 Norris Trophy winner for eight consecutive years

24 One to hang with
26 Miller's need
27 N.Y.S.E. listings
28 Green Hornet's sidekick
29 "Yikes!"
30 Pulls in
31 Prefix with god
32 Zip
33 Kind of votes a candidate wants
34 Stubbly
37 Cardholder's woe
38 That, in Toledo
41 ___ the Hyena of "Li'l Abner"
42 Foot, to a zoologist
44 Popular bathroom cleaner
45 First pope with the title "the Great"
48 Fixed fashionably

49 Summer month in South America
50 Pianist Claudio
51 Change, as an alarm
52 It may precede a chaser
53 They may swivel
54 Self-assembly retail chain
55 Ice sheet
56 She said "Play it, Sam"
59 "I know what you're thinking" skill
60 "If I Ruled the World" rapper

by Andrea Carla Michaels and Peter L. Stein

ACROSS

1 Vision that isn't real
6 Areas of urban decay
11 Country singer Ritter
14 Ahead of time
15 Vietnam's capital
16 Vietnam ___
17 A-team
19 Provision for old age, in brief
20 Footballers' measures: Abbr.
21 Pay attention to
22 Excellent, in slang
24 Abruptly dump, as a lover
25 Curly-haired dogs
26 Composer's work for a film
30 Caribbean resort island
31 "Sesame Street" airer
32 Realtor's favorite sign
36 Five-digit postal number, informally
37 Slow-moving primates
41 ___ de Janeiro
42 Canadian gas brand
44 Former Mideast inits.
45 "Come on!" and "Go!"
47 Portuguese, for Brazilians, e.g.
51 Waltz composer
54 Love god
55 Fireplace floor
56 Spew
57 Drunk's road offense, for short
60 "Star Trek" rank: Abbr.
61 Really steamed . . . or what the ends of 17-, 26- and 47-Across are?
64 Conk
65 Map close-up
66 "Boléro" composer
67 "___ questions?"

68 Show just a little bit of leg, say
69 Winding

DOWN

1 Go against, as someone's will
2 Antibug spray
3 Makes a boo-boo
4 Gore and Green
5 Like dragons and centaurs
6 Yiddish for "small town"
7 Cooking fat
8 Prefix with cycle
9 Kipling's Rikki-Tikki-Tavi, for one
10 Milan mister
11 Band majorette's move
12 Country star Steve
13 Pictures at a dentist's

18 Actress Ward
23 Fruity drinks
24 Triangular sail
25 Banned pollutants, briefly
26 Labyrinth
27 Literary Leon
28 Dines
29 Church feature seen from a distance
33 Not a copy: Abbr.
34 In ___ of (replacing)
35 One teaspoonful or two caplets, maybe
38 Surpass
39 Stadium cheers
40 Relatives of mopeds
43 "The Rubáiyát" poet ___ Khayyám
46 E.R. or O.R. workers
48 Barbie doll purchase
49 What a couch potato probably holds

50 Oakland paper, informally
51 Biblical queendom
52 It's inserted in a mortise
53 Hoarse
56 Hot times on the Riviera
57 One who might receive roses at the end of a performance
58 Timespan for The Economist
59 How thumbs are twiddled
62 Airport worker's org.
63 Light brown

by Susan Gelfand

ACROSS

1 Dudley Do-Right's org.
5 Banjo sound
10 Video recorders, briefly
14 Anticipatory cry
15 Tend to, as plants
16 "So true!"
17 Disk-shaped sea creature
19 Bit of dialogue
20 Oral hesitations
21 Bruins' sch.
22 High-I.Q. crew
23 Actress Carrere
24 Shift blame to another
27 More posh
29 Approx. takeoff hour
30 Bashful
31 Routing abbr.
32 Immeasurably vast
35 Chowder ingredient
40 Tater Tots brand
41 Santa ___ (hot California winds)
43 Exclamation in Berlin
46 Leatherworker's tool
47 Current unit
49 Hit that just clears the infield
53 Short smoke?
54 Turkish money
55 Jean who wrote "The Clan of the Cave Bear"
56 Hydroelectric project
57 "He loves," in Latin
58 Auto-racing designation
61 "Scrubs" actor Braff
62 Not abridged
63 Baseball great Musial
64 Ones who've been through divorce court
65 Horseshoers' tools
66 Pain in the neck

DOWN

1 Stone discovery site
2 "Ben-Hur" racers
3 Global agricultural company
4 Advanced deg.
5 Kind of garage
6 Masons' creations
7 Muscular Charles
8 Union with 3+ million members, in brief
9 Junkyard dog's greeting
10 Novelist Carr
11 Pretty good grade
12 Stand-up guy
13 Deceitful
18 Hornswoggle
22 Battlefield doc
25 Rival of Edison
26 WWW code
28 "For more ___ . . ."
32 Hot dog topper
33 U.K. lexicon
34 Sound of thunder
36 Golf hazards
37 Wields a needle
38 Short reminiscence
39 ___ Trench (deepest point on Earth's surface)
42 Orange part, e.g.
43 In flames
44 Part of a book where you're unlikely to stop
45 Poet who originated the phrase "harmony in discord"
47 Indigenous Alaskans
48 Pell-___
50 Courtroom rituals
51 Feds who make busts
52 Ruin, informally
58 Stole material
59 "Not ___ bet!"
60 African slitherer

by Doug Peterson

ACROSS

1 With 69-Across, 1930s-'50s bandleader
5 Brand name in the kitchen
10 Suit to ___
14 Bellicose deity
15 One who's "toast"
16 Comparison word
17 Japan, to the U.S., once
19 Sleek, in car talk
20 1966 Mary Martin musical
21 Fleet elite
23 Ex-lib, maybe
24 "I'm ___!" ("Can do!")
25 Views that reality is a unitary whole
29 ___ Martin (cognac brand)
32 Ancient Greek sculptor of athletes
36 "Golly!"
37 Hogwash
39 Eagle's claw
41 Place for une île
42 Brickyard 400 entrant
43 Use weasel words
44 All there
46 Makes a cat's-paw of
47 Sizzling sound
48 "Baby Baby" singer, 1991
51 Sushi-rolling accessories
53 Good-humored
58 Carbon 14 and uranium 235
62 Subtitle of 1978's "Damien"
63 Shark on some menus
64 1976 Eric Carmen hit
66 Pulitzer-winning author Robert ___ Butler
67 Homeric sorceress
68 Word with family or fruit
69 See 1-Across

70 Made bearable
71 Criteria: Abbr.

DOWN

1 Oral vaccine developer
2 Take for ___ (hoodwink)
3 Copycat's cry
4 Old Connecticut whaling town
5 Science for farmers
6 See 50-Down
7 Wintour of fashion
8 More than desire
9 One with yellow ribbons, maybe
10 Game maker since 1972
11 Courtroom antics, e.g.
12 Sandwich man?
13 Fourth book of the Book of Mormon

18 Esau's descendants' land
22 Brass or woodwind: Abbr.
26 Chinese menu notation
27 Start of a rumor report
28 Ancient city that lent its name to a fig
30 Tool for a duel
31 Actor Mike
32 That you should feed a cold and starve a fever, and others
33 Explorer John and actress Charlotte
34 Snowy peak of song
35 Creamy beverage
38 Former German president Johannes
40 "Cool!"
45 Ate up, so to speak

49 Popular social networking site, and this puzzle's theme
50 With 6-Down, 1994 Olympic gold medalist in downhill skiing
52 Thing to do on Yom Kippur
54 Endows (with)
55 Hard to combine, chemically
56 Was indisposed
57 Thomas Hardy's "___ Little Ironies"
58 "Don't worry about me"
59 Part of una casa
60 London Magazine essayist
61 Some cameras, for short
65 Pre-A.D.

by Dan Schoenholz

172

ACROSS

1. 2006 boorish film character from Kazakhstan
6. Castle-defending ditches
11. David Letterman's network
14. Smells
15. Suffer ignominious defeat, in slang
16. Feedbag tidbit
17. Second- or third-string player
19. Actress Hagen
20. Cyclotron particles
21. Interest-grabbing
23. "Apologies"
27. "As old as the hills" and others
28. What wheels do on an axis
29. Talk to flirtatiously
30. Screwballs
31. "God ___ America"
32. Photo ___ (when pictures may be taken)
35. Son of Seth
36. Audio censor's sound
37. Molecule component
38. Broadband connection inits.
39. Lewis's partner in an expedition
40. Stiller and ___ (comedy duo)
41. One-horse town
43. Explorer Hernando
44. One showing diners to their tables
46. Indian baby on a back
47. Spider's cocoon, e.g.
48. Suspect, to a cop
49. "Norma ___"
50. Presider at a meeting
56. Stock debut, for short
57. Newsstand
58. Decorative fabric
59. Highest non-face card
60. Spread, as the legs
61. Assail

DOWN

1. Dylan or Dole
2. Praiseful poem
3. Director Howard
4. Lob's path
5. Gift shop apparel
6. George who was the first president of the A.F.L.-C.I.O.
7. Items fitting in rowlocks
8. Place to enter a PIN
9. Man's jewelry item
10. Narrow passageways
11. Boob tube lover
12. Wash oneself
13. Remains
18. Had on
22. Fort Worth sch.
23. Annoyed
24. Time periods lasting about 29½ days
25. Police informant
26. Acorn producers
27. Where rouge goes
29. Office worker
31. Lacking individuality
33. Skin openings
34. Some air pollution
36. Kind of stock
37. Prefix with dynamic
39. Music store fixtures
40. Tots
42. Tie-breaking play periods: Abbr.
43. Complain
44. ___ badge
45. Open-mouthed
46. Cheerful
48. Leaning Tower site
51. Yahoo! competitor
52. ___ v. Wade
53. Use the start of 17- or 50-Across or 11- or 25-Down?
54. Suffix with schnozz
55. What 51-Down connects to, with "the"

by Randy Sowell

ACROSS

1 Defeat, barely
5 Word on a bar worker's jar
9 Gem
14 Pasta or potato, for short
15 Savoie sweetheart
16 Still in the game
17 Brag
18 Beekeeper played by Peter Fonda
19 Recurring melody
20 Tiger and Elin Woods's 37-Across order?
23 Super, slangily
24 Sign on a locked lavatory
25 Vast amounts
27 It might start "E FP TOZ LPED"
30 Party that's a wow
31 Posh
32 One pitied by Mr. T
33 Doo-___ music
36 Actor's rep: Abbr.
37 Cocktail called "the elixir of quietude" by 4-Down
40 1950s campaign nickname
41 ___ 'easter
42 Apple originally marketed to schools
43 New car sticker fig.
44 Figure of Greek myth with a statue at Rockefeller Center
46 1889 statehood achievers, with "the"
49 Ringtoss game
51 A marathon has about 26 of these
52 Runnin' Rebels' sch.
53 Paula Abdul's 37-Across order?
58 "Later, amigo!"
60 French cleric
61 Foot: Prefix
62 It's not good to run one
63 Potter's oven
64 Mineral in hemoglobin
65 The hapless Corleone
66 Things that modest people lack
67 "Peter Pan" fairy, for short

DOWN

1 Shoe company founded in Denmark
2 "Phooey!"
3 Small cavern, in poetry
4 "The Elements of Style" updater
5 Sign after Aries
6 "Please help me with directions!"
7 Jigsaw puzzle element
8 Be "it," in a game
9 Wing it, musically
10 Skips the dos before the I do's?
11 O. Henry's 37-Across order?
12 Aquafina rival
13 Some turns and boxing punches
21 Opposite WSW
22 Wise old Athenian
26 City known as Colombia's sports capital
27 Pizazz
28 "Car Talk" dubbed it "the worst car of the millennium"
29 Popeye's 37-Across order?
30 Avril Lavigne's "Sk8er ___"
32 Consumer protection agcy.
34 Vegetable in Cajun cuisine
35 Livens, with "up"
37 Cheesy sandwich
38 Collect
39 Dorm figures, for short
43 Frenzied place at a rock club
45 Recorded for later viewing
46 Cisco Kid's horse
47 "The X-Files" figures
48 Big beer buy
49 Hearty drink
50 Hypnotized or anesthetized
51 Head honcho
54 Help oneself to
55 Garr of "Tootsie"
56 Noodles with tempura
57 Medium-rare steak color
59 B'way success sign

by Keith Talon

174

ACROSS
1 Specialty
6 1970s sitcom that included Carlton the Doorman
11 "___ you one"
15 "___ Majesty's Secret Service"
16 Hatch in the Senate
17 Country music pioneer Ernest
18 Boarding place?
19 Test group?
20 Attempt
21 Short trip
22 Civil War inits.
24 Some footnotes, for short
26 Person on your bad side?
29 Cannoli ingredient
32 Contradict
33 Flower of the buttercup family
35 Gmail alternative
36 Passeport info
38 "Mazel ___!"
39 Green gem source
41 Some surprises . . . and what you'll find in the circled areas of this puzzle
45 Israel's Dayan
46 ___ Miss
47 Superscript number in math: Abbr.
48 More than -er
49 Woman in Sartre's "No Exit"
52 Number two: Abbr.
56 Doughnuts are fried in it
58 Short piano piece
60 Shoe brand named for an antelope
62 Former N.B.A. star Unseld
63 Hip-hop's ___ -A- Fella Records
64 It's better than ace-high

66 Tchaikovsky's black swan
68 Madison Sq. Garden player
70 Woodworking tool
71 Branch gripper
72 Regular's request, with "the"
73 Goes on and on
74 Religious assembly
75 Word-processing command

DOWN
1 Took the cake, perhaps
2 Smitten
3 "Fantaisie" composer
4 In the know, old-style
5 Standing
6 1915 Literature Nobelist ___ Rolland
7 Realm ended by Napoleon: Abbr.
8 "Yes ___?"
9 Confute

10 Tylenol competitor
11 "___ die for"
12 Defeat in a don't-blink contest
13 Tate and Bowe were once champions of it: Abbr.
14 Decline
23 Person often pictured with crossed legs
25 Where trays may be stacked
27 "Dune" director David
28 Irritate
30 Santa's sleighful
31 "Is that ___?"
34 Bris parties
37 Michael of "Caddyshack"
40 American in Paris, perhaps
41 Singer Feliciano
42 What a record may have
43 "Another time, perhaps"

44 Designer Geoffrey
45 Kind of school
50 Cousins of clogs
51 Subwoofer's zone
53 Bright spot in Canis Major
54 Back-country winter transport
55 Take on
57 They did it
59 Invite to one's penthouse, say
61 Oven
64 Meddle
65 Org. with a sign at many motels
67 Head of Buckingham Palace?
69 Secretive org.

by Pete Muller

ACROSS

1 Listings in a dr.'s calendar
6 Number of Muses
10 Best guesses: Abbr.
14 Nary ___ (no one)
15 Grandson of Adam
16 March Madness org.
17 Parting words from the Everly Brothers
19 Unrestrained revelry
20 "Clean up your ___!"
21 "___ Baba and the 40 Thieves"
22 "___ me, Father" (confessional phrase)
23 Parting words from the Lone Ranger
28 Card game for two
29 "Telephone Line" rock grp.
30 Diminutive suffix
31 ___-Coburg-Gotha, former British royal house
32 Heavenly body
33 Gorillas
34 Parting words from the Terminator
38 Degs. for corporate types
41 ___ Lingus
42 Hula dancers wiggle them
45 Building wing
46 Suffix with labyrinth
47 Reply to "Am not!"
49 Parting words from the von Trapps
52 Laughs
53 Forbid
54 Bowling stat.
56 Western Indian tribe
57 Parting words from Donald Trump
61 Halliwell of the Spice Girls
62 Claudia ___ Taylor (Lady Bird Johnson)
63 Director Kurosawa
64 Fruity drinks
65 Dennis the Menace, for one
66 Not tidy

DOWN

1 Four-line rhyme scheme
2 Human spirits
3 Horace's "Ars ___"
4 Bath site
5 Foxy
6 Nervous ___
7 How French fries are fried
8 Oct. follower
9 Language suffix
10 W.W. II bomber ___ Gay
11 Homer Simpson type
12 Common house event before moving
13 Agrees
18 Sunrise direction
22 Pal
24 Vertical line on a graph
25 Hershiser on the mound
26 Subject follower
27 Isle of exile
32 "___ the ramparts . . ."
33 "Go fly ___!"
35 Fritz who directed "Metropolis"
36 Hamburger meat
37 "___ your food" (mother's admonition)
38 Yiddish for "crazy"
39 Like a stomach after an all-you-can-eat buffet
40 Fully focused and attentive
43 North Star
44 Crossword doers
46 ___ and outs
47 Mount where Noah landed
48 Artist Magritte
50 Place for camels to water
51 Touches
55 "Hello" Down Under
57 Talk noisily
58 Bullfight cheer
59 Clan: Abbr.
60 '50s prez

by Jay Kaskel

ACROSS

1 You might fix one yourself at a bar
6 Abbr. after a lawyer's name
9 Blog additions
14 Dance partner for Fred
15 Little, in Lille
16 "99 and 44/100% pure" soap
17 Place for knickknacks
18 "What ___ to do?"
19 Link
20 Thief in a western
23 Rm. coolers
24 ___ -de-sac
25 Suffix with Orwell
26 Bard's "before"
29 Some metal frames
32 "Dancing Queen" group
35 Penn, e.g.: Abbr.
36 They're red or blue, on some maps
37 Emergency strategy
39 N.L. cap letters
41 "All About ___," 2009 Sandra Bullock bomb
42 Main lines
44 Canon camera line
46 "___ Tu" (1974 hit)
47 Parliamentary procedure guide, familiarly
50 Outcomes of some QB sneaks
51 Bacon runoff
52 Suffix with penta-
53 ___ few rounds (spar)
56 Unclear outcome . . . or what can be found literally in 20-, 29- and 47-Across
59 Hip-hopper's headgear
62 Battery for many penlights
63 Modular elements
64 PayPal money, e.g.
65 Chain part: Abbr.
66 Little Munster
67 SALT subject
68 To date
69 Accomplish, biblically

DOWN

1 The younger Obama girl
2 Specially formed, as a committee
3 Lascivious looks
4 Tell- ___ (some bios)
5 Reason for a merchandise return
6 Adornments on officers' shoulders
7 Coll. terms
8 "Knock that off!"
9 Pesto ingredients
10 In the strike zone
11 Beantown or Chi-Town team
12 Play about Capote
13 Part of CBS: Abbr.
21 They intersect in Montréal
22 TV husband of Phyllis
26 Perfumery compound
27 Christopher of "Somewhere in Time"
28 Slalom paths
29 "À votre ___!"
30 "I'm outta here!"
31 Fills to the gills
32 In pieces
33 Red Cross supply
34 Verbal digs
38 A bouncer might break one up
40 TV boss of Mary Richards
43 Record label for Booker T. & the M.G.'s
45 Gin flavoring
48 Like a Turkish bath
49 Came next
53 Go like a flying squirrel
54 Super Bowl XXV M.V.P. ___ Anderson
55 Item in the plus column
56 Communion service
57 See socially
58 "Go back," on an edit menu
59 TV room
60 World Food Day mo.
61 "Norma ___"

by Peter A. Collins

ACROSS

1 Intimidate
6 Group of eight
11 Jazz style
14 Mary of "The Maltese Falcon," 1941
15 Rose ___, group with the 1977 #1 hit "Car Wash"
16 Bibliophile's suffix
17 2010 Guinness world record at 1,689 lbs.
20 "Well, ___-di-dah!"
21 Cybermemo
22 Put up
23 Yoga posture
24 Stockbrokers' orders
25 1975 Pulitzer-winning critic
28 Successor to Frist as Senate majority leader
29 2010 Guinness world record at 11 ft. 6 in.
36 Director Lee
37 Time on end
38 Shake a leg
39 2010 Guinness world record at 72 lbs. 9 oz.
44 Court legend
45 Stirs up
46 Mario Puzo best seller
49 Actor Lloyd
52 Restaurant reading
53 Yard menaces
54 Staff's partner
57 2010 Guinness world record at 115 ft.
60 Roxy Music co-founder
61 Mr. who squints
62 Stand out
63 Part of A.A.R.P.: Abbr.
64 A whole bunch
65 "Navy Blue" singer Renay

DOWN

1 Willy Wonka's creator
2 Where whalers go
3 Home of the city Bountiful
4 Topaz mo.
5 Adriatic port
6 Director Welles
7 Terra ___
8 Font contents
9 Prefix with puncture
10 Class clown's "reward," often
11 Lay in the hot sun
12 Standing by
13 What suspenders suspend
18 Disney deer
19 Gucci rival
23 1978 World Cup winner: Abbr.
24 "The Gondoliers" girl
25 Mideast carrier
26 ___ fides
27 Mech. expert
28 Mysterious character
30 "I Am . . . ___ Fierce," #1 Beyoncé album
31 Place for un béret
32 May honoree
33 Indian spiced tea
34 Challenge for Jack and Jill
35 Snaky swimmers
40 Country crooner Brooks
41 Values
42 Seriously bad-mouthed
43 "___ appétit!"
46 Orangish yellow
47 Northern terminus of U.S. 1
48 Grain disease
49 At all, in dialect
50 Mishmashes
51 Part of an itinerary
53 Homeowner's debt: Abbr.
54 Costa ___
55 It's often operated with a dial
56 Strike out
58 Erie Canal mule
59 511, to Caesar

by Robert A. Doll

ACROSS

1 Cow's offspring
5 U.C.L.A. player
10 Bank no.
14 Margarine
15 Copy, for short
16 What's seen in "Saw"
17 Football alignment named for its shape
19 "___ a Song Go Out of My Heart"
20 Impertinent
21 Bed-and-breakfast
22 Muslim's God
23 Elvis ___ Presley
25 Drug that's a downer
26 Top choice
31 Sign in a boarding-house window
32 "Yes, captain!"
33 Good "Wheel of Fortune" purchase for STRING BIKINI
34 Drano ingredient
35 Undeveloped
38 Heckle or Jeckle of cartoons
42 Lay waste to
45 "Light" dessert?
48 Went nuts
49 School near Windsor Castle
50 11th-century conqueror of Valencia
51 Number on a golf hole
53 Starbucks size that's Italian for "twenty"
57 Fruity drinks
58 Sci-fi hero in the 25th century
60 Circus shelter
61 Stan's pal in old films
62 Puccini's "Nessun dorma," for one
63 Captain Hook's henchman
64 To the point, ironically
65 Classic theater name

DOWN

1 Foldable beds
2 ___ Romeo (Italian car)
3 Ones born before Virgos
4 Abandon
5 Item under a blouse
6 Color again, as the hair
7 Go ___ smoke
8 Do a post-washing chore
9 Oui's opposite
10 Nimbleness
11 Property securing a loan
12 Manufacture
13 Restraining cord
18 Ancient Athenian sculptor
22 Samoan capital
24 Frequent, in poetry
25 Cheer for a bullfighter
26 School org.
27 Charged particle
28 It might be marked off with police tape
29 Rutherford B. ___
30 Ogle
34 Big fib
36 Biographical datum
37 Itsy-bitsy
39 Skilled entertainer
40 Where to enter this puzzle's answers
41 Indy 500 service area
42 Same old same old
43 From the beginning: Lat.
44 The "sour" in sweet-and-sour
45 Shoe grippers
46 Poker variety
47 Sleeveless jacket
51 Word on a door handle
52 Org. protecting individual rights
54 Literary Wolfe
55 "___ are for kids" (ad slogan)
56 "___, old chap!"
58 Go up and down, as in the water
59 On Social Security: Abbr.

by Bob Johnson

ACROSS

1 Deep-six
5 Crosswise, on deck
10 Movie lot sights
14 "Beat it!"
15 Martini's partner in wine
16 Turkish title of old
17 Not stuffy
18 Pesky swarm
19 H.S. math class
20 Keypad forerunner
22 Safecracker
23 They, in Thiers
24 Coarse, as humor
26 Knock down in rank
30 Term of address from a hat-tipper
32 Seat of Marion County, Fla.
33 Ghana, once
38 Company that makes Lincoln and Mercury
39 Afternoon fare . . . or a hint to the ends of 20-, 33-, 41- and 52-Across
40 Eliciting a "So what?"
41 Body suit shade, perhaps
43 Community of plant and animal life
44 Blossoms-to-be
45 Glossy fabric
46 Absolutely perfect
50 Mineo of "Exodus"
51 Zap in the microwave
52 One of two in a Christmas song
59 "Axis of evil" land
60 Stiller's partner in comedy
61 Like thrift shop wares
62 Snowman's prop
63 Vows locale
64 Came into a base horizontally
65 Give off
66 Down and out
67 Broadway honor

DOWN

1 Peter the Great, e.g.
2 Kent State locale
3 Do a laundry chore
4 ___ beans (miso ingredients)
5 Pattern named for a Scottish county
6 Wall Street buys
7 Morales of "La Bamba"
8 Terrier in whodunits
9 Isn't completely honest with
10 Lecherous figure of Greek myth
11 Everglades wader
12 Chicken piece
13 Drooping
21 Meter maid of song
25 Onetime Jeep mfr.
26 Tip, as a hat
27 Earth Day subj.
28 Foal's mother
29 Cutlass or 88
30 Haunted house sounds
31 Mont Blanc, par exemple
33 Well-behaved
34 Article that may list survivors, in brief
35 Burn soother
36 Common bar order, with "the"
37 "That was ___ . . ."
39 Movie double, often
42 "Def Comedy Jam" channel
43 Seat at a barn dance
45 Job interview topic
46 Take potshots (at)
47 Jewish holiday when the book of Esther is read
48 Cousin of a giraffe
49 Basic belief
50 Fine fiddle, for short
53 River to the Ubangi
54 Credit card statement figure
55 Do some housecleaning
56 Capital on a fjord
57 Way to a man's heart?
58 Whirling water

by Sarah Keller

180

ACROSS

1 Ninny
5 Actor Danny of "The Color Purple"
11 Jungle menace
14 "___ 911!" (former Comedy Central show)
15 Dub over
16 English novelist Radcliffe
17 Abbr. before a name in a memo
18 Promptly
19 Like zinfandel wines
20 Chokes after bean eating?
23 No room at the ___
24 The Engineers of the N.C.A.A.: Abbr.
25 Not all
27 Gave up
29 Monk's karate blows?
34 Business card abbr.
36 Shade of blue
37 When clocks are set ahead: Abbr.
38 Movie finales featuring actress Miles?
41 ___ Lanka
43 In ___ of
44 Fr. holy woman
45 Result of a sweetener overload?
48 Wife of Hägar the Horrible
52 Tints
53 China's Chou En-___
55 Metalliferous rock
56 Modern educational phenomenon . . . or a hint to 20-, 29-, 38- and 45-Across
62 The Windy City, briefly
63 Fearsome wooden roller coaster at Six Flags Great Adventure
64 Plains Indian
65 Cool, man
66 Nearing midnight
67 Johnston in 2008–09 news
68 Broke a fast
69 Newly fashioned
70 Harriet Beecher Stowe novel

DOWN

1 Like some irony
2 Sloppy kiss
3 Mean
4 Lots and lots
5 Congregation
6 Soup bean
7 Not duped by
8 Futile
9 Novel on which "Clueless" is based
10 Recite rapidly, with "off"
11 Peevish states
12 Interstate entrances
13 "Pick a number, ___ number"
21 Hospital attendant
22 Noncommittal suffix
26 Approx. number
28 Time off from l'école
30 Per ___
31 Magazine featuring 47-Down
32 Alamo competitor
33 "Sex and the City" actress Nixon
35 Not of the cloth
38 Like some tomatoes
39 Abbr. in help-wanted ads
40 Exclamation before "I didn't know that!"
41 Library admonishment
42 Camp in the wild
46 That, to Juanita
47 ___ E. Neuman
49 Hang around
50 Pronounced rhythm, in music
51 Origin of the phrase "Beware of Greeks bearing gifts"
54 Unassisted
57 ___ Xing
58 She, in Cherbourg
59 Twosome
60 ___ Scotia
61 Tattled
62 When doubled, a dance

by Anna Shechtman

ACROSS

1 Growing older
6 Tool for horses' hooves
10 Protective wear for lobster eaters
14 Region of ancient Asia Minor
15 "Hmm . . ."
16 Amo, amas, ___ . . .
17 Blue things that make some people turn red?
19 "Dear ___"
20 Sound systems
21 Actor/rapper ___ Def
23 Seedy loaf
24 Metal in a mountain
25 Nine-to-five gigs, often
27 Frequently, to Donne
30 Ran, as colors
32 "Othello" villain
33 Title for a prince or princess: Abbr.
34 Tennis's Nastase
35 As one
37 "___ the ramparts we watched . . ."
38 Womanizer
40 "___ Loser" (Beatles song)
41 Donkey's sound
43 "Give it ___!"
44 20-vol. reference work
45 Jacob's first wife
46 Not the original color
47 Soon-to-be grads: Abbr.
48 Company with an industrial average
50 Relentless nine-to-five gig, e.g.
53 "Norma ___"
54 "My gal" of song
55 Easiest to beat up
59 Yemeni seaport
61 Wrangler product
63 Toy dog, briefly
64 Coup d' ___

65 "___ to the Moon" (first science fiction film, 1902)
66 Formerly, in old usage
67 Singer McEntire
68 Sheds feathers, e.g.

DOWN

1 Helps
2 ___ alone (have no help)
3 Concerning, in a memo
4 Explosive compound, in brief
5 More festive
6 Spanish rivers
7 Request
8 Appeared to be
9 Cuban coins
10 Ewe's cry
11 Confused situations
12 Bill Clinton was the first one elected president
13 Eye woes
18 Ordinary fellow
22 Thin
25 Record spinners . . . or a hint to 17-, 25-, 38-, 48- and 61-Across
26 Quick boxing punch
27 Cry of anticipation
28 One who mooches
29 How long the N.C.A.A. basketball tournament lasts
31 Architect Maya
34 Some potatoes
35 It protects the tympanic cavity
36 Rascals
39 Colorado tribe
42 Journey to Mecca

46 Undo, on a computer
48 Hang loosely
49 Perennial presidential candidate Ralph
51 Fix, as a printer's feeder
52 Connect with
55 Falafel bread
56 ___ of Sandwich
57 Vexed state
58 Baking soda amts.
60 Mesh
62 Arrest

by Oliver Hill

ACROSS

1 No-no
6 Late football star and FTD pitchman Merlin
11 Driver's lic. and such
14 Take forcibly
15 Sluggo's comics pal
16 Thing to pick
17 BAD
19 Buck's mate
20 Two cents' worth
21 Morales of "La Bamba"
22 Capitol Hill worker
23 BED
27 Name to the cabinet, say
30 Comic-strip light bulb
31 Van Susteren of Fox News
32 Ajax or Bon Ami
36 Weed whacker
37 BID
39 Movie pal of Stitch
40 Strange
42 River pair
43 At the drop of ___
44 "Animal House" beanie sporters
46 BOD
50 Exclude
51 Late singer Horne
52 F.D.R. power project: Abbr.
55 Blood-type abbr.
56 BUD
60 Versatile vehicle, for short
61 For all to see
62 Not quite round
63 Place that's "up the river"
64 Hobbyist's knife brand
65 Doesn't hoof it

DOWN

1 Rolaids alternative
2 Province of ancient Rome
3 Like the proverbial beaver
4 Tolkien beast
5 Shakespeare character who goes insane
6 Having no intermission
7 "___ en Rose" (Edith Piaf song)
8 ___-cone
9 Old French coin
10 Albany is its cap.
11 The movie "Wordplay," for one
12 L.E.D. part
13 High, pricewise
18 "This ___ outrage!"
22 "Shane" star

23 Slow-cooked beef entree
24 Some flooring
25 Wroclaw's river
26 Neptune's realm
27 Ottoman Empire chief
28 "No ___!" ("Easy!")
29 Hammer part
32 North-of-the-border grid org.
33 Rat on the Mob
34 Sommer in cinema
35 Woman depicted in "The Birth of Old Glory"
37 Neighbor of Yemen
38 Some are saturated
41 Letter after pi
42 Beat to death, so to speak
44 ___ Vallarta, Mexico
45 Checkout annoyance

46 Like some toasters and children's books
47 Overdo it onstage
48 "Christ is ___!" (Easter shout)
49 Say without thinking
52 Fly-catching creature
53 Show of hands, e.g.
54 Spy Aldrich
56 Symbol of slyness
57 Sch. founded by Thomas Jefferson
58 Gumshoe
59 56, in old Rome

by Sarah Keller

183

ACROSS

1 Japanese beef center
5 Speck in the ocean
10 Visitor to Mecca
14 Sources of gold, e.g.
15 Clichéd
16 Holder in the Obama cabinet
17 Bye lines?
18 Prickly plant
19 Looney Tunes manufacturer
20 Metaphorical target of attacks
23 Roundup animal
24 Speck in the ocean
25 Tribesman of Kenya or Tanzania
29 Broccoli ___
31 It makes jelly gel
32 Grab most of
35 Captor of Wendy Darling
38 Bears, in Baja
40 Boxer Ali
41 ___ Stanley Gardner
42 Game show originally titled "Occupation Unknown"
45 The Cisco ___
46 ___ Beach, Fla.
47 Bit of dust
49 Oslo Accords partner of Yitzhak and Bill
50 George Harrison's "All Those Years ___"
52 Some border patrol cops
56 Dance with fiddlers and a caller
59 New Mexico native
62 One of 101 in a googol
63 Cuisine that includes pad see ew
64 It may let off steam
65 Grande ___ (Québec's main drag)
66 Diary fastener
67 Unwanted engine sound
68 Richter scale event
69 Sawbuck halves

DOWN

1 Mentholated smokes
2 Go round and round
3 Color that blends well
4 "Sanford and Son" aunt
5 Amazon.com ID
6 Compensation during a work stoppage
7 "Rawhide" singer Frankie
8 Poem of lament
9 La., e.g., from 1805 to 1812
10 Ibuprofen target
11 Circumference section
12 Olympian Thorpe
13 Beverage store buy
21 ___ II (razor brand)
22 Eclipse, to the impressionable
26 Image on many a birth announcement
27 Garlicky sauce
28 Sporting tattoos, slangily
30 Like Indian summer days
31 Forte's opposite
32 Cowboy's greeting
33 Milo of "The Playboys"
34 What a shut-out team may lack
36 Up to, in ads
37 Severance package payments?
39 Trying hard
43 "Slumdog Millionaire" garb
44 Sicilian spewer
48 Kitt in a cabaret
50 Like a ballerina
51 Movie bomb of 2003
53 Post-surgery regimen, for short
54 "Give it a rest!"
55 Errata
57 Vitamin label amts.
58 Agenda part
59 ___ + 4
60 Altdorf's canton
61 ___ troppo (moderately, in music)

by Adam Cohen

184

ACROSS

1 Angers, with "up"
6 Forest
11 Protrude
14 Disney's "little mermaid"
15 Facing the pitcher
16 French "a"
17 Recipe guideline for a hot dish
19 Railroad stop: Abbr.
20 Cozy lodging
21 Lure for Simple Simon
22 Smidgens
24 Persian Gulf leader
26 Family divided by divorce
30 Barbers' tools
32 Deep hole
33 Fat used for tallow
34 Captain of Jules Verne's Nautilus
35 Name in a family restaurant chain
37 Football scores, for short
38 High-stakes draw in Las Vegas
41 Place for a baby to sit
44 Fish often destined for cans
45 Medical success
48 Gear for gondolas
50 Gradually slowing, in music: Abbr.
51 Pacific island garment wrapped around the waist
53 Pastrami, for one
56 Greek liqueur
57 Fainthearted
58 Spain's Costa del ___
60 Ob-___ (med. specialty)
61 Rope-a-dope boxer
62 "Sure, go ahead" . . . and a literal hint to what's found in 17-, 26-, 38- and 53-Across

67 IV adjusters
68 Oil directly from a well
69 12" stick
70 Golf peg
71 Entered via a keyboard
72 Chasm

DOWN

1 More risqué
2 Certain triathlete
3 Treat as a celebrity
4 "Yikes!"
5 Sales receipt
6 Transaction at a racetrack
7 Slugger Mel
8 Kimono closer
9 Hoover ___
10 Gertrude who wrote "Rose is a rose is a rose is a rose"
11 Hot off the press
12 Wild
13 Dishes for doll parties
18 Penpoints
23 Cries of excitement
25 Frolic
27 Do surgery
28 Old Testament books labeled I and II
29 Sicilian erupter
31 Tooth or plant part
35 Jeans fabric
36 Family rec facility
39 Many a northern Iraqi
40 Continental currency
41 Skill that no one has anymore
42 "Now We Are Six" poet
43 Declaration sometimes made with crossed fingers behind the back

46 More or less
47 They help digest food
49 Vacation at Vail, maybe
51 Store (away)
52 Dead ducks
54 Formal decree
55 Queried
59 Turkey's currency
63 Give it a shot
64 Dine
65 "___ on a Grecian Urn"
66 Rubber ducky's spot

by Lynn Lempel

ACROSS

1 Muscat's land
5 Asset
9 Coffee choices
14 Clinton's 1996 opponent
15 Woodcarver's tool
16 Tortoise or hare
17 Actress Swenson of "Benson"
18 ___ de vivre
19 Milo of "Romeo and Juliet"
20 Astronomer's aid
22 Means
24 With 41- and 54-Across, group with a 1967 ballad version of 39-/41-/42-Across
26 Word after "does" and "doesn't" in an old ad slogan
27 Glass on a radio
28 Audio input location
33 Wraps (up)
36 One who can't keep off the grass?
38 One of the Mannings
39 With 41- and 42-Across, 1964 Beatles hit
41 See 39-Across
42 See 39-Across
44 "The Star-Spangled Banner" preposition
45 Join the staff
48 Pinnacle
49 Keeps from happening
51 Western defense grp.
53 Broadcast
54 See 24-Across
59 Women, quaintly, with "the"
63 12:30 a.m. or p.m., on a ship
64 Bubbling
65 Cord material
67 Et ___
68 Zellweger of "My One and Only"

69 Button between * and #
70 Fronted, in a way
71 Piglike
72 Look inside?
73 Some jeans

DOWN

1 Keats, for one
2 The 6 in 6/8/10, e.g.
3 Pond buildup
4 Close call
5 Some are flannel
6 Parkinsonism drug
7 Israeli arm
8 Appear
9 See 40-Down
10 Having less forethought
11 Repeated message?
12 Thistle or goldenrod
13 Ladies of Spain: Abbr.

21 Damage
23 Villa d' ___
25 Earliest time
29 Edit menu option
30 Job rights agcy.
31 Grad
32 Marriage, for one
33 Word before "You're killing me!"
34 Fancy pitcher
35 Bra insert
37 Lemony
40 With 9-Down, group with a 1962 hit version of 39-/41-/42-Across
43 Really enjoys oneself
46 About, on a memo
47 "Private - keep out"
50 Isn't all the same
52 O'Neill's "The Hairy ___"

55 Old Testament prophet who married a harlot
56 Martinique volcano
57 Dior-designed dress
58 Strips in front of a window?
59 Old MacDonald had one
60 Busy as ___
61 Table salt is composed of them
62 PlayStation 2 competitor
66 Auto loan inits.

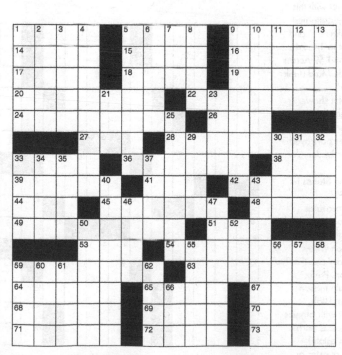

by Peter A. Collins

186

ACROSS
1 Flexible blades
6 Machines that run Panther or Leopard
10 Bean curd
14 Prefix with brewery
15 Home of King Harald V
16 Eye part
17 Part of a drug lord's income, maybe
19 Burping in public, e.g.
20 Eye part
21 Field of expertise
22 Small particles
23 Shogun's capital
24 Fruity soda
26 "Slumdog Millionaire" setting
28 Still
29 Watch furtively
30 Res ___ loquitur
33 You might get your feet wet with this
34 Boldly patterned warblers . . . and a hint to 17-, 24-, 50- and 59-Across
38 Minute Maid drink brand
41 Big film shower
42 Eye shade
46 Powerless
49 Singer portrayed in film by Jennifer Lopez
50 Rolling Stones hit of 1967
54 Liq. measures
55 Prepare to recite the Pledge of Allegiance
56 Hidden valley
57 "Comin' ___ the Rye"
58 Trillion: Prefix
59 Certain mason
61 City in Utah
62 Prefix with physics
63 Many-___ (large, as an estate)
64 Half, quarter or eighth follower
65 ___-bitsy
66 ___ nova

DOWN
1 Insignia
2 Amassed
3 Rental car choice
4 Cupid's Greek counterpart
5 Stuff sold in rolls
6 Actress Mary Tyler ___
7 Co-star of 6-Down in 1970s TV
8 Cloudless
9 ___ milk
10 Cassiterite, e.g.
11 Like a good speaking voice
12 Deft touch
13 Base entertainment
18 When doubled, a fish
22 When Emperor Henry IV was dethroned
24 Fred Astaire prop
25 Oenophile's concern
27 Staten Isl., for one
30 Doctrine
31 Educ. group
32 "Yakety ___," 1963 hit
35 Target of Pierre's prayers
36 Place with a gym
37 "The best pal that I ever had," in song
38 Author Zora Neale ___ of the Harlem Renaissance
39 Not yet born
40 1966 musical based on "I Am a Camera"
43 Gentle breezes
44 Sides accompaniers
45 World Series-winning manager of 1981 and 1988
47 How famous people are known
48 Brit. company name ending
49 Went under
51 Everglades wader
52 Skirt features
53 Break down
57 ___ Bell
59 Ascap alternative
60 Science course requirement, maybe

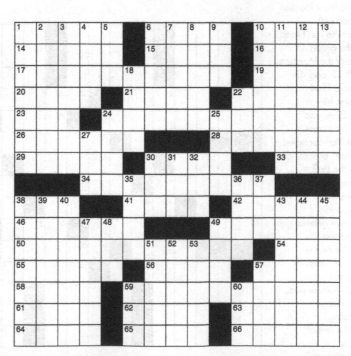

by Gary Whitehead

ACROSS

1 The Crimson Tide, informally
5 Swiss peaks
9 Rand McNally product
14 Author Haley of "Roots" fame
15 "___ Caesar!"
16 Result of an armistice
17 1980s TV series starring Michael Landon
20 Confused
21 Fill to excess
22 Sail holder
23 A sharpshooter needs a good one
25 Golf pro Ernie
27 2002 Tom Hanks/Paul Newman film
36 Easter roast
37 Actress Sorvino
38 Organization for geniuses
39 Japanese port
42 Catch red-handed
43 Cranium contents
44 Parking space adjunct
45 Elevator inventor Elisha
47 Big Japanese computer maker: Abbr.
48 Onetime Alaska boondoggle
52 One in a blue state majority: Abbr.
53 A pair
54 Yard entrance
57 Time of danger for Caesar
61 Occupied, as a lavatory
65 Traveler's option . . . or what you won't get on a 17-, 27- or 48-Across?
68 Near the center
69 Burden
70 Rough-___ (not smoothly finished)
71 Impoverished
72 Reserved parking space for an exec, maybe
73 Bones, anatomically

DOWN

1 ___ Men ("Who Let the Dogs Out" group)
2 Touched down
3 Computer capacity, in brief
4 Cutting part of a lumberjack's tool
5 Idea person's exclamation
6 Puts down
7 ___ bread
8 One-armed bandit
9 Animal that beats its chest
10 Professional truck driver
11 Volcano's output
12 King beaters
13 Already in the mail
18 Word repeated before "Don't Tell Me!"
19 Obey
24 Pop's partner
26 What a do-it-yourself swing may hang from
27 Oblique-angled, four-sided figure
28 Western, in slang
29 Classic violin maker
30 ___ grigio (wine)
31 Muse of love poetry
32 Israel's Yitzhak
33 Nonsensical
34 Willow whose twigs are used in basketry
35 F.D.R. veep John ___ Garner
40 Blushed
41 Encourage
46 Drunkard
49 Send out, as rays
50 Hitler started it: Abbr.
51 Top dog
54 Sheepish look, maybe
55 Popular steak sauce
56 Something to sing along to
58 Go south, as a stock market
59 "___ kleine Nachtmusik"
60 Thing on a cowboy's boot
62 Hawaiian instruments, informally
63 Stitches
64 Sicily's Mt. ___
66 Drought-stricken
67 "Shame on you!"

by Mark Feldman

188

ACROSS

1 Pet rocks, once
4 Prebirth event
10 Message runner
14 Top-of-the-charts number
15 It may come before the end of a sentence
16 Not get merely by accident
17 Intermittent, as a relationship
20 Former host of a nightly TV show taped in Burbank
21 Sunburned
22 Lift the spirits of
23 Spearheaded
25 Plumlike fruit
27 Leaves the main topic temporarily
35 Playground retort
36 Pub deliveries
37 Apply brakes to
38 Org. with audits
39 Gearbox option
42 Day of anticipation
43 ___-do-well
45 One you dig the most
46 More exquisite
48 Start to exit an Interstate
51 Old El ___ (food brand)
52 Simile connection
53 Fall bloom
56 Resinous tree
58 Stick it in your ear
62 Trade places . . . or a hint to parts of 17-, 27- and 48-Across
66 Smuggler's unit
67 Francis of old game shows
68 Show hosts, for short
69 Dish simmered in a pot
70 Negotiator's refusal
71 Dig in

DOWN

1 Jester
2 Rice who wrote "The Vampire Chronicles"
3 College V.I.P.
4 Place to relax
5 Arrangement of locks
6 River of Normandy
7 Alternative to an iron
8 Little help?
9 Whistle blower, in brief
10 Limbs for movie pirates
11 Tiny battery
12 Sand
13 Feminine suffix
18 Uses an iron or a 7-Down, say
19 Time in earth's history
24 Get an ___ effort
25 Quadraphonic halved
26 Scottish miss
27 Last step at a bakery
28 Delhi wrap: Var.
29 Beginning
30 Arizona tribe
31 Pain reliever brand
32 ___ Kagan, Obama nominee to the Supreme Court
33 Caesar's nine
34 Impudent nobody
40 Terrestrial salamanders
41 Bad grades
44 Aid for skiing uphill
47 Modern dweller in ancient Ur
49 Crack officer?
50 Hot breakfast cereal
53 Questions
54 Loretta of "M*A*S*H"
55 Scrabble piece
56 Bow out of a poker hand
57 "Now it's clear"
59 Big book
60 Member of a Pre-Columbian empire
61 It's attention-getting
63 ___ Solo, Harrison Ford role
64 Voting yes
65 ___ Aviv

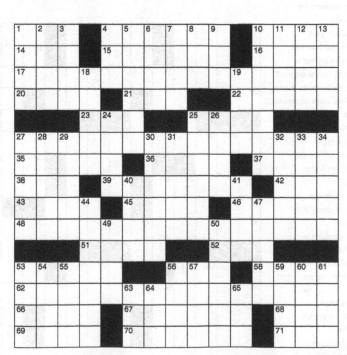

by Jill Winslow

ACROSS

1 ___ Cohn, 1991 Grammy winner for Best New Artist
5 Rent-___
9 "War is not the answer" people
14 Elizabeth Taylor role, in brief
15 Khrushchev's impromptu gavel
16 Slightly ahead
17 Followed the Hippocratic oath, in a way
19 Either of two peaks in Greek myth
20 Sporty, powerful auto
22 Collapsible place to collapse
23 Not idling
24 "It's ___!" ("I give up!")
26 Racy, low-budget film
31 "Cool" amount
34 Checked out
35 Beatlemania reaction
36 Plebe's place: Abbr.
38 Check for freshness, in a way
41 Ladies' man
42 Ladies' man
44 "___ bien!"
46 Slot-car track section
47 Undergarments that show a little of the chest
51 101
52 Software instruction file heading
56 Easter lead-in
58 Messages on an Apple device
61 Youngest-ever French Open winner Michael ___
63 Some Election Day surveys
64 It may bring a tear to your eye

65 Word on a biblical wall
66 Sheryl Crow's "___ Wanna Do"
67 Fake-book contents
68 "With a wink and ___"
69 Closing bell org.

DOWN

1 Early 15th-century year
2 Many a day laborer
3 Make even deeper
4 ___ eel
5 Common car door fixtures, once
6 Activity in a virtual room
7 Simplest of choices
8 Send a tickler
9 Hollow-point bullets
10 ___-out clause
11 Yea-or-nay event
12 Prefix with skeleton
13 Pants part
18 Midwest air hub
21 Knock over, so to speak
25 Some eaters at troughs
27 Half a score
28 One of TV's Bunkers
29 Notes in pots
30 Reaches 0:00:00 on a countdown clock, say
31 Sportscaster Albert
32 Scissors, for "cut," on a PC
33 Knucklehead
37 Prefix meaning 27-Down
39 Common party night: Abbr.
40 Discovered after a search, with "out"

43 "Go ahead" hand gestures
45 High, as a price
48 Bit of advice
49 Conceptual framework
50 Margaret Mead interviewee
53 Waste time
54 Rumor sources?
55 Bovine in ads
56 Some PX patrons
57 "Yikes!"
59 Beasts in a span
60 Spanish boy
62 Seasonal quaff

by Joe Krozel

190

ACROSS
1 Leftover bit of cloth
6 "The Zoo Story" playwright Edward
11 Manx or Siamese
14 "Remember the ___!" (cry of 1836)
15 Sounds SSTs made
16 Color shade
17 "It ain't hard!"
19 Ill temper
20 Go like a bunny
21 Wedding dress material
22 Kind of sleeve named after a British baron
24 With 46-Across, "It ain't hard!"
25 Chop-chop
26 Nadir's opposite
29 School time when kids aren't studying
30 Without an escort
31 Irritated
32 Potpie vegetable
35 Playful bites
36 Tennis great Monica
37 Source of linen
38 Big beagle feature
39 Farm tracts
40 Work like a dog
41 Be against
43 Hung around
44 Singer Flack or Peters
46 See 24-Across
47 Mama Cass ___
48 Autobiographer's subject
49 Follow the coxswain's calls
52 Sidewalk stand quaff
53 "It ain't hard!"
56 Not Rep. or Ind.
57 "The Odd Couple" slob
58 Bird on a U.S. quarter
59 B'way sellout sign
60 Attempts at baskets
61 Live in fear of

DOWN
1 Pageant entrant's wear
2 Advertising award
3 Multistory parking garage feature
4 Guitarist's accessory, for short
5 Foul the water, e.g.
6 Taken ___ (surprised)
7 Get whipped
8 Drag queen's wrap
9 Hugs tightly
10 Made a getaway
11 "It ain't hard!"
12 Hearing-related
13 Pint-size
18 To ___ his own
23 U.S.O. show audience members
24 Rackets
25 T. ___ (fearsome dinos)
26 Grey who wrote westerns
27 Charles Lamb alias
28 "It ain't hard!"
29 C.S.A. general
31 Vice ___
33 Roof overhang
34 Abruptly dismissed
36 Like many tartan wearers
37 Pajamas' rear opening
39 Pertinent
40 Like a taxidermist's work
42 Rock and Roll Hall of Fame architect I. M. ___
43 Without an escort
44 Uses a Kindle, e.g.
45 Like a big brother
46 Tarot card readers, e.g.
48 Ad-libbing vocal style
49 Violent 19-Across
50 State with a panhandle: Abbr.
51 Whacked plant
54 ___-friendly (green)
55 Indy 500 entry

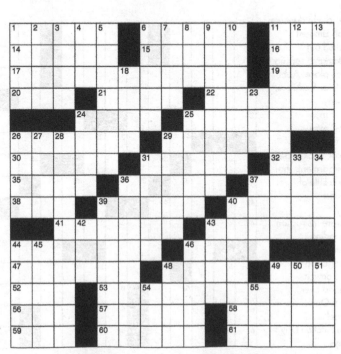

by Fred Piscop

ACROSS

1 Fresh talk
4 Female TV dog played by males
10 Alphabet enders, to Brits
14 Letters on a wanted poster
15 Sitcom pal of 46-Down
16 Plains Indians
17 Kitten call
18 Governing body of a municipality
20 South-of-the-border outlaws
22 Conductor Zubin
23 12:50 or 1:50
24 Bay Area law enforcement org.
26 1965 Vivien Leigh movie
29 Gateways or Dells, briefly
32 Georgia home of the Allman Brothers
33 Baseball Triple Crown stat
34 Excellent, slangily
35 Safe havens
36 Word game . . . or a word that can precede the starts of 18-, 26-, 43- and 54-Across
38 Suffix for the wealthy
39 ___-Ball (arcade game)
40 Rawls of R&B
41 Strait of Hormuz vessel
42 "The buck stops here" prez
43 Old comics boy with the dog Tige
46 Rope fiber
47 Board game turns
48 Briquette residue
51 Delivery entrance, maybe
54 Center of attention around a campfire, say
57 Palm Treo, e.g.
58 Deborah of "The King and I"
59 Deck treatments
60 Often-replaced joint
61 Swing in the breeze
62 Hallucinogen-yielding cactus
63 To this point

DOWN

1 Souvlaki meat
2 Swedish home furnishings chain
3 Hockshop receipt
4 Make privy to, as a secret
5 Many
6 Remove, as a branch
7 Confessional list
8 Abbr. in co. names
9 Fair-hiring letters
10 Like most urban land
11 Impress deeply
12 Two-thirds of D.I.Y.
13 Ward of "The Fugitive," 1993
19 Stereotypically "blind" officials
21 Topple from power
24 Cries out loud
25 Move like a moth
26 Box-office hit
27 Pays attention
28 "Are you in ___?"
29 Field of Plato and Aristotle
30 Rod with seven batting championships
31 Howard of satellite radio
34 Like sorted socks
36 Market surplus
37 Nozzle site
41 "Heads" side of a coin
43 At it
44 The Brat Pack's Estevez
45 Porcupine or gopher
46 Former boyfriend of 15-Across
48 Queries
49 Ratatouille or ragout
50 Bar mitzvah dance
51 Leave in stitches
52 Occasionally punted comics canine
53 Totally absorbed
55 Dose amt.
56 Summer on the Seine

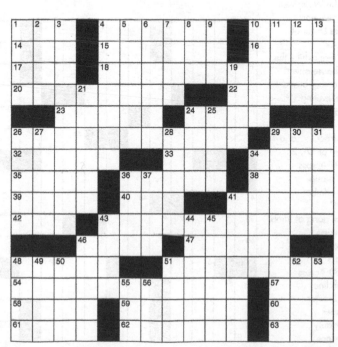

by Barry C. Silk

ACROSS

1 "Still mooing"
5 Old flames?
10 Forage storage
14 Old flames
15 Job made almost obsolete by voice recorders
16 Privy to
17 Tots
19 Upper hand
20 Plaza de toros cry
21 First murderer
22 "Entourage" agent Gold
23 Moor's deity
25 Make fine adjustments to
30 Home of the Stars
32 Fictional airline on "Lost"
33 Wine label datum
36 "It's ___-brainer"
37 "On the Waterfront" Oscar winner
41 Actress Larter of "Heroes"
42 Stars that exhibit the "lighthouse effect"
43 Tortilla chip brand
46 Need leveling, perhaps
50 With 60-Across, ink a contract . . . or a feature of 17-, 25- and 37-Across
53 Shop group
54 Trellis climber
55 "Drat!"
57 "Usual gang of idiots" magazine
58 One of Spot's masters
60 See 50-Across
63 Graph line
64 Film director Kershner
65 Fit for duty
66 Substance
67 Kind of question
68 Line to Penn Sta.

DOWN

1 Time-consuming task for a musketeer
2 Armpit, anatomically
3 Pass along, as gossip
4 Ballpark fig.
5 Away from harbor
6 Stiff-upper-lip sort
7 Temporary tattoo dye
8 St. Louis-to-Cleveland dir.
9 "Sending out an ___" (much-repeated line in a Police hit)
10 Jagged mountain range
11 Hoosier
12 Captain's journal
13 Diet-drink calorie count
18 Toast at a bar mitzvah
22 Mt. Rushmore neighbor of Teddy
24 Menlo Park middle name
26 Pricey seating areas
27 Winter fisherman's tool
28 Salon job
29 Prefix with -cide
31 Attach with a click
34 Target for Teddy Roosevelt
35 Feel awful
37 Morlocks' victims, in an H. G. Wells story
38 Birthplace of eight U.S. presidents
39 Roughly
40 Publisher's 13-digit ID
41 Billboard displays
44 Buy gold, e.g.
45 Water pistol or popgun
47 Bahamas getaway
48 Temporary wheels
49 Win over
51 Sharp products, for short
52 Opposite of "take out"
56 Setting for the movie "Sister Act"
58 Problem for a copier
59 Send packing
60 Handyman's letters
61 Miner's find
62 "U R funny!"

by Alex Boisvert

ACROSS

1 Some British sports cars, briefly
5 Contest specifications
10 Third piece of a three-piece suit
14 Baghdad's home
15 Separately
16 x or y, on a graph
17 In ___ of (replacing)
18 Copy, for short
19 Wang of fashion
20 Dreamy state
22 "Star Trek" weapon
24 The Beatles' "Abbey ___"
25 Schreiber who won a Tony for "Glengarry Glen Ross"
26 Broadcast with little room for mistakes
29 Unshackle
33 Card that may be "in the hole"
34 Early morning hour
36 Exxon merged with it
37 Appear
39 Provide with a blind date, say
41 Anti-attacker spray
42 Politico Palin
44 Aired again
46 Stag party attendees
47 Clearly confused, e.g.
49 ___ party (sleepover)
51 Pinnacle
52 Green gem
53 Isn't an odd one out
56 Gilda Radner character on "S.N.L."
60 Side x side, for a 4-Down
61 Hacienda material
63 Fizzless, as a Coke
64 Long skirt
65 Lethal cousin of the cobra
66 $50 for Boardwalk, in Monopoly
67 Founded: Abbr.
68 Put in prison
69 Pair with a plow

DOWN

1 Jack's partner in rhyme
2 Mozart's "Il mio tesoro," e.g.
3 Celt or Highlander
4 Equilateral quadrilateral
5 One in a million
6 Overturn
7 "Columbo" org.
8 Make a boo-boo
9 "Cut that out!"
10 "Hubba hubba!"
11 They've gone their separate ways
12 Retired racehorse, maybe
13 Peter the Great, e.g.
21 Oodles
23 Captain's place on a ship
25 Ring-tailed primate
26 Rodeo ring?
27 Mountaineer's tool
28 Small American thrush
29 Go past midnight, say
30 First president not born in the continental U.S.
31 Words to an attack dog
32 2008 Olympics tennis champion Dementieva
35 Copy, of a sort
38 1961 hit for the Shirelles
40 Owner of the largest bed Goldilocks tried
43 Pueblo Indian
45 Zilch
48 Put a new title on
50 Curly ethnic hairstyle, colloquially
52 "Star Wars" villain ___ the Hutt
53 Renown
54 401(k) cousins
55 Communicate like many teens
56 Fail miserably
57 Trebek of "Jeopardy!"
58 What moons do after full moons
59 Abbr. before a name on a memo
62 Beaver's construction

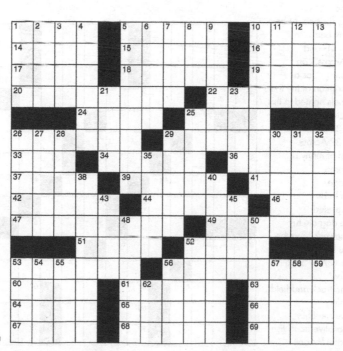

by Joel Fagliano

ACROSS

1 AARP or the National Rifle Association
6 Without: Fr.
10 French city in 1944 fighting
14 "Bird on ___" (1990 film)
15 Lafayette's state?
16 Singer India___
17 Kind of code
18 Super star
19 Poetic foot
20 Asian cat
23 Blue Jays, on a scoreboard
24 Net
25 Heroine of Verdi's "Il Trovatore"
27 Euro forerunner
29 Slo-o-ow leak
31 Santa ___ winds
32 Makeshift seat at a rodeo
34 Penn, for one: Abbr.
35 Alarm bell
39 With 41- and 43-Across, cop cruiser . . . or a description of the five animals named in this puzzle
41 See 39-Across
43 See 39-Across
44 Form of many a diploma
46 Smidge
48 Sign to be interpreted
49 "The dog ate my homework," maybe
50 "You love," to Livy
52 Thurman of "Pulp Fiction"
53 Some track-and-field training
57 Move stealthily
59 Decorative pond fish
60 Shamu, for one
64 "Back in the ___"
66 Porky Pig, e.g.

67 Building usually without a 13th floor
68 Penury
69 "La Belle et la ___" (French fairy tale)
70 At ___ for words
71 Actress Sedgwick of "The Closer"
72 Cornerstone abbr.
73 Like the review "Hated it," e.g.

DOWN

1 Track units
2 Wilson of "Wedding Crashers"
3 Like some vision
4 Melee
5 Bellowed
6 Potential enamorada
7 On
8 Like some exercises
9 Ogle

10 ___ tai (drink)
11 Poetic Muse
12 Island near Java
13 Equus quagga
21 Prominent features of Alfred E. Neuman
22 "What should I ___?"
26 ___ cheese
27 Wanes
28 Class after trig
30 One of the 2008 Olympic mascots
33 Cause of a beach closure, maybe
36 Flight training equipment
37 Thing
38 "99 Red Balloons" singer, 1984
40 "Hogan's Heroes" colonel
42 Made less intense

45 1970 #1 hit whose title follows the lyric "Speaking words of wisdom . . ."
47 Bob ___, 2008 Libertarian candidate for president
51 "Who cares?"
53 Polecat
54 Actress Parker
55 Choir support
56 Tart fruits
58 Intact
61 Former Mississippi senator Trent
62 Minus
63 Ultimatum ender
65 Nutritional abbr.

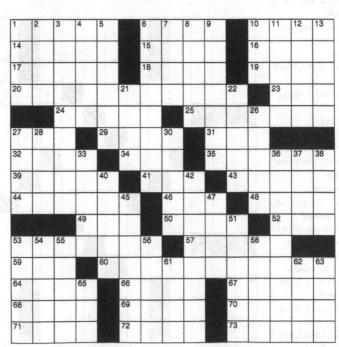

by Peter A. Collins

ACROSS

1 Harry James's "___ the Craziest Dream"
5 Knotted up
9 Bedding item
13 Marisa of "The Wrestler"
15 Georgetown athlete
16 Rabbit punch target
17 Conk the "You Were Meant for Me" singer?
19 Major in astronomy?
20 Attempts, with "at"
21 Did improv
23 Rogers and Bean
25 The "A" of A.D.
26 Truckers' breaks
30 Has contempt for
33 Dernier ___
34 Goes well with
36 Org.
37 Cause of head-scratching, perhaps
39 1943 penny material
41 Architect Saarinen
42 House arrestee's bracelet site
44 Instrument that's usually played cross-legged
46 Tbsp., e.g.
47 Some farm machinery
49 "Billy Budd" and "Of Mice and Men"
51 Radiate
52 Nike competitor
53 Pigeonholed, in moviedom
57 Site of a 1976 South African uprising
61 Speller's words of clarification
62 Scratch the "2 Legit 2 Quit" rapper?
64 Car door ding
65 Cousin of an eagle
66 Sends to blazes
67 Torah holders
68 Floored it
69 Defense grp. since 1949

DOWN

1 Trigger finger problem?
2 Dance done to "Hava Nagila"
3 Andy's partner in old radio
4 White Label Scotch maker
5 Everyday article
6 Early caucus state
7 Checked out
8 Miss Ellie's soap
9 Revolver feature, perhaps
10 Protect the "Kiss From a Rose" singer from the cops?
11 Cathedral recess
12 Drink in "Beowulf"
14 Bars at Fort Knox
18 Festive
22 Quechua speaker
24 Rotisserie parts
26 Programming class locale, perhaps
27 "Three Sisters" sister
28 Amuse the "Get the Party Started" singer?
29 Oktoberfest memento
31 Singer of the "Casta diva" aria
32 Tartan hose wearers
35 Play by a different ___ rules
38 Mendeleev's tabulation
40 Like an inaugural ball
43 Children's author Carle
45 Do a musketeer's job
48 IHOP servings
50 Wyatt Earp, e.g.
53 "Look what I did!"
54 River through Flanders
55 Break one's resolution, say
56 ___ Modern (London gallery)
58 Austen classic
59 Camper's carry-along
60 Roughly
63 Got hitched

by Kristian House

196

ACROSS

1 Doctrine
6 "___ of the D'Urbervilles"
10 Bit of hair standing up
14 Targeted, with "in on"
15 Fe, on the periodic table
16 Burn soother
17 Nimble
18 Entangle
19 Fort ___ (gold repository)
20 "Go!"
23 Doctor's charge
24 Glimpsed
25 Big name in copiers
26 "Look how perfectly I performed!"
27 Vigorous
31 Aviated
34 Web address, for short
36 Wood for black piano keys, once
37 V.I.P.'s transport
38 Separate . . . or a hint to this puzzle's theme
41 Razor brand
42 Billy the Kid, for Henry McCarty
44 Bygone Russian space station
45 "Fargo" director
46 Messed up, as a message
49 Eat like a bird
51 Anglo-Saxon writing symbol
52 No. starting with an area code
53 Firms: Abbr.
56 Sherlock Holmes phrase, when on a case
60 Horse's halter?
61 Temperate
62 ___ ball soup
63 Big rabbit features
64 Salinger heroine
65 Animal that plays along streams
66 Shade of color
67 More's opposite
68 All set

DOWN

1 Grain husks
2 Scalawag
3 Author Zola
4 Farmer's place, in a children's ditty
5 Black Sea port
6 Dance in "The Rocky Horror Picture Show"
7 Cleveland's lake
8 Vile
9 Underhanded
10 Surprised and flustered
11 Bone that parallels the radius
12 Groceries
13 Moniker for a Lone Star cowboy
21 Italian city where "The Taming of the Shrew" is set
22 Sharpen, as a knife
26 Going in side-by-side pairs
28 Mr. ___, John P. Marquand detective
29 About, on a memo
30 Greenish blue
31 Old Glory, for one
32 Reader's Digest co-founder Wallace
33 Arab ruler
35 Take it on the ___ (flee)
39 Dangerous ocean currents
40 Oak and teak
43 Hit hard, as a baseball
47 Tooth cover
48 Death
50 Hullabaloo
53 Terra ___ (tile material)
54 Seeped
55 Tale
56 Southeast Asian cuisine
57 Tooter
58 Classic street liners
59 Destiny
60 Drenched

by Jill Denny and Jeff Chen

ACROSS

1 Voice above tenor
5 Cross : Christianity :: ___ : Judaism
9 Interior design
14 Cries from Homer Simpson
15 Very very
16 Going brand?
17 Number between eins and drei
18 Neeson of "Clash of the Titans"
19 Track-and-field events
20 *"Ocean's Eleven" actor
23 Follower of spy or web
24 Any Beatles song, now
25 *Tweaks
28 Enters Facebook, maybe
30 Annoys incessantly
31 Female flock member
32 N.B.A. nickname
36 Film units
37 *Small sci-fi vehicle
40 Rapper's crew
43 Director Apatow
44 Obstruction for salmon
47 Culmination of a Casey Kasem countdown
49 Book size
52 *"Get Smart" device
56 Toothpaste with "green sparkles"
57 Falsity
58 *Blastoff spot
60 Uses sleight of hand on
62 Head of Québec
63 French girlfriend
65 Aerodynamic
66 Tied, as a score
67 "Boy Meets World" boy
68 Late
69 Organize alphabetically, say
70 Chips in the pot

DOWN

1 Carpenter's curved cutter
2 Uncalled-for insult, say
3 U2 guitarist
4 Brother and husband of Isis
5 Arias, usually
6 Robin Hood or Jesse James
7 "Same here"
8 Director Polanski
9 Obama, e.g.: Abbr.
10 Performed, as one's duties
11 Purify
12 Quaker breakfast offering
13 Prescriptions, for short
21 Keanu Reeves's role in "The Matrix"
22 Middling grade
24 Chilean cheer
26 Poi source
27 Aves.
29 Foreign policy grp.
33 Pilgrimage to Mecca
34 Kwik-E-Mart clerk
35 Proof ending
37 Well-regarded
38 Fall through the cracks?
39 A.S.A.P.
40 A TD is worth six: Abbr.
41 "So beauuutiful!"
42 Unwanted plot giveaway
44 "Yeah, like that'll ever happen"
45 Groveled
46 Blondie, to Alexander and Cookie
48 Rangers' org.
50 "That's awful"
51 Fleecy fiber
53 Hall's musical partner
54 ___ Laredo, Mexico
55 Go in
59 50 ___ ("Candy Shop" rapper)
60 Winter clock setting in Nev.
61 Heavens
64 Storm center . . . or, phonetically, letter that can precede the ends of the answers to the five starred clues to spell popular devices

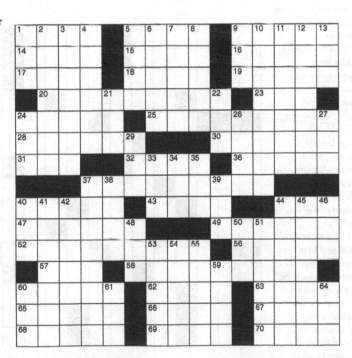

by José Chardiet

ACROSS

1 Veracruz's capital
7 Its motto is "Semper paratus": Abbr.
11 Bonobo, for one
14 You can count on it
15 Kelly of "Live With Regis and Kelly"
16 Word with band or sand
17 Command to a French composer at an intersection?
19 Conciliatory gift
20 Pen
21 Tickle response
22 Uccello who painted "The Battle of San Romano"
24 Don Corleone
25 Loading locale
27 City south of Luxor
30 Command to a Hungarian composer at the piano?
34 Activities
36 Jacques Cousteau's middle name
37 "Tippecanoe and Tyler ___"
38 Move like mud
39 Sophia of "Marriage Italian-Style"
41 Fringe benefit
42 Sch. supporter
43 Author who famously ended a short story with the line "Romance at short notice was her specialty"
44 Cell on a slide
46 Command to a German composer on a baseball diamond?
49 Lessen, as fears
50 Jay Gatsby's love
51 Mayberry boy
53 Leaf holders
55 Czar of Russia between Feodors
57 Initials at sea

60 Snap, Crackle or Pop
61 Command to an Austrian composer on a scavenger hunt?
64 Freudian concept
65 Adm. Zumwalt, chief of naval operations during the Vietnam War
66 Word before a sentence
67 Guerra's opposite
68 Does, e.g.
69 "Woo-hoo!"

DOWN

1 Injures with a pencil, say
2 Somewhat
3 Unlike a go-getter
4 Point of no return?
5 Green skill
6 Plus

7 What an addict fights
8 Symbol of simple harmonic motion
9 Tax pro, for short
10 Bachelorette party attendees
11 Hard core?
12 Game involving banks
13 Fair
18 Denny's competitor
23 Talent agent ___ Emanuel
24 Roof topper
26 Relative of an aardwolf
27 Make one's own
28 Truth, archaically
29 1939 title role for Frank Morgan
31 Like much poetry
32 1964 title role for Anthony Quinn
33 Hungarian wine

35 Hearty helpings of meat loaf, say
40 "Go ahead"
41 It may be + or −
43 Moved, as a horse's tail
45 "But of course!," in Marseille
47 Symbol of strength
48 Device making a 53-Down
52 "Little" digit
53 Sound made by a 48-Down
54 Kurylenko of "Quantum of Solace"
56 Febreeze target
57 Succor
58 Parcel (out)
59 ___ terrier
62 Hearty quaff
63 Take in slowly

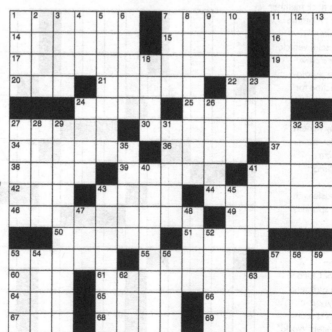

by Will Nediger

ACROSS

1 Point that marks the beginning of a change
5 Rainbows, basically
9 Blunder
14 Palo ___, Calif.
15 Jacket
16 Affliction said to be caused by worry
17 One of 12 for the Alcoholics Anonymous program
18 Robust
19 More courteous
20 Special offer at an airline Web site
23 Japanese electronics brand
24 Scottish castle for British royals
29 Special offer at a supermarket
32 "___ your age!"
35 Scuba tankful
36 Midwest tribe
37 Depressed
38 Place for phys ed
39 "The Murders in the Rue Morgue" writer
41 Depressed
42 Way too weighty
44 Arrow shooter
45 Attempt
46 Special offer at a diner
50 Element with the symbol Ta
51 Rotini or rigatoni
56 Special offer at a car dealership
59 One of three people walking into a bar, in many a joke
63 Fox's "American ___"
64 Sir Geraint's wife, in Arthurian legend
65 François's farewell
66 Mission control org.
67 Prince Charles's sister

68 ___ pole (Indian emblem)
69 Campbell who sang "Rhinestone Cowboy"
70 Corrosive alkalis

DOWN

1 Groups on "Saturday Night Live"
2 The "U" of UHF
3 Writer Gertrude
4 Opium flower
5 Yearn (for)
6 What buffalo do in "Home on the Range"
7 .45, e.g., for a firearm
8 Upright, inscribed stone tablets
9 TV western that ran for 20 seasons
10 Muhammad ___, opponent of 53-Down
11 TV monitor?

12 Lawyer's charge
13 Blunder
21 Bit of real estate
22 Santa's helper
25 ". . . ___ quit!"
26 Henhouse perch
27 Egypt's Sadat
28 Like many old water pipes
30 What a farmer bales
31 Edge
32 Skyward
33 Snake that a snake charmer charms
34 Sixth-grader, usually
38 Flower also known as a cranesbill
39 Campaign pro
40 "Wise" bird
43 Put in rollers
44 Having two methods
47 "Shine a Little Love" rock grp.

48 Really angry
49 Passer of secret documents
52 "What ___!" (possible response to 20-, 29-, 46- and 56-Across)
53 ___ Liston, opponent of 10-Down
54 Bale binder
55 Much of Chile
57 Sniffer
58 Verve
59 Double-crosser
60 Hubbub
61 Chomped (on)
62 Busy one?

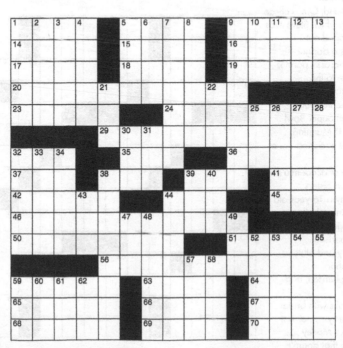

by Freddie Cheng

ACROSS

1 Tiny scissor cut
5 Sphere
10 Annoyance at a barbecue
14 Lug
15 "I'm outta here!"
16 Aachen article
17 Nice through and through . . . or not
20 Mother, in Milan
21 Pin's place
22 Charlemagne's dominion: Abbr.
23 Like some stares
25 Levy on cigarettes and booze
27 Really digs . . . or not
33 Woman who raised Cain
34 58 minutes past the hour
35 Hogwash
38 Portland, Ore., college from which Steve Jobs dropped out
40 Uses a dagger
42 33-Across's partner
43 Invite to the penthouse, say
45 Some Iroquois
47 2008 Super Bowl M.V.P. Manning
48 Most wretched . . . or not
51 One of academia's Seven Sisters
53 Many a 16-year-old Southern belle
54 Bridge expert Culbertson
55 Maryland athletes, for short
59 Shepherded, in a way
63 Speaks with brutal honesty . . . or not
66 Rock's Mötley ___
67 Club that doesn't beat much

68 "L' ___ c'est moi": Louis XIV
69 Terse order to a chauffeur
70 Evaluate
71 Title girl in a 1922 hit

DOWN

1 Flower stalk
2 Exploding star
3 Couple on a gossip page
4 Learner's ___
5 Priestly attire
6 Train transportation
7 Singer James
8 Kind of tide
9 "Gunsmoke" star James
10 ___-Xer
11 Certain vigilante
12 End of ___

13 Bygone communication
18 America's Cup entry
19 "Can I give you ___?"
24 Some evergreens
26 Writer Ephron
27 Juno's counterpart
28 Connecticut and Virginia, in Monopoly: Abbr.
29 Defect
30 Monopoly purchase
31 Japanese seaport
32 Book of the Apocrypha
36 Buddies
37 Give off
39 Nicknames
41 Bit of watermelon waste
44 11th-grade exams, for short

46 Ingemar Johansson or Ingrid Bergman
49 Tater Tots maker
50 Funnyman Conan
51 Climbing legume
52 Old Oldsmobile
56 Itinerary parts: Abbr.
57 Bonus
58 "The Bicycle Thief" director Vittorio De ___
60 Bus driver on "The Simpsons"
61 Lab container
62 "Cómo ___?"
64 Stan who co-created Spider-Man
65 Lock opener

by Peter A. Collins

The New York Times

Smart Puzzles

Presented with Style

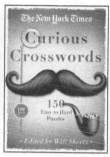

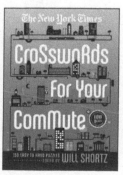

Available at your local bookstore or online at www.nytimes.com/nytstore

St. Martin's Griffin

1

```
C H A T   S O L E   R A P I D
H A L O   A V O N   A M E B A
A M E N   F E E D   G O D O T
S L U G G E R W I L L I E
M E T A L   K E N Y A   S D S
S T S   U Z I   G E N E T I C
    P E E L E     L A N A
P A L E Y E L L O W C O L O R
U R A L     S P O O N
P U L L T A B   O E R   P A T
A T A   A R E A S   G E O D E
  L A B R A T S M I L I E U
S N A R L   T R U E   I N S T
E R N I E   L I M A   O T T O
C A D E T   E A S T   T E E N
```

2

```
A C T E D   W A I L   R S V P
L A H T I   E M M A   O H I O
D R E A M A B O U T   B O A T
E G G   E T C   S E G U E
N O A H   L A B   R E S H O T
  P A J A M A B O T T O M S
  L A S   R U N S   R I P
E P S O M   S T Y   M I N T S
D O H   P A P A   K A T
A L A B A M A B O R D E R
M E D I C I   S L O   M A S S
  O S K A R   D N A   M C I
N E W T   B E A M A B O A R D
O V E R   L A V A   O R D I E
R E D O   E D E N   O B A M A
```

3

```
S P O K E   S K E E   A B B A
L E C A R   P O U R   K A E L
I N T R O   C O R A   I S N O
G R E A T L A K E S   N I N E
H O T T I E   K E Y   L I V
T D S   C A E S A R S W I F E
  S A R A H   S L I C E R
M A G I   T O N   P A R A
A D O N I S   J U D G E
G H O S T W R I T E R   S T U
N E D   O A K   N O S P I N
A S I S   P E R R Y W H I T E
T I D Y   P L I E   S E R T A
E V E N   E L L A   U R A L S
S E A S   D Y E D   P A L E Y
```

4

```
Z E A L   P E T E   M K T S
A R I A   E X A L T   A N E W
P A L M R E A D E R   R U L E
  B A L M   C U B I C L E
R E F   M E S H   M A S K S
E X I T E D   A P P E A L
L I N E N   S N E E R   E T S
A L G A   C A D E T   A B U T
Y E E   D A N S K   M I A T A
  R E B U K E   P E G L E G
O P A L S   T M E N   L E E
C L A S S I C   U N L V
A L I T   N A I L P O L I S H
S I N E   G R A T A   A S H E
T E T R   E M I L   D O U X
```

5

```
T S P   L U I G I   A S S E T
O T O   A G R I N   S O C I O
P A K   P L A N T   A S O N E
D R E S S I N G U P   U T E S
O V A T E   E R A S E S
G E T A   H O R N R I M M E D
  S C A R Y   Z E A L S
E N C   H M O   D I E   N I L
F O R T E   L I N D A
F R I E S A N E G G   M I F F
  B A S S E T   C O M E R
D E B T   K I S S M E K A T E
A L A R M   G L E A N   G I N
W A G E R   H I T I T   E S C
S L E E T   S P I N S   S H H
```

6

```
  S A G   F I G H T   M O B Y
A C N E   A C R I D   O R L E
M O A N   T E E N S   I B I S
P U L L A H E A D   F R A T S
E R Y   L O S T   C R E C H E
R E T R I M   W H O O S H E D
E D I E   E H U D S
  C A P T A I N A H A B
    R E S T S   M I R A
A N I S E T T E   H A T R E D
M A R T Y R   W H O M   D V D
A P E R S   S H O W C A S E S
Z O N E   S L A N T   B E A T
E L I A   R O L E O   R E L O
D I C K   O B E Y S   A D S
```

7

```
C A R A F E  ▪ A B C S ▪  A H S
C L E V E R  ▪ M E A L ▪  L E I
C E S A R R O M E R O ▪ T Y R
▪ T I M ▪ G O T O ▪ S I D E
C H A L I C E ▪ ▪ B A T M A N
E A R ▪ L E A H ▪ X R A Y S
O D E S S A ▪ R E N E E ▪
▪ J A C K N I C H O L S O N
▪ A I S L E ▪ I S S U E D
F L A R E ▪ O D E S ▪ T W O
J O K E R S ▪ T E A R O S E
O T I S ▪ C H I C ▪ R E F
R I N ▪ H E A T H L E D G E R
D O T ▪ O N Z E ▪ E N D A S H
S N O ▪ T E E M ▪ S A Y S S O
```

8

```
A B R U P T ▪ L A I R ▪ T S O
P R O M O S ▪ A I D E ▪ A B E T
B A N A N A S P L I T ▪ G O A T
▪ I R I S ▪ I C A N S O
E L I T E ▪ L E M O N C R E A M
L O S E S I T ▪ A A A S ▪ S L A
I C A R U S ▪ A C H ▪ A T T N
▪ A P P L E C R U M B L E ▪
T I C S ▪ D U O ▪ A R C A D E
I N N ▪ O M A R ▪ S P O O K E D
C H E R R Y M A S H ▪ W A S P S
K O W T O W ▪ E A R N ▪
L U T E ▪ O R A N G E C R U S H
E S O S ▪ R O B O ▪ B O U R N E
D E N ▪ D E E R ▪ S W E L L S
```

9

```
A L A W ▪ S T O A T ▪ O W E S
S E G A ▪ T O M C A T ▪ H O M O
T I O S ▪ E R E N O W ▪ D R I P
A F G H A N P R E S I D E N T
▪ S N O O T ▪ N R A
G R E A T G R A N D P A R E N T
R I A L S ▪ E X A M ▪ T O O
I A T E ▪ T R A G I C ▪ S H O W
E T E ▪ S H E D ▪ I N A N E
G A R A G E D O O R O P E N E R
▪ L T D ▪ N O R S E
▪ T H E S E C R E T G A R D E N
H O A X ▪ A R I S T A ▪ S E X Y
S U Z I ▪ D A M I E N ▪ A M E N
T R E S ▪ B E E N S ▪ T I D Y
```

10

```
C H E F S ▪ W I P E ▪ I D O L
U B O A T ▪ A P E X ▪ D E M I
D O N Q U I X O T E ▪ E N I D
▪ B R E D ▪ C H A N T S
S I D E B A R ▪ G R A T I S
U S O P E N ▪ L O A V E S
R A C E D ▪ M O N T E ▪ Q B S
G A T E ▪ F O R G E ▪ E U R O
E C O ▪ E L V E S ▪ B R A I N
▪ R E T A I N ▪ G A M I N G
▪ S Q U A R E ▪ P A R A D E S
C O U R S E ▪ Z E R O ▪
E L I E ▪ D A I R Y Q U E E N
D I N K ▪ U N T O ▪ U R G E S
E D N A ▪ P A I N ▪ E N O L A
```

11

```
A B A C I ▪ T A C T ▪ O M A N
M A C O N ▪ O S H A ▪ P O L O
P A L M S ▪ M E I R ▪ A B I T
▪ S U B U R B A N M A L I B U
▪ A L A ▪ O A F ▪ L I P
M U S T A N G E S C A P E
A P U ▪ R A I L ▪ R O H A N
H I N T ▪ T A C O S ▪ P O K E
I N D I A ▪ I D O S ▪ M I X
▪ A C C O R D E L E M E N T
S K Y ▪ T O E ▪ T A U
H Y B R I D V E H I C L E S
A R E A ▪ L I R A ▪ O L L I E
R I S K ▪ E V I L ▪ W A L L Y
P E T E ▪ S E C T ▪ S H A K E
```

12

```
S M A R T S ▪ P A R ▪ S I M S
A C T I I I I ▪ I O U ▪ O N I T
C H O P S T I C K S ▪ N E N E
R A M ▪ S R O ▪ H E A D E R
E L I S E ▪ A T T E N T I O N
D E C I D E ▪ R E T A B L E
▪ T I R A D E ▪ L A R
▪ T H E E N V E L O P E
A P O ▪ O R S I N O
P O L E C A T ▪ Z A P A T A
O N E M O M E N T ▪ N E T W T
S C R E W S ▪ U S A ▪ T O T
T H A R ▪ T A K E M Y W I F E
L O N G ▪ E N E ▪ E A G L E S
E S T E ▪ L E D ▪ N O N A R T
```

13

```
S C R E W ■ A L S O ■ S P E W
O H A R A ■ N O O N ■ L A V A
F O U R M I N U T E M I L E R
A O L ■ P L O D ■ O V I N E ■
■ ■ D U L Y ■ C L I E N T S
H A R E M S ■ W H I R R ■ ■
E V A C ■ S H I N E ■ B A G
F O R O L D T I M E S S A K E
T W A ■ A R O S E ■ P R I M
■ S M A R T ■ P L A I N S
D E S P I T E ■ R E A M ■ ■
A L I E N ■ P E A S ■ P S I
F O R E A N D A F T S A I L S
O P E D ■ A I R E ■ O R L O N
E E N S ■ P E E R ■ S K E E T
```

14

```
B O N D S ■ V A S T ■ B E T A
O P E R A ■ I C K Y ■ O X E N
A R T S Y ■ S H A R P T U R N
R A W ■ S H O E ■ E A D I E
S H E P H E R D S C A N E ■
■ I A I M ■ E A S Y ■
A N G S T ■ B A R K ■ C S T
B Y H O O K O R B Y C R O O K
C U T ■ W I G S ■ H A D T O
■ A V O N ■ L O G E ■
S W I N G I N G P U N C H
F L E A S ■ T O S S ■ A H I
R A C K E T E E R ■ H E M A N
A N T E ■ A R M S ■ O V E R T
T E S S ■ B A S E ■ P E S T S
```

15

```
A B B A ■ D I R T ■ F A X
C A R U S O ■ I N A W H I L E
A D O R E R ■ S C H A E F E R
R E W O V E ■ C A S ■ C T R S
■ ■ R E O P E N ■ S H H
C L E A N S E R ■ V I E W E D
H E I S T ■ A N N E X ■ H A R
A V G ■ H O C ■ O T T ■ E G O
N E H ■ D R E A D ■ H E E L S
T E T R A D ■ N E T S A L E S
■ H A Y ■ A N S W E R ■
S S N S ■ S R O ■ O N H I R E
C H O P S U E Y ■ A S A S O N
O U T S H I N E ■ M E R M A N
T E E ■ A T A D ■ T Y R A
```

16

```
G O F I S H ■ R B I S ■ M I Z
P U E B L O ■ A L D A ■ A C E
S I M E O N ■ P A L M T R E E
■ ■ T A K E T H E B A I T ■
A P U ■ N E D ■ A N N ■
L E N D ■ D U M P S ■ S E T H
M O D E L ■ C A R P S ■ G I A
O P E N A C A N O F W O R M S
S L R ■ M O T E T ■ F R E E S
T E T E ■ R E S E T ■ B E L L
■ H A W ■ G U S ■ N Y E
■ G E T R E E L E D I N ■
C A S S E T T E ■ O N E T W O
A G E ■ N O U N ■ R A I S E R
B A A ■ S N I T ■ S I N K E R
```

17

```
B I N D S ■ A S A P ■ A M A T
I N L A W ■ O H N O ■ M A X I
C R E D I T L I N E ■ O P E N
S E R E N E ■ P O T B E L L Y
■ ■ D A M ■ S A B E ■
A N G E L ■ I A M ■ S A L S A
G A R T E R S N A K E ■ E A R
A C E D ■ N U T R I ■ F A T E
S H E ■ B A S E B A L L F A N
P O N T E ■ E S L ■ E A S Y A
■ L I A M ■ E G O ■
A C I D R A I N ■ E T O I L E
M A G I ■ C R I M E A N W A R
A S H E ■ H E L P ■ R E O I L
J E T S ■ O D E S ■ D A N C E
```

18

```
E S C R O W ■ A M A J ■ B B Q
S E L E N A ■ G O T O ■ E A U
T R E E E X P E R T S ■ S A O
D I A S ■ E N S ■ E D T ■
■ F R E E E N T E R P R I S E
■ ■ S E X ■ O H A R A S
A M I ■ E T H A N S ■ C R T S
D O N T S E E E Y E T O E Y E
M S G R ■ N E S T L E ■ D R S
I H E A R D ■ ■ L A I ■
T E N N E S S E E E R N I E
■ E S C ■ W W W ■ D M Z S
W A R ■ K L E E E X H I B I T
A D A ■ O V E R ■ E U G E N E
S O L ■ N I P S ■ R H O D E S
```

19

```
A B O D E . L O G I C . L S D
D E B I T . A C T O R . E Y E
O L I V E R S T O N E . A N N
S T T E R E S A . M E R C Y .
. . R N A . . A V O N . . . .
M A R G A R E T S A N G E R .
E L I E L . S E P I A . C O D
D O N S . S P A I N . S O M E
E N S . T A I L S . M U L A N
. G E O R G E S H E A R I N G
. L E A D . . Z E E . . . . .
P A N D A . . I M I S S Y O U
U S A . T O M S M O T H E R S
L I V . E F I L E . R O A N S
P A Y . D A T E S . O T H E R
```

20

```
M O T H . S U B R A U . O R A
O N C E . P L A N E S . R A G
D O U B L E E A G L E . I F I
. . . A W E E . A D R O I T .
S N E E Z E . D R U . U L N A
M I N D E D . A N D R E S .
O G L E . T R I C E . S I P
T H I N G S W I T H W I N G S
E T S . A H I N T . G E N A
. I T A L I C . P R O S I T
K N E W . P E G . A O R T A S
O G D E N S . O N I T . . . .
D A M . A I R F O R C E O N E
A L E . I D E A T E . G W E N
K E N . F E A R E D . G N A T
```

21

```
A L I T . D E L A . A M E N
N A D A . A G O R A . M E G A
T W E N T Y O N E S W I N G S
I N A T U B . I N T H E U S A
. . . E N Y A . A R E . . .
I T A . E D O M . O N T I M E
N O L I . A R A T . C O C O A
T W E N T Y T H R E E K I D S
R I N G O . A E O N . E L E E
A T E A M S . R O T H . Y S L
. . A O L . P R O D . . . .
S I N A T R A S . U N W I S E
T W O F O R T H E S E E S A W
L I M A . Y E A S T . E T R E
O N E R . X M A S . B O A R
```

22

```
A T A L L . C L A N . U S E S
M A R I A . L I V E . N E A T
T I M E K E E P E R . F E T A
. . S E L F P R O M O T E R
A U N T . A T I T . I R O N S
D R O O P S . . G A M . . .
A I R . A T E M P O . E R I E
M A G A Z I N E R E A D E R S
S H E L . C A R E S S . H A S
. . C O S . . E S T A T E
S T R A W . A S T A . I B E X
P E O P L E P E R S O N .
E R G O . M O N E Y L O V E R
W R E N . U R S A . D R E A M
S A T E . S T E T . S E E R S
```

23

```
C A S T . S S T S . F E A S T
O L I O . U H O H . L A N C E
N E E R . R E L O . A C T O N
J U S T D E A L W I T H I T .
O T T E R . . M O S . S T S
B S A . A C U M E N . S K I P
. . S W A M I . I C I E R
. T O O B A D S O S A D .
C L E A N . S P A W N . . .
H E A P . I N T A K E . S A T
A C C . E R E . A R E N A
. T H E M S T H E B R E A K S
P E E V E . P A C E . A B L E
O R S E R . A L O E . L E E R
E N T R Y . Y E L P . M E T S
```

24

```
H A L F . J E U . T R A D E
I C I E R . U R N . S E V E N
Y E N T A . D I S C O V E R Y
A R C T I C O C E A N . R N A
. . . E S O . A R G O . . .
. T R A N S A T L A N T I C
M O H S . G E L . S E I K O
A P R . A T E A M . M E A
N I E L S . P D A . H O A X
N E W Y O R K H A R B O R .
. E T U I . S A O . .
M I A . H E N R Y H U D S O N
A M S T E R D A M . E L I T E
C U T E R . E T C . R U N T O
S P I C E . R E A . M O O N
```

25

```
R E M   R A W E G G   A D D S
E L I   A Z A L E A   C R A P
C O L D T U R K E Y   R U D Y
O I L I E R   Z E R O G
U S E R   E T T E   A B B O T
P E R E Z   O A R   M A U V E
      R A T O N   B A T S I N
R E F   M I L K D U D   T D S
A D L I B S   T U N A S
U N I T E   J O E   N A S A L
L A P A Z   O P T S   H O P I
    F L I E S   A L I N E S
M A L I   C H E R R Y B O M B
B L O C   R E S I G N   R E O
A L P S   U S O P E N   A N N
```

26

```
C E D A R   T A L O N   I V S
E L U D E   E N E R O   N O T
L O O S E C A N N O N   T W A
      P L A C I D   O T H E R
V I C E   S H E L   N O E L S
I N H A L E   E C O N O
S T O K E   R E A P   I F A T
T E C   D E E P S I X   F R A
A L K A   A B I E   I L I E D
    A W A R E   V I E N N A
S A B E R   L O B E   S G T S
I N L E T   A L L I E S
G T O   H A R D A N D F A S T
M I C   R A M I S   N A M E S
A S K   O H Y E S   A T S E A
```

27

```
R A L P H   W A L D O   R A J
I C I L Y   A P A I R   U K E
O C T A D   D U B A I   S R A
      T R A   E M E R S O N
N A T H A N I E L   N E O N S
A T E   S I T U   P T L
C H E W   M E R   L A I R S
L O U I S A M A Y A L C O T T
  S P L A T   S E I   S W A Y
  I W O   I O N S   E I N
O W L E T   H A W T H O R N E
T H O R E A U   S O B
H I D   E L M E R   W A L L E
E N G   T I A R A   E M A I L
R Y E   H E N R Y   D A V I D
```

28

```
T R A I T   C E D E   C A S A
A A R G H   A L O E   A L I S
W I L L I A M M C K I N L E Y
S L O U C H E S   N A I V E
      K E R   D A T A S E T
J A M E S M A D I S O N
E L A T E   I S H   A C H
R I G H T O N T H E M O N E Y
K A I   G O T   A S K E D
  S A L M O N P C H A S E
M U S T S E E   O R A
A N N O Y   P R O R A T E D
G R O V E R C L E V E L A N D
M I R E   B O A S   N A F T A
A G E S   I S N T   A N T S Y
```

29

```
E R I K   O M N I   O C C A M
R A M A   R E A M   E L L I S
I S M Y   C A M P G R O U N D
S P O O R   D E A L   S E G O
  B L E E D   R E C E D E S
H E A D Q U A R T E R S
A R T   D O Z E   Y E C C H
I R E D   S T I L T   T H R O
R Y D E R   N O A H   A A A
  T H A N K S G I V I N G
S P A R E M E   S T I N K
A O K I   O U T S   S P E C S
B L I T Z K R I E G   E D A M
L A R U E   O R C A   R U S E
E R A S E   N E T S   S P E E
```

30

```
S W A B   E M M A S   S A C K
H A V E   R O A C H   P R A Y
A C E D   N O R T E   Y E L L
W O R L D S E R I E S G A M E
      A U T R Y   P A L
G O T M E       D A T U M
R H O   L E T S G O   S O S A
I A N S   M O U N D   S P A R
T R E E   T E M P E R   O I L
S E D E R       I N F R A
    B O K   A A L T O
B A S E B A L L D I A M O N D
A X I L   H O M I E   A G U E
B O Z O   L O A M S   A R K S
A N E W   O N S E T   M E E K
```

31

```
RAY   GALL   EVENUP
EWE   OWIE   VALISE
TAM   SWIMMINGBAN
ARESO   MELBA
GENTLEBEN   URGES
   ROXY   DOR   ALT
LILI   UNO   REILLY
USEDCLOTHINGBIN
MODELT   TIE   EASE
PUT   ASA   SNIT
STOMP   CESTSIBON
   ATSEA   ITALY
HOTCROSSBUN   RIM
ARARAT   TAFT   EVE
DROOPS   SHOO   SET
```

32

```
MAMAS   GAD   MISS
AMANA   IPOS   ACTA
LITTLEJOHN   REAL
   ASTROS   EASTLA
ASHY   LETTERHEAD
SHA   NES   ORT   AGA
CURIO   ABASE
HEIRTOTHETHRONE
   TAPES   ORION
USA   BET   COW   LIZ
SARDINECAN   AGRO
EXCITE   ONEIDA
ROAD   ROYALFLUSH
INDO   SUER   SEGAR
DYES   TRY   OREOS
```

33

```
GAMMA   WIZ   MESTA
ALIEN   ADE   EXTOL
RANAT   SEA   SPORT
BRITISHALEHOUSE
   EEL   NESTOR
COOTIES   TIDE
APRON   AHA   DNA
PUBLICEDUCATION
ESS   ROZ   DIDTO
   PAIN   OLDCOIN
ASWARM   ANT
CHARGEDPARTICLE
RISKY   RAG   ENROL
INTEL   ICE   STARK
DEERE   PER   TOMES
```

34

```
LIMO   BAWL   WHIM
ODOR   OBOE   SHONE
BOONDOCKS   HOODS
   NORMS   SERAPES
COSTA   SEGA   LEE
ASH   NEUTRON   ADS
BLOCKAGE   IKE
SOTS   SHEDS   ABED
   TEE   PETSTORE
NET   GOULASH   USC
EDU   RUNE   ORFEO
PICKETS   SERIF
ASSET   OOHANDAAH
LOONS   LEIS   ENDS
INNS   DRAT   STAT
```

35

```
WEILL   HOOP   FACT
AMTOO   EDNA   ESAU
ROSEGARDEN   SIRS
   ABITE   TOTALS
DAD   CHIVASREGAL
OREL   NIP   AROSE
CLASSA   NAAN
OLDTIMERSGAME
   ORIG   HERALD
AREUP   CAT   MISO
SAUSAGEROLL   NET
STRATA   FETAL
THOU   SHIFTGEARS
DEPS   PAVE   ERNIE
AREA   STYE   NODOZ
```

36

```
BOY   IMALL   SABLE
ANA   NIVEA   AURAS
DUMBSDOWN   TRENT
ESSO   WWI   GEORGE
   TREASURER
MICHAEL   SENATOR
ONDECK   KEG   OVO
BARRE   TIS   VINOS
IWO   IRA   JINGLE
LEMONDE   JACKSON
   SALESSLIP
BROWNE   OBI   OHOS
RABAT   CRASHTEST
AGILE   MECCA   ALE
DEEDS   ISHOT   POP
```

37

```
ROLFE   ASSN   SACK
OPERA   SHOO   AURA
MAXES   FOXMULDER
ALLEYCAT  ALTIMA
   UBOLT  HASBEEN
LATINI  AIMTO
ACHE  FALL   EXTRA
PRO  XFACTOR   EEL
PEROT  HOST   EXGI
   NEMEA  HEAROF
COVERED   VENTI
OSIERS   PERMITME
MAXYASGUR   ENTRY
AGEE  URNS   STEER
SEND  POKE   HORDE
```

38

```
PEAKS   IAMBS   RIB
INUIT   VIOLA   ETA
TET(RA)HEDRON   CUR
   OKIE   SOMEONE
SYL  (RAH)MEMANUEL
WOOD   DUEL  TIPSY
IRAE  PEW  LEG
GENE(SIS)  (BOOM)ERS
   PUN  SOW   AXES
ADMEN   BLOB   STAT
GRANDPOO(BAH)   EMS
HARDEST   LYNN
AWL  CHEERLEADER
SEE  KARMA  NITRO
TRY  SWOOP  AFORE
```

39

```
PITCHY   CICADAS
INROAD  OLDKNICK
SKILLS  GOESINTO
ASCOT  ERDA   GOR
  KNEWTESTAMENT
   DOC   ETE
BREW  LEWD  TRESS
LADYOFTHEKNIGHT
USUAL  CAFE  TOYS
   TAN   ENO
KNOTFORPROFIT
IOS   WOES  FLIES
COMELATE  CALLME
KNITPICK  TIEDUP
SECANTS   ARREST
```

40

```
FEMA   SNAP   HASTA
AXES   POLE   ACTOR
RISK   EDIT   SQUAT
 THEEASTERBUNNY
   DIK   ERI
STP  GOB  FLOTSAM
TOOTHFAIRY  TINE
INLET  HOO  SALON
CYAN  SANTACLAUS
KARACHI  HBO  STA
  CHI   DUE
BELIEVEITORNOT
EYEON  SPAM  TOUR
ARGUE  TOME  EZRA
MESSY  EDEN  RENT
```

41

```
MARIO  BARGE  KPS
AMEND  ETHEL  WAC
CACTI  COATS  ATA
  YOUCAMPAIGNIN
PFC  MUM  SNEEZED
DELA  ZEROG  LANA
QUELL  ADRY  ATL
  POETRYYOU
DAT  SLOE  SACKS
INRE  SWEEP  RHEA
STENCIL  XES  EGG
GOVERNINPROSE
UNI  IONIA  NURSE
SIN  ERECT  ILIAD
TAO  DESKS  CUOMO
```

42

```
AMOR   IMAC  CSPAN
RARE   NASH  ZORRO
CLAM  TRIOCEREAL
HATE  RCA  OCT
EYED  OENOPHOBIC
RADII  ASAP  FONZ
  MACAU  KEG  ORA
CHOLER   RAPIER
LAV  SIR  DYLAN
ERIS  ZINE  ANGST
OMENCOMICS  AMIR
  EEN  NET  CAGE
FEDERALTAO  ETNA
AMAZE  OHSO  ACED
TUBES  USED  SHES
```

43

A	G	E	N	T		C	A	S	T		O	G	L	E
T	O	N	E	R		O	T	T	O		L	I	E	S
H	A	S	T	Y		C	O	U	G	H	D	R	O	P
E	L	I			A	O	L		A	T	I	L	T	
N	I	G	H	T	F	A	L	L		M	E	T	A	L
S	E	N	I	O	R	S		E	S	L		A	R	E
			T	R	I		T	A	U		A	L	D	A
		K	I	T	C	H	E	N	S	I	N	K		
E	M	I	T		A	A	A		P	V	T			
P	E	N		C	N	N		W	E	A	S	E	L	S
A	N	G	L	O		S	K	I	N	N	Y	D	I	P
	T	S	A	R	S		A	N	D			I	N	A
T	H	I	N	K	T	A	N	K		A	M	B	E	R
O	O	Z	E		E	D	G	E		M	I	L	N	E
O	L	E	S		T	O	A	D		P	R	E	S	S

44

S	I	C	E	M		S	A	G		S	A	W	I	N
I	N	A	D	V	A	N	C	E		A	G	O	N	Y
T	A	K	E	P	L	A	C	E		T	O	M	E	S
O	W	E	N		O	P	T		S	U	R	E		
N	E	D		T	H	E	S	O	P	R	A	N	O	S
			B	O	A			Z	E	N		S	P	H
A	L	I	E	N		M	O	O	N		E	L	I	A
M	O	N	E	Y	L	A	U	N	D	E	R	I	N	G
E	G	O	S		E	D	I	E		V	I	B	E	S
B	A	R		I	R	T			H	E	N			
A	N	D	I	L	O	V	E	H	E	R		R	D	A
		E	L	L	Y		Q	A	S		S	U	E	R
L	U	R	I	D		R	U	N	S	C	A	R	E	D
A	F	T	E	R		R	I	D	E	S	H	A	R	E
W	O	O	D	Y		S	P	Y		A	L	L	E	N

45

A	D	D	O	N		U	T	A	H		R	O	M	A
P	R	I	M	O		S	O	S	A		A	D	A	M
B	E	E	R	B	R	E	W	E	R		M	I	R	E
S	I	M	I	L	A	R		A	D	D	R	E	S	S
			E	V	I	L		L	A	O				
F	R	A	T		I	D	I	D	I	N	D	E	E	D
R	A	D	I	O		G	A	N	G		B	L	O	
O	N	E	T	W	O	T	H	R	E	E	F	O	U	R
S	T	P		L	U	S	T			R	A	N	D	I
T	O	T	H	E	T	E	E	T	H		D	Y	E	S
			O	R	B		R	H	E	A				
T	A	L	L	Y	U	P		R	A	M	P	A	G	E
E	M	I	L		R	O	T	O	R	O	O	T	E	R
S	O	T	O		S	L	A	B		N	O	R	M	S
S	K	E	W		T	O	P	S		G	R	I	S	T

46

L	A	M	B	S		O	R	G	A	N		L	T	D
U	S	A	I	R		L	E	A	S	E		I	R	A
C	O	C	K	A	N	D	B	U	L	L		F	U	R
K	N	E	E		O	P	A	L		S	L	E	E	K
Y	E	S	D	E	A	R			B	O	A	S		
			S	H	O	C	K	A	N	D	A	W	E	
J	A	B	B	A		L	I	B		I	V	E	S	
E	L	L	A		P	R	E	X	Y		D	E	E	P
E	T	A	S		A	A	A			T	A	R	D	Y
R	O	C	K	A	N	D	R	O	L	L				
	K	E	N	T			F	I	C	T	I	O	N	
Y	A	L	T	A		I	S	L	E		A	F	R	O
A	L	I		L	O	C	K	A	N	D	L	O	A	D
L	E	S		O	R	B	I	T		N	O	L	T	E
E	X	T		G	I	M	M	E		A	N	D	E	S

47

	A	D	E	N		P	E	T		D	U	B	S	
O	C	U	L	I		E	L	I		E	N	L	A	I
D	U	R	A	N		P	O	D		B	L	I	N	G
O	R	A	T	O	R	S		E	N	T	E	N	T	E
R	A	N	I		G	I	T	M	O		A	G	A	R
			O	J	S		W	A	V	E	S			
B	O	O	N	E		W	I	R	E	P	H	O	T	O
U	S	A		T	W	I	N	K	L	E		N	E	W
C	U	F	F	L	I	N	K	S		E	R	O	D	E
			R	I	G	E	L		A	S	O			
E	S	S	O		A	L	E	R	T		S	K	U	A
S	P	U	M	O	N	I		I	M	E	A	N	N	O
S	U	G	A	R		S	O	N		K	N	O	C	K
A	R	A	G	E		T	A	G		E	N	C	L	S
	T	R	E	O		S	R	O		D	E	K	E	

48

S	H	A	R	P		H	U	N	A	N		M	F	A
H	I	R	E	R		O	S	O	L	E		A	I	T
H	A	M	M	E	R	T	H	R	O	W		A	N	T
	L	A	Y	L	O	W		E	T	A	L	I	A	
P	E	G		L	L	A	M	A		R	O	T	I	
C	A	N	I		F	R	O	S	T	N	I	X	O	N
S	H	A	C	K		D	E	I	C	E				
		C	H	E	E	S	E	C	L	O	T	H		
			A	R	N	E	L		S	T	O	P	S	
R	A	B	B	I	T	E	A	R	S		A	U	R	A
O	M	O	O		P	S	A	L	M		S	E	X	
S	P	Y	D	O	M		N	O	O	S	E	S		
T	E	T		J	A	C	K	S	T	O	O	P	E	N
E	R	O		O	S	T	E	O		E	L	E	N	A
R	E	Y		S	C	R	A	M		D	I	T	T	Y

49

```
R A J   D I G I N   A B B E Y
O N O   I R A T E   Q U O T E
P O I   P O L E V A U L T E R
E D N A   N A M E T A G
R E T Y P E S   O S I R I S
    H E L D   M A N   N E S T
T H E S E   L A I C   G A T E
W A N   B E A T L E S   D O W
E L A L   L I E S   T R I O S
R A V I   T R Y   N E O N
P S Y C H O   D A M A G E D
    E A R P L U G   D R E W
A G E N T O R A N G E   O R E
W O R S E   O W N E D   O I L
L O R E S   S N O R T   M E L
```

50

```
G U M T R E E   S L Y   P I C A
E N C H A N T   T E E   I D O L
A D D E D I N   A T T H E E N D
R O L F   G A V E   I P A N A
      I B M   A L A S K A
A L A N B A L L   W H E N A L L
R E H A B   E I T H E R   S E A
E V E L   I S S A I D   A K I N
N I A   C O S E L L   V N E C K
A N D D O N E   K E E P A W A Y
      U N S E A T   D S L
L A I R D   B O R E   Y O D A
O F T H E D A Y   O N A S S I S
A R E A   I R S   S I M I L E S
D O R M   G A S   A C E S O U T
```

51

```
J C R E W   C A T T   D I S H
A Z U R E   A M A H   U N T O
R A D I A L T I R E   A D A M
S R I   S U N   H O T L I N E
      S E M I T E   R E A D Y
A M A H L   P R E F I X
L A R O S A   E L E P H A N T
G N A W   C R E S S   A L O E
A S B E S T O S   S O U T E R
      R A S T A S   P S A L M
H A Y D N   A P P L E T
E V E R E S T   L O N   B R A
N A N A   P I R A T E F L A G
C I T I   C O O S   R H O N E
E L A N   A N K H   S A C K S
```

52

```
W E S T   E Q U A L   A S U
A V E R   N U R S E D   P E P
R I G A   L I G H T S P E E D
P L A Y M A T E   S T E R N A
      F O C I   S C A T
A S Q U I E T A S A M O U S E
P A U L   G A L A S
E X O   A L D E N T E   Z I T
      C R O O N   N O N O
B L U E F O O T E D B O O B Y
O O P S   B A I T
U N M A S K   R O D C A R E W
G E O R G E S A N D   B E T E
H R S   T R E N D Y   I A T E
S S T   R A T S O   T R A P
```

53

```
C A I R O   O R E   E L B O W
A L L E N   F E Z   G O O S E
R O O S T   F A I R Y D U S T
A M I E   I N A P E T
F A L C O N C H E S T   I R E
E R O T I C A   A Q U A
      L A S E S   A L U M S
F A T H E R K N O W S B E S T
I L I A D   S L O A N
R E E D   T W E E Z E S
E X O   F A L L H A R V E S T
    N E A R L Y   O R C A
B R E A K F A S T   F L O O R
A B O V E   M O O   A V E R T
D I N E D   A L E   N E S T S
```

54

```
T O N   S A F E   H A S B R O
I D A   L I E N   O S H E A S
P I C T U R E O F W E A L T H
S E L I G   S O N   D A T A
      A G H A   G O G O
S O P R O U D L Y W E W A I L
L A L A   L E I   L Y N D A
A K A   B A S E W I T   S Y D
S I N A I   U A L   P E L E
H E A D F O R T H E W I L L S
      O F L A   L A I N
C H I P   D J S   N T E S T
H A S T E M A K E S W A S T E
A R L E N E   A N T I   S U R
T I E D O N   T E E N   O B I
```

55

```
S A M S   A C H E   H A I T I
A S A P   R O U T   O D D E R
Y O G U R T S M O O T H I E S
O N D R A F T   N I C E
K E A   Y U L E   L A R O S A
    H O L Y M A C K E R E L
B R I A N   B R A E   M A I
L O T S   P L A I N   B A R K
A B S   T A I L   T E N S E
H O M E R S I M P S O N
S T E N O S   S O O N   C E Y
    T U G S   O B T R U D E
A N D A B O T T L E O F R U M
B R O I L   E W E R   D I C E
E A G L E   P O D S   S E E N
```

56

```
L E S   M A R V   A N I T A
A R T   L O U I E   D E N I S
I D A   O R S O N   W A N D A
R E G I N A   S A R A   I A N
    N E L L   A R I E L
S T A N L E Y   A L E C
C O R E Y   C A R L   E R M A
O M A R   P E R R Y   C H E T
P E T E   L U K E   I R E N E
    A D A M   A N N E T T E
    K A R E N   R O S A
A N N   M E R L   T A M A R A
R E N E E   A A R O N   R O D
C L A R A   I L E N E   A L I
A L L E N   N A T E   B E N
```

57

```
H E L M S   A G E   S M O C K
A D I E U   X E D   T O M E I
S W O R D L I L Y   A R E N T
P I N E S O L   A R A L
E N E   B L O W D R Y E R S
D A L E S   A R I D   S T O A
    W O N   A L S O   T A P
    N E W W O R L D O R D E R
D I X   S H E L   N E E
I N T O   A L A I   S T A P H
F E E L D R O W S Y   N I A
    R E A M   L U C K I E R
B R I A R   F I E L D W O R K
A D O R E   A R T   L A N C E
M A R Y S   Y E S   V I S E D
```

58

```
A M B I   A T H O S   L I S A
W E A N   T E M P O   A R I D
E A S T E R N M E D I C I N E
S N E E Z E S   A M U S E S
    R I S E   A S S N
    C E N T R A L H E A T E R
W H O S E   S P O T   I V E
H A R T   R E T O P   C L A N
A L F   S O L O   A R E N T
M O U N T A I N B I K E R
    A I D E   E N I D
S C A R F S   S P R E A D S
P A C I F I C I S L A N D E R
E R A T   D O R I A   Z O L A
X E N A   E L R E Y   A G T S
```

59

```
S I M P   A N A L O G   A D Z
E S S O   M A R I N A   F R A
E A G E R B E A V E R   I O N
M O R T A R   L I F T   C I I
    I C O N   N O H   I D E
P L A C E S T O G O   B O S S
R A F   W E S T   T M A N
O S T I A   B T U   I M A G E
    E L Y S   O S A S   D O G
S O R E   T H I N G S T O D O
E N S   L O O   A R E S
A S H   A R N O   E N T I T Y
M I A   P E O P L E T O S E E
A T V   P U R I S T   P E A T
N E E   S P E E D O   S E M I
```

60

```
A L G A E   P O P   T H E P O
B O A R D G A M E   H E R O N
L A N D G R A N T   C A R L A
E N G   E E R I E R   D O L L
    C R Y   B R A D   R O O
H A L O S   G U I N E A P I G
E D E N   S A S   G A R R
R O O M K E Y   R E D P O N Y
    T E E N   W E D   E N I D
S T O N E D E A F   P L E A S
E E L   P U L L   L A S
V A S T   P A L A I S   J L O
E S T A B   P O L O S H I R T
R E O I L   S P O N G E B O B
S L Y L Y   E S T   O M E N S
```

61

R	O	A	L	D		B	O	A	T	S		J	E	T
A	R	N	I	E		R	O	L	E	S		A	X	E
M	A	D	M	A	G	A	Z	I	N	E		S	I	X
			A	R	M	I	E	S		R	O	S	A	
S	C	H		M	E	D	S	T	U	D	E	N	T	S
C	H	O	S	E	N			R	A	S				
A	A	R	P		H	E	A	D	T	O	T	O	E	
M	I	D	A	I	R	R	E	F	U	E	L	I	N	G
P	R	E	T	T	I	E	S	T		E	T	R	E	
	T	A	T			A	I	S	L	E	S			
M	O	D	E	L	T	R	A	I	N	S		E	D	T
O	D	O	R		A	U	N	T	I	E				
R	I	G		M	U	D	S	L	I	N	G	I	N	G
S	U	E		A	N	O	S	E		T	A	L	I	A
E	M	S		C	A	N	I	T		O	N	E	N	D

62

D	E	N	I	M		L	E	G	O		P	I	S	A
A	N	I	T	A		O	R	A	L		A	N	O	N
H	O	P	S	T	E	W	A	R	D		R	U	L	E
			M	I	N	K	S		A	K	R	O	N	
E	L	F	E	S	T	E	E	M		S	P	E	N	T
S	A	L		S	O	Y		E	T	A	L			
S	T	O	L	E		S	L	I	P	U	P	S		
E	C	R	U		B	R	I	D	E		G	L	E	N
	H	A	S	B	E	E	N		U	S	A	G	E	
	H	A	N	A		K	A	T		N	N	E		
W	A	I	F	S		P	I	N	D	O	C	T	O	R
I	N	D	U	S		S	O	A	P	Y				
S	K	I	N		M	A	L	L	M	I	N	D	E	D
P	L	O	D		A	B	E	L		A	D	A	G	E
S	E	T	S		P	E	T	S		N	I	N	O	N

63

J	U	S	T	T	R	Y	M	E		S	T	J	O	E
A	S	W	E	S	P	E	A	K		A	W	A	K	E
B	L	A	C	K	M	A	G	I	C	W	O	M	A	N
S	T	R			S	E	N	A	T		U	P	I	
	A	D	A	S	H		G	R	O	U	P	I	E	
		B	A	R	B	Q		V	I	N				
W	H	I	T	E	H	O	U	S	E	T	A	P	E	S
A	R	T			Z	A	P			O	V	A		
R	E	D	B	L	O	O	D	E	D	M	A	L	E	S
			T	E	X		S	C	I	F	I			
O	N	A	W	H	I	M		P	A	R	T	B		
M	O	A		A	D	O	U	T			R	O	Y	
A	L	L	O	V	E	R	T	H	E	P	L	A	C	E
H	A	T	E	R		A	N	A	H	E	I	M	C	A
A	N	O	D	E		N	E	W	S	P	A	P	E	R

64

D	E	N	Z	E	L		L	P	G	A		D	A	S
I	C	E	A	X	E		A	R	A	W		E	S	P
C	O	C	K	A	N	D	B	U	L	L		A	T	E
E	L	K		M	O	U	R	N	S		T	R	I	X
D	I	S	K		M	E	I		A	H	S			
			R	O	O	M	A	N	D	B	O	A	R	D
V	I	S	I	B	L	Y		G	A	R		N	A	E
O	N	E	S	I	E		R	U	S	T	I	C		
I	T	A		W	A	C		P	E	P	T	A	L	K
D	O	W	N	A	N	D	D	I	R	T	Y			
	O	O	N		R	O	Z		X	R	A	Y		
B	I	R	D		B	A	N	Z	A	I		O	T	O
A	N	T		R	O	C	K	A	N	D	R	O	L	L
I	C	H		B	A	K	E		K	A	R	N	A	K
T	H	Y		I	T	S	Y		A	S	S	E	S	S

65

J	I	V	E		C	A	G	E	Y		R	E	B	
E	B	O	N		A	B	O	V	E		M	E	R	E
R	O	L	L	E	D	O	V	E	R		A	T	I	T
K	S	U		L	E	D			S	T	A	T	S	
	M	I	S	T	E	R	N	I	C	E	G	U	Y	
A	L	E	V	E		P	E	D	R	O				
R	O	T	O		A	U	S	S	I	E		F	O	P
L	O	W	R	E	N	T		T	O	W	L	I	N	E
O	N	O		I	C	I	E	S	T		O	X	E	N
		A	N	O	L	D			B	L	E	S	S	
B	R	A	V	E	N	E	W	W	O	R	L	D		
I	O	W	A	N			I	C	I		C	U	R	
R	A	M	S		A	N	O	T	H	E	R	O	N	E
D	R	A	T		D	E	N	T	E		A	S	T	I
S	S	N		S	A	T	Y	R		E	T	O	N	

66

S	L	E	D		L	O	C	H	S		I	M	A	X
W	I	F	I		A	S	Y	O	U		S	A	X	E
A	L	F	A		S	H	A	W	N		A	U	L	D
B	A	R	N	E	S	A	N	D	N	O	B	L	E	
		O	N	O			A	I	D	E				
G	E	N	E	N	T	E	C	H		A	L	D	E	R
H	A	T		S	E	T	H		M	Y	L	O	V	E
O	R	E	L		S	E	A	L	Y		A	G	I	N
S	T	R	I	C	T		K	A	R	O		W	A	D
T	H	Y	M	E		P	A	P	A	J	O	H	N	S
		E	L	K	S			A	L	I				
	H	A	R	L	E	Y	D	A	V	I	D	S	O	N
S	O	L	I		A	C	E	L	A		S	T	Y	E
O	P	E	C		T	H	E	O	C		A	L	E	N
W	I	C	K		S	E	R	T	A		W	E	R	E

67

```
A C D C   C A C T I   L E S T
S H I V   A P A I N   A S W E
T A X I   P A N E S   U S E R
A R I   M O T O     P R E E N
  M E E T T H E P A R E N T S
  C A S E Y   O R A L
E R R S     G L A D   H M S
M E A T A N D P O T A T O E S
T O T   L A O S     O P T S
    B O N N   P A I R S
M E T E O U T J U S T I C E
A D O L F     A R T E   O R O
T I N T   P A S S E   S T E T
E T T E   A M O U R   A C C T
S H O D   L I N E N   O H T O
```

68

```
O P T I C   S C A L A   O R B
A L U L A   P A L E S   N I L
T A L L S T O R I E S   U F O
E N S   P E T S     O N S E T
S E A A I R     D A R E
    D A R K V I C T O R Y
A N N A N   R E S T   N E A T
L O A M   B O N U S   L A K E
P A P A   A N O S   F A L S E
  H A N D S O M E S U M
    T I E R   A L P H A S
P R E S S     F E L L   A B E
L O U   M A T I N E E I D O L
O A R   A V I A N   S T O V E
P R O   Y E N T A   T O N E S
```

69

```
G L A D   D O F F S   A B A S
R I M E   U R I A H   D A N L
A B E L   D U B L I N O H I O
H I N T S   S A L E   R M S
A D D   T I N   N O R   A A H
M O S C O W I D A H O   I L E
    A L I T O   E N I D
  A T H E N S G E O R G I A
P L A N   I R R E G
A L T   R O M E N E W Y O R K
R O T   E N E   E S E   L I E
A C E   V E N T   D R I V E
P A R I S M A I N E   O V E N
E T E S   A C R E S   M I R E
T E D S   N E E D S   P A A R
```

70

```
C P A   P L A Y   A N S E L
O I L S   D O M E   S C H M O
M A I M   Q U I L T P I E C E
I N T O W   S L Y   S L E W
C O O K I E S H A P E   F E E
    E G G O   T O T A L
A R O D   A S K   T R I M S
P A P E R D O L L O U T F I T
T E P E E   M A P   S E X Y
  O L M E C   K E P T
M A S   S T O R E C O U P O N
E Z I O   N A H   I D O L S
C U T T H A T O U T   I N D Y
C R E T E   E D G E   O D I N
A E S O P   D A H L   S E C
```

71

```
D E K E   A L O T   S A L S A
I M A C   M O O R   A D O U T
A U N T S E L M A   L O I R E
  G O A L   P I G   T R I
S K A   S I G H T U N S E E N
O A R   E A R   L E E R Y
W H O A   A T R A I N
N O G U T S N O G L O R Y
  A R I S T A   R O O D
R A I S E   N S A   S L Y
M I D N I G H T S U N   E K E
A B M   S E W   R O B B
R E I N S   M I X E D N U T S
S Y R I A   I N X S   A S I A
H E E L S   N E X T   I H O P
```

72

```
O D D   S H U   T A R   T O E
C A R L T O N   E X E G E T E
T H E L A R K   M I N E R A L
A L W A Y S I N P O E T R Y
    N S Y N C   M E S A
C O M O   D A G     A C I D
O V O   M O N A R C H T O B E
M E N   A W E   E A U   T O M
B R O N T E S J A N E   T O O
O T T O   S E T   Y A K S
  O B O E   S W A L E
  S N O B B I S H M A N N E R
F O O D I E S   I M I T A T E
G R U Y E R E   T A N L I N E
H E S   S T E   E N E   L A D
```

73

```
S I E G E   F L I E R   S A T
I N A L L   L E D G E   P R O
N A T A L I E W O O D   E E R
U N E D I T E D     C L E A N
S E N   S E C   B A A A E D
      H O M E C O M P U T E R
U N P I N   R A P S   R A Y
T E R M   B L E S S   P A C E
A R E   C L O D     S O P H S
H O T C H O C O L A T E
    T R A C K   E T A   I M S
C R Y I N     S C O T S M E N
H U B   C O U C H P O T A T O
I T O   E N S U E   R O G E R
P S Y   S E E M S   S W E D E
```

74

```
D I L L   B A T C H   O C T A
O N E I   E B O L A   D A I S
S T A R   M A B E L   E M M A
A U D A C I T Y O F H O P E
G R E   N N E   S E N A T E
E N R O B E S   J E W   I O N
    O R C   P O E   E G G O
S O F A   B I D E N   S N O W
O V A L   E L F     B A R
R E M   C E L   I N T U I T S
T R E N C H   N O W   V A T
  P R E S I D E N T O B A M A
L A I C   V E D A Y   A L A S
V I C K   E L I T E   E R L E
I D A S   S L E E T   R Y E S
```

75

```
A R C S   C E L S   S C A R F
T E R I   E X I T   A L F I E
O N A N   D U N E   B A T O N
M O N G R E L E M P I R E
I I I   E S T   O N E R U N
C R A W L   P A L   T Y N E
    A I L   A M I D   O U T
  C U R C U R R I C U L U M
A L L   S T E T   E C O
M A T T   I C Y   K N O B S
O D I O U S   P S I   L A P
  M U T T V I L L E N I N E
E N A C T   I D E A   I V A N
L A T H E   A L A N   T E N D
S T E E R   L E S T   E R A S
```

76

```
N A G A T   O N T V   N A D A
F U R O R   H E H E   O X E N
L E E R Y   S W I T   A L A N
  L E T S N O T G O T H E R E
    N A T E   H E R S
S E T S   R E V   S E A B E D
A C H   S T A I R   M R L E E
Y O U M U S T B E J O K I N G
O L M A N   S E D E R   N S A
K I B I T Z   S O T   E D Y S
    N A I F   E S T D
I D I D N T H E A R T H A T
D I O R   H O A X   O A T E S
E S T A   E L S E   O N E A L
S H A G   R E E D   P E S K Y
```

77

```
C A P P   T E A S E T   F S U
A L O U   A C T O N E   I T S
M I L L E B O R N E S   R Y E
A N K L E S   A I R T A S E R
Y E A R N E D   A G E N T
    A S T O R   I R O B O T
D O W N Y   Z A L E S   O K S
E R I K   D E M O S   T R I P
M S N   B E N I N   M A N E S
S O D D E D   S E D A N
    B E L I E   R A G T O P S
P R O W L C A R   B O R R O W
E A R   J A S O N B O U R N E
S I N   A T T L E E   M I Z E
O D E   R E S E E D   S N I P
```

78

```
T I E R   S O U L   S U R E
E R N O   H A N E S   U S E D
M A I D M A R I A N   S U N G
P E G G E D   O N A S P R E E
    M E L   I N N K E E P E R
H E A R T E N   E N C
A L T S   P T A S   S T P A T
L E I   T I E G A M E   I G O
O C C U R   L O R E   T A O S
    N A B   A W N I N G S
J U A N P E R O N   I N O
E M M A P E E L   E L Y S E E
L I A M   C H I L D S T O Y S
L A Z E   H A V E N   I L E S
O K E D   B E T A   M O R E
```

79

```
C A J U N   A B L E   C A R T
A M A Z E   M A I D   O V E R
M A R I O N E T T E   P O L O
      N I N T E N D O W I I
C R A B   C S I   O U S T S
R E C I P E   E D I C T
E R R O R   C R A C K   E S T
M A I S O U I   S H A L L W E
E N D   B R A S H   G O T I N
    C A N O E   A E S O P S
S H O O T   V E T   S N E E
M I C H E L L E W I E
O R E O   S U R E E N O U G H
G E A R   A G E R   Y A H O O
S E N T   T E D S   A S F O R
```

80

```
A C T S   B R A S   A B B E Y
M E A L   E A C H   Q U O T E
A L L A   D I R E   U R B A N
S I L V E R D O L L A R
S A Y S N O   L A V   T W O
      G O D S   W I T H E R
  P E R M A N E N T W A V E
A V O N   R A D   I T E M
N E W Y O R K G I A N T S
O L E A R Y   S E L A
N O R   I A M   G I G G L E
    I S N T I T I R O N I C
Z I P P O   I D E E   N O V A
A P R O N   D O E R   E M I R
G O O D S   A L M S   R E D D
```

81

```
G A W K   H D T V   E J E C T
A L O W   A R I A   V E R D I
R E N A I S S A N C E F A R E
B E K I N D   I O N E
    K I B O S H   I G A
A S S T   B A D H A R E D A Y
T H E A I S L E   B E L I Z E
C E N T S   E S P   S I D E A
O R I E N T   S A D T O S A Y
S P O R T S W A R E   T O T E
T A R   L I N K E D
    S M O G   P O T P I E
R I G H T T O B A R E A R M S
A S I A N   U R G E   T O O T
T O N G S   T O A D   A S K S
```

82

```
A M I S   T E T R A   I T L L
R E D O   A G R E E   D R A Y
T W O V I R G I N S   E I R E
E L L I S   G T O   C A D S
    E L E C   S P E L L
B A T T E R U P   S T A V E S
A I R   S A R A N   C R E D O
T S A R   T V S E T   E N G R
E L V E S   E T A I L   U A E
S E E P E D   S T E E L E R S
    L E X U S   O S H A
J A V A   S A T   A T S E A
O B I T   T R A D E R V I C S
E L S E   E G R E T   I N C H
L E A R   D E A N S   A G E E
```

83

```
B A T H   T R E A T   S H O D
A F R O   N O R T H   I O W A
S O O T   O U N C E   X M E N
R O U L E T T E   C H E E S E
A T T I M E S   B R A S S
    N U S   A R O O   T A M
A P S E   C R A W L   E L M
B A L S A   O S U   E V A D E
I C E   B A C O N   I D O S
T E E   L R O N   T E L
    P O E M A   V E R I S M O
P A S T R Y   M A N O F W A R
A L O T   A R O M A   I A N A
C A F E   N I N O N   E M I T
T S A R   T O A S T   R I C E
```

84

```
J A B B A   E G O   S T A G S
O C E A N   A R T   C A R E T
W H A T A C R O C   A K I T A
L O L   P U S S   S L E A Z Y
S O L D E R   S P L A Y
    O S L O   H E R O I C S
E N A C T   S K Y E   U G L I
L O B O   T W I S T   R O U T
A S O F   H A T E   S P R E E
N E U T R A L   D E C I
    H A N D S   T I C K E T
B I S E C T   W A N E   E L Y
A D O B E   P A C A N I M A L
S O F A R   A L I   C R A T E
S L A Y S   X E D   E E L E R
```

85

```
P L I E   ■ C I G A R ■ B L A M
R O S Y   ■ O M E G A ■ R E P O
I R A E   ■ K A R A T ■ O X E N
S N A P D E C I S I O N ■ ■ ■
M A C A O ■ ■ P O N T I F F
■ ■ T R A P S ■ M E T E R
C R A C K L E W A R E ■ I L E
R O T H ■ P R I D E ■ O S L O
E M O ■ P O P M U S I C I A N
D A N T E ■ ■ S E T A T ■ ■
O N E A R T H ■ M U L T I ■
■ R I C E K R I S P I E S ■
Q T I P ■ E L I O T ■ L E N O
E S A I ■ L I N D A ■ E T O N
D O N T ■ L O G E S ■ T O R E
```

86

```
M A K E R ■ E T A S ■ I D O L
A G I L E ■ D E V O ■ N A D A
J A W E D ■ D R A W ■ T R I X
■ R I C H E A R T H T O N E ■
■ ■ T O T ■ A A R P ■ ■ ■
C M I ■ T H E A R T O F W A R
H A N D S O A P ■ T O R M E
U G L I ■ S T O N E ■ R A V E
R O A S T ■ R E V A M P E D
N O W H E A R T H I S ■ S T Y
■ T A R A ■ ■ T A S ■ ■ ■
■ B R O K E N H E A R T E D ■
G R O W ■ N O E L ■ U R B A N
A I D E ■ A U R A ■ L I B Y A
P E E L ■ S T A N ■ E P S O N
```

87

```
Z A P S ■ C A T ■ S H I F T
I D E A ■ G O R E ■ M A N I A
P L A N ■ R O T C ■ E S S E X
P A R K C I T Y U T A H ■ ■
O I L ■ R E I ■ M E R ■ A D O
■ R E V E R S E S P L I T ■
■ Q U O T E ■ O E D ■ R A N I
L U N G E ■ B A H ■ M O C K S
A I D E ■ D O M ■ P E S K Y ■
N E U T R A L S H A D E ■ ■
A T E ■ E L I ■ A L I ■ C A B
■ D R I V E M E C R A Z Y ■
A D I E U ■ I L L S ■ A G U N
L I N E N ■ A B E T ■ N E R O
G E A R S ■ N E T ■ G R E W
```

88

```
F A W N S ■ C H A W ■ C O L E
A L E U T ■ A O N E ■ E R I C
R U B B E R B A N D ■ L A V A
M M M ■ N O I R ■ P E T E R
■ A R O U N D T H E B E N D ■
A S S I S T S ■ E E R S ■ ■
N A T O ■ ■ A C R O ■ H I E
T H E T I E S T H A T B I N D
S L R ■ M L L E ■ ■ A R T Y
■ H A H A ■ B A R R E L S
M U N I C I P A L B O N D ■
A B E T S ■ M I L A ■ G S A
T O R T ■ C U M M E R B U N D
E A V E ■ S N A P ■ E R N I E
S T E R ■ I O N S ■ R A S P S
```

89

```
T O P A Z ■ M A A M ■ T W E R P
A M I G O ■ O M N I ■ I O N I A
L A T I N ■ W I G G L E R O O M
C R A N E O N E S N E C K ■ ■
■ ■ G R R ■ T O O L ■ L E G
M A P ■ S T Y X ■ N I A G A R A
I T E S ■ H O B O ■ S O D O M
S W A L L O W O N E S P R I D E
H I R E E ■ X K E S ■ P E E R
A L L D O N E ■ P E G S ■ S S S
P L Y ■ P E S T ■ T A X ■ ■
■ H A W K O N E S W A R E S
P A P E R T I G E R ■ O N E N O
F J O R D ■ M A I N ■ U D D E R
C A P O S ■ O S L O ■ T O A S T
```

90

```
P R I M E R ■ T M I ■ C E D E
L A R E D O ■ I O C ■ A T O M
A D O R E S ■ P I E ■ R U N T
T I N ■ N E W S S T O R I E S
O A F ■ ■ O T T E R ■ ■ ■
S L E D ■ A M E ■ A D A P T S
■ N O F E A R ■ ■ A M U S E
L E C T E R N ■ S P I N N E R
S T E E R ■ P I C N I C ■ ■
T O S S U P ■ O S S ■ O H M S
■ ■ L A I L A ■ ■ B O P
V O L L E Y B A L L S ■ O R I
E T A S ■ O E R ■ A R A W A K
T O R A ■ L A I ■ S T I L L E
S E A T ■ A M S ■ S A S S E D
```

91

```
E E R I E   T R A M P   G P A
S P U R S   E A S Y A   O E D
P I N K P A N T H E R   L P S
  T R I N I     B R E A D S
C O I N   R E G I S   R B I S
S M O G   W A R N   B R U C E
T E T   S A R I   L O G O N
    P U R P L E C O W
A C R I D   L I L T   B O O
T R E K S   N E R O   S E X Y
M O D E   C A S E S   T A I L
  U P R O O T   E L A N D
I T O   W H I T E R A B B I T
R O N   N A V E L   P L A Z A
A N Y   S N E A K   S E G E R
```

92

```
D I S M A Y   M A S K   T R Y
E L A I N E   O M N I   H I E
F O U N T A I N P E N   A S A
O N C U E   D E L E   R T E S
G A Y E   M I T E R J O I N T
    T R A     S O D S
A S H   E M A I L   C E A S E
C H A M P A G N E C O O L E R
H A L A L   E N N I S   L E G
  F R A U     T E L
H O K E Y P O K E Y   I R A N
O W N S   T U N A   A N I M E
L E O   W A T E R I N G C A N
E N T   O K R A   T O U C H E
S S S   N E E D   S N A I L S
```

93

```
10 C O M E   10 L A W   A S K 10
L O P E Z   S A R A   D A I S
E L E N I   T W I G   A B L E
T A L O N   E N D O W M E N T
    R E A P     N R A
10 C L A S S   B A S I N E T S
L E A H   A B E L   S T A R E
A L B   I N O R O U T   T E N
S L A Y S   S T E R   M E A T
T O N E L E S S   S T A N D 10
    S E N     B A A L
S A N D S T O N E   S A L S A
I S E E   A R E A   T B I L L
T O R A   I M E T   E A S E L
10 F O R   L E D 10   D R A W 10
```

94

```
S M E L L   S C U L L   H O G
I G L O O   H O S E A   A C E
T R Y T R Y A G A I N   N E E
    T E M P S   D E G A S
C A D E N C E   S A L T I N E
O N O R   A R M E N I A N
V I N Y L   E L A N   T S P
E S T   I M I T A T E   H O E
Y E S   G A V E   S P E W S
    T I A M A R I A   O R E O
B O O K M A N   N I P P E R S
R U P E E   P U R E E
I N N   N E V E R S A Y D I E
E C O   T O I L E   L E A R N
F E W   S N I T S   E S S E S
```

95

```
A A R P   G L I B   A R S O N
R I A L   O O N A   Q U E U E
U S D A   S C A N   U S E R S
B L A C K H A W K   A S I
A E R I E   L E A H   O N E S
    D I G S   B A G   G L O
G I G O L O   E L I A   R I B
U R L   L A W Y E R S   E T E
T O A   O T H E   D O D D E R
E N S   R E I   J O V E
N Y S E   E Z R A   E L A T E
    W S J   B U C K N A K E D
R I A T A   A L O U   Y I P E
A R L E N   N E B R   E R I N
F A L S E   G R I T   D A D S
```

96

```
X E N I A   M O R K   B Y R D
A L O N G   O N E I   L E A N
N I E C E   R E A D   U L N A
D O N A L D R U M S F E L D
Y T D   I R O N   M G M
    A M Y W I N E H O U S E
A L I B I   T E A   N I T A
N O N S T O P   O L D D E A R
E C T O   S O W   O A S T S
W A L L A C E B E E R Y
  U N U   Y L E M   I Z E
  N A T A L I E P O R T M A N
B E B E   A B A A   O A S I S
A R A L   T I T S   O T E R O
R O S Y   E S S O   M A T E R
```

97

```
M A O   A R T S   J O I N T S
A R R I V E A T   A G R E E D
S I G M A C H I   M A I T A I
T E A S   O O P S   U S S R
S S N   K N E E H I G H
  M O I     N U D E   M D S
A L U M N A   D S T   C O A T
W I S E G U Y   H A I R D Y E
E R I N   R A W   G L U E O N
S A C   P A P A   L D L
  C L E A R S K Y   P R E
  L I S A   T H E O   A L O T
M U D P I E   E V A N B A Y H
I N L A N D   R E L I A N C E
A G E N T S   O R A L   E E L
```

98

```
G R A S P   B A S E   A Q U A
L A S E R   U R L S   C U P S
A G I L E   S E A T   T O S S
D U F F Y S T A V E R N
      O I L     O O H E D
  F I N N E G A N S W A K E
  D E L     O B O E   Z I A
G I L L I G A N S I S L A N D
U S O   A S I N     E R G
M C N A M A R A S B A N D
P O S T S     O A R
    H O G A N S H E R O E S
A S E A   I T O O   T E R R A
L A W N   G O T O   H A S I D
A X E D   S P A N   A L O N E
```

99

```
A P E R S     S I R E   R E P
R O D E O   I N N E R   A G E
R I D D L E C A K E S   I R A
    T I M O R   K E R N E L
M I R A   I N L A W   C A T S
O N A P A R   L E G A L
N A V E L   M O T E L   C A M
E N E   P R O V O K E   O R E
T E N   H U L A S   A S H E N
  I P A N A     S N O O T S
A L M A   T R A L A   P L E A
M E A D O W   L I N E R
B A G   R O W I N G P A I N S
E V E   C R A C K   I N D I E
R E S   S K Y E   C O O P T
```

100

```
B L A M E   P E R T   C E L L
R O L E S   I C E R   A Q U A
A G E N T   C O P A   S U M O
T O S S A S A L A D   T I P S
    A T T Y   S E G A
A C T   E R U P T   A V A S T
B R E T   I N A   L O O K M A
B A T H   P E T C O   T I E S
A Z O R E S   C R O   E T A T
S Y N O D   C H E F S   A R E
  W A S H   S A P S
B A J A   P I T C H A T E N T
O L A F   I S E E   C A M E O
R A V I   T O R N   E V I A N
G N A T   E X I T   K E R R Y
```

101

```
L A U D E D   L A I   S M E E
E L N I N O   I N K   T A T A
A D D S T O   S T E W A R D S
P E A C H F U Z Z   A N G S T
T R Y   R U S T   M R T
  H O S S   D A S H I N G
A L I E N   T O U R   E S A U
P U P A E   E T S   K M A R T
S L O T   J E T T   A A N D E
O L D S O U L   M A N N
  T N T   R O E G   A D S
C A I R O   C O P S A P L E A
A L S O R A N S   O R I G I N
P E A K   A B E   P O L I C E
P E K E   A C S   S O L D E R
```

102

```
B O L E   R C A S   J E S S E
O P E N W E A V E   E T A T S
C A T C H E S G L I T C H E S
A L S   A L B   A N S E L M O
    B R E A   S U E T
S C R A T C H E S I T C H E S
T O O H O T   S I T   A L A
U C O N N   I T E   A D R A G
M O S   R N A   A R I S T A
P A T C H E S B R I T C H E S
  H I V E   O M I T
A N T I G U A   U H S   S R A
M A T C H E S S T I T C H E S
A T O L L   O N E G A T I V E
D O P E Y   N O S H   N A S A
```

103

```
J A M B   E M I L   A R M E D
E S A I   R E N O   L E O N A
S I N G L E O C C U P A N C Y
T A E B O   W H I R   S O S
      A L S     G O O
D O U B L E I N D E M N I T Y
I T T Y   E D I E   A S T R A
G T E   S P E N C E R   I A L
A E R I E   A J A X   A N N I
T R I P L E L A Y E R C A K E
      L A T     S A C
  S H E   T A C K   C E L I A
Q U A D R U P L E B Y P A S S
V E R G E   E U R O   T O N I
C R E E D   X E N A   S S T S
```

104

```
H T T P   S O L E   S C U F F
E I R E   A V O W   T O R R E
R A I N   R A R E   A R N A Z
B R O C C O L I R A B E
S A S H A Y S   P L A T E S
      A L A   O D I E   A L P
R U N N I N G B E A R   T I E
A T I T   E O E   R U H R
K I X   B A R E M I N I M U M
E C O   O H M S   M E G
S A N D R A   O P I A T E S
      R E B A M C E N T I R E
L I V E D   M O E T   O B I E
A M I G O   F R A U   N E C K
S P A S M   M E N S   I R A S
```

105

```
B I O L   B O S C H   M A C E
R A R E   O R T H O   A L A S
E M A G   B R E E D S H I L L
A N N U L S   W A S H O
D O G M A   S A P   A G A T E
S T E E R   T R O U   A L M A
      E D I T   T E N D E R
E C U A D O R   M A R Y A N N
G A S L O G   A S H E
A R I L   S E V E   S H E E P
L E A S T   M O C   T I L D E
      I O N I C   R U D E S T
N E W Z E A L A N D   E V E S
F R E E   S I D E A   H E L I
L A B S   H O O T S   I N S T
```

106

```
S L E D   A L M S   D A Z E D
P E P E   L E A H   O B A M A
E G O S   I A G O   M A G U S
W A X I N G P O E T I C
S L Y   U N T O   E N I G M A
      A L E   S A G   L E X
  F U L L D I S C L O S U R E
E L L A   B O O   L E I S
W A N I N G I N T E R E S T
E R A   I R S   R A W
S E R E N E   S O U P   M A R
  N E W H A M P S H I R E
A B C T V   A B E T   E N T S
T U T E E   U R G E   L E O I
M Y R R H   L E A D   M O O N
```

107

```
F R I S K   Z A C K   A S E A
W I C C A   U P O N   C U L T
D O E R R   L E V I   C A V E
  T R E A S U R E T R O V E S
    W O N     W I S E S T
T R I C K O R T R E A T
N O V A E   H A H A S   M M E
U T E P   T I M O R   J O E L
T O S   W A N E D   A E O N S
    T R I E D A N D T R U E
S O L E I L     E M B
T R A C T O R T R A I L E R
R A S H   R O M A   R A R E R
A T T N   E W A N   E C L A T
P E S O   D A N G   S K E D S
```

108

```
C A B O T   D A B S   C A S H
A L E R O   E L L E   A L A S
L O R I S   E D O M   N E X T
L U N G C A P A C I T Y
      A A R P     H O U S E
S K I M   C U R T A I N R O D
M A G I C   R A R E R   A L I
I B N   E M P R E S S   N A T
T O O   T A L I A   T R U C E
H O R S E S E N S E   U S E D
S M E A R     O N C D
      M A I D E N V O Y A G E
U M P S   T O R O   N A S A L
Z E R O   E S A U   G R I N S
I R O N   M E S S   A D A G E
```

109

```
M Y S T   ■ C A S T ■   S P A M
R O T O R ■ O B E Y ■ E R G O
B U R M A ■ R A C K E T E E R
U R I ■ I M P ■ E X T E N T ■
R E C K L E S S ■ C O N D O ■
N I T E ■ T E C H I E ■ S A N
S T E V E ■ ■ H A L L S ■ ■
■ ■ R I C K R O L L I N G ■
■ ■ N O O I L ■ ■ N O E L S
H A M ■ C O B A L T ■ B R E T
A R U B A ■ R O C K S T A R ■
R O S A R Y ■ O U I ■ R K O
R U C K S A C K S ■ S Q U A B
I S L E ■ W H E E ■ S E D G E
S E E R ■ S I G N ■ D E E S
```

110

```
S P E E D ■ L I L T ■ Z E A L
A L I K E ■ I N O R ■ A L T A
J A G G E D E D G E ■ I L E S
A C H ■ P O N Y E X P R E S S
K E T T L E S ■ ■ L E N T O
■ ■ B O Y S ■ B A L E ■ ■
B R A T ■ ■ D O G P A D D L E
L O L A ■ M E N U S ■ R I O T
T O L L P L A Z A ■ I S T O
■ ■ E B R O ■ I K E S ■ ■
A S T A R ■ ■ A T E D I R T
M A R C U S W E L B Y ■ D E O
O X E N ■ H I D D E N G E M S
R O V E ■ A N N E ■ E R N I E
E N I D ■ G E A R ■ S E T T E
```

111

```
M G S ■ P A N D A S ■ P F F T
E L O ■ O B O I S T ■ E R I E
G O U N D E R T H E K N I F E
■ B L A S T ■ T E R I ■ S T N
C A M P ■ ■ B O R N W I T H A
B L U E I C E ■ ■ A I R ■ ■
S I S ■ N I E C E ■ ■ A S S
■ S I L V E R S P O O N I N
M C I ■ ■ S T O N E ■ D A S
■ ■ P A C ■ C O N C E P T
O N E S M O U T H ■ H O P E
F A N ■ B A B E ■ M O O R E
F O R K I T O V E R B U D D Y
A M O I ■ E L Y S E E ■ E T A
L I N T ■ S T E A D Y ■ R O Y
```

112

```
J O U S T ■ J O E Y ■ J O S H
O P R A H ■ E N N E ■ A R E A
J E S S E J A M E S ■ N E A T
O L A ■ M A N Y ■ I D I O T S
■ ■ J A Y S ■ T K O S ■ ■
■ A B A S E ■ H U N G J U R Y
S L A C K ■ M E N O ■ O N E A
E L M O ■ J C R E W ■ P I N K
R O B B ■ E G O S ■ P L O T S
F R I J O L E S ■ G A I N S
■ ■ A B L E ■ M A N N ■ ■
H A R V E Y ■ F A L A ■ A L I
A L A I ■ J O E J A C K S O N
H U R T ■ A L T O ■ H I T O N
A M E S ■ R E A R ■ E X A M S
```

113

```
T A C O ■ S M A R T ■ A B R A
A L A N ■ P U S H Y ■ B E E P
T I N K E R S H O R T S T O P
A T A P R I C E ■ R O A S T
■ ■ A T L ■ L I A R ■ ■
E V E R S S E C O N D B A S E
N E R V E ■ ■ H O N E ■ S P A
I T I S ■ T R I M S ■ S P I T
A C C ■ O R E L ■ S I C E M
C H A N C E F I R S T B A S E
■ ■ U T E S ■ E T O ■ ■
O B A M A ■ ■ B R A I N I A C
D O U B L E P L A Y C O M B O
D A R E ■ G O T T I ■ M A L T
S T A R ■ O L S E N ■ E X E O
```

114

```
D I T S ■ E V E R ■ C O B R A
E V R Y ■ M A X I ■ A D O U T
M A I N ■ B L A C K P E A R L
O N A ■ D E S C E N T ■ ■
T O G A E D ■ T R I ■ K E E L
E V E N T ■ M A S T ■ I M N O
■ ■ N A P A S ■ T A K I N G
A S T A I R E ■ R E W I R E S
D I A B L O ■ N O R A D ■ ■
A T I E ■ B O O M ■ R E M I T
N U L L ■ L O G ■ I D E A T E
■ ■ P E L T E R S ■ S R S
S A N T A M A R I A ■ S A I L
O D E O N ■ L I N T ■ P L E A
Y E G G S ■ A L E E ■ P A D S
```

115

```
M A S K   H U M U S     E F O R
U N T O   U N A P T     T R I O
S C A R   S A Y N O     H E L D
T H R E S H   B E M I N E
D O R A T H E E X P L O R E R
O R Y   P U P   T S E   I W O
    K A S E M       A D E N
  J O E T H E P L U M B E R
H U N G     H E N C E
A D E   S A C   E T D   A L A
R O S I E T H E R I V E T E R
  L O C K I N   T I N H A T
I S I N   I N T E L   D O P E
D E C I   N U R S E   E M I R
E X E C   S P E E D   D E N Y
```

116

```
I C E R S   T O M B   D E A F
S A M O A   I N G A   U C A L
P R I M P   G I R D   L O R I
S T R A I G H T   G A L L O N
      N E A T   C U N N I N G
S T R O N G   C L Y D E
A H A   S E A L E   A S H E S
W I S E   S P E A K   S I C K
S N A C K   S A N E R   G H I
      L O S E R   N A C H O S
S I M I L E S   B A N A
O N A P A R   S L I P P E R Y
L U G S   A S T I   A T R I A
I S M E   P E E N   S O B E R
D E A D   H A R D   T R E N D
```

117

```
N I N E   O L A N   P A S S E
O N O R   T I N E   E M P T Y
L A M A   T O N E   S M I T E
E T A S   O N U S   T O R E
S I N E W   L O G   I R A
S E S S I L E   N A P S T E R
    S O R E   L A T E S T
S T A N D A R D W O R K D A Y
P E R I O D   S O R T
I S T H M U S   P E E V I S H
N T H   P C B   D O L C E
  F O R T   O R B S   I L E X
C L U E R   F O R E   D I N O
O E S T E   F I R E   O N E S
S W E D E   S L R S   F I V E
```

118

```
L A L A   J E T S   O R B I T
E T A S   A R O N   D E L C O
G E T T I N G C O L D F E E T
I M H I P   S K O A L   S S T
O P E N E D   T W O   S H E
N O R   C U E S   S T A Y E R
  H A N D I N   T O E S
  C H I C K E N I N G O U T
F O A L   N A T I O N
E R R O R S   I S B N   E M I
R N A   A O K   S E A M A N
U P S   I N R E D   I T E R S
L O S I N G O N E S N E R V E
E N E R O   N O A H   A G E R
S E D A N   A L L Y   M E L T
```

119

```
B I D E N   C L I O   O N A N
A D A N O   A E R O   R E L Y
D O N T M O V E A M U Z Z L E
F I G   S C I     P R O P S
I D E D   T A R S A L   E T A
T O R I C   R I C H   W R A P
  T U B   N A P   E C R U
  B U Z Z I N G T A B L E S
K A T E   T E L   H A L
I S I S   O M E N   R E C U R
D S L   P H O T O N   S A S E
  T I E T O   L E S   M E D
F U Z Z A N D F E A T H E R S
U B E R   E Y E S   E E R I E
N A D A   Y E W S   P R A D A
```

120

```
C P A S   S L O P   C U F F S
H E M P   T O N E   U T I L E
A R E A C O D E S   P E R O N
R U N N I N G A T A B   E S T
    K N E E L   M O S E S
M R D E E D S   I B A R S
G O O D     O V E R A C T S
M A N   K E Y W O R D   A H H
T R O P I C A L   B P O E
  T E N O R   D E B E E R S
  D E I G N   D O P E S
T I N   L O S E C O N T R O L
S A T I E   U P I N S M O K E
A N E R A   M O L Y   A X I S
R A R E R   S T E M   N Y E T
```

121

```
L A K E   H E M P   G A M M A
I D E S   O B I E   A V I A N
S H E S A L A D Y   Z E S T Y
T O N E R   N I O B E
S C E N T S     T A B A S C O
      Y O U R E S O V A I N
C A P S   P R E     S A L T S
A N I N   S N E R D   I S E E
V I S O R   V E E   L A S T
I M A B E L I E V E R
L E N S M E N     R E C T O R
    N A C H O   A L I V E
J A B B A   H E S A R E B E L
A L I E N   E L L Y   A I R E
B E N E T   S L O E   T A T E
```

122

```
T A N   E R U P T   B A B A R
A S A   R A T I O   A R U B A
D I S A R M A N D H A M M E R
A F A R   S H A D E   A P S E
      A T E     R O N
D I S M I S S A M E R I C A
A N T I C   M O O S E   A V E
T K O S   B E R R Y   S P A T
E E L   N E A T O   M A R I A
  D I S B A R A N D G R I L L
    A C T     A R T
I M A M   O A T E R   R I L E
D I S B A N D O N T H E R U N
O C E A N   I N N E R   A M Y
L E A S T   N E E D S   S P A
```

123

```
C U B S   D I V A   F U Z Z Y
U S O C   E M I T   O K I E S
R E F I   A N E W   R E P E L
B U F F A L O W I N G S
S P O I L S   L E I   I D O
    L I L Y L I V E R E D
E D N A   N A E   N E G A T E
T R U R O   G M S   N O N E T
A L B I N O   E U R   S I R S
T A B L E T E N N I S
S O Y   C O X   D A Y S P A
    J U S T A D D W A T E R
N A B O B   O P A L   C A S T
O M A N I   L O D E   H I T S
D I G I T   S P A R   T R O Y
```

124

```
C A S H   D E B R A   F E S T
A C L U   E N T E R   A M I E
C R U M B C R U S T   J A G S
T E M P E R A S   D W I G H T
I S P   R I G   B E A T
    C R E E P Y C R A W L Y
E N J O Y S   A T O M   H U E
P E A T   I C E   D A T A
I A N   L A N E   S A U T E S
C R E D I T C R U N C H
    R O T H   S O T   R P I
B A N A N A   R A W O N I O N
A G O G   C R A B C R E O L E
R E D O   K U K L A   A T O P
E D E N   S T E E P   P S S T
```

125

```
C Z A R   M A T H   F E S T
R E L O   R A D I O   O N C E
O R E O   E X U L T   O L A N
C O C K T A I L   T A T A R S
    S O D   T A I L P I P E
U T E   L E S   R E A R
P I P E D R E A M   S I T O N
S N I P   S L Y L Y   N O P E
Y A C H T   D R E A M T E A M
    E U R O   T R A   S L O
T E A M G A M E   D D E
I M M E S H   G A M E C O C K
N A I R   R E A V E   A M A N
G I G A   A R D E N   R O B E
E L A L   H E S S   D O S E
```

126

```
A R M A N D   E M B A R   P F C
B E A V E R   V E R S E   A O L
A P T I T U D E T E S T   L U X
F R E S H M A N S E N A T O R
T O Y   U S S   M A M I E
  S O P H O M O R E J I N X
S N O W   U R N   N O T
C O L L E G E S T A T I O N
D O O   R A P   E S S E
J U N I O R P A R T N E R
S T E N T   B A I   S A P
  S E N I O R D I S C O U N T S
A I L   T H E I M M O R T A L S
M G S   I N A N E   L E E R A T
I N E   S O R E N   A S S E S S
```

127

```
Z E R O   B O W S   S L A B
A X E S   O L E O   C O R E
P I N T   O L I N   A V I D
S T E E L E M A G N O L I A S
    R O B   H E M A N
J I B   T O A S T S   G T O
A D A P T O R     S C A T
B I G M O M M A S H O U S E
B O G S     S T O P P E R
A M Y   G R O P E S   S R I
    J A N E T   R E S
P R E L U D E T O A K I S S
R E A L   A L A I   I N L A
A N N O   C L O D   R O O F
M O S T   T O S S   T R E E
```

128

```
S W A P   P A R T B   D A M
R O W E D   I T I S I   O R E
T R A D E S C H O O L   T E A
A S K   C U S S     L O M A N
S T E E L E   D A N Z A
      B A R T E R S Y S T E M
I K N O W   W R O T E   R D A
S P A N   D I A N A   V I D I
L A N   M A N S E   S I X A M
E X C H A N G E R A T E
    Y O R K E   N E W A G E
D I D O K   S A K E   N O G
D O R   S W I T C H P L A T E
A W E   U B O A T   S A M M S
Y A W   P A N G S   M E E T
```

129

```
J A B   C O R G I   A M T O O
A L E   O D E O N   B I E R S
C I R   B O A R D   O X E Y E
K E E P O N L O R R Y I N
U N T I L   U A E   T I C S
P S S T   C O N G A Q U E U E
    A L O U D     U P S E T
H A M   O P T   A M I   T D S
E L U T E   E X U D E
W I S E B L O K E S   L I M P
N E I N   A C E   V I D E O
    C A T C H S O M E Z E D S
H U B B A   R O T O R   A L I
A R O L L   E U R O S   L E T
P I X E L   S T O N E   S Y S
```

130

```
S T E V E   J A C K   I B M
E R R O R S   A L E E   N E A
C O N A N O B R I E N   J A Y
T D S   I N A G E S   L E N O
    L E S S O N   A E S I R
M I M I   I N T I M A T E S
A T P E A C E   O N E
J O H N N Y   C A R S O N
    T A M   D E N E U V E
A B O M I N A T E   S N A G
S O L O S   G I B E A T
H O S T   R E D U C E   P R O
T H E   T O N I G H T S H O W
O O N   A N T E   O N T I M E
N O S   P A A R   A L L E N
```

131

```
M I C   T O N I   I M P A L E
I N A   I D I D   N A R N I A
S K I L O D G E   G L I D E S
S E R E   S H O R E L E A V E
M Y O P I A   O M A R
    E A R P   M A R   A R F
S N O W L E O P A R D   J O E
T A B   M A N   A P R
A T E   S O P H I A L O R E N
B O Y   H U E   A T O P
    Y E T I   A G E N T S
S P E E D L I M I T   R O A N
C A N A D A   S R I L A N K A
A N D R E W   G A L E   O E R
M E S S R S   S E T S   S N L
```

132

```
M A L A R I A L   G A N D H I
O N E H O R S E   I B E R I A
N O N S T O P S   A S W A R M
Y D S   B E S T   E T T E S
    S H O R   J O N S
E P C O T   S M U T   H E M
U L E E S   A L A R   M I M I
T W E N T Y S I X S T A T E S
I A T E   A M E X   O L M E C
L Y E   G N A R   A F T E R
    J A G R   A G U A
V I S O R   A C M E   A R C
A N T I C S   H O T C O C O A
I R A N I S   I C E C R E A M
N E C T A R   C O N C O R D E
```

133

```
T E S T   C O P E S   L A Z Y
A X L E   A W A R E   A R O O
S P O T   D E L L A   B I O S
T O W   D E N S E F O R E S T
E S C O R T S     A P E
    O N U S   T O R E A D O R
A B O M B   J E W E L   U P A
J A K E   H O M E R   A M I N
O R E   S O A P S   E B B E D
B A R I T O N E   S L E W
    N A S   O I L L A M P
O B T U S E A N G L E   I I I
L O R I   G L A R E   E T N A
E X I T   O A T E N   L E O N
G Y M S   W R E S T   O R S O
```

134

```
A C E S   A F B S   S T U D S
D O L T   M O A T   T U T E E
H A I R S P R A Y   O B E S E
O C T A L   T E R M P A P E R
C H E W E D   D O N G S
      P E O N   N O A   D S L
I N M O T I O N   P H O T O
V I A L   S H O R T   A M Y S
A N G L O   G O E S N E X T
N O S   U M P   W A N D
      S T I E S   R E S A L E
C A K E W A L K S   A T B A Y
A M A T I   L I N E D A N C E
P I L O T   E N I D   N E E R
E D E N S   T K T S   D R Y S
```

135

```
S T U F F   E T O N   M C C I
L I N E A   R A F T   A H A B
I N D E X   R U T H E N I U M
G E O   P O R E   L I N I
H A N K A A R O N   S L A I N
T R E A T S     R E A S O N
    R O S E A T E   E N E
  B A R A C K O B A M A
B O A   G U A N A C O
E N C O D E     T E A B A G
T E T R A   S U P E R B O W L
  M E A L   E V E S   R N A
F O R T Y F O U R   H U M I D
E R I E   R U L E   I N A N E
D E A D   A L A S   T O N G S
```

136

```
S N A R E   J E A N   A F A R
A E S O P   U C L A   S I M I
P H I L I P R O T H   S N I P
S I T E   E O N   B E I G E
      P A T R U B E R T S O N
S P I L L S   A B A S H
M E T A L   E U R O S   L A M
E A S Y   P R M E N   D I K E
E T A   W A R P S   L E N I N
    S T E N O   D E P E N D
P I E R R E R E N O I R
E M C E E   L I E   I V E S
D A R N   P A U L R E V E R E
A G E D   R I D E   G E N I E
L E T S   O D E S   O S I E R
```

137

```
R U N O F F   S A W S   C A B
S T A P L E   C R O P   O L E
T A M P E R P R O O F   M C I
    E S E   E A S E   S M O G
S O T   C O P P E R P L A T E
I N A H E A P       I E S T
R E P O   T E R R A C E
  S E M P E R P A R A T U S
    B U S S I N G   E N T S
  P A R R     C U D D L E S
P A P E R P U S H E R   I M S
E R A S   A N T E   Y A K
R I C   S U P E R P O W E R S
P A H   A S I A   S U N L I T
S H E   P E N D   I T S Y O U
```

138

```
A C T A S   A L P   S I E G E
S H A L T   B I C   C L A R A
T I K K I   C M L   I O T A S
O N E A R M   B A M   I S N T
    C L I M B   B A L L A D E
T R A I N S E T   R I O T E R
D A R N   G R A M S
S T E E R   T U B   P I P E S
    U C O N N     T R E E
W I E S E L   K E R O S E N E
E N D U S E R   R E N A L
T H E N   O A R   O L D A G E
T A N G O   N O R   O A T E N
E L I T E   B O O   A T E S T
D E C O R   Y T D   N E S T S
```

139

A	P	E		H	I	T	C	H		A	D	E	P	T
E	R	S		A	C	U	R	A		R	E	V	U	E
S	I	S	I	S	E	N	O	R		A	B	A	T	E
O	M	E	N		J	A	P	E		M	I	N	T	S
P	A	N	A	M	A			F	I	T				
			C	M	A	J	O	R	S	C	A	L	E	
S	L	O	P	S		T	U	N	E		A	X	O	N
H	O	B	O		F	A	L	S	E		R	E	N	O
E	V	I	L		E	L	I	E		I	D	L	E	S
S	E	E	Y	O	U	L	A	T	E	R				
			E	N	D				N	E	T	T	L	E
P	A	S	S	E		O	R	C	A		A	R	A	B
E	L	I	T	E		S	E	A	B	R	E	E	Z	E
W	I	L	E	Y		H	E	L	L	O		E	E	R
S	T	O	R	E		A	L	L	E	N		D	D	T

140

A	L	T	A	R		T	A	P	S		H	G	T	S
D	I	O	D	E		A	L	O	T		A	R	A	L
Z	Z	T	O	P		L	O	L	A		D	O	R	A
				P	U	N	C	H	A	N	D	J	U	D	Y
L	E	F	T	B	E		A	R	L	O		C	Y	S
I	M	A		L	E	E			E	T	C	H		
S	O	C	K	I	T	T	O	M	E		F	O	C	I
A	T	T	I	C		U	A	E		R	O	M	A	N
S	E	C	T		H	I	T	T	H	E	S	A	C	K
			H	E	L	I			S	E	A		R	T	E
A	W	E		E	G	G	S		E	L	I	X	I	R
D	E	C	K	T	H	E	H	A	L	L	S			
M	A	K	E		I	N	O	N		I	A	M	B	S
E	V	E	N		Q	U	O	I		F	I	E	R	Y
N	E	R	O		S	S	T	S		E	D	G	A	R

141

S	T	A	H	L			T	A	B		A	O	K
A	I	R	I	E	R		O	H	N	O		N	R	A
D	R	U	G	D	I	C	T	I	O	N		J	A	R
R	O	T	H		P	A	T	E		E	B	O	L	A
			S	H	O	W	O	F	A	D	O	U	B	T
L	O	V	E	I	S			P	R	Y				
R	I	O	A	C	T	I	V	I	T	Y		T	P	K
O	S	I	S		L	A	Z		P	R	I	E		
N	E	D		R	O	L	L	E	R	B	L	I	N	G
			C	O	W			H	O	A	X	E	S	
M	A	I	L	I	N	G	D	R	E	S	S			
A	C	R	E	S		E	Y	E	S		M	O	D	I
B	A	A		T	A	K	E	O	U	T	A	N	A	D
E	S	Q		E	L	K	S		S	H	T	E	T	L
L	E	I		R	A	O			U	V	R	A	Y	

142

L	I	M	O		P	A	A	R		I	N	C	U	R
E	C	O	L		O	N	C	E		S	O	U	S	E
G	O	O	D	N	I	G	H	T	S	S	L	E	E	P
O	N	T	H	E	S	L	Y		T	U	T			
			A	G	E	E		P	R	E	E	M	I	E
N	O	T	B	A	D		K	R	I	S		O	C	T
O	R	B	I	T		S	N	I	P		S	U	E	Y
B	E	T	T	E	R	M	O	U	S	E	T	R	A	P
U	I	E	S		O	I	L	S		R	A	N	G	E
T	D	S		L	O	L	L		H	O	R	S	E	S
S	A	T	H	O	M	E		M	O	T	T			
			D	W	I		G	E	N	I	U	S	E	S
B	E	S	T	K	E	P	T	S	E	C	R	E	T	S
O	L	I	V	E		D	O	A	S		N	E	U	T
T	I	P	S	Y		A	S	S	T		S	K	I	S

143

A	I	D	E		F	I	J	I		B	A	N	K	S
G	R	O	G		O	R	A	N		I	Q	U	I	T
H	O	W	G	O	E	S	I	T		R	U	N	N	Y
A	N	N	E	X		L	E	N	D	I	N	G		
			D	E	C	K		R	O	B				
A	H	A		N	O	W	A	N	D	A	G	A	I	N
C	A	M	S		L	A	M		T	A	W	N	Y	
E	L	O	C	U	T	I	O	N	P	H	R	A	S	E
R	E	C	O	N		N	O	R		B	R	E	T	
B	R	O	W	N	B	A	G	G	E	R		E	T	S
			E	B	B		O	P	A	L				
	J	E	E	R	S	A	T		J	I	B	E	D	
W	E	B	T	V		C	O	W	P	A	L	A	C	E
I	R	A	T	E		U	N	I	T		A	C	H	E
Z	I	N	E	S		S	E	G	A		C	H	O	P

144

E	L	M	I	R	A		S	C	A	M		S	H	E
L	I	O	N	E	L		T	H	R	I	L	L	E	R
S	N	O	C	A	P		S	I	N	C	E	R	E	R
		N	A	C	H	O			O	H	M			
N	O	W		H	A	D	J		A	U	G	H	T	
E	V	A	D	E		D	A	N	G	E	R	O	U	S
D	E	L	I	S	H		C	O	O	L		N	N	E
I	R	K	S		A	S	K	M	E		J	E	T	T
C	L	I		F	L	O	S		S	P	A	T	E	S
K	I	N	G	O	F	P	O	P		A	M	O	R	E
S	E	G	A	R		N	U	L	L		O	S	S	
			P	E	P		N	O	M	A	S			
A	L	O	E	V	E	R	A		A	T	C	O	S	T
F	A	L	S	E	T	T	O		M	O	T	O	W	N
B	Y	E		R	E	E	K		S	P	I	N	E	T

145

```
M E L O N   W A L T   E M M A
E X U D E   A R I A   F O E S
L I B E R A L B E N E F I T S
S T E R O I D       P U R E E
        D O I   W I S E S T
S E T T E E   N I E C E
I C I E R   E D N A     S P F
M O D E R A T E D R I N K E R
P L Y   G O N O   G U I L E
    P L A N T   M O T T L E
M O H A I R   S R I
A V E R T       E M E R A L D
C O N S E R V A T I V E T I E
R I C E   A I D A   A B O V E
O D E S   S N A G   N A M E D
```

146

```
R E A M   F E L L S   B R A
A N V I L   L A S S O   R A M
J O E S A T U R D A Y   Y I P
A C R O B A T   T B I L L S
S H Y   O M E G A   E S C
    F R E D R I C A P R I L
N O T E S   E D E N   E D U
E L A N   A N N A N   E E L S
R E X   P L O D   U N M E T
D O R I S E V E N I N G
    E R A   A L L O T   B A N
T A L E N T   E T R U R I A
E L I   D O N N A A U T U M N
A G E   Q U I P S   E A T E N
R A F   S T A R T   H E D Y
```

147

```
R O B   B I N G E   S C R A M
O P E   I D E A L   C R U D E
B E E   N E W T O   H A D I T
I R R I G A T E   E M M E T S
N A G S     P N O M
  H A S A H E A R T   E W E S
S O R   M E M B E R   D E V A
C U D   C A B O V E R   S A L
U S E S   R E V U E S   T N T
D E N T   T R E E S T U M P
    A A H S     R O I S
C H A S M S   R U M P U N C H
H A S H E   T U B E R   R O E
A S H E N   O M E G A   O N E
S H E D S   S P R A Y   E E N
```

148

```
A D L E R   G A R T H   D A T
C R U D E   A L O H A   R O O
M A N U A L L A B O R   A R K
E G G   M I A M I   D A N T E
    P E R S O N A L L O A N
A R M A D A     W I G
P O U R     S P O O F   E B B
S P I R I T U A L L E A D E R
E E R   G E E S E   N I T A
    E N E     Z A N T A C
D I A G O N A L L I N E
R O T O R   L E O N A   A P O
A W E   A L L T U C K E D I N
M A S   N A O M I   I R E N E
A N T   T O T E S   N E S T S
```

149

```
C R I M E   G A R P   C H A F F
H A R E M   O R A L   H A L L E
A T A L E O F T W O C I T I E S
R E Q   R A R E   A R E T E S
    S I T E   D O R A
  L E T T H E M E A T C A K E
W A L R U S   E L K S   L I R E
A B I E S   E S P Y   S I L A S
R E Z A   W A S H   A T C O S T
  L A M A R S E I L L A I S E
    P A T S   A G R A
P T B O A T   E G A D   F R O
F R E N C H R E V O L U T I O N
C O A C H   O R E O   S A L V E
S P R E E   T E N N   T R E E S
```

150

```
B A N J O   L O C A L   M U M
O C E A N   O C H R E   E N O
F R U S T R A T I O N   N P R
F E T C H E D     A G A T E S
    H E X   M O R T G A G E
A C T A S   S U R   H A L
M O E   L E T S G O   I N K S
I T M A Y B E T A K E N O U T
E S P N   B L A N D A   T H E
    T I X   M R S   S T E N T
F A S T F O O D     S T R
U N F A I R     M E L I N D A
N I A   L I B R A R Y B O O K
G O T   E B O N Y   M A I Z E
O N E   S I N A I   E L R E Y
```

151

T	O	M	S		W	A	R	T	S		D	E	J	A
I	N	I	T		E	L	I	O	T		E	X	A	M
E	T	N	A		B	L	A	I	R		S	P	R	Y
R	O	O	T	O	F	A	L	L	E	V	I	L		
	P	R	U	N	E			S	T	A		O	R	C
		S	E	E	Y	A		C	L	O	S	E	R	
R	A	T		S	T	E	M	T	H	E	T	I	D	E
A	T	R	A			A	N	O			T	V	A	D
L	E	A	F	T	H	R	O	U	G	H		E	S	O
P	A	N	C	H	O		T	R	Y	O	N			
H	M	S		E	R	S			M	Y	E	Y	E	
	P	L	A	N	T	M	A	N	A	G	E	R	S	
S	H	O	E		E	R	I	C	A		A	S	I	A
E	A	S	E		T	E	R	M	S		T	E	E	D
T	R	E	K		S	W	E	E	T		E	S	S	O

152

I	R	I	S	H		T	O	M	S		E	A	R	P
M	A	R	L	O		A	R	A	T		X	B	O	X
A	R	O	A	R		L	E	G	A	L	P	A	D	S
M	E	N	W	A	L	K	O	N	M	O	O	N		
S	R	O		T	U	B		U	P	A		D	O	A
	N	E	I	L	A	R	M	S	T	R	O	N	G	
		D	O	L	C	E			H	E	N	I	E	
K	I	R	I		S	K	I	D	S		L	S	T	S
I	C	O	N	S			G	O	T	T	I			
W	E	C	A	M	E	I	N	P	E	A	C	E		
I	R	K		A	L	G		A	L	I		M	A	O
	F	O	R	A	L	L	M	A	N	K	I	N	D	
A	F	O	R	T	I	O	R	I			T	I	L	D	E
B	E	R	G		N	O	O	N			E	L	I	O	T
E	D	D	Y		E	S	N	E			D	O	O	R	S

153

A	M	M	O		T	R	O	T	S		A	C	I	D
L	O	A	F		R	O	X	I	E		E	D	N	A
E	O	J	F	R	A	Z	I	E	R		S	P	U	R
P	R	O	T	E	M		D	R	E	W		L	I	T
H	E	R	O	D		J	E	O	N	A	M	A	T	H
		D	I	E		D	E	C	A	Y				
O	J	E	B	I	D	E	N			O	T	E	R	I
L	A	V	A		S	P	E	N	D		T	R	O	D
E	R	A	S	E			O	E	J	P	E	S	C	I
	P	I	T	A	S		A	S	H					
E	J	O	C	O	C	K	E	R		O	F	U	S	E
N	O	R		N	E	I	N		A	N	U	B	I	S
A	L	A	S		S	L	O	P	P	Y	J	O	E	S
C	I	T	E		I	L	L	E	R		I	A	N	A
T	E	E	N		T	S	A	R	S		S	T	A	Y

154

M	I	R	E	D		H	A	F	T	S		C	R	O
A	C	E	L	A		A	W	A	I	T		H	I	C
P	U	B	L	I	S	H	O	R	P	E	R	I	S	H
			E	Q	U	A	L		P	R	A	N	K	S
F	U	N	R	U	N		S	C	E	N	T			
O	N	O		I	D	I		A	R	S	E	N	I	C
R	T	E		R	A	M	P	S			D	O	N	O
M	A	X	F	I	E	L	D	P	A	R	R	I	S	H
E	M	I	R		O	S	A	G	E		S	O	O	
R	E	T	I	R	E	S		R	E	N		E	L	S
		T	E	N	T	H		G	E	T	S	E	T	
G	L	A	Z	E	R		U	S	A	G	E			
L	O	U	I	S	I	A	N	A	P	A	R	I	S	H
I	N	N		E	C	L	A	T		D	R	E	A	R
B	E	T		S	H	I	N	E		E	A	R	L	S

155

M	U	M		A	S	A	P		G	A	M	E	S
O	N	O		F	O	N	D	A		A	G	O	G	O
W	I	T	H	O	U	T	Q	U	E	S	T	I	O	N
G	S	H	A	R	P			R	A	P				
L	O	R	I			T	S	A	R		A	R	M	
I	N	A	L	L	L	I	K	E	L	I	H	O	O	D
			I	A	M	I			D	A	L	A	I	
M	A	Y	B	E	Y	E	S	M	A	Y	B	E	N	O
S	W	E	E	T			U	T	I	L				
N	O	T	L	O	O	K	I	N	G	S	O	H	O	T
	L	I	T		S	E	T	S			N	I	G	H
		U	S	N		C	O	U	P	L	E			
A	I	N	T	G	O	N	N	A	H	A	P	P	E	N
I	D	E	A	L		O	Y	O	S		I	R	E	
M	O	O	D	Y		W	E	P	T		E	S	T	

156

J	A	I	L	S		A	F	A	R		S	O	S	A
I	N	L	E	T		R	O	T	E		I	R	O	N
M	A	K	E	A	S	T	R	O	N	G	C	A	S	E
			R	I	O		T	I	E	A	K	N	O	T
S	A	C		N	A	B		G	R	O	G			
C	R	O	P	S	P	R	A	Y	E	R		E	N	O
H	E	M	I		Y	O	R	E		E	N	R	O	N
U	T	E	N	N		N	B	A		T	A	I	L	S
L	O	T	T	E		C	O	S	T		A	N	T	I
Z	O	O		S	H	O	R	T	W	I	N	D	E	D
	T	A	S	E		Y	I	N		S	S	E		
O	N	E	S	I	D	E	D		S	C	I			
N	O	R	W	E	G	I	A	N	T	H	R	O	N	E
I	R	M	A		E	R	N	E		E	A	S	E	S
T	A	S	S		D	E	K	E		S	Q	U	A	T

157

ALLIN · BEARD · CFO
LOOIE · ARTOO · ARR
TOWNANDGOWN · RIB
APPS · IGOR · ANDES
· SHIITE · ILIED
· STARSANDBARS
SPITS · HMO · LIP
ION · YOKOONO · ECO
NOT · MAE · BERET
GLOOMANDDOOM
· TOWIN · OREIDA
FADED · NOTA · TUBA
ABE · WEARANDTEAR
ILE · ALTAR · DELTA
REP · YIELD · EDSEL

158

DISCOS · ATE · AGOG
ENTAIL · SUR · WIPE
NEATLY · SPACEBAR
SPIN · COATI · ELM
· TRAFFICCONE
· PLAN · ENDIN
OUT · AUDITS · ORNE
KNUCKLESANDWICH
ATTU · TRIXIE · PHI
YOULL · IFAT
· PARADEFLOAT
ASS · HEWED · MOWS
ICECREAM · ENTREE
DAMP · SRO · ROOTER
ARIA · EDS · ARMADA

159

EQUI · JAMB · SLEPT
BURT · ALOU · PODIA
BIDE · CLAM · ICING
· PUMPKINPIRATE
· RAN · NIL
GERBIL · LIFT · SHE
ALOUD · WOKE · AMID
SUPREMEBERATING
EDEN · ELBA · GORGE
SER · LADY · TANKER
· PEN · SET
· ERRATICTHERED
BLOOD · SOAR · AMOR
ABOVE · TATA · GIZA
YEMEN · OXEN · STET

160

ERGO · DOLED · EWOK
DEAN · EBOLA · MAGE
IMTERRIBLYSORRY
TIEGAMES · LATTES
· AVAS · JIVE
LENTIL · WAGE · GPS
ATEIN · SASH · SALT
IHAVENTGOTACLUE
ROLE · ARON · DRAMA
SSE · TMAN · WEASEL
· BREW · RASP
VETOED · PASTIMES
ITSWORTHTHERISK
ETAL · ORDIE · OCTA
WARS · PESOS · NEAT

161

SAMSON · SAY · MADD
ICEAXE · PGA · OLAY
POWDERROOM · JIMI
SPLENDOR · GABON
· SKYDIVING
NATALIE · ORNE
ANALOG · WHYS · SSN
BABYONEMORETIME
STU · SOLD · UNITES
· TERI · UNGLUES
NAVYSEALS
ALERT · AERATION
MEGA · KINDOFBLUE
EVAN · INK · TRAITS
DENT · ANY · SOREST

162

GESSO · SRTA · NOHO
ELIAS · HOOD · INON
NEARTOONESHEART
EMMA · NUIT · ACDC
SEENBUTNOTHEARD
INS · ASS · TIS · RUE
STEER · WON · SEXY
· NORTHEAST
OTTO · OHO · PAILS
PRO · SUE · KIA · COL
PARTHENONFRIEZE
LEIA · WHOA · PRED
EARTHSHATTERING
ALOU · TART · LANGE
TASS · STAY · SYKES

163

M	A	C	A	W			T	W	A	S			G	L	E	E
P	L	U	T	O			Y	O	R	E			M	A	R	X
H	A	R	O	L	D	R	O	M	E				A	M	A	T
				F	R	O	Z	E			A	C	A	S	E	
S	O	N	O	M	A			Y	E	L	L			Z	E	N
P	R	O	P	A	N	E			A	T	T	E	S	T		
E	L	L	E	N	G	L	A	S	G	O	W					
D	Y	A	N			O	N	A				E	C	H	O	
			I	R	V	I	N	G	B	E	R	L	I	N		
I	C	E	T	E	A			S	A	P	P	O	R	O		
N	O	L		S	T	O	A			S	I	S	T	E	R	
A	L	I	S	T		B	R	O	I	L						
R	A	C	E			J	A	C	K	L	O	N	D	O	N	
O	D	I	N			A	M	E	R			G	U	I	D	E
W	A	T	T			N	A	D	A			S	T	E	E	D

164

A	L	A	S	K	A			A	M	S	O			P	T	S
T	A	R	T	U	P			S	A	Y	S			R	O	W
C	H	A	R	L	E	M	A	G	N	E			I	M	A	
O	R	B	I	T		O	H	I	O			S	V	E	N	
				P	U	B	L	I	C	D	O	M	A	I	N	
R	O	S	E	R	E	D				S	W	A	T			
E	S	P			D	I	M	S			O	R	E	C	K	
C	H	I	C	K	E	N	C	H	O	W	M	E	I	N		
D	A	C	H	A		G	M	E	N				Y	A	O	
			E	A	T	S			P	E	U	G	E	O	T	
A	U	G	U	S	T	A	M	A	I	N	E					
G	R	I	D		A	G	A	R			A	T	P	A	R	
A	G	R			B	R	A	I	D	E	D	M	A	N	E	
T	E	L		A	V	I	D			C	O	A	R	S	E	
E	S	S			T	E	N	S			U	N	D	E	A	D

165

F	L	I	P			D	R	O	P			F	R	O	M	
L	O	R	E			D	O	L	L	S			D	I	N	O
O	G	R	E			E	N	D	U	P			A	N	A	T
W	E	E	D	S			R	E	G	I	S			S	I	T
			G	E	E	S	E			S	E	A	L	E	R	S
B	L	U	E	S	T	A	R				S	T	E			
A	O	L			E	G	I	S			Y	E	T	I	S	
D	I	A	G	O	N	A	L	P	A	R	K	I	N	G		
E	N	R	O	N		N	E	A	T				M	O	T	
			A	T	F			S	C	O	O	P	E	R	S	
S	A	N	D	A	L	S			E	Z	R	A	S			
A	R	E			P	E	E	L	S			I	S	H	O	T
L	U	R	K			E	X	X	O	N			T	A	M	O
A	L	D	O			R	E	V	U	E			A	R	A	M
D	E	S	I				D	I	T	S			S	E	R	B

166

H	O	P	I				S	C	O	T			F	L	A	W
O	V	A	L	S			E	O	N	S			R	O	S	A
S	I	N	E	W			P	A	C	K	L	I	G	H	T	
E	N	D		A	N	I	S	E			O	N	S	E	T	
D	E	A	D	H	E	A	T			H	U	G				
			B	A	I	T			M	O	D	E	L	T	S	
S	P	E	L	L		O	A	R	S				Y	O	U	
P	L	A	Y	I	N	G	W	I	T	H	F	I	R	E		
C	A	R			I	L	L	S			A	U	N	T	S	
A	T	S	T	A	K	E			O	L	E	G				
			I	C	E			O	L	D	F	L	A	M	E	
S	P	A	D	E		K	N	E	E	D			W	A	X	
H	O	L	Y	S	M	O	K	E			A	M	A	N	A	
U	R	D	U			C	O	E	D			Y	O	K	E	L
L	E	A	P			S	K	Y	S			B	E	S	T	

167

A	T	O	M	I	C			A	C	T	V			C	D	S
R	I	V	E	R	A			B	O	R	E			H	E	N
C	A	I	N	A	N	D	A	B	E	L			E	R	A	
			N	O	R			B	E	D	L	A	M	P		
O	B	I			P	A	L			S	T	O	P	I	T	
H	A	N	D	L	E	B	A	R				S	O	S	O	
S	C	R	E	E	N			M	E	G	S					
	H	E	A	T	E	D	B	L	A	N	K	E	T			
			A	R	O	D			R	E	I	N	I	N		
I	C	E	D			B	A	L	D	E	A	G	L	E		
G	A	M	E	O	N			S	A	E			R	E	D	
E	N	A	B	L	E	D			I	N	A					
T	O	I			S	W	I	T	C	H	B	L	A	D	E	
I	L	L		O	L	G	A			O	C	E	L	O	T	
T	A	S			N	Y	S	E			E	S	T	A	T	E

168

A	R	O	M	A			C	L	A	P				A	D	O
B	E	L	O	W			R	O	M	E			P	R	O	P
A	C	E	I	N	V	A	D	E	R				R	I	O	T
C	O	O	S		E	V	E	N			W	E	A	R	S	
I	N	S	T	O	N	E			C	H	A					
				R	I	N	G	C	H	I	C	K	E	N		
D	E	M	U	R			R	O	U	G	H	A	G	E		
E	L	O	N		D	E	I	S	M			E	T	A	T	
M	A	S	S	L	E	S	S			P	R	O	D	S		
I	N	T	H	E	B	O	T	T	L	E						
			A	N	T			Y	E	S	D	E	A	R		
S	H	I	V	A			F	I	D	O			I	N	R	E
H	I	K	E			E	L	L	B	I	N	D	E	R	S	
O	P	E	N			S	O	S	O			A	U	R	A	E
T	S	A			P	E	A	L			S	P	O	U	T	

169

D	R	E	A	M		S	L	U	M	S		T	E	X
E	A	R	L	Y		H	A	N	O	I		W	A	R
F	I	R	S	T	S	T	R	I	N	G		I	R	A
Y	D	S		H	E	E	D		G	N	A	R	L	Y
			J	I	L	T		P	O	O	D	L	E	S
M	U	S	I	C	A	L	S	C	O	R	E			
A	R	U	B	A		P	B	S		S	O	L	D	
Z	I	P		L	O	R	I	S	E	S		R	I	O
E	S	S	O		U	A	R		C	R	I	E	S	
		M	O	T	H	E	R	T	O	N	G	U	E	
S	T	R	A	U	S	S		E	R	O	S			
H	E	A	R	T	H		E	M	I	T		D	W	I
E	N	S		F	I	T	T	O	B	E	T	I	E	D
B	O	P		I	N	S	E	T		R	A	V	E	L
A	N	Y		T	E	A	S	E		S	N	A	K	Y

170

R	C	M	P		T	W	A	N	G		C	A	M	S
O	H	O	H		W	A	T	E	R		A	M	E	N
S	A	N	D	D	O	L	L	A	R		L	I	N	E
E	R	S		U	C	L	A		M	E	N	S	A	
T	I	A		P	A	S	S	T	H	E	B	U	C	K
T	O	N	I	E	R		E	T	D		S	H	Y	
A	T	T	N		C	O	S	M	I	C				
	S	O	F	T	S	H	E	L	L	C	L	A	M	
		O	R	E	I	D	A		A	N	A	S		
A	C	H		A	W	L		A	M	P	E	R	E	
B	L	O	O	P	S	I	N	G	L	E		C	I	G
L	I	R	A	S		A	U	E	L		D	A	M	
A	M	A	T		F	O	R	M	U	L	A	O	N	E
Z	A	C	H		U	N	C	U	T		S	T	A	N
E	X	E	S		R	A	S	P	S		P	E	S	T

171

S	A	MY		A	M	A	N	A		A	T	E	E	
A	R	E	S		G	O	N	E	R		T	H	A	N
B	I	T	T	E	R	E	N	E	MY		A	E	R	O
I	D	O	I	D	O		A	D	M	I	R	A	L	S
N	E	O	C	O	N			O	N	I	T			
		M	O	N	I	S	M	S		R	E	MY		
MY	R	O	N		MY	O	H	MY		T	R	I	P	E
T	A	L	O	N		M	E	R		R	A	C	E	R
H	E	D	G	E		S	A	N	E		U	S	E	S
S	S	S		A	MY	G	R	A	N	T				
	M	A	T	S			J	O	V	I	A	L		
I	S	O	T	O	P	E	S		O	M	E	N	I	I
M	A	K	O		A	L	L	B	Y	MY	S	E	L	F
O	L	E	N		C	I	R	C	E		T	R	E	E
K	A	Y	E		E	A	S	E	D		S	T	D	S

172

B	O	R	A	T		M	O	A	T	S		C	B	S
O	D	O	R	S		E	A	T	I	T		O	A	T
B	E	N	C	H	W	A	R	M	E	R		U	T	A
			I	O	N	S		C	A	T	C	H	Y	
I	M	S	O	R	R	Y		C	L	I	C	H	E	S
R	O	T	A	T	E		C	H	A	T	U	P		
K	O	O	K	S		B	L	E	S	S		O	P	S
E	N	O	S		B	L	E	E	P		A	T	O	M
D	S	L		C	L	A	R	K		M	E	A	R	A
	P	O	D	U	N	K		C	O	R	T	E	Z	
M	A	I	T	R	E	D		P	A	P	O	O	S	E
E	G	G	S	A	C		P	E	R	P				
R	A	E		C	H	A	I	R	P	E	R	S	O	N
I	P	O		K	I	O	S	K		T	O	I	L	E
T	E	N		S	P	L	A	Y		S	E	T	A	T

173

E	D	G	E		T	I	P	S		J	E	W	E	L
C	A	R	B		A	M	I	E		A	L	I	V	E
C	R	O	W		U	L	E	E		M	O	T	I	F
O	N	T	H	E	R	O	C	K	S		P	H	A	T
			I	N	U	S	E		O	C	E	A	N	S
E	Y	E	T	E	S	T		B	L	A	S	T		
L	U	X	E			F	O	O	L		W	O	P	
A	G	T		M	A	R	T	I	N	I		I	K	E
N	O	R		E	M	A	C			M	S	R	P	
	A	T	L	A	S		D	A	K	O	T	A	S	
Q	U	O	I	T	S		M	I	L	E	S			
U	N	L	V		S	T	R	A	I	G	H	T	U	P
A	D	I	O	S		A	B	B	E		P	E	D	I
F	E	V	E	R		K	I	L	N		I	R	O	N
F	R	E	D	O		E	G	O	S		T	I	N	K

174

N	I	C	H	E		R	H	O	D	A		I	O	W	E
O	N	H	E	R		O	R	R	I	N		T	U	B	B
S	L	O	P	E		M	E	N	S	A		S	T	A	B
H	O	P		C	S	A		O	P	C	I	T	S		
E	V	I	L	T	W	I	N		R	I	C	O	T	T	A
D	E	N	Y		A	N	E	M	O	N	E		A	O	L
		N	O	M		T	O	V		B	E	R	Y	L	
	J	A	C	K	I	N	T	H	E	B	O	X	E	S	
M	O	S	H	E		O	L	E		E	X	P			
E	S	T		E	S	T	E	L	L	E		A	S	S	T
D	E	E	P	F	A	T		S	O	N	A	T	I	N	A
	R	E	E	B	O	K		W	E	S		R	O	C	
P	A	I	R		O	D	I	L	E		K	N	I	C	K
R	A	S	P		T	A	L	O	N		U	S	U	A	L
Y	A	K	S		S	Y	N	O	D		P	A	S	T	E

175

```
A P P T S ▓ N I N E ▓ E S T S
A S O U L ▓ E N O S ▓ N C A A
B Y E B Y E L O V E ▓ O R G Y
A C T ▓ ▓ A L I ▓ ▓ B L E S S
▓ H I Y O S I L V E R A W A Y
▓ E C A R T E ▓ E L O ▓ U L E
▓ S A X E ▓ O R B ▓ A P E S
▓ ▓ I L L B E B A C K ▓ ▓
M B A S ▓ A E R ▓ H I P S
E L L ▓ I N E ▓ A R E T O O
S O L O N G F A R E W E L L
H A H A S ▓ ▓ B A N ▓ A V G
U T E S ▓ Y O U R E F I R E D
G E R I ▓ A L T A ▓ A K I R A
A D E S ▓ P E S T ▓ M E S S Y
```

176

```
S A L A D ▓ E S Q ▓ P O S T S
A D E L E ▓ P E U ▓ I V O R Y
S H E L F ▓ A M I ▓ N E X U S
H O R S E R U S T L E R ▓ ▓ ▓
A C S ▓ C U L ▓ I A N ▓ E R E
▓ ▓ ▓ S T E E L T R U S S E S
A B B A ▓ S T A ▓ S T A T E S
P L A N B ▓ S T L ▓ S T E V E
A O R T A S ▓ E O S ▓ E R E S
R O B E R T S R U L E S ▓ ▓ ▓
T D S ▓ F A T ▓ G O N ▓ G O A
▓ ▓ ▓ M I X E D R E S U L T S
D O R A G ▓ A A A ▓ U N I T S
E C A S H ▓ M T N ▓ E D D I E
N T E S T ▓ Y E T ▓ D O E S T
```

177

```
D A U N T ▓ O C T A D ▓ B O P
A S T O R ▓ R O Y C E ▓ A N A
H E A V I E S T P U M P K I N
L A H ▓ E N O T E ▓ E R E C T
▓ ▓ A S A N A ▓ T R A D E S
E B E R T ▓ ▓ R E I D ▓ ▓
L O N G E S T M U S T A C H E
A N G ▓ A E O N S ▓ H I E
L A R G E S T M E A T B A L L
▓ ▓ A S H E ▓ ▓ R O I L S
O M E R T A ▓ N O L A N ▓ ▓
C A R T E ▓ M O L E S ▓ R O D
H I G H E S T H I G H D I V E
E N O ▓ M A G O O ▓ E X C E L
R E T ▓ S L E W S ▓ D I A N E
```

178

```
C A L F ▓ B R U I N ▓ A C C T
O L E O ▓ R E P R O ▓ G O R E
T F O R M A T I O N ▓ I L E T
S A S S Y ▓ I N N ▓ A L L A H
▓ ▓ A R O N ▓ ▓ O P I A T E
P I C K O F T H E L I T T E R
T O R E N T ▓ A Y E A Y E ▓
A N I ▓ L Y E ▓ ▓ R A W
▓ M A G P I E ▓ R A V A G E
C H E R R I E S J U B I L E E
L O S T I T ▓ ▓ E T O N ▓
E L C I D ▓ P A R ▓ V E N T I
A D E S ▓ B U C K R O G E R S
T E N T ▓ O L L I E ▓ A R I A
S M E E ▓ B L U N T ▓ R O X Y
```

179

```
T O S S ▓ A B E A M ▓ S E T S
S H O O ▓ R O S S I ▓ A G H A
A I R Y ▓ G N A T S ▓ T R I G
R O T A R Y D I A L ▓ Y E G G
▓ ▓ ▓ I L S ▓ E A R T H Y
D E M O T E ▓ M A A M ▓ ▓
O C A L A ▓ G O L D C O A S T
F O R D ▓ S O A P S ▓ B L A H
F L E S H T O N E ▓ B I O M E
▓ ▓ B U D S ▓ S A T E E N
S P O T O N ▓ S A L ▓ ▓
N U K E ▓ T U R T L E D O V E
I R A N ▓ M E A R A ▓ U S E D
P I P E ▓ A L T A R ▓ S L I D
E M I T ▓ N E E D Y ▓ T O N Y
```

180

```
T W I T ▓ G L O V E R ▓ B O A
R E N O ▓ R E N A M E ▓ A N N
A T T N ▓ O N T I M E ▓ D R Y
G O E S O U T O N A L I M A
I N N ▓ R P I ▓ ▓ S O M E
C E D E D ▓ L A M A C H O P S
▓ ▓ T E L ▓ N A V Y ▓ D S T
▓ V E R A E N D I N G S ▓
S R I ▓ L I E U ▓ S T E
H O N E Y C O M A ▓ H E L G A
H U E S ▓ ▓ L A I ▓ O R E
▓ G R A D E I N F L A T I O N
C H I ▓ E L T O R O ▓ O T O E
H I P ▓ E L E V E N ▓ L E V I
A T E ▓ R E M A D E ▓ D R E D
```

181

```
A G I N G ■ R A S P ■ B I B S
I O N I A ■ I S E E ■ A M A T
D I R T Y J O K E S ■ A B B Y
S T E R E O S ■ M O S ■ R Y E
■ ■ O R E ■ D E S K J O B S
O F T ■ B L E D ■ I A G O
H R H ■ I L I E ■ E N B L O C
O E R ■ D O N J U A N ■ I M A
H E E H A W ■ A T R Y ■ O E D
■ L E A H ■ D Y E D ■ S R S
D O W J O N E S ■ R U T
R A E ■ S A L ■ P U N I E S T
A D E N ■ D E N I M J E A N S
P E K E ■ E T A T ■ A T R I P
E R S T ■ R E B A ■ M O L T S
```

182

```
T A B O O ■ O L S E N ■ I D S
U S U R P ■ N A N C Y ■ N I T
M I S C H I E V O U S ■ D O E
S A Y ■ E S A I ■ A I D E
■ P L A C E T O S L E E P
A P P O I N T ■ I D E A ■
G R E T A ■ C L E A N S E R
H O E R ■ O F F E R ■ L I L O
A B N O R M A L ■ B A N K S
■ A H A T ■ P L E D G E S
P E R S O N S B U I L D ■
O M I T ■ L E N A ■ T V A
P O S ■ F U T U R E B L O O M
U T E ■ O V E R T ■ O V A T E
P E N ■ X A C T O ■ R I D E S
```

183

```
K O B E ■ I S L E T ■ H A J I
O R E S ■ S T A L E ■ E R I C
O B I T ■ B R I E R ■ A C M E
L I G H T N I N G R O D ■
S T E E R ■ K E Y ■ M A S A I
■ R A B E ■ P E C T I N
H O G ■ C A P T A I N H O O K
O S O S ■ L A I L A ■ E R L E
W H A T S M Y L I N E ■ K I D
D E L R A Y ■ M O T E ■
Y A S I R ■ A G O ■ N A R C S
■ V I R G I N I A R E E L
Z U N I ■ D I G I T ■ T H A I
I R O N ■ A L L E E ■ H A S P
P I N G ■ S E I S M ■ A B E S
```

184

```
R I L E S ■ W O O D S ■ J U T
A R I E L ■ A T B A T ■ U N E
C O O K I N G T I M E ■ S T A
I N N ■ P I E ■ I O T A S
E M I R ■ B R O K E N H O M E
R A Z O R S ■ P I T ■ S U E T
■ N E M O ■ D E N N Y ■ T D S
■ P O K E R G A M E ■
L A P ■ T U N A S ■ C U R E
O A R S ■ R I T ■ S A R O N G
S M O K E D M E A T ■ O U Z O
T I M I D ■ S O L ■ G Y N
A L I ■ I T S O K W I T H M E
R N S ■ C R U D E ■ R U L E R
T E E ■ T Y P E D ■ A B Y S S
```

185

```
O M A N ■ P L U S ■ B R E W S
D O L E ■ A D Z E ■ R A C E R
I N G A ■ J O I E ■ O S H E A
S T A R M A P ■ M E T H O D S
T H E M A M A S ■ S H E ■
■ I R A ■ O U T E R E A R
S E W S ■ S T O N E R ■ E L I
T W I S T ■ A N D ■ S H O U T
O E R ■ H I R E O N ■ A C M E
P R E V E N T S ■ O A S ■
■ A I R ■ T H E P A P A S
F A I R S E X ■ O N E B E L L
A B O I L ■ B A S T ■ A L I A
R E N E E ■ O P E R ■ L E N T
M E S S Y ■ X R A Y ■ L E E S
```

186

```
E P E E S ■ M A C S ■ T O F U
M I C R O ■ O S L O ■ I R I S
B L O O D M O N E Y ■ N O N O
L E N S ■ A R E A ■ M O T E S
E D O ■ C H E R R Y C R U S H
M U M B A I ■ E V E N S O
S P Y O N ■ I P S A ■ D E W
■ R E D S T A R T S ■
H I C ■ I M A X ■ H A Z E L
U N A B L E ■ S E L E N A
R U B Y T U E S D A Y ■ P T S
S T A N D ■ G L E N ■ T H R O
T E R A ■ B R I C K L A Y E R
O R E M ■ M E T A ■ A C R E D
N O T E ■ I T S Y ■ B O S S A
```

187

```
BAMA  ALPS  ATLAS
ALEX  HAIL  PEACE
HIGHWAYTOHEAVEN
ATSEA  SATE  MAST
      AIM     ELS
ROADTOPERDITION
HAM    MIRA  MENSA
OTARU  NAB   BRAIN
METER  OTIS    NEC
BRIDGETONOWHERE
   DEM      TWO
GATE   IDES  INUSE
ROUNDTRIPTICKET
INNER  ONUS  HEWN
NEEDY  PERK  OSSA
```

188

```
FAD  SHOWER  PAGE
ONE  PAROLE  EARN
ONAGAINOFFAGAIN
LENO  RED   ELATE
     LED   SLOE
ISOFFONATANGENT
CANSO  ALES  SLOW
IRS  REVERSE  EVE
NEER  FAVE  FINER
GETONTHEOFFRAMP
      PASO  ASA
ASTER   FIR  QTIP
SWITCHPOSITIONS
KILO  ARLENE  MCS
STEW  NODEAL  EAT
```

189

```
MARC  ACAR  DOVES
CLEO  SHOE  UPONE
DIDNOHARM  MTIDA
VEIGHTTBIRD  COT
INGEAR  NOUSE
  RRATEDBMOVIE
MIL  EYED  SWOON
ACAD  SNIFF  STUD
ROMEO  TRES  ESS
VNECKTSHIRTS
  BASIC  README
NOR  IPHONEEMAIL
CHANG  EXITPOLLS
ONION  MENE  ALLI
SONGS  ANOD  NYSE
```

190

```
SCRAP  ALBEE  CAT
ALAMO  BOOMS  HUE
SIMPLEASABC  IRE
HOP  LACE  RAGLAN
   DUCK  RAPIDLY
ZENITH  RECESS
ALONE  VEXED  PEA
NIPS  SELES  FLAX
EAR  ACRES  SLAVE
  OPPOSE  STAYED
ROBERTA  SOUP
ELLIOT  SELF  ROW
ADE  PIECEOFCAKE
DEM  OSCAR  EAGLE
SRO  SHOTS  DREAD
```

191

```
LIP  LASSIE  ZEDS
AKA  ELAINE  OTOE
MEW  TOWNCOUNCIL
BANDITOS  MEHTA
  TENOF  SFPD
SHIPOFFOOLS  PCS
MACON  RBI  PHAT
ARKS  GHOST  AIRE
SKEE  LOU  OILER
HST  BUSTERBROWN
  JUTE  MOVES
ASHES  SIDEDOOR
STORYTELLER  PDA
KERR  STAINS  HIP
SWAY  PEYOTE  YET
```

192

```
RARE  ASHES  SILO
EXES  STENO  INON
LITTLEONES  EDGE
OLE  CAIN  ARI
ALLAH  CALIBRATE
DALLAS  OCEANIC
  VINTAGE  ANO
 EVAMARIESAINT
ALI  PULSARS
DORITOS  WOBBLE
SIGNONTHE  UNION
  IVY  DARN  MAD
JANE  DOTTEDLINE
AXIS  IRVIN  ONEA
MEAT  YESNO  LIRR
```

193

```
J A G S . R U L E S . V E S T
I R A Q . A P A R T . A X I S
L I E U . R E P R O . V E R A
L A L A L A N D . P H A S E R
. . R O A D . L I E V . . . .
L I V E T V . L E T L O O S E
A C E . S I X A M . M O B I L
S E E M . S E T U P . M A C E
S A R A H . R E R A N . M E N
O X Y M O R O N . P A J A M A
. A P E X . J A D E . . . . .
F I T S I N . B A B A W A W A
A R E A . A D O B E . F L A T
M A X I . M A M B A . R E N T
E S T D . E M B A R . O X E N
```

194

```
L O B B Y . S A N S . M E T Z
A W I R E . E T A T . A R I E
P E N A L . N O V A . I A M B
S N O W L E O P A R D . T O R
. . C L E A R . L E O N O R A
E C U . D R I P . A N A . . .
B A L E . S T A . T O C S I N
B L A C K . A N D . W H I T E
S C R O L L . D A B . O M E N
. . L I E . A M A S . U M A .
S P R I N T S . P R O W L . .
K O I . K I L L E R W H A L E
U S S R . T O O N . H O T E L
N E E D . B E T E . A L O S S
K Y R A . E S T D . T E R S E
```

195

```
I H A D . T I E D . S H A M
T O M E I . H O Y A . N A P E
C R O W N J E W E L . U R S A
H A S A G O . A D L I B B E D
. . R O Y S . A N N O . . . .
P I T S T O P S . S C O R N S
C R I . S U I T S . A S S O C
L I C E . S T E E L . E E R O
A N K L E . S I T A R . A M T
B A L E R S . N O V E L L A S
. E M I T . F I L A . . . .
T Y P E C A S T . S O W E T O
A S I N . C L A W H A M M E R
D E N T . K I T E . D A M N S
A R K S . S P E D . N A T O
```

196

```
C R E D O . T E S S . T U F T
H O M E D . I R O N . A L O E
A G I L E . M I R E . K N O X
F U L L S P E E D A H E A D .
F E E . S A W . I K O N . . .
. . T A D A . D Y N A M I C
F L E W . U R L . E B O N Y
L I M O . A P A R T . A T R A
A L I A S . M I R . C O E N
G A R B L E D . P E C K . .
. R U N E . T E L . C O S
. T H E G A M E I S A F O O T
W H O A . M I L D . M A T Z O
E A R S . E S M E . O T T E R
T I N T . L E S S . R E A D Y
```

197

```
A L T O . S T A R . D E C O R
D O H S . O H S O . E X L A X
Z W E I . L I A M . M E E T S
. B E R N I E M A C . C A M .
O L D I E . F I N E T U N E S
L O G S O N . . E A T S A T
E W E . S H A Q . R E E L S
. E S C A P E P O D . . .
P O S S E . J U D D . D A M
T O P T E N . Q U A R T O
S H O E P H O N E . G L E E M
. L I E . L A U N C H P A D
P A L M S . T E T E . A M I E
S L E E K . E V E N . C O R Y
T A R D Y . S O R T . A N T E
```

198

```
J A L A P A . U S C G . A P E
A B A C U S . R I P A . B O X
B I Z E T S I G N A L . S O P
S T Y . T E H E E . P A O L O
. . V I T O . W H A R F . .
A S W A N . P L A Y L I S Z T
D O I N G S . Y V E S . T O O
O O Z E . L O R E N . P E R K
P T A . S A K I . A M O E B A
T H R O W B A C H . A L L A Y
. D A I S Y . O P I E . .
B O O K S . B O R I S . H M S
E L F . H A Y D N G O S E E K
E G O . E L M O . G U I L T Y
P A Z . D E E R . Y I P P E E
```

199

C	U	S	P	█	A	R	C	S	█	G	A	F	F	E
A	L	T	O	█	C	O	A	T	█	U	L	C	E	R
S	T	E	P	█	H	A	L	E	█	N	I	C	E	R
T	R	I	P	L	E	M	I	L	E	S	█	█	█	█
S	A	N	Y	O	█	█	B	A	L	M	O	R	A	L
█	█	█	T	H	R	E	E	F	O	R	O	N	E	█
A	C	T	█	█	A	I	R	█	K	I	O	W	A	█
L	O	W	█	G	Y	M	█	P	O	E	█	S	A	D
O	B	E	S	E	█	█	B	O	W	█	█	T	R	Y
F	R	E	E	R	E	F	I	L	L	S	█	█	█	█
T	A	N	T	A	L	U	M	█	█	P	A	S	T	A
█	█	█	N	O	M	O	N	E	Y	D	O	W	N	█
R	A	B	B	I	█	█	I	D	O	L	█	E	N	I	D
A	D	I	E	U	█	N	A	S	A	█	A	N	N	E
T	O	T	E	M	█	G	L	E	N	█	L	Y	E	S

200

S	N	I	P	█	A	R	E	N	A	█	G	N	A	T
T	O	T	E	█	L	A	T	E	R	█	E	I	N	E
E	V	E	R	Y	B	I	T	A	N	A	N	G	E	L
M	A	M	M	A	█	L	A	P	E	L	█	H	R	E
█	█	█	█	I	C	Y	█	█	S	I	N	T	A	X
H	A	S	T	H	E	H	O	T	S	F	O	R	█	█
E	V	E	█	T	W	O	T	O	█	T	R	I	P	E
R	E	E	D	█	S	T	A	B	S	█	A	D	A	M
A	S	K	U	P	█	E	R	I	E	S	█	E	L	I
█	█	A	B	S	O	L	U	T	E	W	O	R	S	T
V	A	S	S	A	R	█	█	█	D	E	B	█	█	█
E	L	Y	█	T	E	R	P	S	█	D	R	O	V	E
T	E	L	L	S	I	T	L	I	K	E	I	T	I	S
C	R	U	E	█	D	E	U	C	E	█	E	T	A	T
H	O	M	E	█	A	S	S	A	Y	█	N	O	L	A